A Prophet
of the People

A Prophet
of the People

ISAIAH SHEMBE AND THE MAKING
OF A SOUTH AFRICAN CHURCH

Lauren V. Jarvis

Michigan State University Press | *East Lansing*

Michigan State University Press
East Lansing, Michigan 48823-5245

LIBRARY OF CONGRESS CATALOGING-IN-PUBLICATION DATA
Names: Jarvis, Lauren V., author.
Title: A prophet of the people : Isaiah Shembe and the making of a South African church / Lauren V. Jarvis.
Description: First edition. | East Lansing : Michigan State University Press, 2024.
| Series: African history and culture | Includes bibliographical references and index.
Identifiers: LCCN 2023021707 | ISBN 9781611864847 (paperback) | ISBN 9781609177522 (PDF) | ISBN 9781628955170 (epub)
Subjects: LCSH: Shémbe, Isaiah, –1935. | Church of the Nazarites—History. | Independent churches—South Africa—History.
Classification: LCC BX7068.7.Z8 S758 2024 | DDC 289.93092—dc23/eng/20230509
LC record available at https://lccn.loc.gov/2023021707

Cover design by Shaun Allshouse, www.shaunallshouse.com
Cover photo: Shembe surrounded by a group of girls and women at Ekuphakameni in the early 1930s.
Photograph used with permission of Campbell Collections, UKZN.

Visit Michigan State University Press at *www.msupress.org*

In memory of Dawn V. Jarvis

Contents

Acknowledgments

I LOVE READING ACKNOWLEDGMENTS. THEY LET ME IMAGINE WHAT SOMEONE ELSE'S life is like: the details and the influences, the people and places that mattered, and the moments when they did. That desire—to imagine another person's life—is what made me want to write this book. I learned while writing it that I do not really know how to revise—only how to re-do. Oftentimes, so much re-doing felt like a burden. But now that I am finally finishing, so much re-doing seems like the biggest privilege. So, let me offer a window into my life and all the people who gave me the space, time, and encouragement to finish.

I'm going to start with family. My mom, Dawn V. Jarvis, passed away unexpectedly as I was nearing the end of this project. So much of the good in my life comes from her fierce sense of what was right and her courage to be different. She was the bravest person I have ever met. My mom as well as Kaye de Kruif, Donna Jarvis, Kathryn Jarvis and Greg Propp, Kimberly Jarvis and James Greene, Jarvis and Tyler Greene (and now their families too) showered me with so much love through it all. So did honorary family. I am looking at you, Erica Edelman. Charles and Virginia Jarvis are no longer living, but their influences are everywhere—from the photos I looked at on my desk to the nagging but loving voice I heard, saying "If I were you, I'd just get that book done." (I'm working on it, Grandma!)

More recent additions to my family made innumerable contributions. Alexander Charles and Dashiell McRae Jarvis-Duncan brought joy, laughter, and much-needed perspective, regularly reminding me that there were more important things than what was wrong with my chapter. Of course, my kids could play such a fulfilling role in my life because I have an equal partner who helped make it so. Al Duncan, there are words. They are all insufficient.

Thank you to the many people who have cared for our kids while we were at work and even, a few times, on vacation. This includes some people already mentioned, especially Dawn Jarvis, Kaye de Kruif, and Donna Jarvis, but also Russ and Sue Duncan, Helena and all of the Pesonens, and the terrific teachers at several day cares and preschools in South Africa and the United States. Alesha Foushee and the women at Childcare Matters in Chapel Hill, North Carolina, have built something so magical. This will sound awkward, but thanks for creating a place where I felt so happy to leave my kids.

I was lucky as an undergraduate to see people who made me want to be a historian—people who cared about students and made it clear why their work mattered. Thanks to Bob Korstad and Karin Shapiro for playing that role then and now. Thanks to Karin, too, for reading so many drafts and talking through so many ideas at Namu in Durham and then over Zoom when the pandemic would not allow Namu anymore.

In graduate school, I was around a cohort of brilliant women in African history, some who stayed in academia and some who moved on. I think of them often. Katie McDonough, thanks for being such a dear friend and for hanging out with me on three continents during the process of finishing this book. Jim Campbell, Sean Hanretta, and Richard Roberts provided many free meals and much goodwill. I am grateful to have been around such gracious people as I tried to figure out what it meant to be a historian.

In South Africa, I owe so much to archivists, other scholars, and countless kind people. My thanks above all to the Nazaretha who welcomed me into their worship services and homes and took the time to tell me their stories. I know that my interpretations of Shembe's life are quite different from theirs, but I also know that their ability to tell his story will always be more compelling and powerful than mine. The inimitable, brilliant Mwelela Cele provided some of the translations that transformed this project, including a key set of articles in *iLanga lase Natal.* Audrey Mbeje is the most talented language professor I have ever met. I was lucky to be her student. A song she taught us in class gave me a last-minute insight about what it meant for a young Nazaretha woman to be called *umakoti* before marriage.

Constance Dlamini Mkhize, thanks for riding around with me to various far-flung destinations (sometimes in the middle of the night), nudging me when I wanted to slink off without knocking on more doors, and providing such wonderful company through it all. The reality of inequality in South Africa means that someone recommended as a house cleaner is, in fact, the most phenomenal ethnographer and interviewer you have ever met. Here's to a future in which more South Africans have opportunities to use their many talents.

A remarkable group of people who study KwaZulu-Natal have been the most patient of listeners and the dearest of friends: Brady G'sell, Meghan Healy-Clancy, Jill Kelly, Liz Timbs, and T. J. Tallie. Thank you for greeting every one of my eureka emails with enthusiasm and for helping me keep my head in the game.

I have the best colleagues, who have encouraged me, laughed with me, and reminded me what is possible in an academic career. From Utah, Beth Clement is the only person who has ever made me nostalgic for faculty meetings—or at least for faculty meetings in her company. At the University of North Carolina, I'm so grateful to Lisa Lindsay and Emily Burrill (before the University of Virginia whisked her away) for being kind role models and good friends in my field. The same applies to Susan Pennybacker in an adjacent field too. Louise McReynolds, Ron Williams, Sharon James, and Corry Arnold have offered so much good advice and commiseration over burgers and generously shared beverages in my front yard. Katie Turk and Molly Worthen are terrific scholars and kind people. I am lucky to count them as colleagues and friends.

To students at Stanford, San Francisco State, Utah, and UNC, I cannot tell you the many ways you have helped me understand South African and African history better. A few among this remarkable crew deserve mention: Sarah Bowers, Georgia Brunner, Kennedy Gandy, Kimathi Muiruri, and Alex Peeples. The graduate students at UNC have also helped me understand my work better and left me marveling at all that they are doing. Thanks to Nancy Andoh, Laura Cox, Kaela Thuney, and Abbey Warchol.

I feel very lucky that so many of the people who have already studied the Nazaretha were kind and encouraging at the prospect of another book about Shembe. Thanks to Joel Cabrita, Liz Gunner, Carol Muller, and Nkosinathi Sithole. Above all, your rich, compelling interpretations made me want to learn more. I'm grateful to many people, some no longer living, who embarked on ambitious projects to record Nazaretha testimonies, songs, and histories to make them accessible, including, again, Liz Gunner and Carol Muller as well as Irving Hexham, Hans-Jürgen Becken, Bongani Mthethwa, G. C. Oosthuizen, and Robert Papini. Because some of these projects involved teams of people, many unnamed in the final result, thanks to them too.

I appreciated feedback from Daniel Magaziner, Derek Peterson, and Robert Trent Vinson on an earlier version of this project as well as the feedback from the anonymous reviewers at Michigan State University Press. Thanks to Peter Alegi for thinking this could be something and to Caitlin Tyler-Richards, whose influence and good ideas helped get me over the finish line.

Along the way, the Fulbright-Hays program, the Mellon/ACLS program, and the Institute for the Arts and Humanities at UNC helped fund my research and this publication.

I will close with convention: despite the many people who made this book possible, the mistakes are, of course, my own.

Introduction

IN 1910, ISAIAH SHEMBE WAS JUST OVER FORTY YEARS OLD. HE HAD ALREADY BEEN A farm tenant, a family patriarch, a sanitation worker, and a wandering faith healer.[1] Most recently, he had become a Baptist evangelist for a fledgling church that sent him to one of South Africa's most dangerous mission fields for African Christians. The trip required not only a new name and a disguise, but some of his own funding too.[2] The cost was one reason why he gave up. His lack of success was another.[3]

But then in 1910, the very year that South Africa became one place on a map, Shembe's evangelical fortunes started to change. He began to find more people who would listen to his preaching or try his healing in places where he faced fewer threats of arrest and vigilantism.[4] By the mid-1910s, he became the leader of his own church, the Nazaretha or Nazarites, a name that referenced "a vow of separation to the Lord" in the Old Testament.[5] Over the next twenty years, that church grew to include tens of thousands of people, with worship sites scattered through South Africa's eastern coast and reaching north into current-day Eswatini.[6] Church membership included people from across many of South Africa's social fractures—race, ethnicity, and chiefdom as well as gender, generation, and geography—if they came, nevertheless, from among those left behind by South Africa's industrializing economy. By the 1930s, people knew of Shembe not only as a church leader but also as a wealthy healer and landowner, as the father-in-law of a Zulu king, and as the father of sons who had attended the best schools open to Africans in segregation-era South Africa. Many knew of him too as someone who had evaded and openly defied state authority with seeming impunity. For his supporters, this added to the scale and scope of his miracles.[7]

In the last years of his life, Shembe's followers spoke as if his stunning success had always been a part of God's plan. Even before Shembe's birth, they said his mother had heard a voice that she would have "a son to be praised."[8] But, to return again to 1910, observers then would have seen someone different: a man who could not read or write, a man who had recently been married to three wives, and a man whose first mission had ended with little to show. They might have guessed that Shembe would soon return to sanitation work.

Shembe's remarkable rise has captivated the attention of many people for nearly a century. As early as 1927, a short article appeared in a South African newspaper, describing Shembe as a "herd boy turned healer."[9] Three years later, the *Illustrated London News* included a feature about Shembe for readers on another continent, puzzling over him as a "man of no learning but great wisdom" whose story was "romantic and inspiring."[10] In 1936, just one year after Shembe died, the first printed book about him appeared in isiZulu, the main language spoken by Shembe and the majority of the people in his church. Edited by one of Shembe's neighbors, the politician and educator John Dube, the book's introduction noted that some people—including Dube himself—"found fault" with Shembe, but that a "person who is followed by so many thousands (as [Shembe] is), who has bought so much land, who has become better off than all the Black people, hawu [wow]! Of such a person the Black people desire to know."[11]

Since Shembe's death in 1935, the continued growth of the Nazaretha Church has helped sustain interest in its founder. Today the church is split between competing congregations, but altogether these rival branches count millions of members.[12] Their ranks include celebrity converts; their dramas inspire television shows; and their events are venues for politicians hoping to consolidate support.[13] In 2017, shortly before becoming South Africa's president, Cyril Ramaphosa appeared sitting on the ground and barefoot (to follow the Nazaretha rules of worship) at one of their largest gatherings. At the event, he requested that church members "pray for the ANC [African National Congress]," South Africa's governing party.[14] His request was a double indication of the world Shembe had helped make—not only because the Nazaretha mattered enough for Ramaphosa to visit, but also because

FIGURE 1. Isaiah Shembe, ca. 1930.

Christianity had become such a taken-for-granted part of life for South Africans that a Black presidential candidate in 2017 would have no qualms asking for prayers.

The first scholarly account of Shembe's life appeared in 1936, the same year as Dube's biography, when a white South African woman submitted her master's thesis in anthropology at the University of Natal.[15] Since then, scholars across disciplines have explored the sources of Shembe's "genius" and talents, focusing on how he "revitalized society" or "constituted a new hybrid regime of religious truth."[16] Recent major revisions of church history have emphasized the roles of texts—written, spoken, and sung—in bolstering Shembe's authority and consolidating the Nazaretha community.[17] And yet, for all of the attention that the Nazaretha have received, questions remain about why and how Shembe became an emblem of a changing South Africa.

By approaching Shembe differently—by following him through the places he lived, visited, and learned to avoid—one draws new insights not only about Shembe's success but also about his world. In his nearly seven decades, Shembe transformed into a prophet of the people in many senses of the phrase: as he absorbed ideas from others around him, managed constraints to make new converts and allies, and crafted popular appeal that resonated with his left-behind community. Along the way, Shembe's actions and decisions expose processes that defined modern South Africa. How, for example, did Christianity saturate public life so rapidly after 1900?[18] And how did South Africa give rise to so many broad coalitions—not only churches such as the Nazaretha but also social-movement trade unions and the multiracial, tripartite alliance of a political party still in power today?[19] Why did men imagined as saviors—whether sacred, secular, or somewhere in between—often stand at the helm of these coalitions?[20] And why, speaking to events in the news in late 2022, might the same president who asked for Nazaretha prayers be embroiled in a scandal over money hidden in his couch?[21] Shembe's life on the move in an industrializing era shows how people laced together the spread of Christianity with strategies of evasion and models of community that continue to shape South Africa today.

The Life of an Individual

Many historians remain skeptical that one life can reveal much of anything about the past. And yet, there is an ongoing turn toward studies of individuals in African history.[22] Most of these accounts sit somewhere outside the field of traditional biography; instead, they use strategies gleaned from critical biography and microhistory to generate meaning by placing one life in broader contexts. As Jacob Dlamini explains in an example of this genre, the story of his subject, a South African freedom-fighter-turned-collaborator, "needs to be painted on a larger canvas."[23]

Within this biographical turn, studies of individuals continue to meet many ends. Some affirm the basic principle of social history: that ordinary people have important things to tell us about the past.[24] Others, including this one, use individuals who were not considered ordinary during their lifetimes to offer new vantage points for understanding periods of rapid transformation.[25] Although Shembe shared characteristics with many people, his exceptional mobility and, with it, his willingness to go places where others would not, make him a compelling, if atypical, subject for understanding a changing South Africa.

Altogether, the many biographical accounts add detail, texture, names, and specifics to the historical record. This may not seem like a significant political intervention to some, but the long-enduring links between the African continent and an imagined absence of individualism still make it one. Shembe lived in a world in which white government officials debated the dangers of attempts to "individualize people who are not fit for individualism."[26] Notions of the primacy of group identity persisted after Shembe died, as evidenced by some of the scholarship that would be written, in fact, about the Nazaretha.[27] Studies of individuals can continue to correct for that long history even as few scholars today would write of a singular "African mind," as some once did.

In this case, too, the life of a particular individual provides a front-row seat from which to observe the emergence of a different kind of leadership.[28] Max Weber defined a certain quality, charisma, to begin explaining these processes. In Weber's formulation, charismatic authority emerged from "powers or properties that are not found in everyone and that are thought to be the gift of God."[29] Charismatic leaders were heroes and miracle workers—people who did the seemingly impossible and, as a result, inspired intense devotion. Their authority was, in Weber's understanding, fundamentally disruptive, untethering people from other connections. Weber saw examples of this authority in a range of figures, from American Indian shamans to the early Mormon leader Joseph Smith, all of whom collected people in new configurations of belonging.[30]

The anthropologist Marshall Sahlins, by contrast, explored not a quality but a category of person: "big men." Based on his research in Oceania, Sahlins sketched out a portrait of people who often had remarkable skills, whether as healers, gardeners, or warriors, but who also maneuvered, politicked, and negotiated to create a following bigger than their families alone. "Big men" were distinctive because they were not chiefs who inherited their authority. As a result, the ties of loyalty and obligation created between "big men" and their followers had to be "continually reinforced." As Sahlins saw it, being a "big man"—or a "fisher of men," as he also called them—was hard work.[31]

Notions of "charisma" and "big men" have moved in many directions since their initial articulations. While once the domain of sociologists and psychologists, the idea of charisma is currently attracting greater interest from historians, who are sketching out the contexts that produced different formulations of charisma as well as the qualities that defined it at different places and times.[32] "Big men," in turn, moved from the anthropology of Oceania to the anthropology and history of Africa in the 1960s and 1970s because it dovetailed nicely with foundational concepts in African studies, including foremost "wealth in people," or the idea that accumulation among African elites came from access to human resources more than private property.[33] As political scientists attended to one-party states and authoritarian regimes on the African continent after the 1960s, the idea of "big men" became more narrowly linked to kleptocratic leaders and patronage politics.[34] In the meantime, scholars in other fields reframed their approach.[35] Historians of Africa are now more likely to ask questions, in the terms Kathryn de Luna has posed, about how leaders *and* followers "crafted dependencies"—that is how they "invented clans, royalty, guilds, and healing cults," for example, through "manipulation of speech and knowledge" as well as "control of material resources."[36] De Luna's framing points to complexity and relationships—between ordinary people and leaders, between ideas and things—that allow for fuller contextualization of an individual's experience.

It is easy to draw parallels between Shembe's life and the different ways that scholars have explained new categories of leadership. Still, Sahlins's idea of the effort demanded of "big men," when considered alongside de Luna's calls for attention to relationships, offers the most helpful framework for understanding Shembe. Put simply, Shembe hustled. His unconventional path to Christianity meant that, from the start, he lacked the knowledge and connections held by many other African Christians and church leaders. As Shembe became an evangelist anyway, South Africa's complicated rationing of authority produced innumerable hurdles. Shembe had to find places where he would not be caught, whether by state officials or vigilantes angry about his presence. He had to find people who might be tractable and then grapple with the many ways that those people might want to use him too. As he moved from place to place, moreover, and pulled people together in one community, he had to manage the resultant conflicts and contradictions as well as the many antagonisms that he and his church accumulated. For Shembe, these efforts were often difficult and dangerous—even after his evangelical fortunes began to improve in 1910. More than once, he came close to disaster. But with luck, savvy, and dogged determinism, Shembe and other members of the church found ways to weave such challenges into the fabric of their community.

Defining an Era

The backdrop for Shembe's life is a mottled map affected by sweeping but uneven change. Shembe's birth in the late 1860s coincided with the diamond rush that jumpstarted South Africa's industrial revolution, drawing people into new patterns of work, community, and daily life.[37] His death in 1935 occurred amid South Africa's recovery from the Great Depression and amid a global rise of fascism that would usher in apartheid in the 1940s.[38] Within this period, 1910 represented an important pivot as the Act of Union made South Africa one political entity.[39] Union had profound consequences in Shembe's life, too, contributing to the turnaround in his evangelical fortunes. And yet, 1910 also represented a midpoint more than an endpoint. Shembe's trajectory and this era of South Africa's history were defined by features cutting across the span from the 1870s to the 1930s.[40]

First was the dramatic realignment of labor and, with it, the wrenching apart of African communities by gender and generation across urban and rural space. Scholars of South African history have shown how African social structures shaped the growth of industrial capitalism and, as a result, why groups of young African men were the first to leave their rural homes to earn wages through migrant work, leaving elder men, women, and children behind.[41] But if the structure of African communities helped mold South Africa's emergent working class, so did a rash of restrictions, some imposed by the state and some imposed by African families, attempting to keep women and children in rural areas—and to keep wage-earning men coming back to them.[42] By the early 1910s, the skewed ratios of African men and women in urban and rural space were peaking in many parts of South Africa. In Durban, for example, a city that Shembe visited as an evangelist, the 1911 census counted sixteen African men for every one African woman.[43] But then, in the early 1920s, African women's movement into cities and towns began outpacing African men's as women found ways to bridge the spatial gaps.[44] It was not just rapid urbanization in general, but particularly the rapid movement of African women, children, and families into South Africa's cities in the 1930s that elicited more urgent calls for "separateness" from Afrikaner nationalists.[45] This movement raised fears that the bulwark that separated African families across urban and rural space was breaking.

Greater connectivity and mobility also defined this period. The interior position of South Africa's vast diamond and gold wealth led to the rapid expansion of infra-structure. This first took the form of more wagons and wagon routes, but an age of railway expansion soon followed.[46] Again, using the approximate year of Shembe's birth as a marker, South Africa had less than one hundred miles of railway in the late 1860s. By 1910, the mileage had increased one-hundred fold: 10,000 miles of railway crisscrossed South Africa, connecting portions of it and bypassing others.[47] And by 1910, a new form of transportation was already becoming more accessible too: the automobile. Through the 1910s, the number of automobiles grew slowly, but then, in the fifteen years between 1920 and 1935, that number increased nearly ten times, from around 20,000 automobiles to more than 200,000.[48] Those cars drove on an expanded road network of more than 80,000 miles.[49] But, as would be a recurrent them in twentieth-century South Africa, intersections of race, class, and gender inflected this era of increased mobility, influencing who could travel where and how.

Greater connectivity meant that some people could move more easily across South Africa's many lingering political and social fractures. These persistent fractures—despite the state's efforts to consolidate and unify—represent a final hallmark of this era. Economic transformations beginning in the 1870s prompted every government in the regions that would become South Africa to adopt new laws and legal codes to manage the movement of laborers, the conquest of more groups of people, and shifting possibilities for profit. As a conglomeration of formerly independent African polities, protectorates, Boer Republics, and British colonies became one place in 1910, the Union government had to grapple with the recent explosion of laws in each region. The Union government also, like many around the world after 1910, attempted to shape its citizens and subjects in more ways.[50] In South Africa, race refracted these efforts, multiplying the need for policies, but so did a host of other social and spatial divisions, marking different categories of people (e.g., "exempted" Africans) and land (e.g., former mission reserves). As a

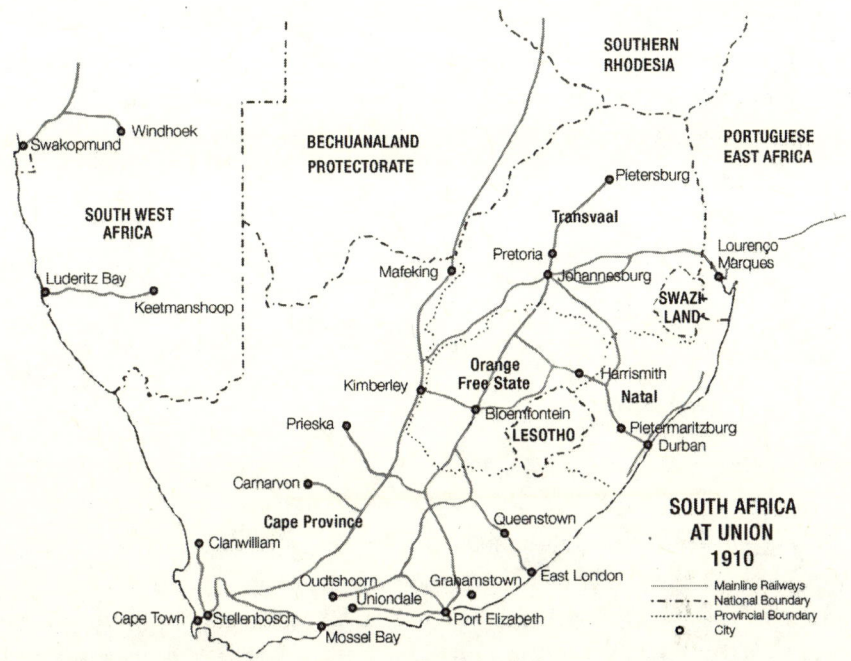

MAP 1. The Union of South Africa with major railways in 1910.

ADAPTED FROM MAP IN *THE CAMBRIDGE HISTORY OF SOUTH AFRICA*, VOL. 2,
EDITED BY ROBERT ROSS, ANNE KELK MAGER, AND BILL NASSON (NEW YORK: CAMBRIDGE, UNIVERSITY PRESS, 2011).

result, local officials often improvised enforcement selectively and muddled through many issues that the new laws had not addressed. In this period, a unified South Africa became a state that perpetrated many kinds of violence and suppression while also allowing loopholes, workarounds, and countless forms of evasion.[51]

What did this mean for Shembe? A great deal. As an evangelist, Shembe's first impulse was to follow the major currents of African men's mobility, moving to a town and then to a big city. Shembe did not begin to experience success, however, until he pushed back against the direction of those currents, moving into rural areas and among people left behind. And even there, he had to tailor his message to fit the circumstances he found, in which African women and children predominated but rural patriarchs still had significant say. That Shembe could try out so many different places—and keep finding new ones when he ran into more trouble—was a testament to the changing possibilities of mobility in an industrializing South

Africa. In Shembe's lifetime, the Nazaretha were a church of the train, growing within walking distance of its tracks. The very ability to traverse so many kinds of borders by train and foot also meant that Shembe moved across microclimates of possibility and restriction. Indeed, even as a changing economy made space for new alignments of people, those people had to find each other and find ways to see across social divides. Shembe himself—through his movement, promises to heal, and example—became one of many sources of commonality, but fissures remained. The next sections turn to the threads that surfaced again and again in Shembe's life—absorbing ideas, negotiating constraint, and cultivating popular appeal—as he navigated this changing world to become a prophet of the people.

Absorbing Ideas

Throughout his life, Shembe adjusted to different circumstances by adopting new ideas. As a boy in the Free State, he picked up an embryonic sense of what it meant to be a Christian while watching and observing his white landlord.[52] As an evangelist in rural Natal, he found ideas from the Bible that he could use to address the circumstances of families anxious about infertility.[53] And as a church leader expanding into southern Zululand, he incorporated ideas about chiefly authority into the organization of the Nazaretha Church.[54] The list could continue, and cataloging every idea Shembe pieced together in an intellectually rich and varied life would be impossible. It is, however, possible to see layers and trace patterns.

Shembe was, like many others born in nineteenth-century South Africa, an astute observer and learner in part because of displacement and dependency. For Shembe, precarity encouraged intellectual flexibility. Whether attempting to secure land for his family, struggling to feed himself, or avoiding the watchful eyes of government officials, Shembe moved through places where he needed patronage, protection, and resources from others. These needs heightened the stakes of finding ways to transform from a stranger to a welcome guest.[55]

As an evangelist and then a church leader, Shembe also pursued specific kinds of knowledge from people around him. One form of this learning related to what was possible in each new place he went: what were the laws, how could one get around them, and who might help? Because survival for Black people in this era of South Africa's history often depended upon such knowledge, he had no shortage of information. Indeed, Shembe was not the only man who learned to change his name at the pass office, put on a new outfit that hid his purpose for travel, or escape state surveillance by heading to the countryside.

Other important forms of learning came from the divine healing revival that Shembe embraced. Earlier methods of healing in the region depended upon rituals of doubt and skepticism, in which healers had to guess at the problems they would need to solve.[56] Revivalism, instead, encouraged people to "report their problems" to Shembe as part of the process of achieving healing. Shembe began to succeed when he found space for large gatherings, where he could collect information about many people's hopes, anxieties, and problems.[57] He could, as a result, speak directly to people in different places, often acting as a mirror for their circumstances because of all the things they had told him.

Over time, absorbing new ideas produced reinventions in Shembe's life and promoted an expanded understanding of who could belong in the Nazaretha community. Again and again, absorbing ideas made absorbing people possible. But the processes that facilitated ideational flexibility also produced contradictions common to the Christian faith. For example, would the Nazaretha be a church of the young women who initially flocked around Shembe and who, like Shembe himself as he became a Christian, had often disobeyed their parents to do so? Or would it be a church of the chiefs in southern Zululand who offered Shembe shelter from state surveillance in the 1920s and were worried about their daughters' behavior? Could it be a church of both? The fact that Shembe had to reconcile such different possibilities leads to the next thread.

Negotiating Constraint

That Shembe negotiated constraint must seem obvious and is already implied by his circumstances. Shembe was an African man with limited formal education living under a series of racist governments. The story of his conversion to Christianity, moreover, involved him rejecting his main sources of authority, both as a family patriarch and a successful farm tenant, to follow God instead. Again, however, Shembe's life reveals creative patterns for negotiating constraint, whether the source of that constraint came from his own family or the South African state.

Movement provided one of Shembe's most important strategies. He came from a community of people who had, in the nineteenth century, been among the most mobile in an age of scatterings. Indeed, his forbears in the Hlubi chiefdom had moved not only when displaced by others but also to find ways to come back together with their chief and each other.[58] Even after Shembe left his family behind, he held onto a possibility confirmed by their history: that, when circumstances did not work out, he would be able to find some place better if he kept moving. But, of course, in the twentieth century, Shembe could go farther, faster. He also had new ideas fueling his movement, including the examples of wandering prophets in the Bible and, indeed, the broader, pervasive cultural associations between journeys and spiritual progress.[59] Still, as he became the leader of a community, he could no longer move everyone with him in times of trouble, and Shembe was obliged to manage the constraints that others faced, too. This made Shembe's continued movement between different outposts of the Nazaretha community one of the strongest threads knitting them together.

Evasion stands out as another, related method for negotiating constraint. Evasion was, in fact, baked into Shembe's and many others' experiences of becoming Christians, as he and they learned that sneaking to follow God was just. The story of Shembe's conversion involved him taking his evasive experiments with Christianity and making them public.[60] And yet, as Shembe encountered a South Africa shaped by indirect rule, settler colonialism, and industrialization, evasion often continued out of necessity. At different moments, his names, his clothes and appearance, his statements, his movements, and his partnerships contributed to strategies of evasion. Sometimes, at the height of his influence, so did welcoming large crowds of people at his church headquarters. As one white official noted in 1929, Shembe was "no ordinary run of small prophet who conducts his doings in secret."[61] This official wrote at a time when the Nazaretha faced state scrutiny for resisting new public health laws and as officials hemmed and hawed about how to respond. Shembe's openness helped the Nazaretha evade punishment because state officials worried about the many people who might be watching the government's next steps.

Finally, compromise and concession represent another pattern for negotiating constraint. Shembe and the Nazaretha shared an impulse with many other communities in the nineteenth and early twentieth centuries: if they could just carve out space to make some of their own rules, their lives would be better.[62] For the Nazaretha, this impulse meant finding many small spaces—some only for temporary use—and then moving people between them. This meant, too, navigating the different laws governing each locality *and* the demands of the people who inhabited it. As the Nazaretha faced pressure from above and below with every move, Shembe needed partners who could help him evade the state.

This circumstance made rural patriarchs an especially important forcefield within the church, whether they were converts or not. By charting the changing notions of gender, marriage, and sexuality in the church over time, one observes Shembe recurrently making compromises with such men in mind.

Shembe's ability to negotiate constraint and manage others' constraints contributed to the growth of the church and to his personal success. This, in turn, demanded that he adapt in other ways. He had come into Natal as an "underdog," whose appeal stemmed from how he was different from other African Christians and elites. Within a decade of his time in Natal, he was a landowner, a known figure, and someone in control of financial offerings from thousands of church members. Over the next decade, he became a celebrity. Shembe's management of his own transformation exposes the final thread of this study.

Cultivating Popular Appeal

In Shembe's first five years as an evangelist, his main task involved finding a place where his distinctive background and message might generate sustained attention. These efforts took him from a rural farm to a small town, then to a city, and, finally, to a cluster of chiefdoms in a rugged, mountainous region north of Durban. In those chiefdoms in 1913, Shembe launched the Nazaretha faith.[63] This was possible because of how his distinctive background and message resonated in a region of many people left behind.

By and large, the people who came together around Shembe remained at a distance from the major transformations of their time. They were rural women and children as well as struggling chiefs and their families and young African Christian men left behind by the possibilities open to people like them a generation before.[64] To some of these people, the church promised charity, care, and even honor in being among the "least of these." To others—and especially the first young women who joined the church—it offered adventure, importance, and an experience that set *them* in motion, as they watched their brothers leave for towns.

From whatever angle one entered the church, the Nazaretha were among many new denominations in South Africa that reframed what it meant to be a good Christian. The Victorian mission model had encouraged African Christians to acquire objects, property, and formal education to mark their spiritual progress.[65] The Nazaretha began to define being a good Christian instead by what one sacrificed,

FIGURE 2. A Nazaretha service in the early 1930s. The uniforms, tablecloths, candlesticks, and vases were products of an industrial age.

PHOTOGRAPH INCLUDED WITH PERMISSION OF CAMPBELL COLLECTIONS, UKZN.

whether medicine, certain foods, or sex.[66] For generally poor, rural people, this was an affordable Christianity. More than that, it was a form of Christianity in which the exemplars of the faith did not have the most, but rather gave up the most.

The Nazaretha were not, however, outside of the transformations taking place in South Africa. They were adjusting to a world in which they might also take the train, eat food they had not produced, learn to read, and wear clothes made from manufactured cloth.[67] Many were adjusting, too, to the problems that accompanied the realignment of their social and economic lives. They grappled with food insecurity, high rates of infant and childhood mortality, and a breakdown of the informal social services that, in good times, had allowed African households to absorb vulnerable people.[68] Many members of the church, like many South Africans, found themselves left behind, ironically, by a system they could not escape.

Still, a shared "left behind" status was never sufficient for the Nazaretha to come together. Other tools that pulled them into a community were products of an industrializing age, if ones that church members sometimes chose between or engaged with selectively. Re-printed photographs let people bring Shembe into their homes, fostering connections with a leader that could feel deeply personal.[69] Mass-produced cloth gave the Nazaretha affordable ways of marking belonging in the form of the simple white robes that became the first church uniforms.[70] Even revivalist "healing homes" resembled modern hospitals in certain respects; they were spaces where sick people with many different ailments came to get expert care and then stayed until they got well.[71] The Nazaretha organized their church headquarters, Ekuphakameni, around similar principles of care, even as they rejected all forms of medicine.[72]

The Nazaretha also came together because of who they were not. Enemies and outsiders helped bind them too. Over the course of Shembe's lifetime, he openly discussed many. Some, such as his neighbor John Dube and the Zulu king *Inkosi* Solomon kaDinuzulu, were the ultimate frenemies: people to whom Shembe wanted proximity to bolster his status but who were uneasy allies at best. At different times, other African Christians, antagonistic chiefs, and people who abandoned the church became enemies. As Shembe walked a dangerous tightrope of evasion and, occasionally, outright defiance, he marked the government as a foe too. When, near the end of his life, Shembe told a white visitor that he "did not believe in the power of the law, but in the powers of God," he juxtaposed these topics (laws and God) intentionally and spoke from the experience of having led defiance of public health laws—and having succeeded (mostly) at avoiding punishment.[73] Such an oppositional approach to the state allowed Shembe to channel popular support at a moment when Africans clamored for a more confrontational response to white minority rule.[74]

Given the complexity of his life on the move, Shembe unsurprisingly sought to control the centrifugal forces around him. He did this through the redistribution of cattle, land, cash, and food; as someone always on the move, he framed himself as a conduit of resources. But Shembe also used crowds and photo opportunities to broadcast who he was through his clothes and possessions. He made foils of the people around him, including members of his own church as well as other celebrities and leaders with large followings. In the last years of his life, one of the most significant symbols of Shembe's self-fashioning came from his modes of transportation. Stories circulated that Shembe refused the ultimate symbol of luxury for the African elite of his time: a motor car. Instead, he kept a collection of "a dozen pairs of worn shoes, and twenty [walking] sticks" as a physical reminder of the miles he had traveled and how he had traveled them.[75] This sent many messages to his people, among them that he would keep moving to seek out others left behind in the places where cars still could not go. These choices dramatized his sacrifices and framed him as the person in the church who had given up the most. Years of carefully crafting a persona built on suffering and sacrifice made it small wonder that some church members considered Shembe, by the time of his death, to be a messiah.[76]

Bodies of Evidence

Like many accounts of individuals in Africa and the African Diaspora, this reconstruction depends upon an exceptional archive. In this case, that archive includes oral traditions and writings that chronicle Shembe's life, journeys, and sermons as well as church members' testimonies of healing. These testimonies detail miracles: events that their speakers narrated as unexpected outcomes resulting from divine intervention, with Shembe always as the source of the divine. Most follow a common pattern: someone was sick or suffering in some way for a long time, that person tried other remedies, but nothing worked until Shembe.[77] The long history of scholarly interest in Shembe and the Nazaretha community means that, in many cases, versions of these oral traditions and testimonies have been written down and translated.[78] It is also possible to find nearly verbatim accounts of healing told by the same person, but to different researchers, decades apart. It is possible too to trace a core set of church narratives, including much of Isaiah Shembe's spiritual autobiography, across decades and find striking similarities through these retellings as well as some significant additions and differences.[79] These sources are, to use Cheikh Anta Babou's phrasing, "living history."[80]

The healing testimonies, in particular, are complicated products of an industrial age.[81] Mass-produced print media created by divine healing revivalists carried examples of this genre around the world as early as the 1890s.[82] But these accounts shared a great deal in common with another genre that proliferated even more widely at the same time: patent medicine advertisements. In South Africa in the early twentieth century, advertisements for patent medicines—including Dr. Williams' Pink Pills,

Zam-buk Ointment, Bile Pills, Reviva Pills, Rapidare Pills, and Dr. Chamberlain's Remedy, to list a few—appeared in print. Many of these advertisements were translated into local languages and took the form of personal narratives explaining success using a particular patent medicine. Sometimes the people who wrote in filled their accounts with specific, if difficult to trace, details. There was, for example, a "Mrs. Susana M. Baneke of Uitzicht, Alberfeldy, Harrismith, ORC" who had been "sick for two years" or a "Mrs. Martha Chere Maloi" who had been "very sick in 1899 and 1900."[83] Other times, however, these advertisements referenced well-known, public figures. The pages of the biggest isiZulu-language newspaper, *iLanga lase Natal*, included a narrative of Shembe's already referenced neighbor, John Dube. He, the ad explained, had "tried many kinds of medicine" for his "liver and stomach problems" until his success with Dr. Williams' Pink Pills.[84] Outside of newspapers alone, patent medicine salesmen took bottles of pills on the road, sharing formulaic testimonials as they attempted to sell their remedies to the majority of Africans who still could not read.[85]

The Nazaretha were one of many groups of people for whom an age of advertising offered new tools for organizing and coordinating claims. These communities found productive slippages between testimony and testimonial as well as between advertisement and personal narrative. As such, the words of one divine healing revivalist who noted that the baby born to her was "an advertisement for Zion [divine healing]," rang truer than she might have meant.[86] Still, the Nazaretha would take a genre, forged in an era of print media and mass production, and turn it into a way of participating in religious life that attenuated the link between Christianity and literacy in their region. Speaking, not reading, would serve as a central act of their faith throughout Shembe's lifetime.[87] This was possible in part because the divine healing revival made the body, as much as the Bible, a source of evidence about sin and morality. Still, the Nazaretha also took healing testimonies and used them alongside other forms for making claims, including praise poems and carefully crafted church histories.[88]

Sources that emphasize miraculous powers might not seem useful for understanding the complexity of an individual's experience. But there are ways of re-grouping and re-ordering the healing testimonies and other Nazaretha sources. The variables within healing testimonies raise useful questions. Why, for example, did accounts of Shembe's earliest healings resemble Jesus's while later ones emphasized curing infertility, something that Jesus—for all his miracles described in the Bible—never did?[89] And what can we learn from tracing the mundane details about where a healing took place and who else was there to witness it? At the same time, the sources provide ways of reconstructing conflict. The Nazaretha readily identified many of Shembe's enemies and antagonists outside of their community and, with more subtlety, contests within. They record who was with Shembe, for example, when the church was still "a very small group of people" who "had no food" and, as important, who was not.[90] With such observations, one can then do what all historians do: coax meaning by reading different kinds of sources with and against each other, whether those sources are oral history interviews, the papers of other scholars who studied the Nazaretha, or correspondence in state archives.

The varied sources about Shembe exist, then, because of an uncomfortable convergence: state officials, members of the Nazaretha Church, and generations of scholars (myself included) have put Isaiah Shembe at the center of the story. This account does so, however, with different goals in mind: to understand what Shembe can tell us about the place South Africa was becoming in his lifetime and the place that it, in many ways, still is.

CHAPTER 1

An Inheritor in the Free State

ISAIAH SHEMBE WAS BORN IN THE LATE 1860S. HE WAS HIS MOTHER'S FIRST SURVIVING son after the births of many daughters.[1] Girls were loved and welcomed additions to polygynous families such as his, but a boy could be an heir. Shembe's mother was his father's senior wife and the person expected to provide an inheritor.[2] And, indeed, Shembe's parents gave him the name Mdliwamafa, meaning "he who eats the inheritance." This name marked Shembe as the son who would, upon his father's death, acquire his father's cattle. The name suggested how Shembe would use the cattle to marry wives who would bear children and continue the lineage. Linking the past to the present and future, those children would offer the sacrifices that appeased the dead, eventually including Shembe's parents and grandparents and then, someday, Shembe himself when his life ended.[3] This was, at least, what his parents envisioned.

For nearly four decades, Shembe played the role assigned to him by his name. In an era of transformation and trouble, he secured land, kept his family together, and did the breakneck work required of African tenants living on white-owned farms in the Orange Free State. Later, he reflected on his life as a young husband and father and described himself as one of a minority of such tenants who had even been "well off."[4] But, in the years following the South African War (1899–1902), Shembe did something unexpected: He renounced his role as the inheritor. Shembe could not read, perhaps had never been to church, and had married three wives, but he said that God had told him, "I want to do my work through you."[5] To do this—to be used by God—Shembe explained to his family, he needed to leave them behind.[6]

Shembe's conclusion was shocking. By way of comparison, some of South Africa's most famous African Christians, many of them about Shembe's age, were thinking about translating Shakespeare into seTswana, channeling funds raised abroad into projects of racial uplift, and drafting petitions to decry the policies of the British Empire.[7] These men were, to be sure, exceptional, but Shembe was even different from less famous African Christians who taught in church schools, served as elders, and led worship services in small towns and mission stations scattered throughout South Africa in the early twentieth century.[8] And yet, looking at Shembe's first decades, one can see how his efforts to live up to the name his parents gave him had a host of unintended consequences that sent him on a different trajectory. As Shembe approached forty, his experiences revealed a bitter irony to the family he left behind. Amid the twists and turns of a rapidly changing South Africa, someone at the center of efforts to stay together might still be wrenched apart.

Hlubi Beginnings

If his parents could not have predicted all that would unfold in Shembe's early life, their history at least gave them reasons to think they could withstand periods of trouble. In the early nineteenth century, their chiefdom, amaHlubi, had been among the largest in southeastern Africa.[9] Amid the violence and political re-alignments of the period called the Mfecane, or the scattering, they were among the people fragmented and displaced. In the late 1810s, their chiefdom experienced an attack that one Hlubi chronicler described like the "breaking of a bottle of atoms," as amaHlubi sought shelter in other chiefdoms, at mission stations, or sometimes by displacing others.[10] But one thing that distinguished amaHlubi from the many other peoples scattered in this period was how large numbers of them found ways to come back and then stay together.[11] They regrouped first in the Zulu Kingdom, the most significant political entity to emerge from the Mfecane. Then, when relations soured with a new Zulu king, amaHlubi made plans to flee again. In the 1840s, they moved into a newly established British colony, just over the border with the Zulu Kingdom: Natal.[12]

Shembe's family played prominent roles in the Hlubi chiefdom for generations. Shembe's paternal grandfather had been a headman and advisor for an earlier Hlubi chief Inkosi Mthimkhulu (ca. 1780–1818). Shembe recalled that this grandfather considered the chief to be "his hero."[13] Shembe's own father eventually became a headman for the next chief, Inkosi Langalibalele (ca. 1815–1889), the leader who stewarded the Hlubi movement into Natal in the 1840s. Shembe said that his father "conducted the weddings of Langalibalele's soldiers."[14] Such a role would not have been simply ceremonial. The "soldiers" referred to regiments of young men. Determining when and whom they married represented one way that chiefs in the region exerted authority.[15] Shembe's father was, then, someone at the nexus of important institutions in his community: marriage, age-regiments, and the chieftaincy. On Shembe's mother's side, too, Shembe had connections to the Hlubi chiefs. Shembe's maternal grandfather was Inkosi Langalibalele's uncle. This made Shembe's mother the great chief's cousin.[16] Thus, for generations, Shembe's family would have been among the people who moved to different parts of South Africa and then to the British colony of Natal as they sought ways to piece a "bottle of atoms" back together.

By the time of Shembe's birth in the late 1860s, members of his chiefdom had been living in Natal for nearly two decades—long enough, perhaps, to think that their days of scattering had come to an end. In Natal, the first expressions of territorial segregation were rural, taking the form of large expanses of land called "locations" (and later "reserves"), where Africans could continue living in polygynous homesteads and under traditional authorities. After moving into Natal, amaHlubi received one of these designated spaces to plant their crops, tend to their cattle herds, and raise their children—the three *c*'s of African prosperity.[17] As a result, the Hlubi chiefdom was one of several groups of Africans who prospered at first, when the settler state was weak and its impositions not yet too onerous. As they had done before in times of abundance, more Hlubi people came back together. Even those who had stayed scattered longer filtered back, joining other members of their chiefdom in the British colony. They had come into Natal around 7,000 strong; by the early 1870s, their numbers had grown to around 10,000 people.[18]

While the Hlubi chiefdom grew quickly, their land allocation from the colonial government did not. Instead, the advance of white settlers hemmed them in. In response, amaHlubi attempted a controlled dispersal, turning to a common set of options among many chiefdoms in South Africa already grappling with land shortages. Some Hlubi families began to look for spots where they might live as tenants on white-owned farms. And some older boys and young Hlubi men began to go away to do migrant work.[19] Young men were already leaving home to earn wages when diamond digging intensified in the early 1870s.[20]

Shembe was born perhaps the very year that white settlers identified the first large diamonds in South Africa. Within five years, South Africa had already exported more than one million carats of that crystalline configuration of carbon. This number was possible not only because of the region's "diamondiferous" geologic veins but also because, by the early 1870s, some 30,000 African men were already making the journey to and from the diamond fields each year to earn wages through migrant labor.[21] Many of these men walked hundreds of miles to a destination that, if the wind was blowing the right way, they could smell long before they saw it: a tent city full of people and their refuse. Already a growing web of laws and white vigilantism meant that the African men who made this journey would be "servants" of white diggers, instead of diamond sellers themselves. But the fierce competition for labor in the diamond fields meant higher wages than many other "servants" earned. It also meant other enticements for the African men who made the journey, including guns.[22]

The many transformations wrought by diamonds played out on different scales and terms. For amaHlubi, the consequences were swift. Shembe recalled that he was "three or four years old" when disaster struck.[23] In 1873, a dispute with the colonial government erupted as young Hlubi men who had been working in the diamond mines began bringing guns back with them into the colony of Natal. For reasons that were not fully transparent but that involved the colonial government's past misdeeds, the Hlubi chief, Inkosi Langalibalele, refused to register the guns or travel to meet with the magistrate.[24] The ensuing dispute revealed the bad faith that, by then, characterized relations between many chiefs and white officials as well as the ways that settler paranoia amplified misunderstandings. As tensions rose, amaHlubi did what they had often done in times of trouble. They prepared to flee—this time attempting to seek shelter across the Drakensberg Mountains in the recently established British Protectorate of Basutoland. Colonial troops caught them in flight.[25]

In the aftermath, the settler government found many ways to punish Hlubi people. Colonial officials tried Inkosi Langalibalele for "treason and rebellion" and then, finding him guilty, sent the once-powerful chief into exile. The government also pressed hundreds of Hlubi people into forced labor and sold their looted livestock at auction for a huge sum of money, amounting to more than £25,000.[26] The most devastating punishment, however, involved the government stripping amaHlubi and their allies of their land.[27] This made Shembe and his family refugees.[28]

In some ways, the fate of Shembe's chiefdom served as a harbinger of the violence and realignments that would befall other African political communities over the next few decades as diamonds (and then gold) changed the politics of the region. Some chiefdoms experienced intensified warfare and then conquest in the 1870s and early 1880s. Others maneuvered and negotiated to try to avoid further violence, requesting "protectorate" status within the British Empire.[29] In many of these cases, the conquests that took place after the 1860s pinned communities to small amounts of land, a circumstance that had serious consequences for people who had, for decades, negotiated precarity through movement to new places.[30] For these people, increasingly, the best option was to send young men out to do work that earned wages, entrenching patterns of migrant labor. But, for amaHlubi, circumstances differed because they were dispossessed of all their land in Natal. This left whole families looking for places where they might rebuild their livelihoods.

How Shembe's family weathered the immediate aftermath of the violence— with its forced labor gangs and confiscations—is unclear. By the late 1870s, however, a surprising option emerged for Shembe's family and many other Hlubi families as well. This option took them to yet another place their ancestors had gone before in times of trouble: the eastern Orange Free State, near a mountain they called Ntabazwe, or the Mountain of the People.[31] Land opened there as an ironic result of Hlubi dispossession. Other Africans were leaving the region because they had received a portion of the old Hlubi territory in Natal.[32] However embattled amaHlubi were by the late 1870s, then, some of them found in the Orange Free State a place to regather once again.[33] And however tumultuous Shembe's early life had already been, his family was headed toward a spot where, if things went well, Shembe might still be able to eat the inheritance someday.

The Terms of Tenancy

In the late nineteenth century, the Orange Free State was one of many regions around the world where a minority class, race, or caste of landowners was attempting to profit from agriculture without labor from serfdom or slavery. In the United States, slavery transformed into a form of sharecropping that trapped Black people in cycles of debt and poverty and that, in Eric Foner's words, "undermined [the] promise of autonomy." [34] In many parts of South Africa, including the Free State, white farmers were undercapitalized at the same time that demand for agricultural goods skyrocketed because diamond diggers needed food, clothes, and other supplies. The white farmers did not have, in other words, access to the technology or credit needed to make their land more profitable or to out-compete African farming families. In this context, African tenant families did not have title deeds, but they did have labor power that white farmers needed as well as the ability, in some cases, to bargain with or withdraw it.[35]

In the eastern Free State, in particular, white farmers often preferred large, polygynous African tenant families. Again, as was common in other parts of the world, agricultural transformations in the region accompanied the growth of a scaffolding of laws that attempted to push economic change in certain directions. The economic "leveling" tendencies among the Boers meant that the Free State government passed a law soon after Shembe's family arrived, limiting the number of African tenant families on any one white farmer's land. Free State lawmakers intended the law to preclude wealthier white farmers from monopolizing access to African tenant families' labor, but the law had a loophole: it counted African households by fathers and husbands—not by mothers or wives.[36] As a result, many white farmers saw large, polygynous families as one way to maneuver around the limits of the law. Some white farmers, as a result, would only accept tenants who brought polygynous families with them.[37]

No matter how remarkable it was that Shembe and his family found an arrangement that supported polygyny near others from their chiefdom, tenancy was difficult for African families. Many Boer landlords were abusive. The Africans who cleared out of the region before Shembe's family arrived had wanted to leave because Boer farmers were "killing several of our people and flogging many including myself," as one chief remembered.[38] Even in the best of these tenancy arrangements, moreover, African families found themselves double farming as they supported themselves and paid rent or offered a share of their crop to the landlord. The sheer scope of the demands placed on African tenants illuminated why large families could be such an asset, whether for white or Black patriarchs, as well as why it helped to have other relatives or members of a shared chiefdom nearby. African families could borrow each other's oxen, African fathers could call upon their adult sons who lived on other farms for help, and chiefly bonds of affiliation could mean the difference between starvation and sufficiency in tough times.[39]

For some, bonds of kith and kin could engender more than simply survival; such bonds could even allow a small number of African families to acquire meaningful wealth as tenants. Although surely an exception, one African tenant family in the early 1900s offered an indication of what was possible. The family included one father, three mothers, eight sons, and eleven daughters. They had so much stock that the senior wife had "split off [moved to another white settler's farm] with 200 sheep and over 50 cattle," while the remaining wives' households had "400 sheep and 70 cattle."[40] Such success was surely what many polygynous tenant families, including Shembe's, hoped to achieve.

For their part, white farmers benefited from the ability to call upon the labor of extended African family networks too. Tenancy arrangements usually required that African wives and children work at different phases of the agricultural cycle. Older boyhood was a time when African tenant sons began to go away to work for white farmers for a few months of the year. These boys could use skills of milking and herding learned at home while also picking up the formal and informal rules of tenancy.[41] Shembe probably would have been nearing twelve when he went to work for his parents' landlord, Coenraad Grabe, for the first time. Shembe's departure took him to another of Grabe's farms and to the land where Grabe and his family lived.[42]

Fitting in on a Boer Farm

Shembe and his parents would have wanted his stints of work with Grabe to go well. Shembe was on the cusp of an age when African boys' behavior could explode into conflict on white-owned farms. It was not uncommon for tenancy relations to break down over debates about how Boer landlords treated (and mistreated) adolescent African sons in arrangements such as Shembe's.[43] Outside of African boys' place in the structural "trouble spots" of Boer–tenant relations, Shembe was not just any tenant son but the inheritor in his family.[44] His stints of work served as an extended, years-long interview to see if Shembe himself might be able to secure a space on Grabe's land or, with Grabe's recommendation, on a farm nearby someday. The same laws that limited the number of African tenant families on any one farm meant that sons always outnumbered the spots available.[45]

In some ways, making the leap to living away from his family—and near Grabe's—would not have been so big for Shembe. The scholarship about tenancy in the Boer Republics portrays how paternalism, violence, and exploitation structured relationships between white landlords and African farm tenants. But this scholarship also underscores how white and Black families in the Free State developed a set of ideas, practices, and structures, some similar and some directly shared.

Patriarchal authority and extended kin networks shaped the norms of family life for landowners and tenants alike. Each group built livelihoods around agriculture and depended on the success of the same crops and livestock on the same land. In the realm of healing and ideas of the supernatural, the scholarship points to many areas of overlap as well. Boers living in the Free State consulted African healers, attended ceremonies to pray for rain, and made their own remedies. They, like African tenant families, also bought patent medicines, looked for signs to understand good and bad fortune, and worried about the effects of supernatural harm, or witchcraft.[46]

Outside of shared practices and ideas, institutions helped Shembe adjust. Indeed, Shembe's social world while away for work drew upon yet another African social formation: the age-set. During his first trip away, Shembe lived and worked with many other boys his age and older who were the children of other tenant families living on the Grabes' land and farms nearby.[47] The older boys among them would have been responsible for socializing and educating a newcomer like Shembe. As they did, some of the forms of education that Shembe received resembled those he might have experienced living in a territorial chiefdom. Shembe remembered, for example, asking the older boys about sex—and being asked in return, "What are you asking that for, child that you are?"[48] But Shembe also received socialization for the terms of tenancy. He had to learn Afrikaans to understand the boss. He likely learned to do new kinds of work as well because tenancy arrangements often demanded a realignment of ideas about gender, generation, and agricultural labor in African families. The other boys might have helped Shembe pick up the informal rules for avoiding an ever-present threat as well: physical violence from white farmers. Shembe described some near brushes with such danger during his first trips away for work.[49]

Whatever similarities white and African farm families shared and whatever structures were in place to help Shembe adapt, some things were quite different. This included the presence of Christians. The Hlubi people who moved into Natal with Inkosi Langalibalele had experienced stops and starts in their contact with Christianity and Christians along the way.[50] By moving to the Orange Free State in the 1870s, Shembe's family entered a region where they were more isolated from Christianity in some ways than ever before. The Free State had fewer mission stations than any other part of South Africa, and, as mentioned, Boer farmers often preferred tenant families who were not Christians and had many ways to enforce this preference.[51] By moving to the Boer Republic, however, Shembe's family moved to a place where a Bible was in every Boer farmhouse and where rituals of Christianity punctuated the Boers' daily lives.

Hide and Sneak Christianity

For the Boers, even more so than for many other rural Christians in the nineteenth century, much of their religious life took place at home. The Boers had historically pushed beyond the boundaries of established states—and beyond the zones where churches dotted the landscape. Even as settler governments followed them, the Boers' land-use patterns placed churches far away. In the 1870s, just as Shembe's family moved to the Free State, the most popular church among the Boers, the Dutch Reformed Church, had only eighteen branches spread out across the 55,000 square miles that made up the Boer Republic.[52] Travel writers described how Boers "living in remote places" (which was most of them) perhaps only went to church "once in three months."[53] In between infrequent church visits were, however, daily Bible readings, prayers before meals, regular devotions, and weekly sermons with hymns. Religious education for Boer children and teenagers took place on the farm, too.[54]

The extent of religious observance on farms impressed otherwise critical outsiders. After spending some time in a Boer household in the 1870s, a Scottish missionary wrote that nothing he had seen in southern Africa "excited [his] admiration" as much as "simple family worship offered daily in many a secluded glen and isolated homestead."[55] Other observers described a more boisterous but, nevertheless, expressive religious culture among the Boers, including "a very regular business of psalm singing, very edifying to them no doubt, but by no means gratifying to an English ear."[56]

Shembe got extra exposure to white Christians because he fit in so well and became a "favorite" on the farm. After his first stint of working for Grabe for six months, he went home and then "the Boss called [him] back, where this time [his] stay lasted a year."[57] If this first call back was a sign that Shembe was not perceived as a troublemaker, over time, it became something more. "Boss Coenraad liked me a lot," Shembe explained, "and all his house, and I too loved them."[58] The Grabes showed their preference by inviting Shembe in for meals: "Sometimes when they were eating they would call me in." Sometimes they would also give him extra food as he sat on the floor: "When they had finished they put my plate down by the table-leg, and I then ate."[59] These acts reinforced the Grabes' authority and sense of racial hierarchy even as they confirmed Shembe's privilege relative to other Africans living on the farm. By inviting Shembe in at mealtime, these acts would have also allowed Shembe to observe the Grabe family praying.[60]

As he gained more responsibility, Shembe got more contact with white farmworkers whom Grabe employed too. This included long herding journeys to take sheep into winter pasture with a white shepherd.[61] Such herding journeys were a remarkably common feature of white and Black lives in a region where sheep represented the "premier industry."[62] Still, there are very few sources to understand what these experiences entailed. It is possible, however, that this was an opportunity to learn about Christianity up-close too—especially because other journeys that took Boer men away from home, including going "on commando," involved regular religious observances.[63]

Whether in the Grabes' home or on the herding journeys, Shembe surely noticed a few things about the faith he was seeing that made it seem accessible, if strange. First, Christianity did not seem to require special intermediaries—other than the adult men who often led the services. This might have reminded Shembe of how things worked in his own home, too, where his father played an important role in leading spiritual interventions with the ancestors.[64] Also, even though Shembe remembered seeing the Grabes' Bible in their home, he might have noticed how children did not necessarily need to read it to be able to participate in the rituals of Christianity—to sing or to pray, for example.[65]

Shembe said later that, during the chunks of time away from his parents, he began acting upon what he observed. Because Shembe did not want others to see him, evasion was built into this early practice. He noted how he snuck out of the boys' communal living quarters when he "found all people already asleep" to pray.[66] And during the day when he prayed, he looked for places where no one would find him. One of his favorite spots at first was a "rocky outcrop" where he could hide among the rocks. But, after some African girls working in the Grabes' home saw him there, he tried the cattle kraal—perhaps because the same girls would not have been allowed to go there.[67]

Shembe's experiences of hiding and sneaking to practice the rituals of Christianity were common. In fact, some foreign missionaries began to think that converts who hid and snuck were the sincerest. As one missionary explained, people mocking the Christian faith "irreverently throw themselves down within in a few yards of the [church] door, and sometimes jestingly ask, 'Where is God?'" People beginning to believe, instead, "hide themselves among the trees and the recesses of the rocks, or in the depths of the ravine, and from thence cry. . . . Give us, Lord, thy favour."[68] Indeed, the extent of this hiding may explain why some African parents fought back with stories of children running into bogeymen when they went out alone to pray. Shembe, however, described himself defeating these forces as a boy, too, telling a "skeleton-man" to go away so that he could pray alone.[69]

Later in his life, Shembe would tell many stories of hiding and sneaking as a boy learning to follow God. For him, these stories conveyed important messages about God's nature. In other examples of hide-and-sneak stories, Shembe recounted learning about God's omnipotence and omniscience when he also stole a belt from a traveler staying with his family and when he took ripe peaches from the white farmer.[70] In each case, only God saw what Shembe did. In the example of the stolen peaches, too, God promised to protect Shembe from harm if Shembe would "look up" as the white farmer circled around the tree where Shembe hid.[71] The story of the peaches broadcasted an idea that would become a defining feature of Shembe's relations with the government, decades after the events described: God protected people who obeyed divine instruction, even when they disobeyed other authorities. Of course, the close fit between the lesson of an earlier event and Shembe's later theology suggests some revision and perhaps even invention.[72] But it is not hard to imagine how the kernels for such stories took root as Shembe entered adolescence and tested out many kinds of authority—whether God's, his parents', the white farmer's, or the older boys' with whom he lived and worked.

Shembe recalled how, as a teenager, he revealed his interest in Christianity to his parents. After a few years of working for Grabe, Shembe participated in a common act of defiance among African children and adolescents who had more experience with Christianity than their parents: he refused to eat the meat sacrificed to the ancestors to heal another family member.[73] In fact, he described such meat as "anathema to me." As Shembe told it, his father did not mind this assertion of independence. "Even father never had any quarrel with me on that; we understood one another," he explained.[74] Shembe's father's response suggested that African parents tolerated a certain amount of exploration. And yet such forms of refusal could gain momentum if left unchecked. Shembe said that his relative recovered anyway, giving him more reasons to doubt his parents' approach to healing.[75]

The Boers were not necessarily the only Christians or sources of information about Christianity on Free State farms. Some African Christians took up positions as tenants, some missionaries snuck onto farms, and certain members of African tenant families went to church with or without white landlords' permission.[76] If Shembe did know African Christians, he, nevertheless, did not mention them and put his early experiments with Christianity in proximity to his first sustained exposure to a Boer family. He recalled that he had begun to pray "just after [his] arrival at Boss Coenraad's home."[77] It had been Shembe's responsibility while he was away not only to work hard but also to be extra-observant, pay attention, and absorb the rules of landlord-tenant relations. His status as a favorite indicated that he did this very well, and he picked up more than his parents intended as a result.[78]

Eating the Inheritance

One might imagine that, as Shembe grew older, he gained more authority to act on his interest in Christianity. He might have had opportunities to go to church, for example. Many young African men in the eastern Free State also moved to towns near their rural homes to earn extra income during the seasons when their labor was not needed on the farm.[79] This would have given Shembe exposure to life in the Free State's segregated locations, which were vibrant centers of African Christianity. For Shembe, however, events did not unfold that way. In the late 1880s, when Shembe was about twenty, his father died unexpectedly.[80] With his father's death, it was time for Shembe to eat the inheritance. Shembe later explained how his mother soon began to make the arrangements for him to marry.[81]

The pressure on Shembe to find a wife so soon after his father's death exposed a confluence of forces. Not only did his name designate him as the next patriarch, but marriage would help him secure land on a Boer farm. After his father had died, Shembe and his mother and younger siblings temporarily moved in with one of his uncles.[82] A home not only for Shembe but for his mother and siblings, then, depended upon him finding a wife, getting married, and becoming eligible for a tenancy arrangement.[83] Some of the pressure, too, might have come from the fact that Grabe had land available if Shembe could marry quickly. At the very least, soon after Shembe's first marriage, he was back on Grabe's land.[84]

Shembe became a household head at a difficult time. In the years after 1890, drought, locusts, and cattle disease swept through the Free State.[85] Then the last British war of conquest in the region, the South African War (1899–1902), broke out. As total warfare enveloped the countryside, the British established twenty-four concentration camps in the Orange Free State alone. More than 60,000 Africans were placed in those camps, which had some of the highest single-month death rates among all of the concentration camps.[86] Tens of thousands of Africans from the Free State—indeed, about half the number placed in the camps—became refugees, with Shembe's family likely among them. These people packed up the things they could carry and herded their livestock away to weather the war in places such as Basutoland and Natal.[87] After the war ended, many crossed back into the Orange

River Colony, as the Free State was known under British military rule from 1902 to 1910. They then attempted to rebuild livelihoods as the British introduced schemes to modernize the countryside. The difficulty that rural dwellers encountered pushed many families, Black and white, into towns in this period.[88]

In a time of widespread hardship, Shembe did well by many measures. Perhaps most striking was how rapidly he expanded his family. Within a year of marrying his first wife, Shembe married another and soon after that another. At some point in the first years of the 1900s, he was engaged to a fourth woman and had a child with her.[89] Shembe's ability to marry stemmed in part from his father's success and, as a result, the effects of his inheritance. Even so, many other sons who had inherited their fathers' cattle had not been able to marry as many women. The first census of the Union of South Africa, taken in 1911, underscored the rarity of his circumstances: out of about 50,000 married African men in the Orange Free State, only 4000 had more than one wife. Fewer than seven hundred men had three or more wives, and most of those men were much older than Shembe, meaning that they had had more time to accumulate the wealth needed to marry so many times.[90]

Through his marriages, Shembe might have also contributed to sustaining his chiefdom. Many of his wives' families had names woven through Hlubi history: Ngwenya, Tshabalala, and Hadebe.[91] In the Free State, as someone whose father and grandfather once advised Hlubi chiefs, he had even married a daughter of "a councillor of the Hlubi chief Langalibalele."[92] Shembe married these women, moreover, as Inkosi Langalibalele returned from exile and imprisonment. Although he never regained the title of chief, his son did, just over the border from the Orange Free State in 1897.[93] Other chiefdoms managed to sustain similar cross-border arrangements, making it possible that this reinstatement in Natal further bolstered a sense of Hlubi-ness among the people in the Free State too.[94]

As Shembe told it, he managed to hold onto a position of relative security on Grabe's farm as well, and his status as a favorite endured. He described friendly pumpkin-growing competitions with his white landlord, charity from the white farmer's family, and a deathbed request from Grabe that Shembe stay to "look after" Grabe's children until they were grown.[95] What is more, even after Shembe and his family were "uprooted" by the South African War, he managed to return to the same land with the same white family who held him in esteem, however tinged by racial hierarchy and paternalism.[96] Amid others' townward migration, this ability to stay on the farm was significant. And outside of his good relations with the landlord and the security of his land tenure, Shembe also described himself as a talented farmer whose crops succeeded. He was especially good at breaking in horses and other draft animals in a place where literal horsepower still moved most goods, people, and machines.[97] Income from such work, in addition to his herds and crops, helps explain why Shembe could later describe himself during his years in the Free State as "well off."[98] Indeed, his family might have resembled the successful tenant family described above in many ways—but not in at least one important way.[99]

During the same time that Shembe did well by many measures, his family also endured startling losses. The most significant were the deaths of his children. In an interview in 1929, Shembe recounted the number of his children who died. His first wife "bore seven children. Four died young. Another died in maturity." His second wife "bore five—three died, two remained." The third "bore me three children—one died, two remain." And the woman to whom he was engaged for a time "bore only one, it died."[100] All told, then, Shembe had sixteen children, of which ten died. In the same interview, Shembe recounted a particularly harrowing period during which three of his sons died in a matter of weeks. The first to die was a boy named John; he was "of the age when boys herd the calves," so probably around eight or older. He "was sick for two days" before he passed away. Then a boy named Frans and another—this one named Thulasizwe—died as well.[101]

It is hard to know how the numbers in Shembe's family compared to other families' losses at a time when infant and childhood mortality was generally high. These deaths revealed the effects of food insecurity, unsanitary water supplies, and new patterns of movement, whether experienced by refugees fleeing war or by the many people moving between town and the countryside.[102] The deaths might have been an indirect consequence of Shembe's work. Horse manure attracted flies, which acted as carriers of an especially pernicious bacteria in the Free State: *Salmonella typhi*, the source of typhoid, or "enteric fever," as it was known then. The disease often struck children who had survived infancy.[103]

Shembe's losses place his success and especially his marriages in a murkier light. On one hand, Shembe had been among the few men able to muster the bridewealth to marry so many women, but he had also perhaps married so many women because he was hoping to have a wife whose children would live. He broke off his fourth engagement after the child born to his fiancée had died as well.[104]

Many Africans in the region understood the deaths of children as an indication of something very wrong: some act of intentional evil or a situation with the ancestors that would demand the assistance of an expert or healer.[105] Whether or not Shembe still considered such possibilities is unknown, but he was likely looking for answers—especially because the deaths of so many children to different wives implicated Shembe himself as the common cause. More than that, they were also children for whom Shembe described great love. He told a story later about how, after one of his sons died, he had stayed up all night with his son's body because he "still hoped for his resurrection."[106] He had to be convinced to bury the boy. It is also possible that the deaths of sons who had survived infancy prompted not just immense grief but also an existential crisis for Shembe. The labor demands of tenancy were such that the absence of surviving sons might have made Shembe doubt whether he would be able to keep up, no matter how many younger brothers or cousins or uncles were nearby to help. But, as Shembe grappled with what his losses might mean for his family, the region where he lived was pulsing with a theology that offered some answers about what had happened to him.

The Making of a Revivalist

As Shembe would tell his life story in the 1920s, he had heard a voice after his father's death, telling him, "Don't marry."[107] He would later say, too, that he had tried to explain his reservations to his mother but that she had insisted he marry anyway, "having paid already so much of the dowry [bridewealth]" for his first wife.[108] Even after Shembe married one wife and then another, he said that his interest in God had not gone away. He continued finding time alone to sneak out and pray. He said that he sometimes, too, heard voices and had dreams and visions that emphasized his disobedience to God.[109] Shembe described tortuous years in which he attempted to muster the courage to do what he thought God was asking in these visions: to leave his family behind to preach the Gospel.[110] It was the deaths of the three sons, one to each wife, that he marked as a breaking point. He said that he asked God, "What sin did I commit that you hit me with such a severe whip?" He said that God told him, "It was you. . . . I told you to separate [from] your wives, for I wanted to speak to you."[111]

Whatever details of Shembe's account are or are not verifiable, Shembe's explanation of what happened offers evidence of his contact with divine healing revivalists.[112] These revivalists argued that Christians were wrong to think that the miracles of Pentecost had come to an end. Instead, God's healing was still promised in the present. A. B. Simpson, a revivalist in the United States, explained, "As salvation is through faith, so is healing." Healing was, again in Simpson's words, "a great redemption right," or something that came from God to those who were redeemed.[113] The darker implication of this message was that bodily suffering resulted from sin. The South African divine healing theologian Andrew Murray explained the link, "The pardon of sin and the healing of sickness complete one the other, for in the eyes of God, who sees our entire nature, sin and sickness are as closely united as the body and the soul." "Sickness," Murray added, "is a consequence of and a visible sign of God's judgment."[114] Shembe's spiritual autobiography would use the events of his life to support a similar position: his sins had brought sickness to him and even death to his children. When he had stopped sinning, moreover, he said he had gotten well. "I was once very ill," he later explained, but "when I became a believer, it left me."[115]

Beyond a few shared ideas, divine healing revivalists debated many things, including whether to break away from their churches to form new ones, whether revivalists should reject all forms of human-made medicine, and even how divine healing happened—that is, whether it occurred instantaneously or through repeated prayer, with the laying of hands or through other methods. This meant that South African revivalists were spread throughout many different denominations and churches. Murray fostered connections to divine healing revivalists in Europe and stayed at a famous "healing home" in London to recover his lost voice after a period of illness. He then returned to South Africa convinced of God's power to heal, but he maintained his membership in the Dutch Reformed Church despite how many others disagreed with him.[116] Similarly, George Weavers was a white missionary from the United States who stoked revivalism among the isiZulu-speaking Congregationalist churches affiliated with the American Board Mission in South Africa. Weavers preached Holiness, a strain of evangelical thought "by which those who accepted the gifts [of Christ] lived free from sin." Weavers also believed that divine healing was possible, however, because he said he himself had been healed.[117] Still other revivalists were affiliated with new denominations, including the largest divine healing church in the United States, the Christian Catholic Apostolic Church in Zion founded by John Alexander Dowie in 1896.[118] But smaller US-based churches sent revivalists to South Africa, too, including the African American–led Church of God and Saints of Christ.[119] A final group of revivalists had no clear affiliation, whether because they rejected organized religion or moved frequently between different groups of Christians.[120]

In some cases, new churches took root because revivalists packaged claims about divine healing with antihierarchical ideas about whose voices mattered and who should be able to lead a church. More broadly, many Christians in the late nineteenth century saw education and training as a potential impediment to evangelism. Consider the words of one mission society convener in Scotland, who, as early as 1878, said, "I am not sure that the farther young men advance in literature and science they are led nearer to Christ."[121] Still, revivalists often took matters a few steps farther, rejecting the notion that any formal training was necessary to preach the Gospel. Maria Woodworth-Etter, for example, a divorced woman living in the United States explained how, in the 1890s, she had "heard the voice of Jesus calling [her] to go out in the highways and hedges and gather in the lost sheep."[122] Woodworth-Etter would go on to become a famous religious figure and one of the originators of the modern Pentecostal movement.[123] Her success underscored how, to many in the revival, a calling from God alone would suffice.[124]

The area around Harrismith became a hub of revivalism because of people whose movements paralleled Shembe's in the years before and after the South African War. In the 1890s, Edgar and Johanna Mahon worked with a group of Black revivalists to begin sneaking onto farms in the eastern Orange Free State to evangelize among the African tenant families living there. When the South African War broke out, the Mahons and their associates weathered the fighting in Natal, preaching divine healing in chiefdoms just over the border in the British colony. If Shembe and his family were among those who also fled into Natal, they would have been very close to the Mahons' preaching field during the war years. Then, after the war, the Mahons were back in Harrismith, the town closest to Shembe. They set up a center for divine healing first on a piece of land within town limits and then, after complaints that they were a menace to public health, farther in the countryside.[125]

On their farm, the Mahons and African co-evangelists began to host large divine healing gatherings several times a year. The attendees were almost all Africans. In many cases, people from farther distances had an easier time coming than people from nearby because of the tight restrictions imposed by white farmers on tenant families' movements. What this meant, however, was that as many as "180 wagons" full of people "all singing the songs of Zion and bringing their sick to be prayed for, or with convicted souls seeking salvation," crisscrossed the region at different times of the year, traveling from as far as Natal and Basutoland.[126] Once they arrived, the people sang, visited, and heard sermons and testimonies. These events would have represented moments when people listened to accounts about the sick and suffering who, again and again, explained how they had tried other remedies unsuccessfully until divine healing finally mended their bodies. Indeed, the organization of these events conveyed a powerful message in a region where rates of literacy were generally still low. At divine healing services, people learned that anyone with a body could interpret some of God's most profound promises—and, in fact, that anyone who had a story would be expected to share it.[127]

The miracles associated with the Mahons ranged from curing cancer and paralysis to mental illness and possession by demons. The people who gathered with the Mahons, however, also told stories of sick and dying children. The Mahons had their own account, which was surely relatable to many, if not as sorrowful as some of the others: they had a baby daughter sick with "croup" who had only gotten well when they "committed their child into God's keeping."[128] Another pair of white revivalists in the region told a story of how they had been tempted to use medicine when "their little Josie had convulsions" and had been sick "for three weeks, during which [her] little life seemed to hang by a thread." Eventually, they said, "the child was healed" through the prayers they had almost abandoned.[129] While such accounts emphasized that healing could come as people steeled their faith, some revivalists said they preached because they had not been so lucky. To return to Woodworth-Etter, she told people how she had come to divine healing as she struggled with the losses of her six children.[130] Other famous revivalists who had themselves been sick as children wove these personal experiences into their testimonies too.[131]

Revivalists used stories of sick and dying children to confirm that God was both loving and judging. Most revivalists believed in an "age of accountability," before which people were not responsible for their sins. Children's innocence meant that they would go to heaven if they died and that their deaths could warn their sinning parents who might not.[132] The consequences of these associations could be powerful for revivalists because of how they linked the fate of children to the morality of parents. Indeed, such associations would contribute to the downfall of one of the United States' most famous proponents of divine healing, the already mentioned Dowie. His daughter's unexpected death in 1902 became part of an accumulating body of evidence among members of his congregation that he was not as godly as he claimed to be.[133] For others, however, these accounts must have offered hope that they could protect themselves from a misfortune that they knew was all too common.

Shembe had reasons to be interested in testimonies about sick and dying children and in a theology that unsettled notions of who could preach. A voice might call anyone to take a message out to the "highways and hedges"—even a polygynous man in South Africa who had likely never been in a church. In fact, the antihierarchical impulses of the revival underscored the possibility that the least likely of messengers could have the strongest connection to God.[134]

Leaving Home

Nazaretha sources are largely silent about how Shembe might have gotten exposure to divine healing while still living on the farm, but there were many possible channels. Revivalists might have come onto the farm where he lived to proselytize, and Shembe's work of breaking in animals would have brought people from other parts of the region to and from him. Shembe described journeys away from the farm too, not only to find spaces to pray in secret but also to access some of the scattered remaining sites of commonage and shared watering holes and rivers in the region.[135] And despite the draconian pass laws in the Free State, African people frequently used roadsides to camp out on journeys.[136] The people traveling the long distances to and from the Mahons' likely would have used these spaces.

The timeline of Shembe's decision to leave his family is also difficult to establish. In his spiritual autobiography, he described a protracted period of trying different arrangements to see if they might satisfy God—keeping only one wife, for example—before he concluded that he had to leave. Shembe's last surviving child was born by 1907, suggesting that he had not left before then.[137] Other sources placed him away from the farm soon thereafter.[138]

In Shembe's account of his departure from the farm, his mother most resisted his plans to leave. His wives had been sad and protested, but it was his mother who asked him if he was "crazy" and kept watch on him to see if he was sneaking off (again) to pray. Shembe recalled how she would sometimes "meet [him] at the gate, asking [him] where [he] had been" as he returned from prayer, although he suspected that she already knew the answer.[139] Perhaps because she was a bridge to the tumultuous Hlubi past—and would have remembered the violence of the 1870s more clearly than he did—she understood acutely the importance of what their family had been able to do in the Free State even if not everything had gone as they hoped. Certainly, she understood what it had meant to give her son the name Mdliwamafa and how none of her other sons would ever likely achieve as much because Shembe had already eaten the inheritance. Shembe's mother stood out as the most important authority he would have to defy to leave. His conversion involved summoning the courage to do so.

Whatever Shembe left behind on the farm, he also carried with him enduring elements of his family's history. The boy who had grown up chosen, as the inheritor, and with a profound sense of responsibility began to tell people as an adult that God had not only chosen him but made him doubly responsible: for his suffering and for saving others. As he began to figure out what to do next, moreover, he held onto a possibility confirmed by his parents' and grandparents' experiences too: the idea that, if circumstances did not work out, he would be able to move again. After leaving the farm, Shembe's first destination was the nearest town, Harrismith.

CHAPTER 2

A Baptist in Town

THE EARLIEST KNOWN PHOTOGRAPH OF SHEMBE COMES FROM HIS YEARS IN Harrismith. In it, Shembe wears store-bought clothes. His ensemble includes a jacket and pants, if not a formal suit. Peeping through the opening of the jacket, one sees a shirt and flouncy necktie. A felt hat sits on his head, and he has boots on his feet. Shembe looks like a farmer dressed up nicely for town. If his clothes seem crisp and new, he had probably owned similar ones when he still lived on the farm. Something Shembe likely had not owned, however, rests on his lap in the photograph: a piece of luggage resembling a doctor's bag. The spread of consumer culture made certain items potent symbols of competition in South Africa. Shembe was using the doctor's bag to broadcast what he claimed to do and whose efforts he claimed to rival.[1]

Shembe is not alone in the photograph. The man standing behind Shembe's right shoulder is a Baptist preacher from the Transvaal named William Leshega. At a time when many portraits showed people in dress that reflected similar levels of social status, the photograph of Shembe and Leshega stands out for its two subjects' differences.[2] In the photograph, Leshega wears a top hat, a minister's robe, and a clerical collar. One of his hands encloses a cane, chosen for style more likely than necessity. In such photographs, many people like Leshega signaled their ability to read by carrying a Bible, dressing in academic regalia, or holdings papers. Leshega broadcasts his ability to read in another way: with a pair of reading glasses draped on a chain around his neck.

Shembe was only in Harrismith for a few years and in Leshega's company perhaps a handful of times in that period. The photograph might have been taken for Shembe's baptism. More likely, it was taken around the time that Shembe was preparing to leave for his first mission, a trip he would embark upon as a Baptist affiliated with Leshega's church.[3] This photograph might have rested against an inside pocket of Shembe's doctor's bag, to be taken out to communicate to people who could not read certificates or letters that Shembe had affiliation with someone who looked official. Leshega's presence made the doctor's bag in Shembe's lap more significant. By standing beside Shembe in the photograph, Leshega sanctioned his claim to heal.

One might imagine the moment of the photograph as a profound success for Shembe. The move to town had thrown him into a space with different demographics, social fissures, and patterns of daily life. Within a few years of arriving in town, Shembe had, however, become associated with a church leader willing to validate his homespun religiosity. In addition to a portrait with Leshega, Shembe also had certificates affirming his role as an evangelist and a designated mission field. And, indeed, all of this was significant—more so because few other places in South Africa would have opened such opportunities to him.

The events that brought Shembe to the moment of the photograph were more complicated. Shembe's early faith, fostered in observation and relative isolation, had not involved much contact with communities of African Christians. In Harrismith he soon learned more about those communities as he struggled to fit in among the nearly 75 percent of African town dwellers who were already Christians.[4] Indeed, perhaps the biggest indication of Shembe's difficulties came, ironically, from the fledgling Baptist Church that made a place for him. Even in Leshega's church, the leadership determined that Shembe could best be used somewhere else.[5] That was why, at the time of the photograph, Shembe likely readied to leave for Durban.

Sanitation Work

Shembe moved to town with a swell of other people—many white but more who were Black—seeking different livelihoods after the agricultural crises of the 1890s and the devastation of the South Africa War. Harrismith, as a result, had seen a 450 percent increase in its African population since 1890 and was close to becoming a majority-African town.[6] Other towns nearby already were.[7] The influx of people prompted anxieties from white officials about how to manage rapidly growing urban populations. Their anxiety manifested in many ways, including in debates about something that increased along with population growth: sewage.[8]

Many small towns in the Orange River Colony (ORC), as the Orange Free State was known from 1902 to 1910, sought to improve their sanitation systems, but the reforms in Harrismith had added significance. The height of Harrismith's connectivity to an industrializing South Africa had come with the opening of the diamond fields. Indeed, those connections helped explain how Shembe's family had done relatively well as tenants in an economy buoyed by transport routes between the diamond fields and the port of Durban.[9] But then, when the gold fields opened, the new railways built to the Rand bypassed Harrismith.[10] Municipal leaders attempted to rebrand the town by making it a site of white leisure, relaxation, and recuperation. There was golf, horseback riding, and fresh highveld air.[11] Outbreaks of disease did not fit the image. Municipal leaders wrote about the need for "some drastic steps," as one resident wrote, to improve sanitation services as a result.[12]

To people from other countries—and especially Britain, where sewage infrastructure was more advanced—these small-town efforts were laughable because the most sophisticated still relied on a "bucket system" instead of piped sewage. One such observer scoffed at how he was "sometimes able to tell the day of the week merely by passing a latrine," or, in other words, based on the strength of the stench in between bucket-service days.[13] The plans for reform and improvements, nevertheless, offer important context for the job Shembe found soon after arriving in Harrismith.

In town, Shembe became a night-soil collector. The work of collecting buckets of excrement, emptying them in a "sewage farm" twice a week in winter and three times in the summer, washing out the buckets, and then returning them for reuse, would have been, surely, stomach-churning.[14] The job, nevertheless, braided together strands of Shembe's personal history. It required knowledge and skills honed on the farm, including care for the draft animals that pulled the night-soil cart.[15] Shembe likely learned on the job, if he did not know already, about the links between sanitation work and attempts to curb epidemics like the one that had recently killed three of his children.[16] This work represented another way that he could make penance for their deaths.

Once again, Shembe seemed to do his job well. Nazaretha Church members described how Shembe made himself a favorite of another white boss and became a foreman of the African sanitation workers in Harrismith.[17] The 1904 census counted fewer than two dozen such African men throughout the Free State, exposing yet another way that Shembe achieved something rare.[18] The job came with benefits other than recognition. For the kinds of work that Shembe could do in town, sanitation paid relatively well. Shembe earned over £3 a month, an amount that was more than the African men working in the gold mines on the Rand at the same time.[19] The job also allowed Shembe to live legally in housing for "the Native employees in the town."[20] Shembe's housing spared him from some of the scrutiny that others faced amid the municipal policing reforms that also accompanied the growth of the African population. And finally, Shembe's job gave him free time in quantities and with regularity that he likely had not experienced on the farm. As a town employee, he had Sundays off year-round; during the winter, when "bucket service" happened less frequently, he had more time free from work.[21]

The job mattered for many reasons in the short and long term. Perhaps above all, sanitation work fostered in Shembe the sense that inward purity and outward cleanliness were linked. Other divine healing revivalists, too, shared an interest in modern sanitation methods, if not modern medicine, for similar reasons.[22] In segregation-era South Africa, sanitation could do more than signal inner virtue, however. It could also offer some protection from a racist state. Years later, after founding the Nazaretha in Natal, Shembe would sit before a government commission and tell officials that "personal cleanliness" was one of his main teachings.[23] White officials had noticed, repeatedly remarking upon the "cleanliness" of Shembe's community even if they saw little else good in his influence.[24] The job in Harrismith gave Shembe technical know-how as well as exposure to the sanitation anxieties of white officials. Of course, the more immediate effects of the job were important too. Sanitation work gave Shembe security while he explored where he might fit among the many Christians in town. Indeed, soon after moving, Shembe realized that this task—figuring out where he might fit—would take time.

Town Christianity

Urbanized African Christian communities existed in what would become the Free State even before the founding of the Boer Republic. In fact, some of the largest mission stations ever established in southern Africa had been in the region in the first decades of the nineteenth century. These mission stations included thousands of people and were organized as towns, with greater density in central locations, schools, and urban infrastructure. As the Boers conquered the region in the mid-nineteenth century, these mission communities did not survive the destruction that came with white settlers' advance, but remnants of them persisted in other ways. In some cases, the Boers founded towns on the ruins of the old mission stations, even using the same names. The looted goods of African Christians, moreover, helped white townspeople establish themselves. And some of the first African town dwellers in the Orange Free State were likely dispossessed mission station residents.[25]

The early presence of Africans who were former mission station residents in need of homes and work might also explain another peculiar feature of Free State towns: the early establishment and entrenchment of residential segregation.[26] This took the form of urban locations in which Africans were cordoned and curfewed off from areas of towns reserved for whites. Some of this pattern resulted from timing: towns and cities established in South Africa in the middle of the nineteenth century had planners who demarcated segregated locations at the time of their founding.[27] And yet, the legacy of this era of town planning left a deeper mark on the Free State than in any other part of South Africa. By the early twentieth century, the towns of the Free State were the most segregated of any in the country and the ones, some have argued, that provided the clearest blueprint for the ambitions of the apartheid city.[28]

The segregated locations were, from the start, expressions of racism. But they also became powerful incubators of African Christianity in the nineteenth century. The very act of moving to town helped prepare some people for conversion through laws about clothes and housing styles as well as the different rhythms of life that allowed Sundays off from work.[29] Moreover, the demographics of Free State towns, with white Afrikaans and English-speaking populations, meant that small towns often had at least four or five different churches by the 1890s: the Dutch Reformed Church, the Wesleyans, Anglicans, Catholics, and sometimes Lutherans.[30] Many of these denominations sent white ministers to tend to white congregants in town while also "overseeing" missions to Africans.[31] Compared to foreign missionaries on mission stations, most of these white church leaders did not have the language skills or the time to monitor the growing number of African congregants—other than perhaps at key moments such as baptisms, weddings, and funerals. This situation points to the most important reason why the segregated locations produced such large African Christian communities: Africans themselves had more figurative and literal space to direct religious change as they creatively maneuvered within the confines of racist laws. Indeed, even the laws that kept Africans off of "white" streets in town also kept white church personnel out of churches and worship spaces in the segregated locations—at least for certain portions of the day.[32] And the locations offered snippets of public space as well as front yards and homes where people could meet and congregate for worship without anyone else directing them.[33]

The communities of African Christians growing in the segregated locations were not uniform. The number of denominations underscores one source of difference already. By the time Shembe arrived in town, that number was growing. In Harrismith in the early twentieth century, members of the Salvation Army, revivalists affiliated with the Christian Catholic Apostolic Church in Zion, and members of the African Methodist Episcopal Church all contributed.[34] The towns of the Free State pointed to a possibility suspected by some sociologists: that competition can help religious movements grow.[35]

Within denominations, fissures of education and status, if not always class and economics, also divided African Christians in the Free State's towns. The clearest evidence comes from depictions not of Harrismith's segregated location but, from the much larger locations of Bloemfontein, the capital of the ORC.[36] Still, this evidence shows similarities to Harrismith. In both places, for example, a "very respectable class" of African Christian men as well as their wives and families had a place at the top of location hierarchies.[37] As one legacy of their mission affiliation, they could read and write in multiple languages, including English.[38] And, of the 10 percent of Africans who could read in the ORC in 1904, the majority lived in towns where some could get jobs that involved literacy.[39] Some of them made up a small, fragile middle stratum, not always better off financially than other Africans living in town and doing manual labor, but with skills that marked their social status.[40] Still others—and, in fact, the majority African church members—fell in neither the top nor the middle categories. Indeed, many of them lived in the countryside and only attended church as the Boers did: when they traveled to town three to four times a year.[41]

The dynamics of Free State towns made churches a backdrop for contradictory processes. In towns, Africans worked out notions of racial inclusion and started to see similarity across many divides.[42] But in towns, people also experienced exclusion across and within racial categories. Some African Christians bristled at the control of white church leaders whose casual racism appeared even in irregular contact—when, for example, "the white minister does not carry [African children] in his bosom as he does white children." Such indignities contributed to many

Africans' reasons for wanting to leave white-led churches behind.[43] But other people in towns might feel excluded, instead, by African Christians who had longer histories of affiliation, more privileged positions in their denominations, and skills that marked their status. Indeed, even in the revivalist denominations that otherwise challenged church hierarchies, African leaders (and many members) could read.[44] As a result, a newcomer in town such as Shembe—one, moreover, who had recently been married to three wives, who had not been to school, and who collected night soil for a living—chafed more from the exclusion of other African Christians than from white church leaders. Africans represented for Shembe the face of Christianity in the locations as well as the gatekeepers if he wanted something more.

Learning and Trying

With so many versions of Christianity on display side by side, Harrismith offered opportunities to learn with and alongside other African Christians. Shembe seemed to dive into the process. His questions related to the recent events of his own life: What happened to children who died unbaptized? They were not sent to hell, he decided, "for they had not yet sinned."[45] What happened to the souls of people who committed suicide, something that Shembe said he had considered during his torturous last years on the farm? He concluded that one "would stay in a prison cell in a very cold place for all the time which [he was] supposed to live" before being "liberated."[46] Other questions related to the tenets of divine healing: who could "preach in the name of the Lord," if God's healing on earth "came to an end together with Jesus and the apostles," and what happened if one still "trusted in native doctors."[47] During Shembe's time in Harrismith, he arrived at a common revivalist position on medicine: no form of healing other than God's was acceptable.[48]

In Nazaretha accounts, Shembe's questions bear hallmarks of later editing by church historians who scoured the Bible for evidence to support Shembe's theological claims. It seems significant, however, that those historians associated this period of Shembe's life with more questioning and exploration than other eras. Shembe had long lacked a social experience of Christianity; one can imagine him seizing the opportunity to learn from the many Christians around him in the segregated location.

Shembe also tried out different denominations, including the local Wesleyan Church. The membership of the Wesleyan Church in Harrismith was large, with more than 1,300 Africans who were already members or "on trial" to join.[49] In a church so big, no single social profile fit everyone in the congregation. That said, the African Wesleyans had a formal church building that hosted "white weddings" for the minority of its members who could afford them.[50] It also had African teachers and leaders who, unlike Shembe, could read, write, and speak English.[51]

A Nazaretha account that, again, shows signs of later editing, encapsulated sources of tension between Shembe and the Wesleyans. The story described Shembe worshipping among the Wesleyans "in his customary skin dress [because] he did not yet put on trousers." (This description pointed to editing: wearing "skin dress" in town would have been illegal at the time.[52]) The story also described how a "white missionary" announced unexpectedly to the entire congregation, "Today, we shall be led in worship by Shembe, son of Mayekisa."[53] The likelihood of a white missionary leading worship among the African Wesleyans matched the likelihood of that missionary spontaneously asking Shembe to preach. Despite the potential revisions, clothes in the account could still be a proxy for the status, education, and religious authority that Shembe lacked in Harrismith.[54] The use of the white missionary in the story also indirectly suggested Shembe's difficult relationships with other African Christians. Part of the miracle of the account involved the white missionary recognizing what the African Christians would not: Shembe's authority to preach.

Shembe's struggles to make a place for himself among the Christians in town offer context for another of his free-time activities. In Harrismith, he began trying out a strategy that he would turn to again when he had trouble finding people who would listen to him: he used the town as a secure base from which to evangelize outside the town's borders. He said that he rode by horseback to the countryside to try to heal people.[55] Shembe targeted places where Africans did not live under white landlords most likely because he was hoping to stay out of trouble in a part of South Africa where "everybody [white] was a policeman." [56] This sent him to a handful of patches of land with absentee landlords and to Witzieshoek, one of the few rural reserves in the Free State set aside for Africans who lived under the authority of chiefs.[57]

By the early twentieth century, Shembe was not the only person traversing the countryside with something to offer. He had company from "insurance agents, motor salesmen, picture-framers, agricultural implement sellers, itinerant eye 'specialists,' quacks and patent medicine vendors." One problem many of these people encountered—especially if they were selling something among Africans—related to long-held notions about mobility and healing. Many Africans continued to think that the best medicines were pursued, not peddled.[58] A person showing up unannounced at someone's homestead with something to sell or offer faced hurdles from the start. These social presumptions helped explain why, later, when Shembe did finally access space where people could come to him, his ministry took off. In the meantime, Shembe, like many divine healing revivalists in the region, began to tell people that he would pray over the sick for free and "take no fees" to make himself more welcome.[59]

Perhaps Shembe also hoped that not charging could help him avoid accusations of fraud. Even so, Shembe, like the traveling salespeople who did charge, still had some brushes with danger. In one case, the family of a girl said he "put [his] hands on her and she died."[60] They hunted him down and brought him back to observe her condition. When she finally seemed to come back to life, the family let Shembe leave.[61] Such circumstances added to the significance of Shembe's horse. Not only could he travel farther faster to evangelize, but he could also get away more quickly in case of trouble.

Although the Nazaretha would not be tentative later, Shembe was modest in his assessment of his abilities during this time of looking for people to heal. What the Nazaretha community preserved are stories of success: Shembe removing demons, raising people from the dead, restoring people's ability to walk, and curing people of skin disease.[62] These examples all have parallels in Jesus's miracles as the Nazaretha used Jesus's example to index the authority of their church leader. Reflecting on his early days of healing, by contrast, Shembe said, "Some were healed, some were helped although they were not healed, some were not healed."[63] For revivalists in the early twentieth century such assessments were not surprising. They did not think that healing always happened immediately, and many argued that effective healing demanded "right conditions" as much as "right prayer."[64] Someone who could channel God's healing might not be able, then, to heal everyone. But Shembe's tentative assessments and his stories of danger underscore how going door-to-door to find people to heal posed challenges. The difficulty of Shembe's situation both in town and in the countryside made the opportunity that came through affiliation with William Leshega's Baptist Church all the more important.

Building an Independent-ish Baptist Church

William Leshega, the man standing in the photograph with Shembe, illuminated the possibilities of a different era of global evangelism amid South Africa's rapid industrialization. Leshega came from a Lutheran community in the Pedi polity in the eastern Transvaal but had left to work in Pretoria in the 1880s.[65] He already lived near the Rand, then, when people began flocking to the gold fields after 1886. In the fifteen years that followed, Johannesburg grew from nearly nothing to a city of around 100,000 people.[66] Towns on the Rand filled in too, with a railway that connected Johannesburg to places such as Boksburg, Springs, and Krugersdorp—and where the combined population growth was higher than in Johannesburg alone.[67] White missionaries and ministers struggling in other placements in South Africa—and in other parts of the world—saw unprecedented opportunity in these numbers. And while, in many instances, the first arrivals set their sights on ministering to white populations, they saw opportunities in the African people who were already the majority demographic on the Rand.[68] Indeed, in some ways the early culture of evangelism on the Rand modeled what had played out in the segregated locations of the Free State: white missionaries unprepared to minister to African congregants quickly made partners with African Christians who could do the mission work that white missionaries could not. As someone who already had a few years of education, affiliation with a church, and the ability to speak English, Leshega made a prime candidate for such a partnership.

How Leshega connected with any of the Baptists freshly arrived on the Rand was not clear; clearer is how the Baptist faith allowed Leshega to advance quickly and bring more African Baptists into the fold. Perhaps unsurprisingly, denominations with the least oversight adapted quickly to a changing South Africa. In fact, the author of a South African Baptist history, a missionary himself, wrote that he did not know and had "never heard how" the Baptist's first white missionary in Johannesburg had gotten there at a time when "the railway did not reach that far, and the expense was very great."[69] The author did note, however, that once this "genial Irish man" got there, "he soon made friends" and began establishing congregations across the Rand.[70] As a denomination that had grown in Europe and North America primarily from recruiting people who were already Christians, the Baptists could make "friends" more easily than others. That is, someone could become a Baptist by accepting full-immersion, believers' baptism, and without having to be "on trial" before being welcomed into the faith. In the late nineteenth century, the same fast-paced approach extended to delegating pastors, deacons, and church leaders, too. The Baptist emphasis on the autonomy of "the congregation, a tight-knit covenanted community of baptized believers," meant, moreover, that Baptist ministers might plant a church in one place and then leave it to be largely "self-supporting," both in terms of finances and growing its membership.[71] Such a sink-or-swim ethic could backfire. It drove many Baptist ministers to pursue posts in other, more financially supportive denominations.[72] But this was not the case for Leshega because of another key resource that the white Baptists helped him access: land.

As early as 1892, the Baptists set Leshega up on a "church farm" in one of the booming Rand districts. If, in some ways, evangelism on the Rand looked like evangelism in the towns of the Free State, the existence of such patches of land where African Christians lived together under a shared denominational affiliation made the Rand a different mission field.[73] Of course, "church farm" was a misnomer because most of the Africans who moved to these pieces of land had little intention of farming. Most sought proximity to wage-earning work on the Rand. But this meant that Leshega had control over a desirable piece of real estate and, with it, a great deal of authority over determining who became a Baptist. Even if the white Baptists who came to visit had questions, who, other than Leshega, could they have asked? And, instead of asking questions, many of the white Baptists seemed happier to write home about their great successes at making converts. In 1892 a white Baptist missionary, freshly arrived in South Africa, wrote to tell his mother of the Baptists' evangelism in the region. On Leshega's church farm, the Baptists had just baptized six more African members, which, the missionary noted, "makes sixty-five altogether since our arrival."[74] For earlier generations of missionaries, this would have been an astonishing number.[75]

Leshega became a Baptist as the first inklings of Ethiopianism spread through South Africa. In the 1880s, many African Christians had seen opportunities in the mission churches recede, fueling the push to leave white-led churches behind. But Leshega's experiences with the white Baptists add complexity to questions about why African Christians did or did not break away from mission churches. After all, some mission bodies exerted more control than others, and some offered more advantages than others. The white Baptists gave Leshega access to land, but otherwise left him largely alone.[76] The missionary who had written home about Leshega's work probably only visited the church farm a handful of times during his stay in South Africa.[77]

Leshega's authority had limits too, though. The same land that propped up Leshega's position also gave the white Baptists final say. After the South African War, Leshega got into trouble with the white Baptist leadership. Some of these Baptists later passed along second-hand information that Leshega had "seduced a young girl of his congregation."[78] Such rumors were, however, so common in relation to African pastors that it is hard to know how to assess them, and the Baptists might have soured on Leshega for any number of reasons.[79]

The loss of his position on the farm was a real blow, if not an end to Leshega's evangelical career. The changing laws after the South African War had brought new administrators into power and left open many questions about what might happen next—that is, which pass laws would apply to whom and what kinds of permissions the government would grant to African ministers.[80] At the same time, if Leshega had not already embraced the idea that God sometimes permitted evasion and the odd misleading statement, he would be compelled to do so very soon to maneuver within and around the many restrictions he faced.

After failing to secure another piece of land where he could replicate his former position, Leshega stretched some truths as he narrowed down on a different evangelical strategy.[81] First, he established affiliation with a Black American Baptist mission society, telling its representatives (or leading them to believe) that he had been formally ordained by the white Baptists.[82] This Black American mission society was stretched more thinly than the white Baptists and yet was more determined to "uplift the native people."[83] The representatives of this mission, who were stationed hundreds of miles away from Leshega, noted that they had "never met [Leshega] in person, but he has been highly recommended to us by several people."[84] Without asking many questions, they added Leshega's name to a list of "missionaries and native helpers" on "whose salaries no money had been pledged," but whom they "trust will be remembered" with donations from Black Baptists in the United States.[85] Perhaps more important for Leshega, however, members of this mission body wrote for him to government officials as he navigated South Africa's complicated bureaucracy.

Leshega likely knew that his new affiliation was risky and potentially limiting. Already, many government officials did not look kindly on Black American–led evangelism in South Africa and were making efforts to curb their influence by denying their ministers and pastors requests for passes and worship space.[86] But Leshega might have realized that the name of his new mission body, the Foreign Mission Board of the National Baptist Convention, did not immediately give away the race of its US-based leaders—and that many officials in South Africa might not bother to investigate it.[87] With letterhead from this ambiguously titled mission society, Leshega got a special pass, limited to a tiny minority of ordained

African ministers. This pass allowed Leshega to ride the trains without needing a magistrate's permission for every journey.[88] It was likely at this point, too, that he bought clothes like the ones he wore in the photo with Shembe, backing up his official, ordained status by putting on a collar and other formal clerical garb as he readied to ride the rails.[89]

As to where to go, Leshega prioritized places where he would not run into any of his former Baptist associates. The ORC had many African Christians who might be convinced to accept the Baptist creed and whose homes in the segregated locations might provide worship space. Within the ORC, Harrismith would have been of special interest to Leshega. The end of the South African War brought regional extensions that tied small towns to the railway's mainline. He could use them to zigzag across the eastern ORC.[90] As important for Leshega, however, was also Harrismith's proximity to spaces not yet connected by rail. Harrismith sat close to Witzieshoek, one of the few pockets of land in the Free State that had been reserved for Africans living under traditional authorities—and where Shembe had already been trying his hand at evangelism.[91]

Leshega and Shembe

Although Shembe did not attract much attention in Harrismith's African Christian communities, he did make at least one friend, a man named Saul Lephuthi. Nazaretha retellings offer few details about Lephuthi, but what the Nazaretha preserved was revealing. Before moving to Harrismith, Lephuthi had been a teacher who held a lower-level leadership position in the Wesleyan Church of another small town in the ORC.[92]

Shembe likely befriended Lephuthi as he attempted to make connections within a more established denomination and to learn more about Christianity. Lephuthi became a conversation partner for Shembe, someone with whom Shembe worked out some of his answers to the theological questions posed above. Lephuthi also became the first of many literate friends who gave Shembe greater access to the Bible.[93]

It was through this "good friend" that Shembe met William Leshega—most likely because Leshega had wanted someone like Lephuthi (instead of Shembe) in his church. Lephuthi's literacy would have mattered to Leshega not only as a marker of status but also as a skill that could help Leshega string together his spread-thin congregation, whether through writing letters to each other, to Baptist foreign mission societies, or to state officials to see what different authorities might allow.[94] And, although Lephuthi did not seem to join Leshega's church, others like Lephuthi did. Some of them would soon sign Shembe's certificate confirming his status as a preacher and evangelist in Harrismith's Baptist Church.[95]

The relationship that Leshega forged with Shembe represented a step-up in affiliation for Shembe and a step-down—or perhaps a step in a different direction—for Leshega. It is not hard to see what Shembe found appealing about Leshega and the Baptists. Leshega could read and write and appeared formal in a way that Shembe did not. The Baptists also allowed for a rapid pace of inclusion with few questions asked about one's background or other theological commitments. The small membership of the Baptist Church meant, too, that early joiners might more easily gain responsibility. By comparison, the Wesleyan church in Harrismith that Shembe attended had nearly three times as many members as the total number of African Baptists in all of the ORC.[96]

Although Shembe had not necessarily been the kind of person whom Leshega hoped to make a shepherd of his flock, Shembe had important qualities from Leshega's perspective too. Here was someone, after all, willing to collect buckets of sewage for a living so that he could share the Gospel in his free time. What is more, Leshega seemed receptive to Shembe's message of divine healing—perhaps in part because he had not heard about it as much already. Areas on the Rand were on the cusp of a Pentecostal revival that included some elements of divine healing, but the region had not seen the same fervor for divine healing revivalism as in the eastern ORC. Soon after meeting Shembe, Leshega began to preach some tenets of divine healing too.[97]

Leshega and perhaps the other Baptists in Harrismith still had a sense, however, that Shembe's talents might be better used elsewhere. The Baptist newsletters that Leshega read might have given him some clues about another option.[98] The experiences of a few African Baptist missionaries in another part of South Africa had captured a great deal of international attention after the South African War, prompting the National Baptist Convention to decry how certain laws in South Africa made their "work to suffer and our workers to experience great trouble, some being imprisoned even."[99] Members of the National Baptist Convention referred to African Baptists who had been kicked out of the British colony of Natal for their evangelism. Leshega and others decided that Natal would be Shembe's destination.[100]

The danger that the earlier African Baptists faced casts shadows on the decision to send Shembe to the British colony. In fact, their harsh treatment raises the possibility that Shembe was being sent there to get rid of him or at least as a test, to see if an unconventional evangelist could make it. But a more charitable reading comes from a few additional factors salient to the decision. Leshega, after all, was someone more practiced at evasion and could help Shembe learn. Moreover, the story of those earlier Baptists' expulsion, as the next chapter shows, suggested that a Natal mission field might, in fact, reward someone who did not wear formal church garb or speak English and who could not read or write. And if all of this might help Shembe avoid Natal's zealous officials, so perhaps would the fact that Shembe spoke a dialect of the same language spoken by the majority of Africans in Natal, the language Shembe still called isiNtu but that others were calling isiZulu.[101] This was the language he had grown up speaking in his Hlubi home.

The Baptists took other steps to prepare Shembe for departure, suggesting a more charitable reading of their intentions as well. They baptized him by full immersion; gave him a "commission" to baptize others into the faith; and, in 1908, filled out the certificate that would confirm his formal role in their church to those who could read it.[102] To return to the photograph that opened this chapter, 1908 was also, then, when Leshega and Shembe likely went to the Harrismith photography studio to create the image that would communicate Shembe's affiliation to other people who could not read. It was possible that Leshega contributed some of the funds for Shembe's fresh-looking clothes and the doctor's bag as part of the send-off too.[103] Either way, the clothes were, at once, an expression of Shembe's differences from other African Christian leaders and a disguise that would help him avoid detection in the dangerous place he was headed.

Leshega might have helped Shembe decide upon a name as the younger man prepared to leave Harrismith. Baptisms were common times for choosing new names, but, because of South Africa's thicket of pass laws monitoring Africans' mobility, so was preparation for travel.[104] Many African men gave fake names when applying for passes as one way to avoid detection and to trick pass officers into giving them additional passes as needed.[105] Records from Natal make it seem likely that the new first name Shembe chose was not "Isaiah," but instead "John." There were many Johns (or Jans in Afrikaans) in the region, making the name generic and hard to track. But, for Shembe, the name was also a reference to the first of his three older sons who had died not long before he left the farm.[106] The name could communicate, too, the form of baptism that Shembe intended to offer—full immersion in the model of John the Baptist.[107] Such a choice would also, then, allow Shembe to show people that he knew something about the Bible despite the fact that he might be evangelizing among people who were more familiar with it than he was.

Just when Shembe settled on his last name is unclear as well, but the combination of new commitments and pass-law strategy surely motivated him to choose a different last name too. His family's "clan name" was Nhlanzi, a name that Shembe would honor later in his life by naming a Nazaretha settlement Nhlanzini, or the Place of Nhlanzi.[108] But, as he prepared to leave Harrismith, he was likely looking for a last name that marked his new start and would be difficult to trace. There is no evidence that anyone ever had the last name "Shembe" before him.[109]

Shembe expressed some reservations about leaving. Perhaps he knew what had happened to those earlier Baptists. (And if he did not when he left Harrismith, he soon would.) The reason he gave for not wanting to go involved his mother. In Harrismith he "could still help [her]."[110] This explanation represented one of many ways that Shembe would show, over the next few years, that he had not forgotten the family he left behind. But perhaps because of what Harrismith had taught him about African Christian communities or because he expected to return soon, he did decide to go. Sometime most likely in 1908 or early 1909, Shembe headed to the local pass office so that he could buy a railway ticket to take the train to Natal's biggest city, Durban.

CHAPTER 3

An Evangelist in Durban

THE BOTHA'S HILL TRAIN STATION COMES UP MORE THAN ONCE IN NAZARETHA accounts of Shembe's time in Durban.[1] Travel writers from the early twentieth century marveled at the construction of the tracks leading up to the station, where some of the "heaviest railway cuttings in Natal are passed" and where it "appears at times as though [railway] carriages will be dashed between the cliffs."[2] Shembe might have been impressed by these engineering feats as well, but, for him, the station was something else: both a literal and symbolic end of the line. Traveling from the city of Durban, it was the last stop on the mainline and the farthest place someone could ride after purchasing just one ticket. In Harrismith, Shembe had used a horse to stretch the possibilities of town while still living within town limits. In Durban, he used the train to do the same for the city. The Botha's Hill station was not only the last stop on the mainline but also a place where one could decide to buy another ticket to keep going back to Harrismith. After about a year in Durban, Shembe did.

One might imagine that a bigger city would be a good place for Shembe, with a greater number of people to respond to his message of divine healing and unconventional background. Indeed, that notion might have influenced Leshega and the Harrismith Baptists' decision to send him away. Leshega might have known how some African Christians more like Shembe were finding ways to expand congregations in rapidly urbanizing areas, especially in the goldmining regions on the Rand.[3] But, then again, Durban was not the Rand.

In Durban, Shembe found himself navigating two sets of extremes. The first related to disdain for African Christians. By the early twentieth century, many white officials at outposts of empire groused about the "trousered Africans" that Christianity had helped make. In Natal, such concern translated into some of the most draconian laws targeted at African Christians not only in South Africa but throughout the British Empire.[4] In fact, Shembe headed into the colony at a time when it was even illegal for him to preach in public and when denominations flourishing in other parts of South Africa stayed away as a result.[5] And, if Natal was especially dangerous for African Christians, Durban was especially dangerous for African men.[6] At a time when city and municipal officials around the world sought ways to manage and control growing urban populations, the approach in Durban did not yet include segregated locations for Africans.[7] Without such spaces, Durban officials kept certain populations—and especially African men—"in their place" by cordoning them off legally instead.[8]

The extremes pushed Shembe out to places such as Botha's Hill, where he could find a different organization of space and authority that was, nevertheless, connected to the city. Even there, however, Shembe made few converts and must have been disappointed by the results. The conditions he encountered in Durban meant that success might be measured by other metrics: the fact that he, unlike the Baptists who came before him, was not caught and the fact that he made connections to people who would help him return to another part of Natal to try again.[9]

African Christianity under Attack

In Natal, white officials' extreme response to African Christianity grew out of the colony's history of missions and land distribution. In few white settler colonies had foreign missionaries been more important to colonial planning than in Natal, where the earliest colonial administrators envisioned missionaries as "indispensable auxiliaries of the government," who would shepherd Africans on the path to Christianity and civilization.[10] This vision of close partnership with foreign missionaries did not pan out. It did, however, translate into mission societies controlling vast tracts of land in Natal in the earliest days of the colony, with some of the first mission stations including 6,000 to 8,000 acres of land each.[11] The American Board Mission, as a foreign missionary firstcomer in the region, received more than 100,000 acres of land altogether.[12] Over time, groups of African Christians—sometimes with foreign missionary assistance and sometimes without—also found ways to acquire property. In fact, the footprint of African Christian land ownership would contribute to Shembe's eventual land-buying success in the region.[13] Long before Shembe began buying land, however, Natal had the highest percentage of mission-controlled land and the highest percentage of African-owned land in South Africa.[14]

In Natal, antagonisms toward African Christians and foreign missionaries took sharper focus as colonial officials pushed for "responsible government" in the early 1890s.[15] To prove to Britain that they should have greater independence in their own affairs, representatives of the settler government emphasized a founding myth. White Natalians would not celebrate the liberal, assimilationist traditions of the Cape, but, instead, the "Shepstone system."[16] Named for Theophilus Shepstone, who was the son of missionaries and one of the planners in the era of close missionary cooperation, this "system" was like many others in colonial contexts: a hodgepodge of policies and improvisations in pursuit of "hegemony on a shoestring."[17] Some of the basic components of this system aligned, however, with later notions of indirect rule because the Shepstone system involved selective interpretations of custom and the use of traditional authority to govern.[18] The 70,000 Africans living either on mission land or on African-owned land could escape some of the authority of this system.[19] They became both a perceived threat and a convenient scapegoat for officials.

Between the early 1890s and 1910, the government of Natal used a range of laws to try to curb the influence of African Christians and foreign missionaries. These efforts extended to chipping away at the privileges of "exempted" Africans, denying Africans easy access to Christian marriage, and choking the missions of funding. More than that, Natal officials made it clear that, unlike in other parts of South Africa, affiliation with white missionaries alone would not help African pastors and evangelists secure additional privileges from the state. Officials used ambiguous phrases such as "under *effective* European control" to ensure this. And for churches "under no European control," options were more limited still. Natal's laws forbade "any Native Minister or member of a religious movement not under European control and not recognized . . . to address meetings or assemblies of Natives."[20] This law made the African Methodist Episcopal Church effectively a banned organization in Natal and would be one reason why Shembe's work was so difficult at first. It meant that, if caught preaching, Shembe—or any other African pastor without white-led mission affiliation—could be arrested, fined, and potentially deported.[21]

Officials intended the new laws to distribute authority back toward chiefs to further emphasize, again, the role of the Shepstone system in promoting good governance.[22] If Natal's planners had once envisioned Christianity as the transformational solvent that would slowly eradicate customary law, now the government attempted to enlist chiefs to eradicate the influence of Christianity. Within a few years, Shembe's experiences with chiefs would show that these efforts often represented too little too late. The intention of the laws was, however, still revealing.

Earlier Baptists in Natal

Why, one might wonder, did African Baptists (or any other African evangelists) bother to show up in Natal amid such an antagonistic legal regime? Two African men with Baptist affiliation, Johnson Benjamin Mfazwe and Funiselo Solani, were among the African Christians who moved into Natal to evangelize there anyway.[23] They came from the Cape, where the presence of white British and then German settlers made it a hub of Baptist activity and where, as on the Rand, Africans had taken control of spreading the faith in their communities and beyond.[24] By the time they entered Natal, these two men, like Leshega, had affiliation with the African American–led National Baptist Convention.[25]

Mfazwe and Solani would later claim that they did not know about Natal's especially harsh laws, which might have been true. Implementation of the laws was spotty, and the patchwork of shifting legal frameworks in South Africa made it difficult for the people enforcing the laws as well as the people maneuvering within them to keep up. Still, white and Black Christians in South Africa exhibited different degrees of willingness to abide by the limits the state tried to impose, and one could often see patterns along denominational lines. Many Baptists, for example, ploughed ahead when, again, members of the African Methodist Episcopal Church, would not. These differences make it seem as if more than ignorance or knowledge of the law determined why some denominations showed up and why some did not.

Whatever Mfazwe and Solani did or did not know about how they were breaking the law, they also likely knew some things that made Natal an attractive mission field for African Christians without strong foreign missionary connections or frequent financial assistance. The presence of more than 140,000 Africans who were already Christians made for many potential recruits.[26] Moreover, the economy of Natal's largest city, Durban, was booming in the 1890s and the first years of the twentieth century, as shipping capacity tripled and brought more jobs with this expansion. A few years of education, as both Baptist men had, could get an African a better-paying job, but Durban also offered *togt* jobs, or casual and day labor, to supplement income if needed. These opportunities for work offered a safety net if evangelism was not successful.[27]

The biggest advantage in Natal related to a certain kind of mobility that could only be conferred on African men from outside of the colony's borders—men such as Mfazwe and Solani and, later, Shembe. Natal's government had for decades sought ways to secure access to Africans' labor despite the better wages that workers often found outside the colony's borders. By the early twentieth century these attempts intersected with railway expansion and led to laws that made it very hard for African men to leave Natal, while making it very easy for African men from elsewhere to enter. As a result, an African man who claimed he wanted to enter Natal to work got an "inward pass" that lasted for one year and that gave its holder permission to use the trains throughout that time.[28] Elsewhere, similar freedom to ride the train without a government-issued pass required for the purchase of each train ticket was a privilege limited to very few Africans: ordained ministers or people with exemption.[29] (Again, that was why Leshega's success at convincing the Black American Baptists of his ordination represented such an achievement; it gave him greater access to the train.) In Natal, then, by claiming to be work seekers, African Christian men got a year of freer movement and opportunities to scout out more territory. If they did well enough to stick around, they could get a new inward pass simply by leaving Natal, returning to a border office with a different name, and applying for another pass that would give them one more year of easy access to the train.[30] Natal officials complained that they had no way to keep this cycle from going on indefinitely.[31]

Mfazwe, according to official correspondence, had come from Port Elizabeth, traveling via ship and entering through the Port of Durban in 1899. Perhaps because of bribes, bureaucratic mistakes, or both, he had managed to get passes for himself as needed (without having to resort to the name-change trick) as well as for his wife and daughter to relocate to Natal.[32] Using Durban as a base, Mfazwe then traveled north and south along the railway. He went into the rural reserves where, like Leshega, he was "usually wear[ing] clerical dress and spectacles" and where he preached a message that "we," as one African observer who heard him recalled, "would be properly baptized, not have our faces sprinkled with water."[33]

Mfazwe had enough success to recruit someone else to help him manage a mission field that would have stretched more than a hundred miles. In fact, his trouble began because of that success. In 1901, Mfazwe wrote a letter to introduce the second Baptist man, Solani, to the magistrate of a district in southern Natal, near the Cape border. The letter explained that Solani was a "preacher + deacon" who had "the authority to baptize and to administer the sacraments of the Lord's supper."[34] Perhaps Mfazwe had written similar letters to magistrates in the Cape? Perhaps elsewhere such letters had worked to smooth over relations, get concessions, or to test out the dangers of a particular mission field? In the Orange River Colony (ORC), Leshega and his evangelists would write similar letters over the next few years that met with polite rejections from officials. "This is not a case," one official wrote in a typical response to Leshega and his affiliates, "in which the privilege can be granted."[35] Emphasizing, again, the extent to which Natal was different, the magistrate who received Mfazwe's letter took offense. Mfazwe did not even say, the magistrate wrote, "to what denomination he belongs . . . + he practically tells me that Solan [sic] is to be allowed the free rein of the district."[36] The magistrate initiated an investigation with the colonial government.[37]

Over the next two years, Mfazwe and Solani struggled in different ways to continue growing their flocks in Natal, but their experiences showed the limited recourse of men in their positions. Solani returned to the Cape, but he continued to fight from across the border. The congregation he had ministered in Natal paid lawyers' fees to try to bring him back; they also paid for Solani to travel to the United States in 1903 to rally support from foreign missionary sponsors.[38] Two years later, when Baptists from around the world convened in London to establish the Baptist World Alliance, Solani's plight appeared on the agenda. It did not help. He stayed in the Cape, where he evangelized and appealed for continued aid there instead. In one letter to the National Baptist Convention from 1911, for example, he asked for money to build a church that could answer "the Englishman" who asked, "Can native people do anything successful without a white man taking charge?"[39] It is not clear if such entreaties, intertwining resources and racial solidarity, ever helped him meet his desired aim.

Mfazwe's errant pass (however acquired) gave him some time before he faced removal. He used it to write Natal officials explaining that any mistakes he had made were "not through disregard of the Pass Law, [but] through ignorance of it."[40]

Mfazwe also wrote to Joseph Chamberlain, the secretary of state of the colonies in the United Kingdom, but, again, to no avail.[41] Mfazwe, who realized that he faced arrest or expulsion, left a few months before his pass expired. He moved north, toward the border with Mozambique, either to chart a new career in trade or to evangelize there (or do both). In 1903, Mfazwe's wife reported to Natal officials that he had died of fever.[42] This might have been a faked death—as part of an effort to give Mfazwe some relief with a new start and a new name by crossing a border.[43] But, even if it was, Mfazwe no longer worked as an evangelist in the region by the time Shembe arrived. Supporting the idea that Mfazwe did die while attempting to escape his pass troubles, Nazaretha accounts described Shembe going to visit Mfazwe's grave soon after he arrived in Natal.[44]

Looking at the experiences of the two Baptist men, one could interpret their story as a reason to stay out of Natal. Yes, the men's troubles sent a warning about the aggressive enforcement of anti-Christian laws as well as the limits of foreign missionaries' advocacy. That said, one could also interpret their story as a lesson about what was possible if one did things differently. It had taken two years for the men to be discovered, and they had only gotten into trouble after Mfazwe wrote a letter to an official. Shembe could not read or write or speak much English, all hallmarks of the "trousered Africans" who provoked so much official ire.[45] Mfazwe and Solani had, moreover, left congregations behind, with members who might welcome someone bold enough to try again and who might understand why that person did not wear "clerical dress," like those who had come before him.

Durban-Bound

After getting his own "inward pass" to enter Natal, Shembe would have gotten on a train perhaps for the first time in his life. Natal's two main railways converged upon Durban in a sideways, slanting *T*. The older of the two lines cut northwest from the port city, connecting to the Orange River Colony. This route had attached Durban's port to the markets opened by diamonds. Shembe rode on this line, sloping down through the steep mountain pass that his parents had traveled up by foot some three decades before when they moved into the Free State. The train would have passed near the old Hlubi territory in Natal as it cut southeast.[46]

Keletso Atkins, Ralph Callebert, David Hemson, and Paul La Hausse have all done important work to illuminate the world of African working men (and some women) that Shembe entered.[47] Since the 1880s, Durban had grown due to factors

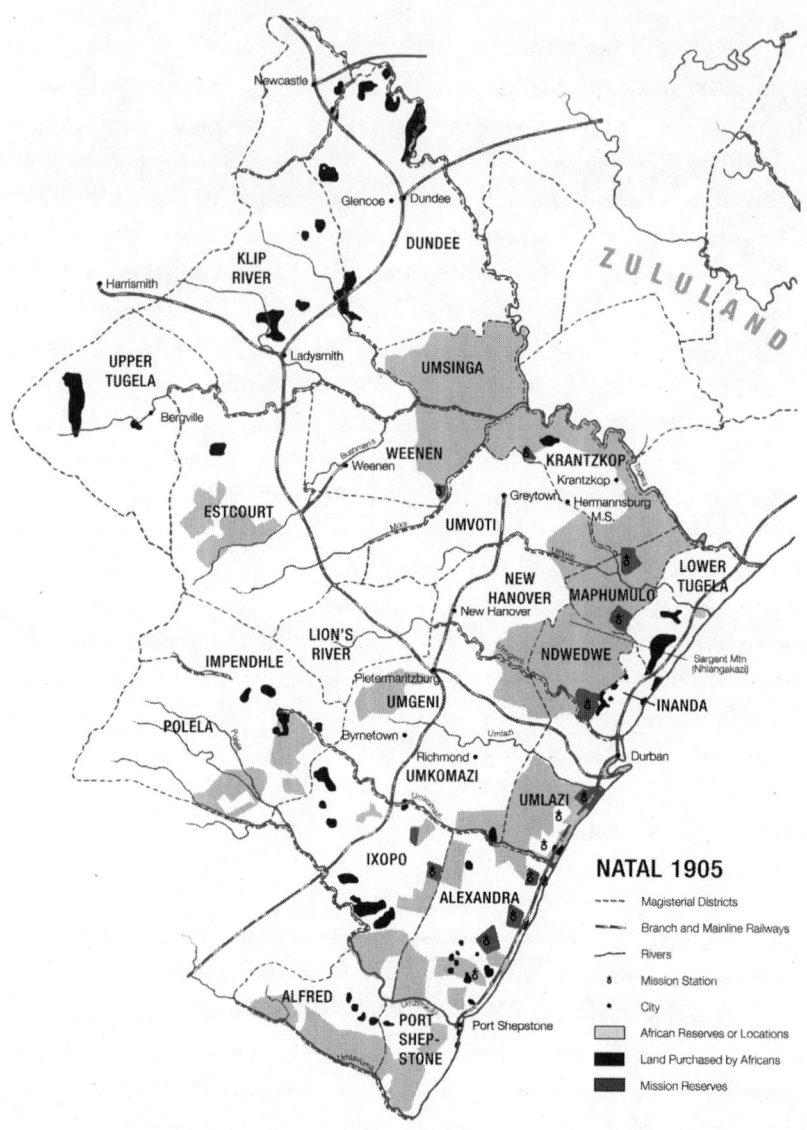

NATAL 1905

- - - - Magisterial Districts
━┿━ Branch and Mainline Railways
━━ Rivers
⚲ Mission Station
• City
▨ African Reserves or Locations
■ Land Purchased by Africans
▨ Mission Reserves

MAP 2. Natal on the eve of Shembe's arrival.

ADAPTED FROM MAPS IN SHULA MARKS, *RELUCTANT REBELLION* (OXFORD, UK: CLARENDON, 1970),
AND JOHN LAMBERT, *BETRAYED TRUST* (SCOTTSVILLE, ZA: UNIVERSITY OF NATAL, 1995).

largely outside of its city limits. Gold mining in the Transvaal had significantly increased the volume of trade at the port without reworking the fundamental structure of an economy built around shipping and sales.[48] At the same time, people from outside of Durban filtered into town, on new terms and for different reasons. More South Asian people moved to Durban as a place to make livelihoods after indenture contracts ended.[49] And for decades African men had already pursued migrant work in Durban, if, by the early twentieth century, doing so was "no longer a source of agency, but a result of impoverishment" in the rural areas they left behind.[50] These movements had increased the city's population to more than 70,000 people, with roughly equal portions of Africans and Indians as well as a white community a bit smaller than the African and Indian populations combined.[51]

Shembe arrived in Durban with strong demographic camouflage. In the 1911 census, nearly sixteen times more African men lived in the borough of Durban than African women.[52] (African women came to town on the weekends to sell beer and to see relations, but they did not count in the census figures.)[53] Shembe's age—he was around forty—made him older than most. As a growing number of older African men sought work in the city, however, he would not have seemed out of place.[54]

In Durban, Shembe did not have, however, the same sets of rural ties as other men. The laws that facilitated Shembe's entry, as someone from outside of the colony, made it more difficult for African men from inside the colony to leave.[55] Most of the African men in Durban, as a result, hailed from the rural reserves of Natal and Zululand. Groups of boys and men from the same rural area would often come to Durban together and then live and work together before, in some cases, returning home to the same region they had left.[56]

What Shembe did have by the time he moved to Durban was a denomination. His experience showed how religious affiliation could help people navigate urban migration. Shembe met up with a group of Baptist men living in the workers' barracks at the Point. Led by a man called Pastor Mathe, these Baptists had been converted by Mfazwe before his forced departure and likely death. The Baptist men were more typical of others in Durban in that they came from the same rural area: in this case, Ndwedwe, a district north of the city.[57]

Ndwedwe had been where some of the earliest foreign missionaries received large allotments of land for mission stations and, therefore, where a minority of African Christians had lived for decades already.[58] Indeed, the presence of those Christians (and their proximity to the train) helped explain why Mfazwe had been successful there. More recently, Ndwedwe had also experienced a different strand of divine healing revivalism than the one in Harrismith. This strand took the form of a commitment to sanctification and the call to give up medicine.[59]

The religious currents in Ndwedwe meant that the Baptist men in Durban would not have understood Shembe's message as especially foreign or necessarily seen him as a strange choice. They would have heard claims like the ones that Shembe was making about God's healing even if they had not yet heard them packaged with the Baptist creed. In Ndwedwe, moreover, children and youths were often the vehicles of revivalism, as another testament to the way that the revival reworked notions of religious authority.[60] Shembe might have represented a restoration of gendered and generational order to them despite how he differed from people such as Mfazwe. And again, they might have appreciated that Shembe was evangelizing in Natal after what had happened to his predecessors.

The support of the Baptist men in Durban changed Shembe's life. A few years after they met him—and after Shembe had given up on Durban and gone back to Harrismith—those men would offer him the funds to return to Natal.[61] Although there is less evidence to draw upon, they surely helped him more immediately after arriving in Durban too. The barracks were a difficult place to live, with one white official saying that he had seen "better stabling for horses."[62] The other men might have made it easier for Shembe to adjust. They likely supplemented his finances too. Shembe had the bad luck of entering Durban during an economic downturn.[63] He would have needed more money as he began to travel farther from the barracks to try to find people who would listen to him and spaces where it was safe for him to talk to them.

Seeking Space in and outside of Durban

When Shembe moved from Harrismith to Natal's biggest city, he moved from one of the most racially segregated urban areas in South Africa to the least.[64] The barracks where Shembe made his residence were exceptional in Durban as one early example of residential segregation in the municipality. Durban officials agreed with white officials in many other parts of South Africa that Africans were "mere visitors" in the city with "no right to share in the same privileges that regular citizens do."[65] But Durban's officials interpreted Africans' status as "mere visitors" differently. Rather than segregating Africans in locations, the municipality "allowed [Africans] to squat in every yard, hole, and corner" in the city, as one police officer complained in 1904.[66]

Most Africans lived, in other words, in backyards, rooms, garages, small apartments, shared houses, and stables rented out by white and South Asian landlords. This "laissez-faire" approach, as municipal leaders termed it, meant that many white and South Asian city dwellers supplemented their incomes from rent paid by African men and, in some cases, paid lower wages because they offered housing too.[67]

Shembe's early explorations of Durban coincided with debates among white municipal leaders about how to manage the city's residential integration as the numbers of Africans and Indians swelled. Already city planners were implementing new policies to segregate South Asian people in the municipality. And perhaps the very year that Shembe moved to the port city, its officials settled on the terms of the so-called "Durban system" that would eventually propel the development of segregated urban locations for Africans in the region. The Durban system gave the city a monopoly on legal beer-brewing and selling to finance segregated facilities.[68] But change was slow. For the first fifteen years, the revenue from the beer monopoly would only produce small experiments in segregated residential space: the construction of additional barracks and tiny "model villages" for African families.[69] It would not be until the 1930s that Durban had segregated residential locations like those in other parts of South Africa—some eighty years after they had been established in the Free State.[70]

In the meantime, the absence of urban locations helped explain the harsh legal regime. Police in Durban seemed to pursue African men with such intensity in public spaces in part because there were so many places where they could not pursue African men in private. Africans living in white-owned stores and backyards were sheltered, to some extent, by private property laws pertaining to white South Africans.[71]

Shembe would have quickly discovered that Africans' residences in the city were important spots for gathering, if he, nevertheless, had a hard time accessing them. It was true that landlords and business owners controlled some of what happened in Africans' living spaces. But the same landlords and business owners often went to houses in the suburbs at night and on weekends. Africans living in Durban regularly invited guests over to their dwellings when their landlords were away as part of what white Durban residents called the "sponging" system. Keletso Atkins noted how such access to city residences depended upon what she termed "homeboy networks," meaning that rural community and kin shaped who got in and who did not.[72] Shembe's example suggested how his denomination had helped him connect to people who were already living together as part of one such group, but there is no evidence that he managed to be "sponged" up by any other African men living elsewhere in the city.

If private space was difficult to access, public spaces were difficult to use, whether under the rubric of laws governing African Christianity or the municipality's many laws criminalizing Africans' activities in the city. Shembe arrived in Durban, too, at a time when the few pockets of improvised public space that existed—and might have provided a buffer from surveillance—had been recently removed. The municipality had cleared out Bamboo Square, for example, where Africans and Indians lived together in an informal settlement, just a few years before Shembe arrived.[73] The streets at night served as another kind of public space, but only for those willing to break the curfew imposed on Africans and risk encounters with the police or the groups of young African men who used these spaces already and sometimes made trouble.[74]

There were other quasi-private and quasi-public spaces in Durban. There were churches and school buildings for Africans that provided the setting for many events, but these structures were the domain of recognized mission communities.[75] Eating houses and beer halls represented other common gathering spots in the city, but they offered no easy solutions either. These spaces had associations with vice that might have been enough to steer Shembe away from them anyway. By the time Shembe arrived in Durban, such sites also experienced police raids as the municipality began imposing its beer monopoly.[76]

The Nazaretha did preserve some stories of Shembe attempting to use public spaces in the city, including the beaches, for baptism.[77] These instances might have represented risks he was willing to take or experiments with what might be possible. Still, his main strategy became looking for ways to escape the danger posed by the many imbricated laws limiting his options. The earlier Baptists had avoided the tight restrictions in Durban by traveling to the surrounding rural districts. But Shembe, whether out of circumstances or strategy, did not venture too far from Durban. This decision allowed him to avoid the cost of more expensive train tickets, and it allowed him to blend in more easily. In rural districts with fewer people passing through, the earlier Baptists stood out in ways that contributed to the evidence eventually used against them.[78] In and around Durban, by contrast, there were African men moving to and from the city and its outskirts every day.

In the company of other African men and wearing clothes like them, Shembe likely walked at first, over the hills that circled Durban's commercial district and into suburbs.[79] He soon started to push farther, however, riding the train as far as one ticket would take him. This brings the story back to Shembe's time in Botha's Hill, the symbolic and literal end of the line.

Making a Convert at Botha's Hill

An early twentieth-century railway guide described the Botha's Hill station as "where a number of natives detrain" because "within easy distance . . . several tribes have their villages."[80] The travel guide suggested that the stop was a good place for white visitors to go to offer "a few beads or cheap pocket knives" to the Africans who lived there in return for "a sufficient stock of artistic negatives to make up an album of views which will delight all who see it."[81] Shembe was not interested in photographing "authentically" African people, but he was likely looking for the different organization of authority and community implied by this patronizing description of things to do on the urban periphery.

Botha's Hill sat near areas demarcated as some of the first "locations" in Natal. In contrast to the Free State, where "locations" were urban, the first locations in Natal were rural. Shembe had, in fact, been born in one in the late 1860s. By the time Shembe returned to Natal decades later, these rural spaces where Africans lived under traditional authorities were called "reserves" instead. Again, the rural orientation of mission stations meant that African Christians already lived in the reserves and Shembe might try out his message about the "baptism of John" upon them.[82]

White officials had more difficulty policing rural areas than the streets of Durban. The region's Code of Native Law deputized African patriarchs with control over space as a result. A chief was responsible in his territory for "cognition and control of strangers not being people of his tribe," and household heads were "constables within the precincts of their own [homesteads]" with the "authority to arrest summarily any person therein."[83] Such intimidating language meant that chiefs and homestead heads had authority, on paper at least, to get rid of Shembe with the backing of the law. But this language also provided the potential for a small opening: if Shembe could find household heads and perhaps even chiefs who would give him permission to be in their space, he might slip through unnoticed by white officials.

Shembe surely hoped that the Botha's Hill area would be more fruitful than the city. And perhaps it was. The Nazaretha offered varied reports of his success, with some saying that he built a congregation and others saying that he "handed over" converts to the churches nearby.[84] That explanation—of "handing over" converts—was common among revivalists throughout the region who, admittedly, did not always see their theology as confined to one denomination. But, for some revivalists, this phrase also offered a way to gloss over the sometimes complicated or unflattering reasons why they left one place behind to try somewhere else.[85]

However many people Shembe might have preached to or baptized around Botha's Hill, he only made one named convert who stuck with him over the next few years, through the founding of the Nazaretha in 1913. The story of Shembe meeting this convert, like many others, included an account of a miraculous healing. In this case, Shembe had encountered "a sick boy" named Peter Mnqayi, who was bed-ridden due to an injury. Shembe purportedly commanded, "Peter, take [up] your bed and walk," and this had sufficed to heal him.[86]

Despite the triumphant tone, the details of the story pointed to lingering difficulties, beginning with how Shembe found Mnqayi. God, purportedly, told Shembe to "alight from the train" at Botha's Hill because Shembe would find someone there who needed healing. Mnqayi's family did not know that Shembe was coming, in a pattern that echoed Shembe's days of going homestead to homestead in the ORC in search of people who would listen. At the same time, the setting of Mnqayi's healing was significant. True, Mnqayi could have been in bed because of the severity of his injury, but a healing inside also meant that it took place away from the watchful eyes of people who might have reported Shembe's activities to some authority. Another detail confirmed the privacy of the scene: Mnqayi's father was the only other person mentioned.[87] Such an encounter was not, then, the kind of "meeting or assembly" that could get an African Christian in trouble in Natal.

And yet, Botha's Hill did foreshadow some things about the places where Shembe would soon see his evangelical fortunes improve. For starters, Shembe had guessed correctly about the role that rural patriarchs might play in helping him—and how they could act as a shield between him and the state. When he did begin to hold those larger, open services, the help of such homestead heads and chiefs allowed him to do it. Moreover, in the young man who stuck with him, Shembe found someone whose story highlighted one of many ways that Africans in Natal were being left behind. Mnqayi himself was younger than Shembe and had some schooling. If he had trouble walking—as the story of his healing suggested— that might have explained why he did not join the other young men his age who commuted from Botha's Hill to work in Durban. As a literate African Christian too,

Mnqayi would have felt the generational crunch of opportunities lost. Not only was the South African government wringing out the privileges once afforded to African Christians, but, as more African Christians became literate, it became more difficult for people such as Mnqayi to use reading and writing as a pathway toward salaried jobs and better options.[88] In Shembe, however, Mnqayi found someone who greatly valued his education and wanted to use his skills.[89]

However significant Shembe's relationship with Mnqayi would soon become, before 1910, it was not enough to keep Shembe in Natal. A Nazaretha account described Shembe, again, at the Botha's Hill train station as he debated buying another ticket to go farther than one fare would allow.[90] The pass laws dictated that Shembe needed to go back to the Free State at some point anyway, whether to stay there or to apply for another pass under a new name. Still, it seems that when Shembe made plans to go back to Harrismith, he was intending to stay there. Throughout his life, Shembe described himself as someone who looked for signs that he was doing what God wanted. It would have been easy for him to interpret his struggles in Durban as a sign to leave.

But then, another set of signs appeared. In 1910, the formation of the Union of South Africa underscored Natal's differences once again. In most parts of South Africa, the Union made laws governing African Christianity more stringent; in Natal, the Union stripped the harshest laws from the books. After 1910, it was no longer illegal for Shembe to lead gatherings in Natal or Zululand.[91]

The Baptist believers from the barracks in Durban seemed to be paying attention. They raised the funds to pay for Shembe's train ticket back soon after the shift in laws. Still, on Shembe's second mission journey, his destination was not Durban. If the Union had loosened the laws about African Christianity, it had done little to change the basic patterns of Africans' lives in the city. Instead, when Shembe left Harrismith again after 1910, he was headed to the men's rural home, to the place where they had first become Baptists. That young convert from Botha's Hill, Peter Mnqayi, would eventually join him there, in the hills of Ndwedwe.[92]

CHAPTER 4

A Guest in the Reserves

To get to the Baptist men's rural home, Shembe took the train from Harrismith to Durban, going the same route he had taken before. From Durban, he entered new territory, traveling by rail at least fifteen miles north.[1] As he disembarked, he moved west. Shembe was approaching topography that slowed down the people trying to move through it. The great-great- and great-grandparents of many of the region's residents had chosen the area for that reason in another set of displacements accompanying the Mfecane.[2] To thwart the military regiments that might follow them, they cut into the hills that travel guides later described as "bold and bluff-like buttresses of nature" with "foaming rivers" coursing through them.[3] Descriptions that focused on what it meant to live in the area, instead of visiting it, referred to the land differently: as "shocking" and "broken" country.[4]

The beautiful, difficult land of Ndwedwe provided a backdrop for some of the most important events in Nazaretha history. In fact, just a few years after Shembe's arrival in the region, he came down from one of the "bold and bluff-like buttresses," like Moses from the mountain, to announce a new set of rules for following God.[5] At the base of that mountain were hundreds of people awaiting him, a sign of the support he had managed to rally as he founded the Nazaretha.[6] Ndwedwe is still, moreover, where thousands of the faithful return each January for a pilgrimage to the same mountain, Nhlangakazi, to commemorate the beginning of their faith.[7] And yet, however important it would become, Ndwedwe must have seemed at first like another place where Shembe might fail.

Nazaretha hymns depicted Shembe's early days in Ndwedwe as a time of loneliness. The first song in the Nazaretha hymnbook chronicled this period of Shembe's life. The hymn detailed how God was,

> his [Shembe's] shield,
> even though he [Shembe] wanders in the Wilderness,
> sleeping in the forests.[8]

These lyrics drew Shembe into biblical narratives, evoking comparisons to the wandering Israelites as well as the solitary sojourns of John the Baptist, Jesus, and others. Over time such references contributed to Shembe's image as a "suffering servant," willing to sacrifice for his people. More immediately, loneliness was an indication of bigger problems. By moving to the countryside, Shembe lost the ability to support himself through his own wages. If he was alone, then he was also looking for the local equivalent of locusts and wild honey. People in isolated pockets of Ndwedwe had good reasons to wonder, as some did, if Shembe was the person eating their goats.[9]

But what Ndwedwe's broken land also gave Shembe was time to keep trying. As long as Shembe was willing to sleep occasionally in the forests and scrounge for food, he could continue to observe people's circumstances, talk to those who would listen, and hide from people who might want to chase him away.[10] He could also try to change people's perceptions: to give them something to talk about other than how he might be stealing livestock. And, although early stories emphasized how Shembe was alone, he, in fact, could already rely on some people as he kept trying—people who helped him by giving him access to space for healing services and ideas from the Bible that fit his activities. When Shembe came down from that mountain in 1913, the rules he shared reflected what he had done to make himself a welcome guest in Ndwedwe's homesteads and chiefdoms.

Finding People Left Behind

Until Shembe entered Ndwedwe, his major movements had been toward South Africa's growing population centers. In Ndwedwe, Shembe found a place defined, instead, by departures and absence. As in many parts of South Africa, the effects of living on tired land coupled with tax demands from the state to erode African homestead production and send more men away, looking for work.[11] If their reasons for leaving had once reflected different ratios of choice and need, Shembe entered Ndwedwe as need pulled more strongly. By the early twentieth century, many men entered employment to secure cash advances that helped their families buy food to survive but that also trapped them in cycles of debt.[12] Still, in part because Ndwedwe was not so far from Durban, the main destination for work, more men had left too; difficulty *and* proximity explained the extent of the departures. The 1911 census pointed to the sharp demographic contrasts that had emerged as a result. In Ndwedwe, for every 100 African men, there were between 146 and 167 African women.[13] These numbers varied depending upon where in Ndwedwe one looked, but they were among the highest in Natal. And even the dramatic ratios did not fully capture the impact of departure in daily life. Many men who left were still counted in their rural homes, while the men living in rural areas skewed toward the young and the old.[14]

The tensions that erupted in rural homesteads in Ndwedwe are well known and resembled struggles on many parts of the African continent where migrant work became an entrenched feature of social life.[15] Fathers and sons fought over control of wages in a system that conferred legal authority to elders but that gave younger men easier access to an increasingly necessary resource: cash.[16] As the men left behind in rural areas tried to keep women from leaving, too, they fought over issues of mobility.[17] Men complained about women staying away too long for church services and spending more time away at beer drinks. Women "returned home at all times of day," one man from Ndwedwe explained, and sometimes "remained away all night."[18] Men also complained of more substantial acts of departure: women running away to mission stations, towns, or the magistrate's office and, in the case of some daughters, running away from the marriages that fathers planned for them. As another Ndwedwe man noted to the magistrate, daughters "who had been carefully brought up by their father, ran off to town."[19] The last complaint—and the reference to girls being "carefully brought up"—underscored how fathers sought to use bridewealth exchanges to shore up the social and economic basis of their authority. If young men could more easily accumulate through work in cities, older men could still accumulate more easily through their daughters' marriages.[20] Many fathers bristled, then, at anything untoward that might make it seem their daughters had not been "carefully brought up" and would lower their prospects for bridewealth.

When fathers did manage to arrange marriages for their daughters, wives and husbands faced new strains, too. Men and women worried about infidelity as they spent more time away from each other. Due to food insecurity, men's extended absences, and perhaps the spread of sexually transmitted infections, married couples had understandable concerns about infertility as well.[21] In the absence of reliable statistics, the problem was hard to measure or track over time. Certainly, people perceived infertility as a problem. In an interview in the early 1930s, John Dube described a broad shift he had witnessed over the past decades in Natal (and that affected him personally), explaining how African women once had many children but "somehow they do not now—they cannot now; they have greater difficulty."[22] The patchy numbers available do suggest that Ndwedwe had an especially low birthrate just as Shembe arrived in the region, a data point that tracked with the absence of so many men.[23] The birth of a child had historically confirmed a marriage because, as the African intellectual Magema Fuze wrote in the 1910s, a child meant that "the mother arrived [in her husband's family] without defect, good and pure."[24] The absence of children or the birth of unhealthy children, in turn, produced additional tensions for married couples and their families.[25] So did the fact that older methods of dealing with infertility—such as marrying another wife—were no longer possible, whether because families could not afford it or thought that polygyny conflicted with their faith.[26]

Chiefs shared the concerns of other rural men because, by and large, they experienced similar problems with their wives, sons, and daughters.[27] But chiefs also faced new challenges. Since the 1890s, the government of Natal had granted chiefs more responsibilities to control territory, collect taxes, and enforce laws but without considering how transformations in rural economies had undermined ties between people and chiefs.[28] This made chiefs answerable for more at a time when they often had a less varied toolkit for compelling action. Chiefs from Ndwedwe had reasons to agree with one representative who, speaking on behalf of all of them to white officials in 1907, said chiefs had become "the government's dogs."[29] The government had, in other words, left them behind too.[30]

Ndwedwe's history of foreign missionaries differed from other parts of South Africa, but in ways that added another wave of departure. Ndwedwe sat within one of Natal's first locations. As a result, the American Board Mission established three large mission stations on its edges in the 1840s.[31] Maintaining the earliest stations was, however, a struggle.[32] Among the small communities of African Christians that grew around them, some people left to pursue economic opportunities elsewhere, moving to places where they could go to boarding schools, buy land, or open businesses—and use the skills associated with Christianity in ways that Ndwedwe did not allow.[33] By the late nineteenth century, foreign missionaries were thinking about leaving, too, whether for cities such as Johannesburg, other outposts of empire, or mission boarding schools.[34]

By then, many African Christians resented the influence and authority of foreign missionaries anyway, and some welcomed the departure. Others were less celebratory. Some held deep connections to foreign missionaries and celebrated what it meant to be in the line of "Grout, Champion, Lindley, Wilson, Venable, and Adams," as one African Christian wrote, in reference to the foreign missionaries who had come to the region.[35] Some understood, too, that the loss of mission stations meant the loss of local resources and services. Missionary education for children in Ndwedwe, for example, had been more available in the 1880s than in the 1910s.[36]

Ndwedwe was also different from some other parts of South Africa because of the intensity of a recent experience of state violence. In 1906, what became known as the Bambatha Rebellion started as resistance to another new tax imposed by the government. In this case, the tax targeted single men in African families—in other words, the sons whose work and wages were already a source of such controversy. Amid the tension that resulted, a few white settlers died.[37] Expecting retaliation, whether for refusal to pay the tax or the deaths of the settlers, many African men armed themselves for battle. They gathered in gorges and forests, the hideouts that would have provided protection from armies of earlier eras but did not stop the excesses of colonial violence in the present. The settler government killed more than 4,000 people and imprisoned or flogged thousands more. In Ndwedwe and neighboring districts, government troops also swept through the reserves, looting and burning homesteads as they made more than 30,000 people homeless.[38]

The aftermath of the Bambatha Rebellion added to the devastation in Ndwedwe and sped up the ongoing exoduses. As Natal officials made sense of what had happened, they turned to a familiar scapegoat: African Christians and the foreign missionaries who could not exert *effective* control over them.[39] This, in turn, contributed to the sense among missionaries in the region that their resources would be better used elsewhere, in places where officials exhibited less "apparent discriminations," as one missionary wrote.[40] The violence sped up the departure of rural men in search of migrant work, too.[41] Given the timing, it was possible that the Baptist men Shembe met in Durban had left Ndwedwe because of the recent violence.

But, as much as Ndwedwe was a place of people left behind, it was also a place where people experienced uneven consequences. The Bambatha Rebellion dramatized this too. In its aftermath, some chiefs were rewarded for their loyalty to the government while others lost significant portions of their chiefdoms or were deposed.[42] And more broadly, not everyone dealt with infertility, not everyone's sons stayed away after leaving home, and not everyone's daughters ran away from arranged marriages. Shembe would soon discover, however, that the people suffering more, relative to others in rural society, would be more receptive to him.

A Homestead Healing

In Ndwedwe, Shembe's Baptist connections did help him at first, especially on the region's eastern edge, where earlier Baptist missionaries had passed through. In this area, the first place where Shembe stayed was likely in the home of someone who was already a Baptist. Once there, Shembe soon found that he could hold a service unlike any he had ever held before—a service that was planned, in the open, and that allowed many people to attend. In an act that was already common in the region, his hosts offered up their homestead as the site.[43]

A description of one of Shembe's early healing services suggests how he used homestead space to draw many kinds of people together. There were, of course, the sick and suffering. Many had problems that were chronic and difficult to solve: "tropical ulcer," "bleeding disease," and persistent head and body pains.[44] Most of these people could arrive on their own feet, but not everyone. One woman, who had a fistula after childbirth, showed up on a sled made of "bags" (perhaps stitched-together maize bags) that her family had pulled because she could "no longer walk or sit or sleep."[45] The presence of such people added to the importance of knowing in advance where Shembe would be; families could plan how to get someone to him. In some cases, too, sick people could also stay for a few days near Shembe. The rural homesteads of Ndwedwe might not have been good for agriculture anymore, but they offered space for camping out. These sites could also offer temporary healing homes for people who took longer to get well.[46]

As important was another category of people in attendance: those who could say that divine healing had made them well. In the early days, this category of people was the smallest. Shembe shared his own story, confirming how he had come to believe in God's healing after so much sorrow and loss.[47] But a new person—someone who attributed his healing not to God directly, but, instead to God through Shembe—was there early on as well. This was Peter Mnqayi, the convert from Botha's Hill, who told people in Ndwedwe the story of how he had once been so sick that he could not walk.[48] The fact that he could now travel by foot into a region known for needing "strong walkers" added to the weight of his account.[49] Mnqayi's story also set a model that others would follow: they, too, would orient their healing testimonies around Shembe, filling in his name for the powerful medicine that had made them well after they had tried many others that did not work.[50]

Finally, there were people who came to the healing services just to see—perhaps because they were curious, skeptical, or already disdainful and looking for ways to disprove Shembe's claims. Whatever their intentions, they were also welcome. Letters to the editor from Shembe's supporters appeared on the pages of the local newspaper a few years later even daring people who did not believe to come, explaining, "If we are being tricked they [the disbelievers] must come and see if there is any deception as other people are saying we are misled."[51] Such invitations not only drew more people but also made claims about Shembe's medicine seem more believable—why would people invite outsiders otherwise?

The presence of onlookers underscored something else significant: how the forms of impoverishment in South Africa gave some rural dwellers more free time—and even perhaps a problem of boredom. This happened slowly and, sometimes, because of changes that did not seem to be signs of growing poverty. Maize, for example, was a much less labor-intensive crop than sorghum. Although less nutritious than sorghum, maize had taken over as the staple grain in the region by the time Shembe arrived.[52] Growing reliance on cash, poor soil quality, and the possibility of buying some food in stores meant that many people farmed less intensively. Because women and children had been responsible for agricultural labor, this might explain, too, another reason for the intensity of the conflicts over women and children's mobility. They had free time in a way that they had not in the past. Certainly, some women and children—and girls, in particular—were among those showing up at Shembe's services out of curiosity, looking for something to do.[53]

The many kinds of people in attendance contributed to a varied exchange of information, starting with information about Shembe himself. People could hear Shembe's life story and weigh in on what they thought about this man who said he once had "wives in the Free State," as one observer reported, but now said that he could "pray for the dying."[54] They could weigh in too on how he did not look or act like other Christian leaders they had seen.[55] While some people opposed

Shembe because he led services despite his family history and lack of schooling, others thought that his story made him more relatable and Christianity more achievable, without the trappings of class and education once associated with mission Christianity. This man who had changed his name and was in clothes that served as a disguise seemed authentic. His story of losing children, too, suggested that he knew what it was like to suffer as many in the region had, adding to his sense of authenticity and relatability as well.[56]

The sick contributed to the exchange of information, too. Shembe asked them to "report" their problems in direct, public exchanges. In fact, this represented one of the most significant ways that divine healing departed from earlier methods of healing in the region. In those earlier methods, people tested a healer's abilities by having the healer guess at the problem afflicting a sick person.[57] In contrast, open exchanges gave Shembe invaluable information about the people he was encountering. The exchanges also let onlookers weigh in on the sincerity of the statements that the sick and suffering made, opening up space for debate. The exchanges meant that not only Shembe's skill but also a sick individual's faith were on trial. Did people call Shembe a "man of God" when they approached him?[58] And how did they respond when Shembe asked them, "Do you believe that God will heal you?"[59] The behavior of the sick gave people grist for assessing success or failure in ways that did not fall only on Shembe's shoulders.

The exchanges of information that took place at homestead healings were transformative, giving Shembe information he needed to understand people's circumstances and spreading word about him. Shembe did not stay at the homestead on Ndwedwe's eastern edge for long, however. He likely had many reasons to keep moving on, but one related to an inconvenience of geography. The portion of Ndwedwe where he hosted the first healings was near the seat of local government, the magistracy, and a place where many sick people coming for a healing service might attract attention from white officials. True, the laws were not as strict as they once had been, but Shembe likely knew he could still get in trouble for any number of reasons. He began to use the homesteads in eastern Ndwedwe as he had used spaces in Durban and Harrismith before: as a base to which he could return. The mountains of Ndwedwe with their spread-out populations made it hard, however, to walk and return anywhere in one day. As he pushed farther into the hills, with a billycan of food, he likely knew that he would have to rough it.[60] But he also had a sense from those first homestead healings of what might be possible.

Prophet Seeks Room and Board, Additional Space for Worship Appreciated

Deeper in rural Ndwedwe and without Baptist friends, Shembe generated over-lapping anxieties as a result of the ongoing crises of homesteads, chiefdoms, and missions. As someone who might ask for hospitality, he posed problems in homesteads without much extra food to spare. As an unattached man traveling through a region absent working-aged men, he raised concerns about sexual impropriety. Some people also wondered if Shembe, as someone who claimed to be a healer, might use "love charms" and "Malay magic" to seduce the women and girls he encountered in the countryside.[61] Outside of Shembe's potential effects on rural women, others worried that he might be another person pedaling false cures, even if he did not have "bundles of medicine" like the other healers about whom local people complained.[62] African Christians of long-established denominations in the region had reasons to worry about Shembe too. The first evidence of Shembe's presence in rural Ndwedwe came from one such African Christian in 1911 who wrote to the local African-language newspaper, *iLanga lase Natal*, to complain about this "polygamist" and "tale-bearer," who "prayed for children" but "they die anyway." The letter-writer wrote to warn others who might soon encounter Shembe, too.[63]

Aware that his success in Ndwedwe depended upon others' hospitality, Shembe attempted to cultivate it by what he said and did as well as what he encouraged others to say about him. He preached, for example, about the possibility of mis-taking a long-lost son for a stranger. This topic resonated, with so many sons gone, and encouraged kindness to Shembe, as a stranger who might just be someone's long-lost son.[64] Shembe, moreover, looked for homesteads to stay where men were present, whether as fathers or husbands, to avoid accusations about why he was wandering around a countryside full of women.[65]

Rumors spread, too, of characteristics that distinguished Shembe from other healers, past and present. Shembe, people began to say, "ate little and charged nothing."[66] This description did a few things. It distinguished Shembe from the many healers who had reputations as demanding guests, milking theirs hosts of resources.[67] The description also kept Shembe from potential prosecution because of the many laws about who could sell medicines and services. He, after all, was not charging anything, although he did take the offerings that people sometimes gave to ensure a good result.[68] People began to hear, too, how small kindnesses to

Shembe brought blessings in abundance and whether or not someone converted to his faith. Indeed, the first example of Shembe promising to cure infertility came from one such story: a family without children in Ndwedwe had offered him a place to sit and drink water on their homestead after he was chased away by an angry party of men. In return, Shembe "blessed them with three sons."[69]

With the help of a few literate young men, Shembe began to emphasize the biblical parallels of his activities in Ndwedwe. When he returned from his journeys, he met up on Ndwedwe's edges with Mnqayi and at least one other younger, literate man from nearby, Ezra Mbonambi.[70] Like Mnqayi, Mbonambi saw Shembe initially as an elder who would appreciate his skills and formal education. Together, the two younger men helped Shembe scour the Bible for pertinent examples. The Old Testament offered a great deal, between its mountains and wandering holy men. But there were also more specific connections to make. For example, in 2 Kings, the woman of Shunem recognized the prophet Elisha as a "holy man of God" and encouraged her husband to make "a small roof chamber with walls . . . so that he can stay there whenever he comes to us."[71] After offering Elisha this hospitality, the woman of Shunem, who had been childless, bore a son. Elisha's miracles continued, moreover, when the boy died and Elisha raised him from the dead. Shembe and his supporters began to use this example to encourage hospitality toward him, telling others that people who opened their homes to Shembe became "like the woman of Shunem."[72]

In part because Shembe was willing to sleep out in the forests sometimes, this approach worked. Many people—perhaps most—still thought he was "a madman."[73] There was no one way, after all, to respond to a wandering prophet who did not eat much and claimed to help people have healthy babies. Shembe found, however, a few additional homesteads where he could stay, whether the people there believed in his message or simply thought that hosting him was a small price to pay for the possibility of receiving a child. Their support also helped Shembe as he began to approach people on the next rung of authority in rural areas: chiefs.

Among Chiefs in Ndwedwe

Once Shembe had a place to stay in a new area and had hosted a few services, he began to meet with local chiefs.[74] In so doing, he sought access to common land where he might hold larger worship and healing services. By approaching chiefs,

Shembe was acknowledging their authority over territory in ways that pointed to a recent shift. If, historically, a chief's authority had come primarily from relationships to people, the colonial government attempted to remake chiefly authority for the purpose of controlling territory.[75] Of course, land and people were linked in the past and in the present. But the laws mentioned in the last chapter that made chiefs responsible for the "cognition and control of strangers" in their territories (or "wards") gave Shembe added reasons to ask for chiefs' permission.[76]

For chiefs, decisions about granting Shembe a worship site could be complicated. Chiefs had historically been responsible for public health and welcoming healers, especially in times of trouble.[77] But healers could also rival chiefs and even usurp their authority. As a result, the greatest chiefs in the region had in the past endeavored to disprove healers or absorb their powers (or both). Of course, chiefs might also look at Shembe and not worry too much. They had seen other African Christians in the reserves come and go.[78] Perhaps they thought it was easier to grant Shembe a site and then let his services dwindle. But chiefs also had to contend with the fact that some people in their territories were still opposed to the spread of Christianity and might not want Shembe (or any additional Christians) worshipping near them. Moreover, if Shembe's activities were discovered, a chief could get in trouble with the government for allowing such a "stranger" in his territory. By approaching chiefs, Shembe not only acknowledged their authority but also asked them to be complicit in sheltering his activities.

With chiefs, too, Shembe found ways to present himself as an easy guest. In fact, Shembe's order of operations—seeking out homesteads first—already did this to an extent, giving chiefs a reason to agree to his presence because some of their people had already welcomed him. But Shembe also smoothed relations with chiefs through his approach to land. Shembe's detractors showed their feelings—and perhaps tried to set him up to fail—by recommending that he receive terrible worship sites. One in Ndwedwe was on a "very difficult" mountain where "nobody goes up" because of the "dangerous wild animals."[79] Another was near a pool of water with a frightful "water snake" that would make baptism in it a challenge.[80] Shembe took these spaces. More than that, too, he did not build anything permanent on them. This decision to avoid formal structures kept chiefs from getting in trouble in case the government swept through the reserves to destroy unregistered churches, as officials had periodically done in the years before 1910. Instead, Shembe and his followers began to use cairns to mark their gathering spots, and those who could afford them began to bring umbrellas in case of rain.[81]

Shembe found ways to speak directly to chiefs' biggest problems. Some of these problems reflected how chiefs' families also dealt with infertility and other difficult circumstances faced by the ordinary people living in their territories.[82] In one chiefdom, for example, the people who began to follow Shembe recalled how "all the many wives of the chief's sons in the entire family of the chief did not have children."[83] Shembe addressed more dangerous concerns, too, including witchcraft. In one account of Shembe's initial overture to a chief in Ndwedwe, he seemed to make a witchcraft accusation against a woman living in the chief's territory. "Here in this house," Shembe purportedly said, "is a woman, who has done an evil thing; and for this reason, the chief became a cripple."[84] To make it clear that he was referencing witchcraft, Shembe added details that associated her with malevolent, supernatural harm: she "came with the fat of wild animals, and all the people were dreaming of witch's familiars."[85]

Shembe's engagement in discussions of witchcraft indicated how hard he was willing to work to win the favor of chiefs. In the past, the removal of people suspected of witchcraft had been one way that chiefs demonstrated their commitment to protecting their people.[86] As a result, chiefs complained bitterly about how colonial laws refused to acknowledge witchcraft but, instead, punished witchcraft accusations. Only a few years before Shembe arrived in the region, a deputation of chiefs from Ndwedwe made their grievances known to white officials, with one wondering "what was meant by the English word 'witch'" if white people said that witches did not exist.[87] The change in laws also meant that, if Shembe did accuse someone of witchcraft in Ndwedwe, he was committing a crime.[88] More than that, by saying that someone else's ill intent could cause another person's physical misfortune, Shembe was offering explanations that did not fit neatly within a divine healing framework. That framework, after all, suggested that an individual's sins caused personal suffering. And yet, by making a witchcraft accusation, Shembe indicated that he would take risks to support chiefs, much as he asked them to take risks for him.

The rewards for Shembe's approach were meaningful. Over time, Shembe got some level of revenge on the people who had stuck him in terrible spots. These sites added to Shembe's reputation because he could show that he and his followers did not fear the malevolent forces that others associated with such places. More importantly, he got sites where, with chiefly approval, he could hold larger, longer gatherings. As more people showed up, they added to the exchange of information about Shembe and offered new kinds of evidence of Shembe's miracles. For example, people at these larger events began to show off the healthy babies that they attributed to him.[89]

Within a year or two in Ndwedwe, the contours of a community forming around Shembe were visible. Among Shembe's strongest supporters were often the very people who had been left behind in multiple ways amid South Africa's broad transformations. The profiles of the chiefs and chiefly families who offered Shembe worship sites affirm this. One was barely hanging onto his position because of the tiny size of his chiefdom deep in the mountains of Ndwedwe.[90] Another had stayed loyal to the government during the Bambatha Rebellion but lost a significant number of people in his territory as punishment for the many who had ·joined the tax resistance.[91] And, just over the border of Ndwedwe in Maphumulo, the family of another chief politicking to get their lineage reinstated welcomed Shembe after the government sent the chief into exile for his involvement in the Bambatha.Rebellion.[92] Chiefs who were doing relatively well, however, did not seem responsive to Shembe.[93]

Church members were left behind in other ways. Perhaps a handful were older homestead heads, and a similar number were the young men on Ndwedwe's edges who helped Shembe access the Bible. But, already, women and girls, some who were Christians already and some who were not, made up the majority of the congregation around Shembe. Their presence was not surprising given the demographic profile of the region. But these people included married, rural women struggling with infertility as well as young, unmarried women looking for something to do as their brothers left for jobs in Durban.[94]

Even if some similarities surface among the people supporting Shembe, the descriptions of them expose their differences as well. Gender, age, and experience with Christianity divided them, as did chiefdoms and material circumstances. Other less obvious characteristics divided them too, including the exclusiveness of their commitments to Shembe. Already, distributions of authority in Ndwedwe meant that Shembe was accommodating people who could help him but might never join his church. It is unlikely that all the chiefs, for example, who gave him space were baptized in his faith, and some of them certainly continued to consult other kinds of healers.[95] The need to reach out to people—and especially patriarchs outside of the church—would continue in part because strategies of evasion in the countryside often depended upon them. Even so, whatever questions remained about how Shembe would accommodate such a variety of people in his faith, he had already built support in ways that were changing how Shembe himself understood Christianity—and how others understood him too.

Becoming Nazarites in Ndwedwe

Scholars have given different dates in the early 1910s for the founding of the Nazaretha. In the absence of clear-cut evidence, many are plausible; all indicate a change of Shembe's fortunes after he came to Natal the second time.[96] Previously unexamined evidence, however, suggests a break with the Baptists beginning in 1913. In February of that year, Ezra Mbonambi—one of those young, literate men, associated with Shembe—wrote to *iLanga lase Natal* to report a large gathering that had taken place in Ndwedwe a few weeks before. In the letter, Mbonambi described Shembe as "formerly of the Baptist church from Ntabazwe [Harrismith]" and offered details about an event at which "over 300 people congregated" and "85 were converted" in an area with many "unclothed"—or people who were not yet Christians.[97] These people included "the whole Nyuswa nation" and the "Hlophe nation," in reference to the two small, embattled chiefdoms whose leaders had given Shembe the most support.[98]

The description of Shembe at the event in 1913 suggests that he and the literate young men affiliated with him were drawing upon biblical examples to announce a new set of rules from God. The letter explained that Shembe had climbed Mount Nhlangakazi, "requested by the voice of God." In Exodus, Moses had communed with God on Mount Sinai, before coming down from the mountain to reveal the Ten Commandments.[99] Shembe did not spend forty days on Mount Nhlangakazi, as Moses had on Mount Sinai, but Shembe's time on the mountain reflected knowledge of other biblically important numbers. Shembe spent twelve days total on the mountain, coming down to greet the people who had gathered on the seventh. And in the Bible, when Moses revealed the Ten Commandments, his appearance was altered, an indication that something significant had happened on Mount Sinai.[100] Likewise, according to the letter writer in 1913, Shembe seemed changed as well: "his skin tone was very dark as if he had risen from the grave"; "his voice was piercing"; and his presence made others "intoxicated."[101] Such descriptions implied that Shembe, too, had just returned from an encounter with God.

The letter from 1913 did not mention the word Nazarite, but the term tied together many ideas that Shembe had been exploring in Ndwedwe. In the book of Numbers, God explained the Nazarite vow to Moses while the Israelites were still at Mount Sinai. The vow offered a set of requirements for "separating from" worldly things in order to "separate to," or consecrate oneself to, God. Nazarites were supposed to avoid strong drink and anything made from grapes. They were not supposed to cut their hair or "go near a corpse."[102] In return for following this vow, Nazarites were described in Numbers as "holy unto the Lord." Other parts of the Bible suggested that this state of consecration produced miraculous results. The story of Samson, who was a Nazarite, and his "great strength"—at least until his haircut—confirmed this.[103] So did the story of Samson's birth. Indeed, the vow of the Nazarite had strong associations with miraculous births in the Old and New Testaments: Samson's mother, "having borne no children," made the vow to raise her son as a Nazarite before he was born. A "childless Hannah" promised that her future son, Samuel, would follow the vow. And Elizabeth, the mother of John the Baptist, did the same before she bore John, her first child, at a time when she was "getting on in years."[104] Altogether, then, the Nazarite vow seemed to offer those who followed it general protection from harm as well as a specific remedy for infertility. Although the word "Nazarite" was not in the letter, then, the idea of a church based on the Nazarite vow was likely what Shembe brought with him down from the mountain.

It was probably around this time too that Shembe chose the name "Isaiah"—and decided to keep it—as yet another sign that things were going well and that he might not need to return to Harrismith again.[105] "Isaiah" referenced God's promise in the Old Testament book of the same name to send a "suffering servant" who "took our infirmities and carried our sorrows."[106] In another chapter, the book of Isaiah also told of a savior who would make it so that the

blind shall see,
and the ears of the deaf be opened,
then the blind shall leap like a stag,
and the mute tongue sing for joy.[107]

Elsewhere, too, the book of Isaiah promised "barren women" that they would experience children in abundance.[108] As with the name "Nazarite," then, "Isaiah" announced theological orientations and opened conversations about his commitments to people, whether they could read the Bible or not.

As with any interpretation of the Bible, Shembe and the people helping him piece together this theology engaged creatively with the ideas they found in the book. As explained in Numbers, the Nazarite vow was often a temporary state for special consecration. Through his new church, Shembe, however, aspired to make the terms of the vow permanent—that is, a set of requirements that people would follow for all of their lives. This shift demanded that the leaders of the early Nazaretha community work out rules for atonement when someone broke the vow; cleansing rituals would, over time, become a central part of the Nazaretha faith.[109] In some cases, Shembe's community also prioritized symbolic acts over absolute commitments to the terms of the vow: Nazaretha men would often have longer hair than others and would grow beards, but they would not necessarily refrain from ever cutting their hair.[110] Shembe and the people gathered around him also packaged the Nazarite vow with common prohibitions in divine healing communities, including prohibitions against eating pork, smoking, and taking any form of medicine.[111] They added other rules from the Old Testament, perhaps assuming that these were also ways that the Nazarites in Numbers honored God as part of their Hebrew heritage and outside of the vow alone. The Nazaretha followed a Saturday Sabbath, called their worship sites "temples," and removed their shoes while on sacred ground. They celebrated Passover, too, and recreated an Ark of the Covenant and holy vessels.[112] Shembe kept, however, the Baptist commitment to full-immersion, believer's baptism as a way of bringing new people into the faith while adding new markers of unity. If the Nazaretha were not yet wearing white robes for worship in 1913, they would be very soon.[113] These robes offered a simple solution to smooth over differences between the "clothed" and "unclothed" already among the Nazaretha congregation.[114]

Scholars writing later often imagined the Nazaretha Church as a repackaging of Christianity that demanded less transformation from its followers.[115] It is true that Shembe, like many others at the same time, widened some of the channels through which people could not only become Christians, but also be perceived as good Christians. Still, the many rules one had to follow in the church suggest that the Nazaretha demanded profound change too. What was so significant, in fact, was not absence of transformation but the kind. African Christians associated with the mission stations in the nineteenth century had often relied on new acquisitions—such as their clothes, homes, and years of schooling (along with the associated costs)—to show their spiritual progress. The Nazaretha relied, instead, on what one gave up, whether medicine, alcohol, pork, or older notions of the correct Sabbath. Sacrifice, then, determined the sincerity of the Nazaretha faith.

Another letter, from two years later, described Shembe doing something else significant at Mount Nhlangakazi. In 1915, he began ordaining ministers to operate under his authority—yet another mark of the establishment of a new denomination. Two of the men ordained were from outside of Ndwedwe, pointing to the rapid spread of the church in neighboring areas as well as south of Durban, in another place where the earlier Baptists had gone. Another of the four men was Peter Mnqayi, the "first member of the church" and the first person who publicly attested to Shembe's healing. Shembe's ordination of Mnqayi stood out as a rare instance in South Africa's history to that point: someone who could not read ordained someone who could. Still, the final person was the most significant for illuminating Shembe's changed status. Johannes Mlangeni was about Shembe's age and could also read and write. In fact, Mlangeni had been one of the people who signed Shembe's certificate affiliating him with the Baptist Church in Harrismith. Mlangeni was also, then, one of the people whom William Leshega had chosen to lead the Harrismith congregation when Shembe had gone to Durban instead. Now Shembe ordained him.[116]

The years after Union produced realignments in many religious communities. By 1914, William Leshega had moved on to be a member of the Pentecostal-inspired Apostolic Faith Mission, leaving the small Baptist congregation in Harrismith to inch along without him.[117] The Zion Christian Church marked 1910 as the year that their founder, Engenas Lekganyane, began having visions from God. In the Transvaal, Daniel Nkonyane left white missionaries who had been affiliated with the Christian Catholic Apostolic Church in Zion to establish a new church in 1911.[118] In the Cape, Enoch Mgijima broke first with the Wesleyans and then with the Church of God and Saints of Christ, founding the Israelites in 1914.

The wave of church foundings in the years after Union shared much in common. They involved men (most often) who promised divine healing and who challenged church hierarchies. If Shembe was one of a few who could not read and write, most of these leaders had less education than African Christian leaders of a generation before. These churches also took root on rural land, whether offered by chiefs or, more often, on patches of freehold.[119] Others squatted illegally on commonage, "away in the locations."[120] These movements comprised people left behind, offering a contrast to the wave of new churches emerging in the 1920s and 1930s that would take root in cities—and especially on the Rand.[121]

The similarities between the churches point to widespread shifts in notions of religious authority. They point as well to the changing ways that disparate people could find each other and the reasons why they wanted to come together. And yet, whatever the Nazaretha had in common with other churches from this time, Ndwedwe changed how Shembe interpreted his calling from God and who the Nazaretha were becoming. The influence of its rural dwellers surfaced in so many ways, from Shembe's use of frightful spaces and overtures to chiefs to his promise to eat little food and cure infertility. Scholars have explained schism among African Christians as the result of factors ranging from the personal ambitions of individual leaders to the splitting tendencies common in the Protestant tradition.[122] But Shembe's example suggests how Africans navigated the fractures of colonized, industrializing spaces and tailored theologies to fit the different, local circumstances they found. The ability to do so would be both a strength and a weakness of the Nazaretha community as it continued to spread out of Ndwedwe.

Ndwedwe's influence persisted as Shembe began moving beyond the region too—and not only because of the enduring significance of Mount Nhlangakazi or the ideas that Shembe took with him. By taking root in Ndwedwe, some of Shembe's most committed followers already came from the demographics overrepresented in rural chiefdoms: women and girls. Although Shembe ordained men in 1915, the next chapter turns to the strong relationships Shembe forged with the women and girls whose contributions were essential to sustaining and spreading the Nazaretha faith in its earliest days, as they left their rural homes to evangelize with him.

CHAPTER 5

A Landowner in Inanda

LINAH MNTUNGWA WAS AN OLDER GIRL FROM NDWEDWE WHO HAD JOINED SHEMBE'S congregation before 1913, while he was still a Baptist. She had probably been around twelve when she went to a healing service near her family's home.[1] She was one of the people who had gone not because she was sick, but because she was curious: she wanted to see. At the service, she remembered Peter Mnqayi telling his story of healing and seeing others who got well.[2] Soon after, she became one of Shembe's most important converts.[3]

Before the gathering at Mount Nhlangakazi in 1913, Mntungwa and some others had left Ndwedwe for a neighboring district, Inanda. Among them were a few men, but their group included many unmarried girls about Mntungwa's age and some married women with their children.[4] They were camped out on the property of an African Christian landlord and rentier because they too wanted to buy land.[5] Mntungwa remembered Shembe saying, "Let us all watch and pray that God may give us a place."[6]

An offer finally came from a man who had a "a small place near the lower end of the school at Ohlange," a reference to a boarding school for African children founded by John and Nokutela Dube in 1900.[7] Mntungwa explained that the man had not yet finished paying for the land and agreed to transfer it to Shembe because he felt "very sorry when looking at the great sufferings of [Shembe]" as he "could not find a place to sleep." While this might have been true, many African landowners fell on hard times; this one might have been looking for a way out of a deal that he could no longer afford. Whatever the full set of reasons for the offer, Shembe told the people with him that God had "heard their prayers." He then asked them to make "a collection to pay off the money which was still due."[8]

Mntungwa was describing the land that would become Ekuphakameni, or the Elevated Place, a name that referenced how the Nazaretha set themselves apart to be closer to God. And if buying the first four-acre plot of land had required connections, luck, and many people willing to pool resources, building something on that land required similar collective effort and sacrifice. With the help of Mntungwa and others, Ekuphakameni grew over the next decade in acreage and significance, rivaling Mount Nhlangakazi in importance.[9]

The last chapter showed how the pursuit of homestead and chiefly hosts changed the community around Shembe amid the founding of the Nazaretha. The pursuit of private property in the 1910s added new facets as well. Land ownership cemented the bonds between Shembe and the young church women who came to live at Ekuphakameni. The placement of their land in Inanda, moreover, drew the Nazaretha into new relations and confrontations. The Nazaretha began to imagine the Indian majority living around them in Inanda as "Samaritans," the helpful strangers who gave assistance in times of need. But the Nazaretha also found themselves near other African Christians whom they imagined instead as the unhelpful priests and Levites who passed by, offering nothing.[10]

Propertied Aspirations

Shembe and the early converts entered the land market at a time of mixed opinions about the value of private property in African communities. True, many people were doing something akin to Shembe and the early converts: making plans to buy land collectively.[11] But other Africans expressed skepticism about such plans. In an interview in 1913, one of the chiefs who had offered land to Shembe in Ndwedwe summarized the opinions of these skeptics, noting, "There are few, if any, [Africans] who can purchase land and keep it. I see for myself that those who purchased land have no land today."[12] This chief had an interest in propping up communal land rights over private property. Still, his statement reflected knowledge of convoluted land laws, complicated legal arrangements, and a political economy that kept most Africans poor.[13]

The chief spoke as a new threat emerged, the infamous Natives Land Act of 1913 (NLA). The NLA was the source of South Africa's most quoted statistics: 87 percent of the land reserved for whites and 13 percent for Africans.[14] Important though the NLA was for clarifying the segregationist commitments of the Union government, it did very little to change the distribution of land in Natal. The damage was done. Already, Africans owned only 1.66 percent of the private property in the province, and that miniscule amount represented a higher proportion of land ownership than in any other part of South Africa.[15] Through the 1910s, the NLA did, however, make private property rights in places such as Inanda especially tenuous. As officials considered which tracts of land to reallocate in pursuit of territorial segregation, they looked to places such as Inanda, where its peculiar history of settlement meant that people of different races owned property sometimes side by side.[16]

Shembe made his first land purchase before the passage of the NLA and several purchases in the risky period after 1913. The NLA might have helped him acquire more land later in the 1910s or at least made others more willing to sell in Inanda because of their concerns about government appropriation.[17] But the fact that Shembe continued to buy land during this precarious period suggested that the risks did not matter much to him.

Shembe's steadfastness in pursuit of private property had deep roots. His life before coming to Natal had been defined by moments and circumstances that emphasized the value of private property, rather than its precarity. His parents had lived through the turmoil of the settler government in Natal stripping a chiefdom of its land. In fact, Shembe might have answered that chief in 1913 with knowledge from personal experience about how fragile communal land claims could be too. And Shembe also understood very well the pressure that Africans faced to secure land tenure without a title deed; he had lived with it for three decades as a tenant farmer.

Owning land allowed Shembe to address questions that had emerged since he decided to stay in Natal too. Land ownership, for example, let Shembe establish a residence without needing affiliation with a chief. This added another layer of protection for chiefs and gave Shembe a place to go if his relations with them soured. Shembe likely had a sense already, too, that private property could give him another way to escape state scrutiny. Governance premised on ideas of indirect rule was ill-equipped to manage Africans living on land they owned; this showed up in many ways for Shembe, including in his tax assessments.[18] Land ownership could give Shembe a way to regather his scattered family as well. Whether he was thinking about this when he and the others were still camped out in Inanda is unclear, but, within a few years, he would bring his family to live on his land in Natal. His mother had passed away by then, but his surviving wives would soon come to live "as sisters" to Shembe with their children.[19] The NLA might have had something to do with this decision, too, since it did the most immediate damage to African tenant families in the Orange Free State.[20]

As important, buying land could give Shembe a way to display his accountability to his spiritual family. At the services in Ndwedwe, Shembe had begun to collect regular church offerings, expecting different amounts from women, men, and girls.[21] And, even though he did not charge fees, the norms of payment for healing in the region meant that some people still made offerings to him in the hope of securing a good result.[22] Buying land and supporting people on it gave Shembe a way to show how he used this money. And, once again, Shembe might shine relative to others. In a context in which many collective land-buying schemes failed, his ability to purchase and then keep land could set him apart.[23]

Still, the most significant reason that Shembe wanted to buy land involved the possibility of building a permanent "healing home," where people could come and stay as they sought divine healing. Before coming to Natal, Shembe had heard about (if not also seen) what the revivalists in the Free State had been able to do with their own piece of land despite the bitter antagonisms of the people around them.[24] Although Shembe had created temporary equivalents in the countryside, his own piece of land would let him open a permanent healing home that welcomed people all year. His ambitions were shared, moreover, by a range of other African church founders and leaders who creatively used the spaces that were available—including, in once case a missionary hospital for lepers—until they figured out ways to access private property too.[25]

If Shembe had many reasons to want to buy land, so did the women and girls who gathered around him. To understand their reasons, however, one must first disaggregate them between married women (often with younger children in tow) and unmarried older girls and young women. Most mothers with children who were a part of Shembe's early community were likely looking for options to address economic and social crises in the countryside. That is, they had likely been abandoned by husbands who did not return from migrant work; had husbands who had died; or were, for any number of other reasons, struggling to make do in stretched-thin rural societies. Their presence in the Nazaretha community reflected how Shembe used notions of charity and care to welcome categories of vulnerable people who had long been welcomed on mission stations. Shembe welcomed them at a time when the number of vulnerable people grew, but rural mission stations could no longer support them. Shembe made it clear early on, however, that he thought that mothers' duties were to their children, preaching of "children who were brought to their graves in the absence of their mothers." These mothers might find a place to stay with Shembe, then, but they should not "roam" about the countryside spreading the Gospel.[26]

For unmarried girls and women without children, the reasons for wanting land both overlapped with and diverged from mothers' and wives'. Family crises and the decline of mission stations also drove some of the unmarried girls and women to consider following Shembe. Still, there is a sense that many girls such as Mntungwa wanted something more than a way to survive in difficult times—and that they were looking for places to go, adventures that paralleled their brothers' who were leaving for migrant work, and communities that valued their contributions. Early on, they had good reasons to think they might find this in affiliation with Shembe.

In many African communities, older girlhood stood out as a time of spiritual and supernatural connections—that is, a time when some girls claimed special knowledge from the ancestors or affliction from spirit possession. In fact, the very porousness that might make girls more open to communication with the ancestors might also make them more susceptible to possession by harmful spirits.[27] Before Shembe arrived in Ndwedwe, the demographic shifts in the region had already opened some space for unmarried youths and girls, in particular, to channel their spiritual energy into church communities—especially as the spirit-filled holiness revival pulsed through the American Board Mission churches.[28]

The Bambatha Rebellion—and its many imbricated crises—interrupted the revival.[29] But Nazaretha accounts in the early 1910s described similar zeal and energy as roving groups of unmarried women and girls traveled with Shembe to evangelize, showed off their knowledge of the Bible, and had spiritual authority respected in their small church community.[30] An older girl's vision, for example, encouraged Shembe to allow the whole Nazaretha congregation to begin climbing Mount Nhlangakazi—instead of just Shembe alone—sometime in the mid-1910s.[31]

South Africa's history included perhaps as many elders and men who doubted girls' claims about the supernatural as it included girls who claimed special knowledge and spiritual affliction.[32] Shembe's willingness to believe girls and young women was significant and stood out as another way that he set himself apart. This willingness emerged from how the divine healing revival made people attentive to surprising channels of religious authority. Again, if a polygynous man might receive a message from God, why not an African girl? Taken too far, this idea could cause chaos and contradictions. And, indeed, in the preceding example about Nhlanga-kazi, Shembe verified the girl's claims, asking others if she was "good" and, "Do you believe what this girl has said?" before agreeing to it. Still, by acknowledging that some girls had visions from God, Shembe could try to channel girls' spirituality.[33]

To some extent, Shembe was also working with the people he had. A dispro-portionate number of unmarried girls and women gathered around him as he was trying to grow his fledgling congregation. He needed their support, and, even so, it was not unbounded. As much as he might endorse the idea that God could speak through girls, too, he only ordained men at Nhlangakazi. As is often the case, girls and young women were negotiating among forms of patriarchy—not breaking out of them altogether.[34]

One perplexing dynamic of Shembe's interactions with girls and young women stemmed from how African women, too, had been and still were powerful healers—in part because of the very associations between girlhood, womanhood, and the realm of the supernatural. Some of these women healers made claims like Shembe's and were nearby. One, for example, did "not know how [she] learnt to pray" but heard an "invisible person" when she was sick and came to believe that "God ha[d] given [her] powers" to heal.[35] It would be naive, of course, to assume that women and girls would only support other women and girls as healers. But it does raise questions about what affiliation with a man could offer the young women around Shembe. Any answers are complex, but access to land for building a different kind of community represents one possibility.[36]

Perhaps the best indication that African girls and women wanted land through Shembe comes from the fact that, as Linah Mntungwa told it, they were willing to help pay for it.[37] But this raises questions about how the young women had money to give. Details about young women's wage-earning work are limited during the first decades of the twentieth century, but it is possible to sketch out some options. Two of the most common jobs for African girls and women, sex work and beer brewing, would have been forbidden in the church.[38] The Nazaretha took root, however, as transformations in the labor market opened new possibilities for African girls and women in areas such as Inanda. As the system of Indian indentured labor on sugar plantations ended, African women and girls had more opportunities to pick up casual labor by cutting cane in the sugar fields. African girls and women could also get work as domestic servants in the homes of people nearby—and perhaps especially among the large Indian population in Inanda.[39] The number of African women employed in domestic service increased in the early twentieth century in Natal, such that, by 1921, women and girls made up nearly 45 percent of domestic workers in an occupation that African men had formerly dominated.[40]

Having money to offer involved more than earning it. The fact that girls and young women could give money to Shembe also pointed to something important about their social obligations and economic relationships with their families. Because of cultural and social pressures for unmarried girls to stay close to home, there seem to have been few expectations in place that girls would contribute to a family's finances. Sons, by contrast, dealt with immense familial pressure to contribute to family expenses—and especially those linked to their mothers' households in polygynous families. [41] The observations of a local sugar baron in 1905 who employed African women might have been correct, then, when he noted that, when an African girl or woman went out to work, "as a great many of them do, she spends the money on herself, invariably, in buying goods or something she requires." [42] The unmarried girls and women who joined the Nazaretha in the 1910s found themselves in a moment when, on one hand, they had more opportunities for work and, on the other, they did not yet have familial expectations about how they were supposed to spend their money. Through the early 1920s—and outside of the purchase of Ekuphakameni alone—Shembe would turn to young women and girls for extra funds when land deals became more expensive than he anticipated.[43]

Although young women's contributions were central to early land-buying efforts, their names did not appear in legal documents. Starting with the purchase of the land that became Ekuphakameni, Shembe alone appeared on the title deeds.[44] Over the next two decades, white officials and some Africans antagonistic to the church criticized Shembe for buying land in his own name, but, in the early years of the church, this decision pointed to the constrained legal framework in which he and the young women operated. Even adult African women were "perpetual minors" under customary law; their names could not appear on title deeds unless they were among the few who had exemption.[45] And, if Shembe's land-buying arrangements did not legally acknowledge the women and girls who made them possible, the same could be written of countless other land-buying schemes in the 1910s. Perhaps some of these others offer hints that African girls and women found ways to get access to land through men as well.

Building Ekuphakameni

As the Nazaretha told the story later, Shembe first went alone to inspect the land that would become Ekuphakameni. Seeing it, he perhaps had new reasons to understand the generosity of the man who sold it. Shembe had been a successful farmer; he knew about the difficulties of making land usable. Although Shembe did not record his assessment of the property, the residents of another famous social experiment in Inanda did. Mohandas Gandhi's Phoenix Settlement had been established in 1904 and was an easy walk away from Ekuphakameni. The residents of Phoenix offered vivid details about the challenges of living nearby. Gandhi's nephew described how the land "had never been ploughed," the winters were "severely cold and breezy," and the summers were "hot and long" in "such a desolate place." At their one regular water source, Gandhi's nephew noted, too, that green snakes hung from the trees, and that it was not unusual to "come across five or six [snakes] in a single day."[46] Millie Polak, one of the early residents of Phoenix wrote with sarcasm of her first night there, recalling, "I didn't realize that the simple life meant living in corrugated iron . . . where so many insects and disagreeable things happening made it difficult to sleep."[47] The closest railway station was 2.5 miles away. The closest store was about as far. Wandering donkeys ate any crops they tried to grow, and the roads were slush for much of the year. Through the 1940s the trip to and from Durban took more than six hours even for those who could afford the bus and train fares to speed it up.[48]

The shared effort to build Ekuphakameni started the day after Shembe saw the land, as he invited the others who had been camped out to come join him. Their first job involved making shelters. And in fact, their dwellings offer the best clues about the demographics of the people with Shembe at the time: they built a large communal structure to house the young women, self-standing rooms for Shembe and Peter Mnqayi, and a multipurpose building that served as a kitchen and the place where mothers and their children could sleep.[49] Their construction tools were a hoe and a measuring stick made of the same braided grass they used to make

FIGURE 3. A scene from Ekuphakameni, near Inanda, in 1930. The rolling hills in the background offer an indication of how the area looked when Shembe and a small group of converts moved into the region ca. 1911.

PHOTOGRAPH INCLUDED WITH PERMISSION OF THE MARY EVANS PICTURE LIBRARY.

many of the buildings.[50] They probably could not have afforded the corrugated iron that Millie Polak had joked about at Phoenix.

Despite ongoing struggles, the Nazaretha managed to transform Ekuphakameni over the next decade into a space that replicated the services of mission stations and healing homes. As mission stations once had, the Nazaretha offered space for the needy and schooling for children.[51] And while missionaries had also offered access to basic medicine, the Nazaretha welcomed sick people to come and stay indefinitely—whether they were converts or not.[52]

Unmarried girls and young women provided services at Ekuphakameni and helped transform it into a place where people would want to stay. They were the teachers at the schools and the people who welcomed new arrivals, doing divine healing triage on sick patients to decide where they should stay and how urgently they needed to see Shembe.[53] If Shembe was away, unmarried girls and women prayed over the sick and suffering too.[54] They also helped maintain the people who came to stay at Ekuphakameni with food and supplies. It is possible that such services offered another way to fundraise—and without running afoul of the laws about who could charge for healing. Certainly, Ekuphakameni's placement in the middle of nowhere often made these supplies hard to get if people did not bring their own.[55] Girls and women also did the daily chores to maintain the space and were the main reason why white observers so regularly commented on the "cleanliness" of Shembe's "model village."[56] These girls and women made Ekuphakameni a desirable place to come in another important way too: by repeating a common claim about Shembe that took on new meaning in a place with so many snakes. Shembe's healing powers, they began to say, "were far stronger than that of a bite from a black mamba" and "no Nazaretha will be killed by a snake."[57] Such promises surely encouraged some people who might be hesitant to make the difficult journey.

Unmarried girls and women in the church did not stay only at Ekuphakameni either. As the Nazaretha bought more land, Shembe sent some of them to other church settlements. The most important new site was a "church farm" on private property south of Durban, called Gospel.[58] A core group of girls moved back and forth between it and Ekuphakameni.[59] Some of the young women and girls, including Linah Mntungwa, also traveled with Shembe on mission journeys through the 1910s. They recruited other people like them who might come to live at Ekuphakameni too.[60]

Within ten years, descriptions of Ekuphakameni suggested that many girls were attracted to the model of life they found there. A police officer patrolling Inanda in 1922 noted that he saw the Nazaretha building a bigger dwelling structure, one that "is sufficiently large to accommodate fifty girls."[61] This was a small number compared to the oldest, most established mission boarding school in the region, Inanda Seminary. The school had been founded in 1869 by the American Board of Commissioners for Foreign Missions and enrolled around 130 students by the late 1910s.[62] But the Nazaretha did draw some students from Inanda and offered formidable competition to other, newer Christian schools for girls that had opened nearby. In 1922, the founder of one of those other schools explained that, had he not closed his boarding school when he did, he would have "lost all of the girls to Shembe."[63]

As unmarried girls and women helped transform Ekuphakameni, they gained experiences that linked them to Shembe. For example, if Shembe was already a "suffering servant" who would sleep out in the mountains, girls and women could say that they too had "suffered greatly and were hungry" in the early days at Ekuphakameni.[64] Indeed, Mntungwa surely preserved the story of the purchase of Ekuphakameni because of how much the site mattered to the Nazaretha faith *and* because of how it reminded people of her role in building it. As others joined the faith later, Mntungwa could turn to accounts of these early days to jockey with them for authority. At the same time, Shembe linked the young women's efforts to buy land to tests of loyalty and, with them, histories of warfare and battle. When, for example, young women gave the offerings he requested to finance additional purchases, he sang songs that drew parallels to the history of the Zulu army defeating the British in 1879.[65] Many groups of people, outside of the Nazaretha, attached land purchases to narratives of conquest and triumph that harkened back to past glories. Again, however, seldom did other people invoking this military history see girls and unmarried women as central to their projects of land reclamation.[66]

Although the work of young women and girls at Ekuphakameni compared in some ways to the work of young women and girls on other mission stations and at other mission boarding schools, Mntungwa and people like her seemed to be arguing something different about pathways toward girls' and women's advancement. Much as the Nazaretha thought that Shembe did not need to be ordained to preach, women and girls used their positions at Ekuphakameni to show that they did not need the formal training as teachers, nurses, and evangelists that other young, African Christian women pursued.[67] Young Nazaretha women, then, offered a model of how to open channels to advancement as they navigated a rapidly changing world—in part out of acknowledgment that narrower channels had long excluded people like them.

Altogether, the girls and young women at Ekuphakameni and other Nazaretha mission stations add complexity to notions of the "modern girl" in the early twentieth century. If consumerism provides one lens for understanding the emergence of modern girls around the world, what, one might ask, of girls and young women who participated less in consumer culture? What of girls who, like those at Ekuphakameni, did not wear the pearl necklaces and cloche hats that marked the "modern girl" in the 1910s and 1920s, but who pursued new possibilities for their lives nevertheless?[68] The girls at Ekuphakameni charted a different path to modernity.

The parallels to more conventional "modern girls" are more striking because, as the next chapter shows, Nazaretha girls provoked anxieties about their sexuality as well. Indeed, elders and men could highlight the unconventional behavior of

Mntungwa and her cohort as well as how their work at Ekuphakameni brought them into contact with many kinds of people outside of their families at the very age when young women began to think about marriage—and when fathers worried most about their sexuality. In places such as Inanda, specifically, many Africans also fretted about African girls and women in proximity to Indian men.[69] In fact, those paying close attention to what Shembe was saying might have known that he welcomed Indian men (and all Indian people) to Ekuphakameni.[70]

Samaritans in Inanda

As Shembe and the young church women worked out their roles at Ekuphakameni, their collective efforts to use and buy more property pulled them into relationships with people outside of their community as well. Another story about the purchase of Ekuphakameni implied the centrality of these relationships from nearly the moment they bought the land. The account chronicled Shembe's first visit to the site, when he had gone alone to see what he was buying. The account did not focus on the snakes, the mud, the wandering donkeys, or anything else about the difficulty of what was in store. It focused instead on an unexpected act of kindness. According to the Nazaretha, Shembe sat "under a kei apple tree until sunset," perhaps planning to spend the night outside. But then "an Indian who lived on the other side of the road . . . had mercy on him and called him into his home, where he gave him a place to sleep."[71] This example of easy hospitality marked a stark shift from Shembe's struggles in Ndwedwe's interior. It also foreshadowed the good relations that Shembe would forge with many of his Indian neighbors in Inanda.

Living in Inanda, the Nazaretha accumulated and even cultivated evidence that Indian people were "Samaritans."[72] In fact, Shembe began to call them by this name, in reference to the helpful strangers who gave welcome and surprising aid in times of need.[73] Church members preserved other stories, too, of Indian people offering shelter, kindness, and jobs as well as rides (a bit later) when sick people needed to get to Ekuphakameni as soon as possible.[74] More than simply helping the Nazaretha, some Indian people also converted to the faith. By the end of Shembe's life, the Nazaretha included several dozen Indian church members.[75]

On one hand, accounts of such good relations between African and Indian people are not surprising. The scholarship about these relations acknowledges how the scant archival record cannot capture the whole story of Indians and Africans who were "friends, drinking partners, criminals, co-conspirators, comrades and lovers."[76] Still, places such as Inanda often stewed Indian-African prejudices in the early twentieth century, as different groups of people "in zones of enforced cosmopolitanism" competed over resources and pushed the state for more.[77] Their strategies often involved attempting to push other racial and national groups down in the process. The year 1913 represented a key moment in these attempts because of the passage of the already mentioned Natives Land Act as well as the Immigration Regulation Act, which placed new limits on Indian people's movement into and lives in South Africa.[78] In this context, some Indians argued that they deserved more from the state because they were more "civilized" than Africans, while some Africans argued that they deserved more from the state because of their indigeneity vis-à-vis Indians.[79]

The reasons for the welcoming tone toward Indians among the Nazaretha were manifold, starting with Shembe himself. Shembe already had a long history of finding ways to forge relationships across divisions of race, geography, ethnicity, gender, and generation. By the time he moved into Inanda, he had become a favorite of a white landlord and then a white employer, the protégé of a sePedi Baptist, an evangelist supported by migrant-working men in a city far from his home, and a guest in the homes of rural dwellers in Ndwedwe. In a place as difficult as Inanda, neighbors (Indian or otherwise) could offer aid in tough times, additional sources of income for the Nazaretha, and access to land.[80]

Shembe's willingness to operate across entrenched social divisions did not mean, however, that he argued for a raceless society or even race-blindness before God. The term "Samaritan" implied foreignness and made it clear that he still saw categories of difference. Shembe joined others who made stark pronouncements against interracial sex, as one reflection that he knew many other Africans were worried about such possibilities.[81] And he echoed a version of a familiar segregationist refrain: that different races were like the spokes of a wheel, but God was still the common center and "loved them all equally."[82] Although Shembe did not talk much about the specifics of heaven (other than what kept someone from getting there), he extended notions of racial separateness to heaven, too, with stories about how it might be segregated as well.[83]

Indian people's perceived differences contributed to why Shembe and the Nazaretha were so welcoming of them. Divine healing revivalism intersected with

Natal's pluralistic healing culture to encourage the Nazaretha to welcome different kinds of people at their church mission stations. Since the nineteenth century, revivalists had looked for stories of God's healing from all over the world as they collated evidence about what they argued was still possible. This dovetailed with how healers made claims in South Africa, often elevating their reputations by appealing to many kinds of people too. One tagline that developed about Shembe made this point. Shembe, his followers, began to say, cured people after they had gone to "White, Indian, and Native doctors" and after those other doctors had failed.[84] The presence of people of other races at Ekuphakameni helped confirm Shembe's reputation as someone whose medicine worked for everyone even when others' did not. Shembe understood this, collecting evidence about his own abilities to show to others. He kept some of the distinctive gifts offered to him by people of other races, and he took photographs of some of them, too.[85]

There are a few accounts of white and so-called Coloured people coming to be healed at Ekuphakameni, but there is much more evidence of Indian people coming to Ekuphakameni and other Nazaretha mission stations.[86] The anomalous demographics of Inanda contributed; Inanda would remain South Africa's only majority Indian district through the 1930s.[87] More broadly, socioeconomic marginality and histories of healing exchange meant that many Indian people who showed up at Ekuphakameni did so for reasons similar to Africans'.[88]

The methods of healing at Ekuphakameni underscore why not just Shembe but wider circles of the Nazaretha—and especially the young, unmarried women—needed to be welcoming of Indians too. The most detailed account of an Indian person staying at Ekuphakameni comes from the early 1920s.[89] It involved a man who had contracted tuberculosis while living close to Durban in an area that had many Indian residents making the transition from peasant producers to a working class.[90] Some, like this man, contracted tuberculosis as they did.[91] In this case, the man tried other care first but heard that "there was a priest at Phoenix named Shembe who heals people of their ailments." The man told his wife that he planned to stay for two weeks "up country" in the hope of getting better.[92] To make the tough journey, he brought his wife too. She stayed with him for several days at Ekuphakameni before returning home to get their small child and then bringing the boy back with her. The details underscore how healing at Ekuphakameni did not just involve brief encounters, then, between Shembe and a sick person but, instead, weeks-long interactions with many people.[93]

The story of the man with tuberculosis hints at other elements of Ekuphakame-ni's appeal and, in fact, how some people might have used it as a space that had little to do with what Shembe and the young church women envisioned. For example, the idea that the man was proceeding "up country"—perhaps for the fresh air—in-dicated how Ekuphakameni could function as a kind of sanitarium for the poor.[94] Some people who went there might have intended to use it for hospice too. In the case of the man with TB, state officials interviewed his wife to get her story after the man died at Ekuphakameni and then a dispute emerged over his possessions. While parts of the interview indicated that the man had gone to Ekuphakameni to get well, other sections painted a more pessimistic picture. At one point, he purportedly told his wife that he "did not care for us [his family] anymore and that he was going to Shembe to die."[95] The broader context makes it possible that some poor, struggling people—Indian or African—used Ekuphakameni as a space to die because they knew that the Nazaretha would take care of their burial. Dying people could spare their families funeral costs as a result.[96]

As mentioned, some of the South Asian people who came to Ekuphakameni to be healed also became Shembe's converts. Fanakalo, a form of simplified isiZulu that allowed Indian employers and African employees to communicate, facilitated the inclusion of these Indian church members.[97] Some of them also took new names to mark their conversion. One Indian woman, for example, became known as Nozinkobe because of the food she ate (izinkobe or corn and bean soup) while she sought Shembe's healing.[98] And a few Indian men assumed the titles of "chief[s] of the Indians" in the church and prayed over the sick. One of them had visions as well that he shared in the church community.[99]

The idea of a "chief of the Indians" points, again, to how race became one organizing principle within the Nazaretha community. Giving Indian men such a role—and respecting their supernatural powers (again, within limits) also let Shembe absorb some of his healing competition too. There were other Indian healers who set up on a piece of land not that far away from Ekuphakameni.[100] Much as Shembe could channel some of the spirituality of young, African women, he could channel the spirituality and healing powers of some of the Indian members of his church—and likely attract more people to Ekuphakameni as a result.

In the early twentieth century, Indian people in South Africa experienced their own processes of religious realignment and consolidation.[101] And yet, racial difference often made an Indian person's decision to seek Shembe's healing or to convert to the Nazaretha faith less of an either-or choice and less of a polarizing decision. Some of the reasons why pointed to another set of engagements in Inanda, where the Nazaretha also found themselves living near other African Christians.

Among Priests and Levites

In the story of the Good Samaritan, it was the priest and the Levite who passed by the robbed and injured Jewish man, offering no sympathy or assistance, before the Samaritan foreigner stopped to help.[102] If Indians were Samaritans for the Nazaretha, Shembe and other members of the early church encountered people whom they imagined as priests and Levites in Inanda, too. These were African Christian landowners, whose similarities might make the Nazaretha expect help from them that they did not offer. Already some African Christians of other denominations had made their criticisms of Shembe known, as they wrestled over theology, influence, and members in and around rural Ndwedwe.[103] In Inanda and other places where the Nazaretha sought land, the sources of competition grew along with the antagonisms.

Many African Christian landowners in Natal made up part of a larger community of African Christians called kholwa, or believers. This term marked more than a commitment to the Christian faith; it also marked connections to a particular era of conversion. The kholwa included people who had converted in the nineteenth century (or were their descendants) and who had affiliation with the mission churches. These people had often converted at a time when foreign missionaries expected adherence to Victorian, liberal ideals as signs of true faith. Thus, accepting Christ stood out, of course, as an essential ingredient for belonging in this group, but so did aspirations of monogamy, square houses, formal education, private property, and store-bought clothes.[104]

Like Christians elsewhere in South Africa, kholwa communities had many fractures. Kholwa debated beliefs, customs, and the roles of foreign missionaries, while economics, education, and denomination divided them too.[105] In Natal, private property divided kholwa as well. The history of land ownership in Natal meant that Africans at the apex of Christian communities did not live in towns, as in the Free State, but instead in the countryside. Moreover, the pattern of land ownership meant that in some cases kholwa people bought land together in collective arrangements in the nineteenth century and then stayed together, trying to hold onto their land, even as economic fractures and different interpretations of Christianity emerged among them.[106] Thus, one might see a kholwa whose family was still committed to monogamy and Victorian notions of respectability living side by side with a kholwa whose family had children who had entered polygynous marriages or become traditional healers.[107] And one could also see certain kholwa who seemed to profit from misfortune, buying up extra land when others among them could not hold onto it any longer.[108] Such proximity between people with divergent views as well as different social and economic possibilities would become an enduring feature of South African life. Segregated townships, for example, constricted geographic stratification along lines of class, keeping wealthy and poor Africans in relative proximity as well. The circumstances of the land-owning kholwa in Natal offered one route to a similar end.

John Dube's name has surfaced frequently in this book already. He stands out as the premier example of the elite kholwa in Natal. Born in 1871, Dube was only a few years Shembe's junior. Dube's family had, however, been among the earliest African converts to Christianity in Natal, and his father, James, had become one of the first ordained African Congregationalist ministers affiliated with the American Board Mission. The younger Dube had grown up attending mission schools, where he learned to read and write in isiZulu and English. He then traveled to the United States and studied at Oberlin College in the 1890s, before returning to South Africa with many ideas about progress, racial uplift, and how he might contribute. By the time Shembe moved into Inanda, Dube had launched a newspaper (*iLanga lase Natal*), established the Ohlange School, and bought significant amounts of land. In 1912, he would also become a founding member of the organization that became the African National Congress.[109]

Dube and others like him sought ways to broaden their struggles against social, political, and economic exclusion in South Africa. And yet, their efforts sometimes took the form of speaking for—not with—the masses of Africans or forging partnerships with other kinds of elites.[110] The paternalism exhibited by members of this group coincided with their attempts to prop up their own privileges relative to other Africans. Jacob Dlamini has shown how this played out in reference to a form of technology also central to Nazaretha evangelism: the railway. As railway tracks spread throughout South Africa, the educated African elite chafed at the restrictions imposed on their use of the trains—and pushed for easier mobility and better treatment in ways that suggested they were "worthy" when others of their race were not.[111]

The kinds of arguments that the educated, African Christian elite made about their access to the railways, in turn, relate back to the sources of animus between some Africans and Indians. Dube, for example, publicly said many negative things about his Indian neighbors in Inanda, and his newspaper contributed to the "undertow of anti-Indianism."[112] Dube's stance reflected competition for resources such as land and, perhaps above all, how the settler state so greedily rationed out privilege. But Dube (and others like him) also surely noticed that when Indian people suggested they deserved more from the state because they were more "civilized," they were arguing what elite African Christians had also argued about themselves.

From people such as Shembe, the educated African elite found themselves under attack from another direction at the same time. Shembe's life already served as a testament to the changed terms of debate as divine healing revivalism produced a different answer about what made a good church leader. Founded in rural, poor Ndwedwe, the Nazaretha faith depended, too, upon a different definition of what made a good Christian: a definition that involved avoiding, not acquiring. Indeed, Shembe preached about this directly, taking aim at one of the most important outward markers of conversion: clothes. As he explained in a sermon, "You must not think because you cover your bodies with clothing that you are Christians." Instead, a Christian was, Shembe said, someone who "pray[s] with a whole heart."[113] While few kholwa would have argued that clothes alone made a Christian, Shembe found ways to ask who the real Christians were.

Part of the problem for Dube and others like him stemmed from the fact that Shembe's message appealed to African Christians in their own denominations. The young kholwa men in Shembe's church had helped Shembe find ways to speak to such people, especially with the detailed knowledge of the Bible they shared. When evangelizing in other landed African Christian communities outside of Inanda, moreover, Shembe easily found landowning homestead hosts, and many of them accepted "the baptism of John."[114] Shembe's promise to bring children appealed to kholwa, too, as when Shembe stayed in a landed kholwa household where the family had "only one" child that they "got from McCord hospital," a reference to a mission hospital in the region and perhaps an indication of a complicated pregnancy or a difficult birth.[115] And even for those less interested in Shembe's promise to bring healthy babies, his reassessment of what it meant to be a good Christian resonated to some in landed kholwa communities too. Many of these African Christians had not managed to acquire the trappings of respectability either and yet often lived among some of the few who had.[116] The message of the Nazaretha faith gave them a way to argue back with their neighbors.

The polarization between the Nazaretha and other denominations emerged from a combination of similarity and difference, but it grew as the Nazaretha came to live near kholwa. As already mentioned, land represented one important domain of competition because the limited amount of land available pushed Shembe and the kholwa toward the same places. More than that, some kholwa landowners tried to block Shembe's access to land. In kholwa communities outside of Inanda, they also arrested him and reported him to their local magistrates.[117] These magistrates, in turn, often made issues more complicated by interpreting the laws surrounding different kinds of people (i.e., "exempted" or not) and property (i.e., mission land or not) in ways that denied popular support—and allowed Shembe to continue evangelizing in places where African Christians harbored the most animosity.[118] Living side by side, competition for members took on new dimensions too. For example, the new boarding school for girls in Inanda that had closed because Ekuphakameni attracted so many of its pupils was another school founded by John Dube.[119]

Disputes in Inanda and beyond led to public mudslinging between the Nazaretha and other African Christians. Some of this played out on the pages of *iLanga*, where kholwa began to question not only Shembe's credentials but also if his followers really were Christians. As one noted, "normal Christian Religious worshipping is done inside the Church," referencing how the Nazaretha worshipped outside.[120] Others suggested that the Nazaretha cherrypicked from the Bible and did not understand its real meaning. The Nazaretha read the Bible as "stories" or as the "newspaper" so that "they can use it for their own arguments with other people."[121] In so doing, these African Christians argued that the Nazaretha missed the broader meaning of the text.

Folded into criticisms about how the Nazaretha read the Bible were other debates about how to advance as a people in the world. On the pages of *iLanga*, one could find some observers outside of the Nazaretha faith cheering it on as "a church for Black people" that would exclude the "white religious leaders who are separating us."[122] But one could find others who worried the opposite. "Our people are becoming a laughingstock because of their many religious groups," one wrote, adding, "It is depressing to see a child crawling to the fire."[123] The same arguments playing out in *iLanga* were not settled among the early Nazaretha congregation either. When Ezra Mbonambi, one of the literate, younger men who had helped

Shembe in Ndwedwe, left the church, he did so on the basis that "members of the Shembe church believe in themselves instead of believing in God."[124] He re-affiliated with a foreign mission body to chart a different course—and took church members with him.[125]

The Nazaretha used *iLanga* to argue back against the people who dismissed them and the people who left. But they also crafted church testimonies and histories to make critiques of these people too. Some of their stories encapsulated particular events and moments of dispute. Some of their accounts also took aim at individuals who came to represent the broader tensions between the Nazaretha and other African Christians.[126]

Dube's proximity and renown made him an easy target for the Nazaretha, but so did some of his personal problems. Dube and his first wife had no children; moreover, soon after the Nazaretha arrived in Inanda a scandal erupted over how Dube had a child with one of his students.[127] Indeed, that student might have been a friend and peer to some of the girls who left Dube's school for Ekuphakameni. The Nazaretha could look to Dube, then, and see the hypocrisy of this elite African Christian who wondered if the Nazaretha were real Christians. The Nazaretha emphasized Dube's hypocrisy in another way, however, saying that he came "at night and requested . . . to be baptized" by Shembe and to ask for a child.[128] Shembe, however, refused to baptize anyone who would not "come with this request at daytime"—or in the open.[129]

The story about Dube's secret interest in Shembe resonated in part because many kholwa did convert and express interest in Shembe in the 1910s. The processes that drove the Nazaretha farther apart from other African Christians would continue to involve proximity in places such as Inanda.[130] But this polarization grew as the Nazaretha adjusted to another layer of conflict—this one with African fathers and elders upset by the possibilities that Ekuphakameni had opened for the girls and young women who helped build and sustain it.

CHAPTER 6

A Matchmaker at Ekuphakameni

IN JULY 1918, A. B. MAJOLA WROTE TO *ILANGA LASE NATAL* TO DESCRIBE A GATHERING
he attended at Ekuphakameni. Majola did not seem to be a member of the Nazaretha Church. He did not mention membership, and Shembe showered Majola with
the special treatment that the church leader often used to make an impression on
visitors. In Majola's case, this included a chair to sit in and hot tea to drink. Following
Christ's order to give of oneself, Shembe even "unexpectedly" offered Majola his
own overcoat on what was perhaps a chilly winter day in the southern hemisphere.[1]

Elsewhere in the world, the Romanovs had recently died at the hands of the
Bolsheviks, and the Germans were launching their last major offensive in World
War I. Majola, whose ability to read and write almost certainly made him a part of
the kholwa community, probably knew about such events. Mobilization for World
War I stood out as a crystalizing moment in South Africa's history, and people were
watching.[2] But, however worldly and expansive Majola's interests might have been,
in July 1918, he also focused on events closer to his home.

In the newspaper write-up, Majola called the gathering a "coming of age"
ceremony for the "daughters of Ekuphakameni." Majola said that he observed a
"line of thirty maidens" engaged in "continuous praising, beating of the drum,
and singing." They were all wearing similar outfits: including "white clothes" with

"green ribbons on their waists." They also held "black umbrellas." "My eyes," Majola noted, "were pleased."[3]

Majola's eyes were also witnessing an event intended to minimize dangerous conflicts that had erupted in the countryside. As the Nazaretha—with their girl-forward approach to evangelism—took their message into new chiefdoms, they faced threats from angry men worried about the church. In response, the Nazaretha accelerated efforts to make Ekuphakameni a place where fathers would *want* to send their daughters—or at least a place where they would worry less about the potential consequences. For the Nazaretha, this meant promising that daughters who went to Ekuphakameni would stay chaste and find husbands—and then communicating these commitments to people outside of the church, including anxious rural fathers and potential marriage partners. The late 1910s and early 1920s represented a time of rapid adaptation, as the Nazaretha mobilized to police young women's sexuality, inculcate church-based notions of sexual morality, and broadcast their efforts.[4]

The Nazaretha took part in one of many overlapping conversations about the behavior and comportment of unmarried girls and women in South Africa and beyond.[5] These conversations often revolved around the same set of questions: What forms of sex and intimacy were appropriate and when? Who should get to decide the terms of marriage? How should girls and women respond to the new possibilities for living their lives in the early twentieth century? And even a surprising, if remarkably common, question related to the others: how should young people dance?[6] The Nazaretha pieced together a set of answers among the most extreme of any group engaged in these conversations—extreme in its vision of sexual morality, its ways of marking and inculcating church norms, and in its punishments for violations of them. And yet, their response shared elements with others' and reflected the extent to which young, unmarried women in the early church challenged how rural patriarchs imagined moral, marriageable daughters.

To return to Majola in 1918, he saw young women who had experienced church-based sex education and socialization. He had likely been invited not only to look for a bride but also to tell others that they could do the same at Ekuphakameni. And if that "line of maidens" he described as engaged in "praising, beating of the drum, and singing" was not technically dancing yet—that is, moving their bodies in a rhythmic way accompanied by music—they would be very soon.[7] In the late 1910s, the first church dances featured young, unmarried women and took place at Ekuphakameni because it was a place that provoked so much anxiety for rural fathers.

Open Questions about Sex and Marriage

Questions of sexuality and marriage had surfaced as problems for Shembe since before he left the Free State farm. Shembe might not have known much about formal expressions of religion then, but he did likely know that many people would see his polygynous marriages as incommensurate with Christianity. After all, Shembe's marriages factored into his explanation of how he had disobeyed God and why he had lost so many children.[8] And yet, as Shembe first moved to Harrismith and then Durban, he entered social spaces in which African men predominated—and in which questions about marriage and sexuality receded from his attention. Since arriving in Ndwedwe, with its majority of women, the need to address questions about Shembe's own sexuality had become readily apparent. By staying in homesteads where husbands and fathers were present and by showing no interest in relationships with women, Shembe helped protect himself from the accusations of sexual impropriety commonly leveled against roving African ministers and healers.[9]

As Shembe began to gain followers in Ndwedwe, their sexual behavior became entangled with his. Whatever gratitude Shembe had for the devotion, labor, and offerings of the young, unmarried girls and women who began to attend his services, he had to know that they stood out as a dangerous demographic for him. If any of them became pregnant, people might make assumptions about him. He had reasons, then, to surround himself with young, unmarried women who were also committed to demonstrating their sexual propriety. As people came to stay at weeks-long healing services in Ndwedwe, questions arose, too, about how Shembe would control people's interactions with each other. One more reason why the Old Testament afforded Shembe so many rich resonances involved its prohibitions against sex. Before Moses climbed Mount Sinai to commune with God and receive the Ten Commandments, he had told the people waiting below to "abstain from sexual relations."[10] Shembe had almost certainly commanded the same at Mount Nhlangakazi in 1913 and would continue to demand abstinence at church events. On at least one occasion, he also threatened to leave—and cut short the healing services—if people did not abide by his rules.[11]

After founding the Nazaretha, the first formal acts of restraining church members' sexuality involved churchmen and the requirement that they be married to be ordained by Shembe.[12] This represented a contrast with Shembe's own expressions of sexual restraint, showing an early way that he distinguished himself from other important men in the church. He, in other words, could maintain standards of celibacy that those other men could not. Still, he expected their sexuality to be confined in monogamous marriage. Making this decision, Shembe employed a logic similar to protestant foreign missionaries'. Mission societies had often sent married missionary couples into the mission field in the hope that marriage would keep missionary men from entering inappropriate relationships while abroad.[13]

Outside of concerns for sexual propriety and the need for each Nazaretha minister to marry only one wife, other questions about sex and marriage remained open to debate in the church—as in many other churches too. Africans adjusted to more ways to marry (e.g., through traditional, civil, or Christian rites) as well as reasons to marry—and whether family choice, romance and attraction, economic factors, or other variables should matter most. They adjusted to shifting legal regimes that altered who could conduct marriages, and they used the continued retreat of foreign missionaries after World War I to take charge of debates about what form marriage should take. On top of these other factors, enduring questions about customs such as polygyny, bridewealth, and initiation remained.[14]

Despite the extent to which many African Christian communities debated appropriate forms of marriage, different churches had other factors to consider. Some churches, for example, had institutional history behind their debates. Some churches also had more legal options. The Union government determined that "in the case of native ministers belonging to purely native churches," officials would "not consider it desirable to plant them on the same footing" as others.[15] The Nazaretha, as a church unrecognized by the government, joined many others whose leaders could not perform legal marriages. That prohibition had not changed after Union.[16]

Perhaps because of lingering uncertainties, Shembe experimented with marriage in a range of ways in his first years in Natal. To return to those days of waiting for land in Inanda, he found another way to make himself an easy, welcome guest. The owner of the land where Shembe and the others were staying had a "wayward son," and Shembe promised to "negotiate for him a marriage."[17] Already, Shembe seemed to have a sense that his mobility and connections to many communities could facilitate marriage arrangements at a time when the divisions of an industrializing society might make it harder to find a suitable marriage partner otherwise. He also took finding marriage partners for the early, young members of his community seriously. Church members explained the eventual departure of Peter Mnqayi, the first member of the church, as part of a longer set of disputes with Shembe that had begun over whom Mnqayi should marry to meet the requirement for ordination. Shembe told Mnqayi that "the Word has said" Mnqayi would not "love this maiden [Mnqayi's choice] even for three months."[18] Mnqayi disagreed about his future wife, marrying her anyway in an act that foreshadowed future disagreements with Shembe.[19]

As Shembe evangelized in Christian communities in the mid-1910s, he also experimented with a practice that would become much more commonplace in the Nazaretha community in the 1920s: offering an advance or even a gift equivalent to bridewealth to facilitate an unmarried girl's movement to Ekuphakameni. A young woman named Gertie Mbambo told how Shembe offered to give her legal guardian money that represented a portion of the lobola she might receive so that she could go to Ekuphakameni.[20] Such an offer echoed arrangements foreign missionaries once made, giving "good compensation" to families as they struggled to get African girls to come to their mission stations.[21] Shembe's willingness to link his compensation to bridewealth, however, represented a difference from earlier missionaries' offers since they had sometimes likened lobola to "selling women."[22] For Shembe, such a proposal stood out as an exception in the 1910s that likely stemmed from Mbambo's status as someone who, she revealed in her story, was both sick and an orphan. Shembe could demonstrate his care for vulnerable people, and her legal guardian might have more openly considered alternate arrangement for her upbringing. In this case, however, Mbambo refused the offer because of her Wesleyan faith.[23]

The account of promising to find a marriage partner, the act of offering bridewealth for Gertie Mbambo, and the dispute with Peter Mnqayi all suggest something else: how Shembe already prioritized fathers and elders in his thinking about matters of marriage and sexuality. In the case of the marriage arrangement for the young man, Shembe made a promise to the father—not to the son who was to be married. And the bridewealth offer for Gertie Mbambo would have involved her legal guardian. The story of the dispute with Peter Mnqayi suggested a stance in favor of elders and fathers, too, albeit in this case with Shembe standing in as Mnqayi's spiritual father. Shembe, the story insinuated, knew better than the younger man and should have been able to decide for Mnqayi.

Shembe's leanings toward elders and fathers in matters of marriage and sexuality stemmed in part from Shembe's positionality. In his forties, Shembe approached elderhood, and he was both a biological and a symbolic father. And yet a series of dangerous confrontations in rural chiefdoms also heightened his interest in appeasing fathers.

Angry Men in the Countryside

Why the Nazaretha had not encountered more angry men in Ndwedwe, upset about the behavior of girls and women in the church, is not clear. True, people had expressed concerns about Shembe's effect on young women and girls, but their anxieties had centered on what he might do—his "love charms" and his "Malay magic."[24] In at least a few cases in Ndwedwe, moreover, Shembe managed to maintain relations with rural fathers after their daughters had left their homes behind to live with him, showing that not all families opposed their daughters' departures.[25] To explain the escalating conflicts outside of Ndwedwe, timing likely mattered. People who encountered Shembe after he had a piece of land where runaway girls could go had more reasons to worry.

Nazaretha accounts of early church history suggest that church members began to encounter more angry men in the mid-1910s as the Nazaretha used the railway to evangelize north and south of Durban. Some of this movement related to the pursuit of private property described in the last chapter, but the Nazaretha did not stay within the bounds of propertied Christian communities as they moved through these regions. They evangelized in chiefdoms nearby and used the railway to target a few specific chiefdoms in other parts of Natal and Zululand, including the chiefdom of the Zulu king in Nongoma.[26]

As the Nazaretha moved into new places, people began to make common refrains that revealed how arguments about young women, mobility, and sexual morality had calcified over the past half century. That is, one could find rural men leveling the same charges that generations of rural men had leveled before, saying that Shembe, in this case, "enticed women away" and that the girls and women who joined his church were "prostitutes and nothing else."[27] The calcified terms of the debate extended to Shembe's responses too. He echoed the words that generations of foreign missionaries had used as they attempted to answer such criticisms. When asked about the large number of women in his community, Shembe said simply that he "never called them." "If a husband or father should come for his wife or daughter," he added, "I would not refuse to let her go, but I wish to say that in no instance has such a demand been made."[28]

The calcified terms of the debate hid differences. Shembe perhaps did not "call" girls and women directly—although the account of him suggesting the lobola offer to Mbambo raises questions about this too. But beyond Shembe's direct involvement, he stood at the helm of a community that used other unmarried girls and women to target more people like them. As the Nazaretha entered new communities in the mid-1910s, they often followed a set pattern. Shembe traveled with a few churchmen and a group of unmarried women and girls to a region where they already had a place to stay. Shembe would then schedule a time for a service, and, during the days leading up to it, the unmarried girls and young women would drum up support, recruiting others to come. Girls, who, by this point, had likely been warned not to attend, might sneak away to go to a service, see people being healed, and hear Shembe's story of evading and then defying his family to follow God. In some instances, too, they might decide to leave home and join the others at Ekuphakameni.[29]

Not only did this model of evangelism prioritize the recruitment of girls, but the Nazaretha celebrated the raucous behavior among the girls and young women as they evangelized on the road—especially when other people tried to harm Shembe. In one case, church girls and women purportedly "stayed outside the prison and prayed for [Shembe]" all night after local men detained him.[30] In another, they wielded improvised weapons to fight off a group of men who came for Shembe with "assegais and fighting sticks" because "a maiden of the Ngcobo family . . . joined the other maidens who accompanied Shembe." After the men "dispersed," Shembe rewarded the young women with words of praise, saying, "My children, you have really destroyed them." He also got them a rare treat to thank them: store-bought bread.[31]

The same Nazaretha account of unmarried women and girls "fighting for Shembe" revealed another way that circumstances were different for the Nazaretha than they had been for white missionaries. African men used violence to push Shembe out of their communities. This had been true in the early days in Ndwedwe too when Shembe traveled by himself. But, by the mid-1910s, Shembe and his fellow evangelists had a harder time hiding when his healing services were advertised in advance at specific sites. Shembe's growing renown brought risks.[32]

The Nazaretha also experienced threats of violence in one especially high-stakes mission field: the chiefdom of the Zulu king. Shembe's relationship with Zulu-ness was always fraught.[33] Still, as a telling indication of the social, cultural, and political importance of the Zulu royal family and Inkosi Solomon kaDinuzulu, the Nazaretha arrived to evangelize at the king's homestead just as the government took steps to expand Inkosi Solomon's authority.[34] By then, the king already belonged to the Anglican Church, and he had many other African church leaders attempting to win his favor. Some of them, in fact, made claims much like Shembe's.[35] Inkosi Solomon did give Shembe a worship site, but the Zulu king showed Shembe little favor otherwise. The Nazaretha noted how "new noise of talking and misunderstanding" characterized their bad relations after some "maidens" in the region were "touched by the gospel and became Christians." Soon after these young women joined the church, the Nazaretha said that a man came with "fire to threaten them."[36] Shembe scaled back his evangelism in the region after another event that pointed to ill-will: someone informed on Shembe to the local magistrate.[37]

Other African men began to fight back in court. In the early 1920s, a case made it to the Native High Court that pitted the authority of patriarchal household heads against the authority of patriarchal chiefs. A household head in Eshowe had welcomed Shembe to host worship services at his home, but the chief opposed these services because "complaints had been made by the whole of the tribe regarding the enticement of their women."[38] This language exaggerated Shembe's opposition, but the threat of "enticing women" still resonated with white authorities. The court threw out the case on a technicality: the judges did not think they had jurisdiction to try it. They agreed, however, that "the authority of the chief has been interfered with and that the well being [sic] of his tribe has been interfered with."[39] This decision made it clear that the technical victory for Shembe might not hold.

Altogether, the challenges from angry men in the countryside were serious. They involved physical threats against Shembe and the possibility of losing access to worship space. They had the potential to derail relations with important people, Inkosi Solomon above all. But Shembe's main demographic at Ekuphakameni—the one that contributed to so much of the trouble—opened opportunities for appeasing some of the same angry men.

The calcified terms of debate in the 1910s and 1920s also hid the broader shifts taking place in African communities. In the 1880s, African men had begun to complain about their wives and daughters' mobility as their sons' departures became more commonplace—and as they still thought it might be possible to keep daughters and wives from leaving too. By the 1910s—the period that represented the height of the gap between rural African women and urban African men—some elder men might have already sensed a changing tide.[40] Certainly, as more women began moving to towns and cities in the 1920s and 1930s, fathers had greater awareness of the limits of their influence—and a sense that white officials could not much help them anymore. Some likely tried harder to keep their daughters from leaving in response. But others might have accepted the idea that, if their daughters were likely to go somewhere, they could at least decide where and why.[41]

Already, Shembe's theology gave him a foundation upon which to build as he made the case that fathers should send daughters to Ekuphakameni. By promising good health and fertility for his followers, Shembe addressed common concerns that grooms' families had about potential brides. In fact, during marriage ceremonies, a bride's father sometimes publicly stated any serious ailments she had experienced. The groom's relatives wanted to know that a healthy woman, who was likely to have children, was marrying into their family.[42] If the Nazaretha could disassociate mobility from sexual immorality, they could draw more attention to the ways Shembe's healing might facilitate marriage and the births of healthy children.

Already, too, Ekuphakameni resembled a relatively new institution in southern Africa: a mission boarding school. As the Nazaretha began to address problems in the countryside, Ekuphakameni became more like one—in other words, a place that isolated one sex of people during a particular phase of their lives with the purpose of giving them additional training and education while under elder (and Godly) supervision. Within this institutional apparatus, the Nazaretha soon wove in many more elements to rebrand the unmarried girls and women in their community.

Socialization and Sex Education

Elizabeth Thornberry's work shows how different conceptual frameworks in nineteenth-century Xhosaland made it difficult for people to come to consensus about what kinds of actions transgressed sexual norms. These frameworks were "custom and familial authority, the spiritual world, liberalism and the individual subject, and race."[43] Natal's African communities had similar frameworks, and Natal was another important locus of conversations about sexuality and sexual violence in South Africa. Still, the Nazaretha reveal another element of the multiplicity of frameworks: they provided many sources from which the Nazaretha might draw to disassociate young women's sexual immorality from their mobility. That is, the Nazaretha could (and did) turn to the text of the Bible, notions of an omniscient God, Victorian purity culture, liberal ideas of personal responsibility, and interpretations of custom as they approached the problem of changing churchwomen's reputations.

FIGURE 4. Shembe surrounded by a group of girls and women at Ekuphakameni in the early 1930s. Older girls are wearing head coverings like the ones in popular depictions of the Virgin Mary. Married women are wearing headwraps, while young girls are wearing no head coverings.

PHOTOGRAPH INCLUDED WITH PERMISSION OF CAMPBELL COLLECTIONS, UKZN.

The Nazaretha began to socialize young, unmarried women by marking them in the church and at Ekuphakameni. A young woman arriving at church headquarters for the first time would have gotten a new church outfit that included not only the standard white robe but also a head covering that looked, not coincidentally, like the ones found in popular depictions of the Virgin Mary.[44] And, much as clothes marked unmarried girls and women, so did strict segregation of space. The few men at Ekuphakameni slept in separate quarters from the many unmarried girls who also, in turn, slept in separate quarters from mothers and children. As whole families started moving to Ekuphakameni in the 1920s, they lived across the road that divided the property. And, as Shembe bought farms and settled more families on them in other parts of Inanda, he kept the young, unmarried women at Ekuphakameni, close to him.[45]

Once at church headquarters, a girl would have noticed, too, the many ways that the Nazaretha marked her and others like her through words as well. Calling these girls and young women "maidens" and "little brides," the church emphasized their chastity and the result Shembe promised for them, marriage.[46] The "little bride" designation communicated something else important. Outside of the church, many African women were socialized for certain periods of intense scrutiny in their lives. The time when a new bride left her own home and arrived at her husband's represented one of these times, as the husband's family tested her loyalty by making demands.[47] By calling unmarried churchwomen "little brides," the Nazaretha sent a message to girls that they entered a period of intense scrutiny too as they left their homes to prepare for marriage.

For supervision at Ekuphakameni, the Nazaretha turned to the age-set, or a group of girls about the same age, to monitor converts' behavior. Ethnographic evidence from many parts of southern Africa suggests the important roles of age-sets as adolescent girls often began moving farther beyond their own homesteads (and away from family supervision) just as pregnancy became possible. Indeed, going farther away from home, whether for daily chores or to attend community celebrations, offered a way of finding someone to marry. For older girls, peers—the same people also moving farther from their homesteads—became a network of co-guardians.[48]

Anthropologists writing in the 1930s in southern Africa explained age-sets in normative terms that must have involved more variation and complexity in real life. But they, nevertheless, described how older girls in an age-set provided sex education, decided when younger girls could begin speaking to boys, and determined when younger girls could engage in the premarital sexual activities (e.g., ukuhlobonga or "thigh sex") common in African communities. Shembe had himself experienced something like an age-set when he went away as a boy to work for Coenraad Grabe and asked the older boys questions about sex. But girls' age-sets also punished those among them who became pregnant before marriage in shameful rituals that marked their expulsion from the group.[49]

The discussion of age-sets in the ethnographic accounts reveals another element of the debates about daughters' behavior. Despite fathers' many complaints about daughters' mobility in the colonial present, unmarried African girls had left their homes on occasion in the past. Fathers who complained were expressing anxieties not only about their daughters' mobility per se but also concerns that these older ways of facilitating girls' movement—and, with it, facilitating marriage—did not work anymore. The Nazaretha attempted to change this.

At Ekuphakameni unmarried girls and women watched each other for violations of sexual norms, reported on each other, and administered some of the punishments to each other.[50] Moreover, the Nazaretha had one representative of this group who acted as a leader and the most important authority among them—although she also answered to Shembe. In the late 1910s, Linah Mntungwa, the older girl who had been with Shembe at the time of the purchase of Ekuphakameni, served in this role.[51] Still, over time, the age-set model no longer fit as neatly because some of the young women who came to live at Ekuphakameni never married or left the church. This kept older women in a cohort in which younger, unmarried girls and women predominated. Again, Mntungwa was the first example of such a person who, as she aged, became more like a boarding school matron, chaperoning her younger church wards, than the leader of the age-set that she once had been.[52]

The Nazaretha also added forms of supervision by requiring regular virginity testing.[53] Physical examinations of young women's bodies had, in the past, offered another way that families monitored their daughters' sexual activities and relationships. Usually, older women performed these examinations after younger women in their families returned from community celebrations.[54] Virginity testing could, of course, be inconclusive. And in times past, families sometimes used such examinations, in turn, to pursue marriage negotiations with a daughter's sexual partner. In other cases, virginity testing could offer evidence of rape or sexual assault that then might be used to hold a perpetrator accountable.[55]

Just when the Nazaretha turned to virginity testing as a form of sexual supervision remains unclear, but the mid- to late 1910s make a likely window of time when Shembe would have wanted to know that girls were "fit to stand before God" in the congregation.[56] Around the same time, some chiefs in the rural regions where the church was growing began to require virginity testing of the young women in their territories, as one chief explained, "to check the rapid increase in immorality and . . . sexual intercourse that is afoot degenerating the young people."[57] If Shembe had not adopted the practice in the church already, he might have picked up the idea for how to appease rural elders from his travels. In both cases, as these chiefs and the Nazaretha turned to physical inspections of young women's bodies, they cared less about how virginity testing could hold men accountable and more about how the practice could compel young women's chastity.

At Ekuphakameni, girls also experienced church-based sex education through parables attributed to Shembe. Some of these parables included instruction about what kinds of sex were allowable. For the Nazaretha non-penetrative sex acts were not permitted before marriage, a decision more in-line with Victorian-era foreign missionaries' thinking about sex than many Africans'.[58] Other parables spoke to the circumstances in and around Inanda, warning young women against the sin of "taking an Indian lover."[59] Still another parable made an example of a girl who held onto love letters after Shembe told her to burn them. Love letters in this story represented evidence of a relationship outside of Shembe's control and perhaps revealed his anxiety about a form of communication that he (and many African parents) could not access without help.[60] The culture of love-letter writing in South Africa at the time also made the genre a challenge to Nazaretha sexual norms: these letters often included graphic, detailed sexual language.[61] Shembe's harsh words against love letters also seemed to confirm something else: in Nazaretha sex education, there is no evidence of sharing knowledge about body parts and mechanics or sexual pleasure, all common topics in age-set administered sex education in the past.[62]

The form of sex education at Ekuphakameni implied additional ways of policing unmarried girls' and women's sexual impropriety. For example, the parables and stories emphasized Shembe's discovery of immoral sex acts. Shembe, the stories suggested, would find out even if the many other methods of reporting and accountability did not work—indeed, his ability to do so represented another example of his divine knowledge. Shembe could purportedly look at a girl and know that she would have sex before marriage, suggesting in one account that a family name their daughter "Ngaphi," meaning "Where will her virginity go?"[63] And, in one of the more sinister examples of Shembe's knowledge, he implied that he knew when a woman might pretend that she had been raped to try to absolve herself of responsibility for an illicit sexual encounter.[64]

The idea of omniscience, in turn, related to punishments. Indeed, discussion of punishments abounded. Some were in this world, as when a young unmarried woman became pregnant and was removed from Ekuphakameni. To add to the shame, the other girls "washed the gates of Ekuphakameni" so that they could purify their community.[65] In other cases, older women spat on girls suspected of visiting boyfriends.[66] The Nazaretha told stories of punishments that came directly from God too—as when a young woman did not want to go to Ekuphakameni and "a thunderstorm came and killed her."[67] Shembe also used threats of hellfire and brimstone. In one account, he described examples of young unmarried women who "had bad habits," "slept with Indians," and "had external intercourse," telling such people that they should "continue abundantly" in such acts so that they would "not regret when [they] would burn in hell."[68] Nazaretha girls and women learned that they could expect punishment, then, whether in this life or after and, in some cases, whether they were members of the church or not.

The intensity of Nazaretha sex education meant that activities at Ekuphakameni not seeming to relate to sex often did. Shembe's exhortations to fill one's hours with hard work had strong moral valences. Nowhere were those valences more apparent than at church headquarters. The work of sewing, sweeping, pulling weeds in gardens, rethatching roofs, caring and cooking for the sick, and so much else that unmarried Nazaretha girls did to keep Ekuphakameni "clean" and running offered an indication of their sexual purity. This work also kept them busy and together so that the girls could keep watch over each other. And, again, Shembe's own experiences of sneaking away as a youth under the loose supervision of an age-set meant that he knew how the girls at Ekuphakameni might find opportunities to do the same.

Shembe's sermons admonishing girls to avoid consumerism contributed directly and indirectly to the program of sex education as well. Some parables warned girls about consumer items linked to dance halls and other sites of casual sexual encounters. In one, a girl with one of these items—in this case a harmonica—died after "dogs devoured her body," in a fate echoing the story of the lustful Jezebel in 2 Kings.[69] Other parables warned against buying things less associated with sex, including "perilous sweets," or candy.[70] As shops filled in around Ekuphakameni, this must have been a growing temptation.[71] Much as girls should abstain from sex, Shembe preached, they should also abstain from unnecessary, wasteful purchases too.[72]

The connections between work, abstinence (from many things), and sexual purity emphasize how the regime of policing sexuality at Ekuphakameni depended upon the broader ethos of the Nazaretha community. Shembe demanded many kinds of sacrifices, spoke about other kinds of people who experienced terrible punishments, and upheld extreme ideas of personal responsibility that applied to everyone.[73] His own spiritual autobiography, after all, informed people that God had allowed Shembe's children to die because of Shembe's disobedience.[74] Nazaretha girls could look around and see examples of the lessons they learned applied to other people, if not always the same intense configuration of surveillance and monitoring they experienced.

The Nazaretha surely knew that other African Christians, too, were experimenting with methods of monitoring chastity and preventing premarital sex. Other churches marked the girls in their community at an "age of discretion" with specific head coverings to make them easily identifiable.[75] The practice of virginity testing moved into other contexts in South Africa, including into cities where groups of mothers also came together to pray for their daughters' purity.[76] And the growing popularity of "white weddings" suggested that many church communities sought ways to reward African women's chastity before marriage. By the 1930s, some of these churches also required virginity testing before women could wear veils at their weddings.[77]

The Nazaretha also celebrated examples of young women who stayed chaste. Girls saw how some of these women ran Ekuphakameni and how, for a time, they enjoyed proximity to Shembe himself.[78] The Nazaretha also venerated other virginal role models, some from the Bible and some biblically inspired. These included not only the Virgin Mary but also figures such as Jephthah's daughter, whose virginity was a central apart of her story of obedience and sacrifice for her father.[79] It might have been at this time, too, that the Nazaretha began to add new layers to the story of Shembe's mother to provide another chaste role model. In the story of Shembe's conversion, she had been the main hindrance as he planned to leave his family behind to follow God. But, by the time of Shembe's death, the Nazaretha were already describing how she had heard a voice saying she, like the Virgin Mary, would "have a son to be praised."[80] In accounts that are more difficult to date, the Nazaretha also described her as a "virgin of Jehova [who] did not commit any sin during the time of her youth."[81] Young women who did not have sex before marriage could understand themselves as emulating the mother of the prophet. As they did, they could also see themselves working toward the main reward that many of them wanted: marriage through the church. Offering that reward meant that Shembe needed to find more men.

From Marriage Woes to Dance Shows at Ekuphakameni

Shembe justified the decision to allow church dances based on his growing familiarity with the Bible—and its most-cited passage in favor of dance: "And David danced before the Lord with all his might, wearing a priestly garment."[82] But, if Shembe could find biblical passages to support the decision, other factors mattered too. Many Africans already associated dance with moments that demanded extra monitoring of young, unmarried women's sexuality.[83] These associations existed because of how dance drew many people together, including outsiders who might be suitable marriage partners.[84]

The number of men that Shembe invited to watch young women dance at Ekuphakameni in the 1910s remains uncertain. Majola, whose letter opened this chapter, did not describe a large crowd.[85] Still, his presence and the few details about the others who attended church dances in the late 1910s support the idea that Shembe first tried to recruit a particular kind of outsider, kholwa men, to watch the dances.[86] They were often nearby in Inanda and might have made respectable marriage partners in the eyes of many fathers—especially if they could offer sufficient bridewealth.[87] Because kholwa were engaged in debates about chastity, dance, and marriage, too, Majola's words that his eyes "were pleased" took on added meaning as he seemed to sanction the Nazaretha approach.[88] At the same time, Shembe's preference for Christian men from other denominations points to another realm of competition with kholwa communities—and Shembe's lingering aspirations to draw more of them into his fold. However proud he might also be of the many "unclothed" in his church, the presence of more kholwa could convince others among them that Shembe was a proper Christian too.

Although the Nazaretha drew upon the social roles that dance once played in African communities, much was different about their dances. By the late 1910s and 1920s, for example, the geography of dance in African communities had already shifted, moving with men toward urban areas. Cities provided space for groups of migrant working men to dance and for the dance halls and beer clubs that caused concerns about sexual morality.[89] Allowing dance among the young Nazaretha girls and women stood out as another way, then, that Shembe included people left behind. Through the church, these girls and women found another analog to what their brothers were doing in cities.

The style of dance that Majola and others saw was different too. The first Nazaretha dance costumes, for example, did not seem traditional. Based on Majola's description of "white clothes" and "green ribbons," they seemed, instead, simple and homemade, using widely available materials and objects that the young women at Ekuphakameni could have sewn.[90] The Nazaretha style of dancing could not be easily glossed as traditional either. An outside observer who saw the Nazaretha dance in the early 1920s made this clear, explaining how they "contented themselves by taking two steps forward, and two steps back."[91] The observer added, "They [the Nazaretha] do not dance as we do."[92] Nor did the church allow for individual expressions of dancing talent as some forms of traditional dancing did.

The absence of individual expressions of talent was significant. It represented one way that the Nazaretha bolstered the importance of the group of girls—their camaraderie and their mutual responsibility. Sometimes in the early days, too, Shembe canceled the dances for all of the girls when one of them had gotten in trouble, showing how he tied dance to mutual responsibility (and social control) in another way.[93] But, without letting any one person stand out, Shembe also had more control over the marriages arranged after church dances too.

Shembe began to play the role of matchmaker after the dances. This involved ensuring that the men who married Nazaretha women offered bridewealth that satisfied girls' and women's fathers. A few Nazaretha accounts from this time described "letters in the mail" as fathers received information about potential marriage matches by post, a common practice among literate Africans at the time.[94] In these cases, fathers learned whom their daughters would marry before the daughters themselves, emphasizing the importance of pleasing fathers—and giving them control over the process.[95]

Majola did not seem to find a bride at the church event in July 1918, but six weeks after Majola wrote to *iLanga*, a wedding announcement appeared in the same newspaper describing two weddings of the "daughters of Shembe."[96] The announcement briefly profiled the brides and the grooms, noting that one of the grooms was a "former member of the Anglican church," a detail that surely rankled the sensibilities of many kholwa readers.[97] Another line from the wedding announcement perhaps sent a message to kholwa readers too: "Both of these weddings were remarkable and they were celebrated. All went beautifully."[98] This suggested that, despite questions that the Nazaretha themselves and other African Christians might have about the forms of marriage that would be recognized in Shembe's church, the Nazaretha were figuring it out.

By the late 1910s, the Nazaretha were already on the cusp of a shift that would bring more men into their church and that, within a few years, would also allow polygynous marriage under certain circumstances. This shift would take some of the pressure off Shembe to find more men for Nazaretha women to marry. Over time, the kinds of men who came to Ekuphakameni to seek brides changed in part because a growing number of kholwa did not see the dancing ceremonies at Ekuphakameni as an appropriate way to meet wives.[99] This pointed to another consequence of the polarization and deepening divides among African Christian communities in South Africa who defined themselves, increasingly, against each other.[100]

As church demographics shifted, the success of Nazaretha efforts to market young, unmarried women as chaste and pure worked well. In a conversation in which Shembe was otherwise largely deferential to a white official in 1923, Shembe said with confidence that the "morals are better" in his community than in others.[101] Moreover, white neighbors in Inanda had heard that the young women at Ekuphakameni had reputations like the "mama kaJesu," or the Virgin Mary.[102] Although the evidence comes from later, Nazaretha women were known by the 1940s as the "most chaste" in Inanda.[103] In an odd way, even a negative rumor about Shembe himself confirmed the shift in perception. Some people purportedly began to say that he had "frozen testicles," which helped them explain why he did not remarry and why the young, unmarried women around him did not seem to get pregnant.[104]

The existence of negative rumors underscored that the Nazaretha approach never convinced everyone. But their approach did convince some fathers, who began to play larger roles in determining that their daughters *should* go to Ekuphakameni. The Nazaretha approach also convinced some mothers. Indeed, although Shembe interacted and negotiated most with fathers, mothers in the early twentieth century shouldered much of the blame if their daughters became pregnant before marriage.[105] By taking responsibility for young, unmarried women and calling them "daughters of Shembe," he shared rural mothers' burdens. As important, Shembe's approach convinced some daughters too. African women had long argued that bridewealth helped them become respected members of their new families. The Nazaretha gave unmarried women a path to secure it at a time when many worried they would not.[106] There was "status gained by the girls," as one observer noted in 1930, when he heard of an especially high bridewealth amount for a young Nazaretha woman.[107] The higher lobola that resulted meant something to fathers, yes, but to daughters as well.

The Nazaretha also benefited from a wider shift in perceptions of unmarried Christian churchwomen. If, through the nineteenth century, many people associated Christianity with loose sexual morals, this was less the case by the 1930s. Anthropologists studying African communities recalled how African Christians were seen as less socially active and, relatedly, less sexually active than their peers who were not Christians.[108] As the influence of foreign missionaries receded in African churches, Africans found ways to change the reputations of churchwomen. African women who had lived lives that challenged what rural African fathers imagined as moral spearheaded some of these initiatives. Sibusisiwe Makhanya, for example, had studied at mission schools in Natal before furthering her education in the United States. As the first African woman social worker in South Africa, she helped launch the Bantu Purity League to keep African girls "pure in the right way."[109] Makhanya, who never married, might have understood the consequences of charting a different course in ways that resonated with Nazaretha girls and young women.

Purity projects often came at a social cost even for the women who agreed with their aims. Although the Nazaretha tried to break up associations between immorality and mobility, Nazaretha women were noticeably less mobile by the mid-1920s. While church members still valorized Linah Mntungwa and while she still traveled to other important church centers, her role became most associated with Ekuphakameni and watching over the young women there.[110] Other important young women of her cohort largely disappeared from church histories after their marriages in part because of Shembe's commands that mothers' first duties were to their children and husbands.[111] Some of the changes taking place among girls and women in the church community stemmed, however, from other sources—and from a new era of relations between church and state.

CHAPTER 7

A Dissident in Southern Zululand

IN JANUARY 1923, THE MAGISTRATE OF NDWEDWE SUMMONED SHEMBE TO HIS OFFICE.
Shembe had been going to Ndwedwe for more than a decade. He had launched
a new faith from one of its mountainsides and led pilgrimages to that mountain
each year, crossing through Ndwedwe in a group that one observer described as
"a swarm of locusts."[1] He—and they—were impossible to miss. Still, Shembe had
never before been called to the magistrate's office.

In preparation for the meeting, the magistrate had received instructions from
his superiors. He was to explain to Shembe the "nature of the causes which led
to the serious trouble at Bulhoek" and to "point out to [Shembe] the possibility
of similar developments if misunderstanding should arise between him and the
Authorities." But, the instructions continued, the magistrate should do this without
"antagonising" Shembe.[2]

The "serious troubles" alluded to an incident with another group of African
Christians, known as the Israelites, who had gathered on common land in the Cape
to await the end of times foretold by their prophet, Enoch Mgijima. As their wait
extended months and then years, they entered a standoff with the South African
government. The "possibility of similar developments" referred to an instance of
state violence on May 24, 1921, which left dozens of the Israelites dead and injured

as well as their leaders arrested and facing trial. [3] The story of the Israelites had drawn the attention of many South Africans—Shembe certainly among them.[4] Making the comparison to the Israelites' situation without "antagonising" Shembe would be difficult.

The meeting in early 1923 marked a new era of church–state relations. The Nazaretha had taken root for a decade when state officials knew something about Shembe and others like him but did not much bother with their goings-on. The lack of interest pointed to Shembe's success at finding safe harbors and avoiding trouble. But the absence of bother also underscored something Shembe could not have known when he came back to Natal after 1910: how quickly officials' war on African Christianity would fizzle out. As early as 1912, officials in Natal, who were already hearing complaints about Shembe from chiefs and missionaries, explained, "unless it can be proved that John [sic] Shembe is preaching sedition," they would not "propose to take any action."[5] The terms of Union and then the emergence of new crises in South Africa focused attention on issues other than African Christians worshipping in arrangements on the edge of legality in the rural reserves.[6]

After Bulhoek, South African officials began reassessing the threats posed by communities of African Christians spread throughout South Africa.[7] The Nazaretha were high on the list for additional surveillance.[8] And although Shembe's theological resemblance to another religious leader first focused state attention on the church, his actions helped hold the focus longer. The push to monitor African-led churches throughout South Africa stood out as one sign of the Union government's attempts to influence more areas of South Africans' lives. Shembe and the Nazaretha soon clashed with state officials over other issues too. The thorniest problems began when a large group of Nazaretha worshippers at Ekuphakameni refused to accept vaccination for smallpox amid an outbreak of the disease in 1926.[9] Despite many new public health laws, state officials, as it turned it out, had few obvious options for what to do next.[10]

The Nazaretha experienced profound contradictions after Bulhoek as a result. Threats from the state loomed over Shembe in the last years of his life. But the same state officials debating how to punish him also propped up his authority with their indecision and, in some instances, with major concessions. And if the state seemed Janus-faced, so did Shembe. He projected bravado, reserve, and righteous indignation, while also showing subtler signs that he was (rightfully) scared. The Nazaretha were already pushing into southern Zululand by the time Shembe appeared before the magistrate in 1923.[11] This movement took on added urgency because the region provided Shembe with a haven from state surveillance. And, as Shembe turned to southern Zululand in another time of trouble, the people of the region reshaped the church.

The Nazaretha and the State of the State in the 1920s

In many ways, the South African state resembled others around the world in the 1920s. Officials in South Africa attempted to exert greater authority over the lives of citizens and subjects through new laws and technologies while those citizens and subjects expressed more radical forms of discontent.[12] In the late 1910s and early 1920s, just as the contours of this predicament took shape, the result in South Africa was state violence—not only at Bulhoek, but also against Black workers in Port Elizabeth and against white workers on the Rand, where the government used an aerial bombardment campaign to break a strike.[13] Although some state officials justified their use of force, the perception that the administration responsible "drip[ped] with blood" propelled a push for better policy and, by 1924, a new coalition government in Parliament.[14]

In South Africa, the common complexities of this global moment took on added dimensions. The administration that came into power in 1924 was, again, like others around the world, advancing the role of the state in public health, education, and immigration but also bolstering the position of white South Africans through labor, land, and welfare laws.[15] These ambitions intersected with the realities of making policy to cover all of South Africa's population groups and fractured spaces. The results often left unanswered questions and big holes.[16]

In the 1920s, the Nazaretha were at the center of at least two challenges resulting from the government's policy expansion. The first reflected attempts to iron out the terms of official recognition for churches after Bulhoek: What *did* a proper African-led church look like and, therefore, which churches should be rewarded by the government with additional privileges?[17] The second related to the expansion of vaccination requirements. New public health laws allowed for conscientious objection from vaccination, but could Africans be among these objectors?[18] For the first question, most officials agreed that the Nazaretha did not look like a "proper" church. Indeed, the Nazaretha so little resembled their definition in part because of all Shembe had done to avoid the state. But this left a large gap for administrators to fill as they worked out the terms for interacting with the Nazaretha outside of the framework for "official recognition." In the case of the second question, state officials used the Nazaretha example to suggest that Africans could, in fact, be conscientious objectors. That decision reflected the legal improvisations taking place based on what officials saw happening "on the ground"; to avoid a problem with the Nazaretha, officials tried to draw them within the bounds of legality.[19] But then officials found themselves further stymied when the Nazaretha refused to register to receive conscientious objector status—most likely because of concerns that it would create a record of these objectors and because the law gave church members no way to shield legal minors from vaccination, too.[20] Again local officials were left to improvise responses that included carrots and sticks. Rather than the steady rule of law, one saw a governing regime that might be used when needed either to entangle or reward individuals and groups.

Several elements stand out for making sense of how state officials managed relations with the Nazaretha in the 1920s and 1930s. First, the state paired threats with concessions. This began with the meeting in January 1923. In that meeting, the magistrate did make the connection to Bulhoek very clear as he threatened Shembe with a fate similar to Mgijima's. "You are in much the same position as the leader of the Israelites," the magistrate explained, adding, "by acting as he [Mgijima] did, [he] forced the government to take action, and now it may be said that this Sect [the Israelites] does not exist."[21] These were frightful words. They prompted from Shembe an extemporaneous exegesis on the many Bible verses he knew about showing obedience to the government.[22] And yet, in private correspondence, officials also admitted that it would probably be "impossible even if desired to suppress this sect." Better, then, an official wrote, to allow them to operate "under certain conditions and rules."[23] Those "conditions and rules" explain why, at the same meeting in 1923, Shembe also received his first concession: the magistrate informed Shembe that he would still be able to lead the annual pilgrimage to Mount Nhlangakazi and could continue to do so in the future as long as he requested permission each year.[24]

Another concession followed soon after. At the time of the 1923 meeting, Shembe was in the process of buying three hundred additional acres of land in Inanda. Although officials initially rejected his application, they overturned the decision, concluding, "It is undesirable that such a man as Tshembe [sic], being somewhat unbalanced and undoubtedly wielding a powerful influence over a large section of the native community should be provided with a grievance (imaginary or otherwise) against the government."[25] Further, it was "advisable" that Shembe be "anchored" since a "stabilising effect is likely to be produced."[26] Officials hoped that, if Shembe had ample amounts of his own land where his congregation could gather, another Bulhoek would not occur. By granting such concessions, officials engaged in patronage politics, using resources to try to secure a desired aim.[27]

As the dispute over Nazaretha vaccination refusal escalated in the mid-1920s, the pattern of concessions and threats continued. The government discussed punishments, issued warnings, and demanded payment of fines—all while continuing to grant Shembe permission to go to Nhlangakazi each year and while allowing Shembe to buy thousands of additional acres of private property.[28] Each purchase required sign-offs at all levels of government—from the local magistrate through the governor-general.[29] And, if dozens of other Africans got similar approvals for land purchases between the mid-1920s and the mid-1930s, Shembe also managed to achieve something rarer with those same sets of signatures. In 1929, Shembe became one of the few Africans permitted by the government to get a mortgage from a bank to finance land purchases.[30]

Shembe did not get everything he requested. Notably, officials denied his application for a permanent pass that would have allowed him freer movement into the eastern Cape.[31] This locked the church in Natal and Zululand, a decision that had significant consequences for its further growth. And yet, one would be hard-pressed to suggest that state officials took a punishing stance toward Shembe since they so often turned to strategies of accommodation.[32]

The second element of the state's approach related to the first: officials engaged in extensive risk assessment. Some officials argued that Shembe represented a threat immediately after Bulhoek, and more joined them after the vaccination resistance began.[33] Still, a number of officials looked at the composition of the church and saw it as "principally female," made up of "fanatics" who were "not political at present" and, therefore, "not a threat at this time."[34] The state's definition of "political" was very narrow: the Nazaretha were not a group of African men who were openly confrontational with white people. It is telling, too, that, as officials assessed the Nazaretha, they looked for evidence of interaction with other people who came closer to fitting this narrower definition. Might Shembe have influence over the Zulu king and his advisors, some asked?[35] Might his vaccination resistance spread to Africans involved in more significant expressions of radical politics?[36] As long as the answers were "no," many officials were not particularly worried about Shembe—at first.[37]

Because the state's definition of politics was shifting, relative, and based on the most immediate risks, it often changed. In the 1930s, officials began to reassess the

Nazaretha and discuss the need for a "a final threat that if Shembe will not conform to the law, the powers of the Supreme Chief will be invoked in order to remove him and some of his principal adherents to widely distant and separate parts of the Union."[38] This happened not only as Nazaretha vaccine resistance approached a decade but also as other perceived threats receded. Shembe's death in 1935 delayed the issuing a "final threat" and reset the process of assessing risk as Shembe's son and successor took over.[39]

The third element is already implied but worth stating: the state's intense focus on individual action and individual authority—above all Shembe's. The "final threat" mentioned above did include Shembe's "principal adherents," but officials otherwise steered clear of punishments involving the people whom they described as Shembe's "deluded and misled followers."[40] Thus, all talk of fines, arrest, banishment, and expropriation centered on Shembe. So did the plans for less punitive measures, including the many meetings in which state officials engaged with Shembe, hoping that one more discussion "might induce Shembe to consider it politic to announce to his people that 'vaccination does not cut the skin' or to find some religious text that will reconcile vaccination."[41] The state's emphasis on Shembe exposed how a fundamental logic of colonialism—rule many through one—saturated church and state relations in this period. More surprising perhaps is the extent to which an emphasis on the individual also extended to how state officials thought about their capacities too. Throughout the decade of Nazaretha vaccination resistance, some officials still held out the possibility that all it would take was one skilled official with an "emphatic and grave warning given in private" to change Shembe's mind.[42] One administrator's persuasive conversation could make all the difference.[43]

The very emphasis that the state placed on the Nazaretha leader underscores one way that the state buttressed Shembe's authority during this period. There were others. The additional land purchases in Inanda allowed Shembe to bring hundreds, if not thousands, of new people into the church in the 1920s. As more African families moved into Inanda to be closer to working men in Durban, some of these people were most interested in the lower rent—estimated at half the average in the area—that Shembe charged on church farms.[44] All of them, nevertheless contributed to church funds and added volume to Shembe's growing following. Indeed, by the 1930s, Ekuphakameni was no longer a place of "principally female novitiates" but a place where "between 400 and 500 Natives are in permanent residence" with "men who work in Durban or on the neighboring sugar estates, whilst the women remain at home."[45] Similar demographics lived on the other church farm in Inanda, on the land that Shembe had received in 1923 to keep him "anchored."[46]

When the government issued threats and did not follow through, the Nazaretha dramatized the encounters as another form of Shembe's miracles that matched the zeitgeist. As the vaccine resistance extended, Shembe gained more radical appeal at a time when people clamored for it. He attempted to ride the wave, telling people that "God has criticized this present government" and that they could disregard what the government told them "when Jehova[h] allows you to do it."[47] If in more conciliatory language, Shembe said this directly to government officials, too, explaining, as one official paraphrased, that the Nazaretha had "taken a sacred oath not to resort to medicine in any shape or form nor to submit their bodies to be cut."[48] Thus, Shembe became someone who did not just evade but who openly defied—and encouraged others to do the same because God's laws mattered more.

At least one official was astute enough to predict the consequences of government inaction and indecision, noting how "delay can only add to the prestige of Shembe."[49] And yet, if one can look back on this period and see that Shembe grew more powerful through his encounters with state officials, this result would not have been apparent or even likely in the moment.

Politics of the Tightrope

Decades ago, Shula Marks introduced the notion of the "politics of the tightrope" to describe how other Africans in Natal, including Shembe's neighbors and rivals, attempted to manage relations with the state. As Marks showed, this approach involved changing positions over time, saying different things to different people, and probing possibilities.[50] Shembe's interactions with state officials point to the ways that those officials engaged in a politics of the tightrope too—and, in fact, how their difficulties and uncertainties created the tightrope for many others to walk upon, including Shembe. As Shembe attempted to keep his balance, his relationships changed; he drew new lines in the sand and reevaluated where—and on what kind of land—the church should grow. He also paired his open defiance with new acts of evasion.[51]

In this era of church–state relations, Shembe easily managed some things with quick thinking. For example, when government informants began showing up at

Nhlangakazi in the early 1920s, Shembe greeted them with words befitting a prophet, saying, "I expected you here" and then inviting them to stay.[52] Other situations were much more dangerous—especially after the dramatic vaccination standoff in 1926. That standoff had ended with only a few members of the church accepting vaccination before the government vaccinators backed down and left.[53] But every church gathering after it had the makings of another showdown. Indeed, Shembe seemed especially worried about the first trip to Mount Nhlangakazi after the mass vaccination refusal. Before the trip, he shared Bible passages about the Israelites (surely no coincidence considering Bulhoek) and told the people gathered, "We go now to the mountain of Jehova[h]; but we do not know if we shall come back because of this evil."[54] He was preparing for the possibility of disaster.

If large gatherings were dangerous so, too, were more personal encounters. Every meeting with government officials after 1926 represented a moment when Shembe had to worry about the possibility of arrest. During this period, Shembe earned a reputation for "wait[ing] as long as he dared wait before going to the Magistrate's office when he was sent for."[55] Sometimes to forestall meetings, he sent word that he was sick.[56] If this did not fit his reputation as a powerful healer, it nevertheless pointed to his concerns about what might happen when he showed up.

During the period of increased scrutiny, Shembe fostered relationships with white South Africans who acted as intermediaries between him and the state. Denis Gem "D. G." Shepstone was among them. Twenty years younger than Shembe and a grandson of Natal's most celebrated administrator, Theophilus Shepstone, D. G. Shepstone would become a provincial administrator, a South African senator, the chancellor of the University of Natal, and a knight in the British Empire.[57] Before he assumed so many titles, D. G. Shepstone's reputation harkened back to his famous grandfather's. By the early twentieth century, Africans remembered the elder Shepstone as someone who had listened in contrast to contemporary administrators who did not.[58] The younger Shepstone described himself too as someone who "deal[s] a lot with the Natives and I hear their complaints and their histories."[59]

D. G. Shepstone was not a government employee when Shembe knew him, but he was a lawyer. Although Shembe hired many white lawyers in the 1920s, Shepstone became the most important of them because he was sympathetic to Shembe's land-buying efforts and well connected among the white elite of Natal's governing circles. As Shembe faced more scrutiny from state officials, Shepstone's efforts included "direct representations" to try to sway decisions in Shembe's favor.[60] Of course, as much as it mattered that someone such as Shepstone would vouch for Shembe, it also mattered that Shepstone, through his own back channels, could communicate to Shembe some of the options that the state was considering. Shepstone helped Shembe do his own risk assessment.[61]

Shepstone's efforts took place mainly behind the scenes, but Shembe developed another relationship with a white sympathizer who acted, instead, as a publicist. Her name was Nellie Wells. She and her husband had relocated to Inanda after financial struggles in Johannesburg in the early 1920s.[62] While her husband took up a post as a school administrator at Ohlange, Nellie Wells pursued journalism, filmmaking, and ethnography.[63] Wells was one of several white women whom Shembe knew and with whom he enjoyed kind relations; a few of them who also lived in Inanda sold him land.[64] Wells tried to get Shembe access to land, too, if in an indirect way. One of her plans involved the creation of a hostel and a settlement where white anthropologists could come study the Nazaretha. As she wrote in a proposal for the hostel, "Shembi [*sic*] is doing sound work in the orientation and preservation of the native as he is, not as Europeans think he is, or ought to be."[65] He was, she added, someone who "allows Christianity to lead civilization," instead of the other way around.[66] Such an assessment revealed an update to long-held fears of the "trousered African:" as Wells summarized, "[T]he world will be the better for the preservation and natural evolution of the Bantu."[67] As Wells mapped her understanding of race relations onto the church, she might have been the first person to broadcast an idea that the Nazaretha themselves and scholars of religion would argue later: that Shembe was purposefully pioneering a middle way between African tradition and Christian advance. Even though her plan for a hostel never came to fruition, it represented one of many ways that she told wider audiences that there was something important to see and celebrate at Ekuphakameni.[68]

As much as Shepstone's personal vouching helped Shembe, Wells's efforts perhaps helped Shembe even more. One government official, muddling through the sticky situation with the Nazaretha, noted how difficult any course of action would be since Shembe was "not the ordinary run of small prophet who conducts his doings in secret." Shembe, instead "holds . . . ceremonies to which Europeans are freely invited, and which are given considerable prominence in the press."[69] This was in no small part Nellie Wells's doing.

In her writing about the Nazaretha, Wells mentioned that Shembe had nothing to do with the "recent troubles" in South Africa.[70] Wells was referencing the most radical expression of African popular politics in the 1920s: the Industrial and Commercial Workers Union (ICU). Even its name—or the abbreviation of it—suggested the more confrontational stance that its members took, with ICU becoming a way of saying, "I see you, white man."[71] With branches scattered across South Africa, membership reached as high as 100,000 as people used the ICU to fight for land, better working conditions, and a host of other issues.[72] State persecution as well as the difficulty of holding together such a large, varied group of people contributed to its rapid decline. The 1920s represented, nevertheless, the height of ICU activity.[73]

The Nazaretha had many reasons to be antagonistic toward the ICU, some of which had more to do with similarity than with difference. In Natal, both groups promised pathways to a better world, pulled together unwieldy coalitions, and promised to buy land for members. Natal's ICU leader, A. W. G. Champion, told people, for example, "Pay your red [ICU] money and let us fight for you . . . come to the ICU and we will buy farms for you."[74] Although, initially, both groups had grown from different catchments of people, this was slowly changing in the 1920s. In Natal, the ICU tended to rally African men and women living in urban areas or African families living on white-owned farms.[75] The Nazaretha did not, at first, have strong followings among either of these groups. But, as African families joined the church, more working men with connections to Durban joined too. Shembe did have some reasons, then, to think that ICU support might be growing among the Nazaretha.[76]

Telling church members to "burn their red cards" indicating ICU membership, Shembe's stance against the ICU seemed resolute.[77] In other statements, however, Shembe criticized the confrontational tactics of the ICU more than their stances.[78] And yet, by publicly drawing a line in the sand against the ICU, the Nazaretha helped protect themselves in the context of their own trouble with the government. Shembe knew that the government would be looking for connections to the ICU and that officials would be more anxious—and potentially volatile—if they found evidence of them.[79]

Other purges in this period showed Shembe trying to consolidate support for vaccination resistance. The same growing membership of men—and especially working-aged men—made vaccination resistance more of a problem in the church than it would have been a decade before. The long history of inoculation in South Africa included examples when some Africans had readily accepted vaccination and some when they had refused it. But, by the early twentieth century, African men were more likely to have access to vaccination and to need it for work.[80] During that dramatic standoff at Ekuphakameni, an African man from one of Shembe's new rental properties led his family over to the side of the government for vaccination because "he would not like to be arrested with his family."[81] After no one else followed—and state officials left—Shembe made an example of that family by preaching against their actions and evicting them from their land. In fact, Shembe used a punishment associated with unmarried women who became pregnant: after expelling the family, the "soil of [Dladla's] fields was carried away by the maidens and thrown into the Mzinyathi River" to remove the impurity they had brought to the community.[82] Other people in the church knew well, then, what might happen to them if they defied Shembe's order too.

Shembe's connections to people within the church changed in response to shifting relations with the state as well. Already, church women and girls were more anchored to Ekuphakameni because of the efforts to appease rural fathers described in the last chapter. And if some unmarried girls still traveled to evangelize and recruit others, they, nevertheless, lost some of their proximity to the prophet.[83] This was a response to threats from the state too: among the many charges that officials batted about, they returned again and again to the idea that Shembe might be charged with "trafficking women."[84] Thus, the very girls and women who helped the state see Shembe as someone who was not "political," nevertheless, found themselves with less access to him as he tried to avoid entanglements that might lead to charges.

At the same time, a new group of people in the church rose in prominence. In part because of gendered and generational expectations about who could speak for the church to white officials, magistrates and other Native Affairs Department employees reported various encounters with "some 40 elders," "some of Shembe's elders" and "Rev. Shembe and his men" in the late 1920s and early 1930s.[85] Until this point, most men had not been reliable partners for Shembe. After the departures of important young men in the 1910s, Shembe had turned to older men to help him manage Ekuphakameni and other temple sites in increasingly far-flung destinations. Some of those older men had left and stolen money from the church, too.[86] But in the 1920s, a group of older men gained a stronger claim to what they had done for and with Shembe as they navigated church–state relations with him. Indeed, if young unmarried women could say how they had suffered with Shembe while building Ekuphakameni, older church men could, after the 1920s, say how they had faced danger with him at the magistrate's office. These men, moreover, began to keep the closest company with Shembe on mission trips.[87]

In this era of church–state relations, private property became a liability for Shembe in a way that it had not been before. It was locatable on surveyed maps, making Shembe easier to find when he was on it too. What is more, officials

FIGURE 5. Shembe (*far right*) dancing with a group of men at Ekuphakameni in the early 1930s.
PHOTOGRAPH INCLUDED WITH PERMISSION OF CAMPBELL COLLECTIONS, UKZN.

discussed removing Shembe from his land or expropriating it as they looked for ways to punish him.[88] Shembe did not stop buying land, however, nor did he pull up the large communities that already lived on his land in Inanda. What he did, instead, was stop settling large numbers of people on the new land he bought after 1926.[89] This decision pointed to a broader reality: in most places, church mission stations were not likely to succeed. Already, the church farms in Inanda were doing much better than the church farm south of Durban, where it was harder to sustain a community away from work and other economic opportunities.[90] But the decision not to settle church members on the thousands of additional acres—and not to celebrate these purchases as providential triumphs—perhaps pointed to Shembe's fears about what the government might do next.[91]

The issue of locatability helps explain why another kind of land started to matter more to Shembe. Shembe had often moved somewhere new in times of trouble. His request to get a pass to evangelize in the Cape suggested that he sought

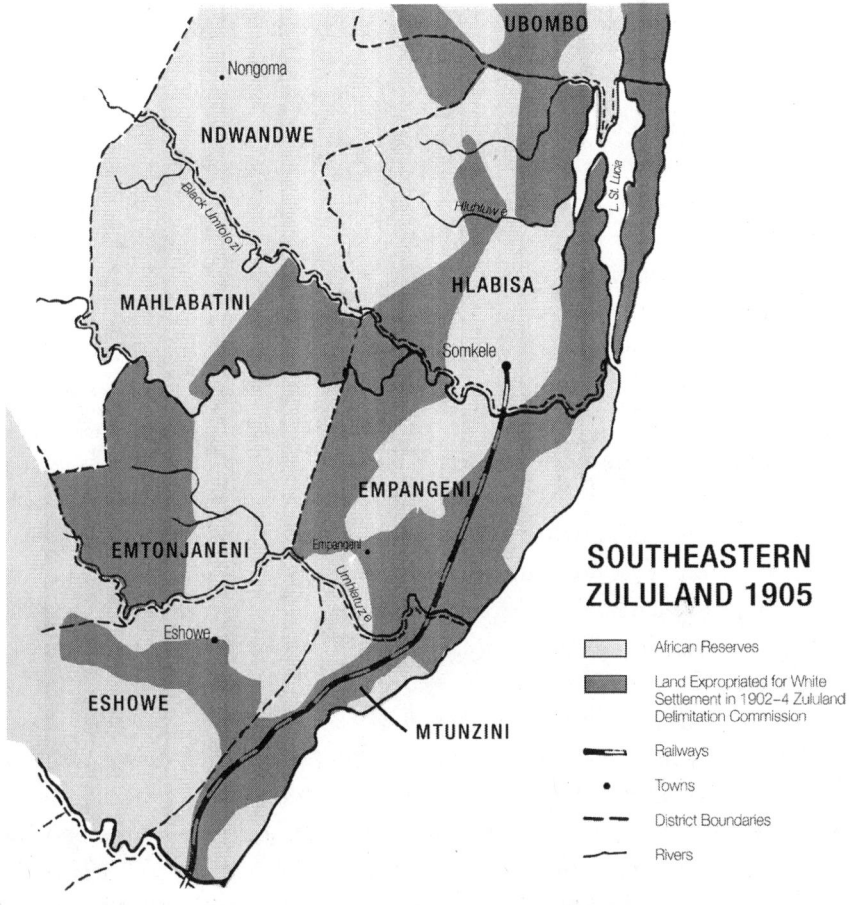

MAP 3. Southern Zululand with major railways and land expropriated for white settlement.

ADAPTED FROM MAPS IN SHULA MARKS, *RELUCTANT REBELLION*, AND ARAN MACKINNON, "THE PERSISTENCE OF THE CATTLE ECONOMY IN ZULULAND, SOUTH AFRICA, 1900–1950," *CANADIAN JOURNAL OF AFRICAN STUDIES* 33, NO. 1 (1999): 98–135.

new options for places to go as the magnitude of his problems with the state increased.[92] When the government denied his request, he began spending more time in another place where Natal officials would have a harder time finding (or following) him: southern Zululand.

The View across the Thukela River

The Nazaretha had already been moving into southern Zululand in the late 1910s. The region sat on the north–south railway that mattered so much to their evangelism throughout Shembe's lifetime. The initial forays into Zululand might have seemed, then, like an incremental progression for church members from Natal. And yet, looking at the whole picture, the extent of Nazaretha growth in Zululand during the last fifteen years of Shembe's life was astonishing compared to what had come before.

Nazaretha expansion was more easily measurable in terms of claims to space than in new members. Consider, however, that by 1935 the Nazaretha established twelve worship sites with the sanction of five different chiefs in southern Zululand. At one, a chief from Mtunzini allowed the presence of "47 huts of all sizes and description," including dwellings built for the chief himself and for Shembe when he visited. "Under the auspices of the Shembe Sect," the magistrate noted, too, that the chief built an unauthorized school that "seriously affected" attendance at the government-aided school a mile away. In another chief's territory in Empangeni, the Nazaretha eventually had a worship site that was estimated at "one square mile," with about "200 huts" and "a very large hall." The chief called this his "place of prayer." In the Nzuza chiefdom, there was a site with "104 huts," where people from Eshowe, Mtunzini, and Empangeni gathered. The worship site in the Mzimela chiefdom was smaller, with only eighteen huts on two to three acres of land, but, again, the chief explained that it mattered to him personally: it was where he and his people went "to congregate . . . to pray to the Almighty."[93]

Much about southern Zululand made it a good place for Nazaretha expansion from the start. Although the Zulu Kingdom's status as an independent polity had delayed some of the shifts that took place in Natal over decades, the later conquest and incorporation of Zululand meant that many people had to adjust more rapidly to sweeping transformations. Zululand was, for example, the site of the last major settler land grab in South Africa's history, with the government "delimiting" more than 2.5 million acres of land for purchase in 1904.[94]

The "opening" of Zululand affected the southern districts especially because the region had land good for growing sugarcane.[95] White settlers increased sugar production in the region and pressed Africans into the worst agricultural land.[96] As in other places where homestead economies faced strains, southern Zululand began to see a larger number of men leaving for migrant work, a process facilitated by expansion of the railway.[97] By 1913, African men made up only 40 percent of the population in one of the districts where Shembe would soon arrive.[98] The people left behind managed new challenges, too, not only from the absence of men and the same resulting tensions as in Natal, but also from changes to the environment. Widespread outbreaks of malaria, for example, accompanied the growth of the sugar industry; district surgeons reported spikes of cases of syphilis too—although this, as in other colonial contexts, might have been misdiagnosed yaws.[99] Whatever the correct diagnosis, the number of cases pointed to widespread ill health.

Chiefs in southern Zululand experienced uneven fortunes too. The personal history of one of the chiefs who would welcome Shembe indicated the difficulties that some had endured in the decades before Shembe arrived in the region. That chief only assumed the title after four other people in line for the chieftaincy had died in about as many years. Perhaps unsurprisingly, his claims to the chieftaincy were not universally recognized, and he experienced continued troubles trying to manage the role, telling the local magistrate that he "could not live with these people."[100] At one point before Shembe arrived in the region, the chief also threatened suicide.[101]

Administrative features of the region could also help Shembe manage his predicament with state officials. The border still delineated a difference of official personnel that Union had not changed. The administration's perception of the centers and margins of Zulu authority, moreover, made southern Zululand a place where the state allocated fewer resources. Better qualified magistrates, for example, worked instead in Nongoma, the "hub of the Zulu universe."[102] Not coincidentally, Shembe had a harder time hiding his activities there.[103] In contrast, Shembe came to understand that he had more leeway in southern Zululand. The extent of the infrastructure that the church built on chiefly land, noted above, offered one indication.[104] Shembe kept these buildings up even after receiving an order from an official to tear all of his structures down.[105] Shembe could avoid the terms of the order in southern Zululand because officials did not know where all of the church buildings were. In fact, officials would not find them until 1940, five years after Shembe's death and nearly twenty years after he had begun spending more time in the region.[106]

Other people used southern Zululand as a space to operate away from state surveillance too. The African Christian author and historian Petros Lamula also evangelized in the region, likely for similar reasons as Shembe.[107] But southern Zululand offered a hideout for activities other than church work: John Dube ran his own secret sugar plantation in one of the same chiefdoms where Shembe received a significant amount of support.[108] "Away in the reserves" people still found many ways to use land outside of the purview of the state.[109]

Of Chiefs, Cattle, Custom, and Conflict

If the Nazaretha moved easily into southern Zululand because of how the region resembled chiefdoms in Natal, differences persisted. Some of them stemmed from histories of antagonism. Africans in the Zulu Kingdom had once reserved some of their harshest insults for Africans in Natal—in part because so many Africans had used Natal, as the Hlubi people once did: to leave the Zulu Kingdom behind. Nor had the people of Zululand forgotten how Africans from Natal helped the British defeat the Zulu army in 1880 or how some of the people fighting with the British had received allocations of land and authority in the messy aftermath of Zulu defeat. Neither the growing appeal of Zulu ethnic belonging in the 1920s nor the possibility of a shared Nazaretha faith fully erased the longer history of how Africans from Natal and Zululand had contributed to making the Thukela River a meaningful border that marked differences of geography *and* belonging.[110]

Zululand was also different because it had more of a rural African aristocracy. Even the chiefs struggling compared to others in Zululand fared better than their counterparts in Natal. The government salaries of chiefs in Zululand were, across the board, higher, ranging from £250 to £350 per year by the late 1920s. With this money, the Zululand chiefs recovered more easily from social and economic crises.[111] Their wealth contributed, too, to growing inequality not only in cash but cattle. As the Nazaretha entered the region, the number of cattle in Zululand had more than recovered from widespread cattle disease in the 1890s, but its distribution had become more unequal, with more cattle concentrated in the herds of the African elite.[112]

Zululand had a different history with Christianity too. In this case as well, the longer independence of the Zulu Kingdom staved off change. Zulu leaders had, through the 1870s, made conversion to Christianity cost the price of citizenship in the Zulu state.[113] After the conquest of Zululand, too, mission communities in the region had stayed small, insular, and isolated.[114] The people of Zululand did not have the same entrenched notions about what it meant to be a Christian that had resulted from more than seventy years of debating this question in Natal. They could also look to the example of the Zulu king, Inkosi Solomon kaDinuzulu, to see one way to be a Christian without as much concern for seeming contradictions with custom. He had, after all, been baptized as an Anglican but still married dozens of wives.[115]

By the 1920s, the Nazaretha already had many ways to smooth over the introduction of new people from different backgrounds. Nazaretha testimonies and uniforms as well as rules about food and worship gave people channels for finding things in common. In fact, the items, sacred knowledge, and ceremonies that marked church members' belonging in the faith increased with the growth of the Nazaretha community in southern Zululand, paralleling the incorporation of new people.[116] The Nazaretha also already had ways of keeping people separate even as they came together. At churchwide events in Natal, for example, people generally stayed divided not only by gender and generation but by geography as well, eliminating some of the potential for conflict.[117]

And yet, the people of southern Zululand changed the church as they brought some of who they were (and how they were different) into the Nazaretha community. As the Nazaretha expanded into southern Zululand, dance became something that all church members did—instead of only the older girls and young women at Ekuphakameni. Stories of Shembe's overtures to chiefs in the region focused on Shembe's promises of healing, as one would expect. But these stories also focused on the role that Shembe played in bringing dance back to rural communities. In one instance, when Shembe suggested a dance, people purportedly said, "Where should we get a dancing dress? Because nobody does still have [them]."[118] People seemed glad, however, to have reasons to dance again even if they had a hard time finding the right clothes. And when they saw their chief dance for the first time in a long time at one of Shembe's services, they "shouted praises."[119]

The rural aristocrats who supported Shembe in southern Zululand began to offer him cattle, allowing Shembe to expand his recruitment of young women at Ekuphakameni by giving fathers lobola advances. The terms of one such arrangement illuminated the basic pattern. Shembe offered a father "7 head of cattle," and "in consideration of [the father's] indebtedness to [Shembe]," the father agreed "to allow [his] minor daughter Hawukile Ngidi, aged about 12 years, to remain with Rev. I. Shembe until she marries." When she did marry, the father would then pay Shembe back "with a deduction of seven cattle from her lobola."[120] Shembe's promise that, at Ekuphakameni, Hawukile would stay chaste and find a husband helped assure her father that he would be able to repay the loan. Hawukile's case represents a rare example because someone wrote down the terms of the agreement and then someone else later gave the contract to a magistrate. But, after investigating, the magistrate learned that "quite a number of young women" at Ekuphakameni had similar arrangements.[121]

Cattle advances were difficult for many families to turn down—especially in Natal, where so few families had sizable herds. Inequality across Zululand and Natal, then, allowed Shembe to make frequent use of these loans as Shembe's trouble with the state added to the pressure he already felt to stave off conflict with fathers. The arrangements raise uncomfortable questions about how the congregation grew "by the children who will be given," as one believer explained.[122] If these loans perhaps smoothed the way for some girls who wanted to make the journey, they also surely pressured or forced others to go to Ekuphakameni. More broadly, the loans also pulled the Nazaretha further into involvement with bridewealth. While few African Christians would have decried lobola by this point, few (if any) other African church leaders played such an active, direct role in orchestrating lobola negotiations.[123]

The movement of the Nazaretha into southern Zululand shifted conversations about marriage in other ways. As Shembe established himself in the region, the church began to allow Nazaretha men to marry more than one wife. The Nazaretha had already been welcoming of people who came to the church in polygynous marriages, which was, again, not uncommon in African Christian communities. Moreover, by the mid-1920s, Shembe's own daughter was in a polygynous marriage—although with someone outside of the Nazaretha faith.[124] Still the support of polygynous chiefs in Zululand and the higher prevalence of polygynous marriage in the region pushed Shembe toward greater acceptance of the practice.[125]

Amid so many changes taking place in the community, subtle signs of conflict appeared. Some of them had to do with where Shembe was spending so much time—and the fact that he could not explain why he needed to be in southern Zululand more often without showing some chinks in his providential armor. Perhaps as a result, Shembe began to explain his movements not by where he thought he might be safer or where he might avoid detection from state officials but, instead, as the work of an "Angel of Zululand" and an "Angel of Mpondoland," who told him when to go north and south. Still, people in Natal seemed to notice the frequency of the calls of the "Angel of Zululand."[126]

Signs of conflict surfaced too in how Shembe announced changes in church policies. Sometimes he made his reservations known, explaining in a sermon in Zululand, for example, "I wanted to introduce monogamy, but you wanted polygamy." Polygyny, he added, "causes poverty because you have to pay the bride-wealth by your cattle." Poverty, in turn, made "aversion," and "people who have aversions do not go to heaven."[127] This explanation allowed Shembe to suggest that polygyny itself was not a sin, if its consequences were. Such an explanation also absolved Shembe of some responsibility as he suggested that he had not wanted the change in marriage policy. Shembe framed his decision to allow lobola in the church in similar terms: a grudging concession because of pressure from below.[128]

Shembe also clarified requirements that hint at his and other church members' reservations about polygyny. Ministers in the church, for example, "should be men who have one wife only," and churchmen should have no more than two wives.[129] Moreover, as Shembe envisioned second marriage arrangements, first wives were to play a crucial role; if a first wife agreed to a second wife, she should go to the church elders to tell them: "I wish my husband to take another wife."[130] This requirement offered one way to make a wife's consent public—and to hold a husband accountable. If she did not agree at first, a husband was to beg, telling her, for example, "I do not find fault with [you] over anything. I simply wish to take another wife." If a husband begged enough times and the wife did not change her mind, the husband might go to church elders to try to get their help in convincing her. While explaining these rules, Shembe also clarified that wives would be allowed to separate, if not divorce. If a marriage "became unbearable," a wife could get permission from church elders to go live with the widows at Ekuphakameni, where such women could also expect support from the church.[131] Difficult though it is to know if people followed these rules, the number of steps and qualifications suggest that Shembe was looking for a way to broker a compromise between the people in the church who wanted to allow polygynous marriage and the people who did not. By requiring that wives give permission for a second marriage and offering them a place to go in case they needed one, he seemed especially concerned about married women and their reservations.

The decision to allow polygynous marriages in the church, again, pushed the Nazaretha farther from many of the African Christians whom Shembe still hoped to convert. But he moved in this direction in another time of trouble as he sought ways to fit in. After the mid-1920s, he needed the chiefs of southern Zululand not only to evade but also to create an alternative locus for the Nazaretha community if the government ever did follow through with a "final threat."[132] If officials, in other words, removed Shembe or stripped him of his land, southern Zululand, where the government knew so little about his activities, could be where the church kept going.

Despite complaints from the Nazaretha in Natal about the influence of the "Angel of Zululand," Shembe did not spend all his time north of the Thukela. Instead, he also made plans to welcome some of those rural aristocrats from southern Zululand at Ekuphakameni. Shembe knew that these chiefs and their people, who had been so eager to dance again, could help him draw a crowd. And although Shembe spent some of his time hiding away from state officials in southern Zululand, he also spent some of it welcoming more people to big events at Ekuphakameni, where the gathered crowds gave him another way to protect himself from trouble.

CHAPTER 8

A Celebrity in South Africa

IN 1930, A PHOTO ESSAY ABOUT SHEMBE AND THE NAZARETHA APPEARED IN THE *Illustrated London News*.[1] The periodical was the oldest of its kind in Britain, although, by 1930, this "unique, large format weekly" no longer had the prominence it held in the Victorian era.[2] Still, Shembe's presence on its pages was a striking testament to the connections he had made and the attention he had garnered in South Africa and beyond. Twenty-five years earlier, Shembe sat in a Harrismith photography studio with a doctor's bag in his lap and William Leshega standing over his right shoulder. On that occasion, he got a photograph that he could carry with him to communicate his affiliation as he traveled to tell others his story. Now his image and story traveled much farther than he himself could carry it: to another country, on another continent.[3]

The list of Shembe's achievements by 1930 was astonishing. The same *Illustrated London News* write-up estimated the Nazaretha membership at 32,000—a number that might have been inflated but that was, nevertheless, impressive for being believable.[4] Even if the number was half that amount, as one official in South Africa guessed it might be, the Nazaretha stood out as the largest of the churches founded by Africans in the 1910s.[5] Shembe had, moreover, purchased thousands of acres of land, perhaps more than any other individual African land buyer among his contemporaries.[6] One of his surviving daughters had married into the Zulu royal family; two of his surviving sons had graduated from prestigious schools.[7] Shembe had recently secured unprecedented levels of support from chiefs in a new region, and the Nazaretha were using their base in southern Zululand to push farther north. They would be nearing Eswatini by the end of Shembe's life, stretching the Nazaretha community across more than three hundred miles.[8] And not only did people bring cameras for photography to Ekuphakameni, but the same journalist who likely wrote the pseudonymous story in the *Illustrated London News* was drafting plans to make a film about him too.[9] The film never came to be, but the plans spoke to the changing possibilities for fame and renown in the last decade of Shembe's life—as well as how Shembe did not shy away from them.

Shembe, of course, still had many problems—some described in the last chapter. But he also had the problem of managing his own success. As Shembe gained authority, with control over vast resources, including land, cash, people, and cattle, it became more difficult for him to be seen by his followers and wider publics as he once had been. Was he still, as a description from 1912 suggested, someone whom people liked because he "does not ask for money and eats very little food?"[10] How could he be when people already thought, as John Dube would write soon after Shembe's death, that the Nazaretha leader had "become better off than all the Black people?"[11]

Shembe managed the transformation through careful crafting of his public image. In the last decade of his life, Shembe found ways to reach bigger and more varied audiences. He shaped the content those audiences saw, sending complex messages through his patterns of consumption and redistribution. His methods of travel, his clothes, and even still what he ate (or did not eat) became a part of this public image too. And, as much as it might matter to Shembe that he could say his story and photograph were being shared in London, he still relied upon comparisons to famous people nearby to position himself among South Africa's celebrities.[12]

The Great Chief and the Great Healer

To describe Shembe as a celebrity is fitting even if the word might seem flippant for someone so important in many people's lives. Shembe was not a Hollywood star written about in gossip columns while vacationing on the French Riviera—a more stereotypical image of a celebrity in the 1920s.[13] But South Africa had its own histories of fame and reputation that shaped how a global celebrity culture of cameras, crowds, and conspicuous consumption developed in the early twentieth century. In that longer history, two kinds of people in African communities were associated with renown that extended far beyond their home regions: great healers and great chiefs.[14] The shared potential for fame and authority among these groups of people helped explain why one could point to historical examples of close cooperation among them as well as examples of intense rivalry and conflict.[15] By the 1920s, chiefs and healers had company, and other kinds of famous people were well known in South Africa too.[16] But the fact that Shembe, as a great healer, was both related to and a rival of the region's greatest chief, Inkosi Solomon kaDinuzulu, marked Shembe's celebrity.

Shembe's relations with Inkosi Solomon had been difficult from the time the Nazaretha arrived in Nongoma in the late 1910s.[17] Nongoma stood out as a site of pushback against Shembe and a place where the behavior of unmarried women sparked the kind of dangerous outcries that made the Nazaretha find new ways to accommodate African men. Shembe's troubles with the Zulu royal family persisted for the rest of his life, however, and despite moments that held the promise of improvement.

In the mid-1920s, the marriage of Zondi, one of Shembe's daughters, to Inkosi Solomon had the potential to reset relations, but the marriage was complicated from the start. The Zulu heir and king already had several wives, narrowing the chances that Zondi would be the most important one.[18] Although the Nazaretha inched closer toward accepting polygyny, church members continued to debate the forms of marriage allowed in their community at the time of Zondi's wedding. Likewise, Shembe still tended to hold himself and the people closest to him to different standards than the masses of church members.[19] This raised questions about why Shembe's daughter would marry a man with other wives. But, at the same time, a marriage to Inkosi Solomon would have been hard to turn down. In the 1920s, the Zulu king married many women to cement partnerships with important families. The people watching the Zulu king's actions could interpret the marriage to Zondi as a sign that Shembe had made it to the upper echelons of African society. And, of course, marriage still had the potential to tie families together through bonds of responsibility and obligation. As a result, many African men hoping to draw upon those bonds offered their daughters to Inkosi Solomon for marriage.[20]

Additional evidence that the wedding represented a moment of promise for Shembe comes from a history written by the Zulu nationalist and intellectual

Petros Lamula and published in 1931.[21] The book ends with a photograph that shows Inkosi Solomon and "the daughter of Shembe," sitting side by side, on their wedding day. The Zulu heir looks ready for high society in London, Paris, or New York, wearing a tuxedo (with perhaps a tailcoat), white gloves, shiny black shoes, and a top hat. At a time when "white weddings" represented an aspiration of many African elites, Zondi is decked out in white, with a formal dress, a voluminous veil, spotless gloves, rows of pearly beads around her neck, and white shoes.[22] (All of the white underscored the success of the Nazaretha purity campaign for young women too.) Both the formality of the clothes and the expense involved pointed to the planning and the importance of the moment. So did the fact that the photograph must have been reproduced for sale or distribution, making it part of the growing body of memorabilia associated with Inkosi Solomon.[23] For Lamula's purposes, the impressive depiction of the Zulu king was more important than the fact that the bride in the photograph was Shembe's daughter, but the Nazaretha could look to the image to indicate Shembe's greatness by extension.

By the time the photograph appeared in Lamula's book, the potential positive outcomes for Shembe were not panning out. The marriage produced no heirs, a difficult circumstance for Shembe to explain considering his reputation for curing infertility.[24] Worse still, Inkosi Solomon made public displays of disrespect toward Shembe that included not showing up at big moments when he was expected and smoking cigarettes at Ekuphakameni.[25] This occurred as, in the late 1920s and early 1930s, both the strain of Inkosi Solomon's position and the privilege the Zulu king had, nevertheless, derived from it were on full display. Inkosi Solomon was drinking a great deal, in debt, and seeking financial support from more people.[26] Likely around this time, the Nazaretha began to say that Shembe had never wanted his daughter to marry the Zulu king in the first place: because Inkosi Solomon "like[d] very much the women and the alcoholic drinks of the Whites" and would "not get old," meaning that he would die young.[27] This interpretation of Shembe's stance toward the marriage provided Shembe with a way to explain why no children had been born. Shembe had himself "close[d] her [Zondi's] womb that she will not give birth to children for [Inkosi Solomon]."[28] The problem was not Shembe's healing but, instead, Inkosi Solomon's bad habits, disrespect, and negligence.

By the time Shembe began to tell others that Inkosi Solomon was a "dead husband" to his daughter, the two men were rivals on more fronts anyway.[29] They competed for influence among and funds from the same rural dwellers. They made different arguments about how to live and participate in the modern world, with the Zulu king emphasizing consumption—of cigarettes, alcohol, food, and clothes, among other things—and Shembe emphasizing sacrifice. They even made competing claims about pathways to better health too, with Inkosi Solomon's image appearing on patent medicine advertisements circulating around Natal, Zululand, and the Rand.[30] Shembe surely saw this as an insult as well.

If Inkosi Solomon and Shembe had an especially complicated history, the impulses that pushed them toward each other and the frictions that drove them apart were more widespread. One can see the possibilities of rivalry and cooperation in the broader pattern of Shembe's relationships with other chiefs. Shembe, after all, wooed and advised the chiefs who supported him and was rumored to curse, threaten, and slander the ones who did not.[31] Moreover, part of the drama of Shembe's relations with the Zulu king also came from how some of those other chiefs—and especially chiefs in southern Zululand—were rivals to Inkosi Solomon who might benefit from his bad behavior or the government's reassessment of his role as the Zulu paramount. Shembe himself made this clear, when, after an insult from Inkosi Solomon, Shembe purportedly said, "I would not be astonished, if Jehova[h] would install another King from the house of other chiefs."[32] Other chiefs from Zululand were suggesting the possibility of a replacement around the same time.[33]

Similar dynamics played out with other kinds of celebrities in this era as well. Shembe's neighbor John Dube was among them, as was a rising star, the local Industrial and Commercial Workers Union (ICU) leader, A. W. G. Champion. Both men had complicated histories with each other, Inkosi Solomon, and Shembe.[34] These local celebrities helped define Shembe's public image because a broader swathe of Africans in the region could follow their goings-on to compare them. And, if general proximity facilitated such comparisons, so did sometimes seeing them in the same crowd.

Surveying the Crowds

That Shembe understood the importance of drawing crowds was not surprising. His interest in Christianity grew in an age when evangelists sought mass conversion through mass communication, whether newspapers in global circulation or individual preachers standing in front of swelling audiences of people. The ability to draw a crowd was also foundational to Shembe's break with the Baptists. Ample space in Ndwedwe allowed Shembe to bring many people together, learn about their problems, and communicate that he was someone who would redirect the movement of people, even if only temporarily, back into the spaces that were otherwise defined by departures. Drawing more people to church headquarters at Ekuphakameni played a critical role in sustaining the early Nazaretha community as well, whether the crowd of girls who came to live there or the crowds of people who sought Shembe's healing. And crowds continued to broadcast Shembe's strength to chiefs considering if they might welcome him and to government officials attempting to compel vaccination.

Shembe's ability to draw crowds resonated because he evangelized among people with their own understandings of the links between large gatherings and the basis of political, social, and economic authority. Older Africans in Natal and perhaps even older members of Shembe's family, if they were still alive, remembered chiefdoms that had hosted first-fruits ceremonies, events installing new leaders, big weddings, and crowded funerals—all of which drew large numbers of people together.[35] Some of them had seen too how the colonial government used crowds to assert authority, whether through the meetings of chiefs called by Theophilus Shepstone or the government commissions that brought people together for fact-finding missions.[36] And, of, course, Indian people living near Shembe in Inanda had histories of gathering in crowds for religious events, meetings with government officials, and, in the 1910s, protest and civil disobedience.[37]

The 1920s witnessed a proliferation of crowds in Natal and Zululand, reflecting increasing urban density, new forms of mobility, and the wide range of causes that brought people together. There were packed ICU meetings and protests as well as crowds that gathered for competitive dances held in Durban among migrant working men.[38] Still, the largest crowds in this period came together in places that were difficult to reach, which added to the impressiveness of their size. These crowds gathered in Zululand for the indabas, or meetings, sponsored by the government as part of a renewed effort in the 1920s to make chiefs useful functionaries of the state. The biggest of these gatherings took place in 1925 and included 60,000 people.[39]

In a time of large gatherings, Shembe's crowds never came close to the scale of the government indabas. His crowds did, however, grow in kind, number, and size. The movement of the Nazaretha into southern Zululand contributed significantly in all regards. As one more sign of Shembe's confidence evangelizing in the region, the church began to encourage crowds of people to wait for Shembe and his traveling companions to arrive at the train stations where they would disembark before entering the next chiefdom on Shembe's schedule.[40] This use of train stations pointed to how Africans made space for themselves in strategic places, knowing, for example, that a group of African men, women, and children, might not raise eyebrows waiting for a train at a rural station in the same way that they would gathering in downtown Durban.[41]

Rural roads provided similar opportunities, and the Nazaretha used these spaces too. After Shembe disembarked from the train, many of the people who had been waiting at the station would then travel with him by foot along the roads, sometimes beating drums and playing homemade instruments to announce his arrival as part of a ready-made parade. These Salvation-Army-style tactics made the Nazaretha presence known in advance. One man in the region remembered how he "heard the sound of the drum, and when we looked there, we saw the people in white gowns."[42] The use of these tactics in the 1920s also underpinned the claims that members of the Nazaretha Church would make decades later over the most contested fan paraphernalia in World Cup history, the horn called the vuvuzela.[43]

Crowds could be dangerous and unpredictable. The crowds of the 1920s made this clear. In some cases, individuals took over otherwise carefully orchestrated occasions, attempting to spin the events for their own purposes.[44] Indeed, Inkosi Solomon proved especially adept at this, when, in 1925, he transformed a welcoming ceremony for the Prince of Wales into a display of his authority as the Zulu paramount. In other cases, crowds turned violent or experienced violence, as when a white mob descended upon an ICU crowd in 1929.[45]

For their part, the Nazaretha had rules for controlling gatherings that helped Shembe manage potential problems—indeed, the same rules that divided people by gender, generation, and geography as well as the rules about who could speak, how, and when, all helped Shembe contain crowds.[46] The presence of outsiders at Nazaretha events meant, however, that the rules did not apply to everyone. Shembe's gripes about Inkosi Solomon pointed to the many ways that the Zulu king, for example, made it clear that the rules did not apply to him when he came to Ekuphakameni.[47] And yet even when things went wrong, Shembe could still use crowds to send powerful messages about his authority.

A Crowd at Ekuphakameni

An event that did not go as planned revealed how Shembe drew crowds at Ekuphakameni to boost his public image while navigating his difficulties with state officials. The Nazaretha described how "an angel told" Shembe to "build [a] house for the Zulu nation" and that the "foundation stone should be laid by the king." Timed to take place during the "July assembly" in 1931, the cornerstone ceremony featured hundreds of Nazaretha, who danced and sang at the event. But then, with perhaps as many as 5,000 people waiting in the crowd and with "the [w]hites and other chiefs" already present, Inkosi Solomon never showed up. If Shembe might have hoped for better from his son-in-law, the Zulu king's erratic behavior was well known by then. At Ekuphakameni, Shembe and the others waited for him for a while before Shembe asked one of the chiefs who had come from southern Zululand to lay the cornerstone instead.[48]

The premise of the event—a cornerstone ceremony—was more significant because of Shembe's troubles with the state. At a time when Shembe knew that government officials were considering ways to punish him, Shembe invited a large crowd of people including "the [w]hites" to come to Ekuphakameni, where he orchestrated an event around the idea of permanence and immovability. That premise alone sent a message to officials, but the event had other layers of significance. The presence of crowds indicated openness, with Shembe suggesting that he had nothing to hide, even as he hid his activities in southern Zululand.[49] One can also imagine the event as a dare, too, showing the government all the people who knew about Shembe and who would know if the state acted against him. The crowds included perhaps as many as two hundred white South Africans, traveling by "charabanc and motor-car" to the event.[50] By inviting large, diverse crowds, Shembe gave himself extra protection against the dramatic standoffs that government officials hoped to avoid with him after 1926; the bustling scene at Ekuphakameni was not the backdrop they wanted as they attempted to change his mind about vaccination. One can also imagine the ceremony as a way of indicating to white officials what Shembe, in fact, told one of the white visitors who came to Ekuphakameni in the 1930s: that "he did not believe in the power of the law, but in the powers of God."[51] That is, Shembe could proceed because he had God's sanction and needed no one else's. Each of these interpretations added to the meaning of the event for Shembe and the people in the crowd.

The possibilities for gathering so many people at Ekuphakameni in the 1920s and 1930s depended upon a broader transportation revolution. While average church members still likely took the train and walked, some were beginning to take buses, taxis, and private automobiles that traversed a growing mileage of maintained roads. But these crowds were possible too because of concomitant changes in how groups of people thought about mobility. Chiefs, for example, turned to mobility as a

FIGURE 6. Young men dancing at Ekuphakameni in 1930.

PHOTOGRAPH INCLUDED WITH PERMISSION OF THE MARY EVANS PICTURE LIBRARY.

FIGURE 7. Shembe (*far left*) with chiefs at Ekuphakameni in 1930. Many of these chiefs hailed from southern Zululand, a region where the Nazaretha experienced significant growth in the 1920s.

PHOTOGRAPH INCLUDED WITH PERMISSION OF THE MARY EVANS PICTURE LIBRARY.

strategy that entrenched their status in ways that differed from a few decades earlier. In the past, ordinary people had often moved to chiefs to show their allegiance. As people came together to offer tribute at first-fruits ceremonies, for example, chiefs offered evidence of the people they could mobilize—literally.[52] But, as migrant working men left rural areas, chiefs began to travel more to see them. This movement not only helped chiefs maintain bonds of affiliation, but it also helped them raise funds. Automobile ownership became one way that a chief could flip the direction of movement while still entrenching his authority and elite status.[53] As chiefs traveled more, this, in turn, led to a reassessment of their attendance at other kinds of events, including at Ekuphakameni.[54] The special gates that Shembe added where chiefs could enter church headquarters were there, broadly, to mark chiefly status but also, more specifically, to accommodate their automobiles.[55]

White South Africans traveled more and for different reasons too. In the 1920s, they were interested in "discovering" their country through cultural tourism. For this purpose, Ekuphakameni was an easy destination.[56] For those who could drive (or be driven), Ekuphakameni was a daytrip from Durban and other suburbs. The manageable distance also made Ekuphakameni a middle ground, a place where white South Africans could go to encounter and observe rural Africans without having to go too far into what many of them still imagined as the primitive, potentially dangerous, unknown reserves of Natal and Zululand.[57] Finally, the work of Shembe's unofficial publicist, Nellie Wells, made Ekuphakameni a vetted space. As Wells wrote about how Shembe turned a "war dance" into a "dance for peace," she helped prepare white visitors for what to expect when they arrived. Her stories also let them know that they would be welcomed.[58]

The Nazaretha perhaps traditionalized dance—or at least made it more spectacular—in this period to attract more people to Ekuphakameni.[59] Shembe and others in the church might have noticed the posters advertising big events in Durban that showed migrant-working men in elaborate dance costumes, many of which included feathers, shields, and other more traditional-looking elements.[60] By the late 1920s, some Nazaretha dance costumes included more fur and feathers too. Others included more interesting assemblages, pairing, for example, pith helmets and cattle-tail whips.[61] During this period, a distinct shift became apparent in the dance ensembles of the people who had been dancing longest: young, unmarried women. In the 1930s young women no longer danced in white robes with green ribbons as described in 1918.[62] Instead, they wore "short scarlet or black skirts decorated with bells and jangling ornaments." They were "naked from the waist except for necklets, armlets, and girdles of beads."[63] Such dancing ensembles reflected a convergence between the growing celebration of tradition among many Africans (including many African Christians) and what white audience members expected to see.[64]

The Nazaretha had company as they used dance to attract attention; for others, too, the combination of crowds and dance also contributed to strategies of protection and rebranding. Just months after a violent mob attacked an ICU crowd in downtown Durban in 1929, the ICU leader A. W. G. Champion invited white members of the Commission on Native Riots to "a Sunday tea party" that involved dancing and singing.[65] Champion hoped to use dance to convince the white public that the ICU was not as dangerous as they imagined at a moment when he also knew that officials were considering how to punish him.[66] Given how closely people such as Champion and Shembe were watching each other, Shembe likely knew how Champion was using dance—and vice versa.

Ekuphakameni had long been a porous space, where the Nazaretha welcomed outsiders, whether they came to seek Shembe's healing or to find brides. And yet, as more outsiders began to come to Ekuphakameni, people in the church likely understood it as, at once, a sacred site but also a space for public display.[67] Other sites—and Mount Nhlangakazi above all—became more important for the sharing of "insider," esoteric knowledge about what it meant to be among the Nazaretha faithful.[68] The continued remoteness of Nhlangakazi and the need to walk several days to get there contributed to its role in clarifying who really belonged to the church and who came just to see. And yet, Ekuphakameni still had significant weight—especially for Shembe because it provided the backdrop for photo opportunities, interviews, and other moments that crystallized Shembe's public image.

Conspicuous Consumption

One of the photo opportunities at Ekuphakameni involved a foot washing ceremony.[69] In the photograph, there are men, sitting on a bench and all clad in white robes. Some of them wear the kehla, or head ring that historically marked marriage in the Zulu Kingdom and made it likely that these men had traveled from Zululand.[70] Rows of men stand behind the ones on the bench, watching and perhaps awaiting their turns. Shembe squats down in front of the man closest to the camera. Shembe's hands look as if they have just dropped the man's feet into a basin or are preparing to remove them and move on to the next feet to wash. This act, of stooping down

FIGURE 8. Shembe washing the feet of church men in the 1930s at Ekuphakameni. Rituals such as foot-washing gave Shembe ways to emphasize his humility and sacrifice for the church community as his wealth and authority grew.

PHOTOGRAPH INCLUDED WITH PERMISSION OF CAMPBELL COLLECTIONS, UKZN.

to wash disciples' feet, gave Shembe another way to imitate Christ—much as he had by offering his own coat to others or by traveling, as he did more and more often in his last years, with a group of other men. The models of Old Testament prophets from Moses to Elisha had resonated for Shembe in the early days of the church, but, by the end of his life, it was Christ's example that offered the richest symbolism and imagery.[71]

In the photograph, the positions of the men took on added meaning because of the politics of sitting. Since the mid-nineteenth century, important African men often had chairs, stools, or other items that lifted them up from the ground.[72] In this photograph, by contrast, Shembe is the person closest to the ground. And yet, this is not an image that broadcasts only the last-shall-be-first reversals so central to the promise of Christianity. Shembe's preaching on cleanliness and purity add another element, emphasizing his ability to decontaminate the souls and bodies of sinners. Shembe's ensemble sets him apart too. He is the only person not wearing a white robe. As striking is the fact that the other men—including those standing behind the seated row—are barefoot, while Shembe wears nice shoes.[73]

The photograph of the foot-washing points to the complex—and sometimes contradictory—posturing in which Shembe engaged as he gained control over vast resources. Consumer capitalism gave Shembe opportunities to broadcast who he was as a leader through a range of items and objects. Indeed, Shembe used them, sometimes to set himself apart, whether from his people or other elites, and sometimes to link himself both to his people and to other elites. And yet in an age when many celebrities turned to consumer culture to craft complex public images, Shembe's self-fashioning also depended upon what he did not consume. Abstention and restraint often distinguished Shembe most from the other important people who might show up in the crowd at Ekuphakameni too.

One might start with the ultimate symbol of having "made it" as an African elite in the 1920s: the automobile. Already, the new needs and uses for cars in segregation-era South Africa were becoming apparent. If not by automobile, the new social logic suggested, how else could a chief get to those government indabas? Cars also represented a way to avoid the indignities of racism in South Africa's public spaces. Bad treatment at train stations united many Africans in their complaints, whether they had to sit outside of the station during rain storms or ride in coal cars when there were no passenger cars for Africans available.[74] Although bad treatment on the roads would become another way of indexing South Africa's racism later in the twentieth century, the early days of automobile ownership and travel seemed to offer an escape—at least for those who could afford it.[75]

Stories circulated that the Nazaretha, aware of the importance of cars, tried to buy one for Shembe. Shembe, however, refused the gift in a public act loaded with meaning.[76] The refusal suggested that he, unlike the chiefs fundraising for automobiles, would not enjoy comfort and luxury at the expense of his people. He backed this up with many other forms of refusal, from his spartan dwelling to the cigarettes he would not smoke and the alcohol he would not drink. But, especially as Shembe began to show signs of aging, his continued mission journeys by train, foot, and sometimes donkey (instead of car) translated into another important element of his public image: the idea that he continued to suffer and sacrifice both for his people and to obey God.[77]

The absence of a car also positioned Shembe in relation to other important people and to his publics. In some ways, refusing a car sent a message that Shembe, too, was excluded. He did not have a place in those big government meetings, where chiefs, government officials, and other important people got together.[78] As he acknowledged this, Shembe also suggested that he would not compete for influence on the same terms as the chiefs who had recently joined his church. This was especially important because of the long history of rivalries between chiefs and healers and because the chiefs who supported Shembe often wanted the same things as him: allegiance, offerings, and obedience.[79]

Refusing a car suggested something about the main demographics of the church too—and who its members still were in the last years of Shembe's life. Impressive though fancy cars might be, they were not useful for getting to many remote parts of South Africa.[80] By rejecting a car, Shembe affirmed that he would still travel to seek out the people left behind. This was also why he kept, instead, "a collection of worn shoes and walking sticks."[81] Shembe was one of many leaders in the 1920s—including his former neighbor in Inanda, Mohandas Gandhi—who rejected the most advanced technology to try to consolidate belonging among followers.[82]

Shembe did accept some nice gifts, though. In fact, he accepted other expensive gifts related to transportation and movement: horses.[83] The culture of horse breeding in Natal made horse ownership a marker of an elite—although in this case horses had associations with the region's wealthy white communities.[84] The decision to give Shembe horses spoke to how well congregants knew Shembe's life story. In the Free State, he had earned a reputation for breaking in horses, being a skilled horseback rider, and traveling by horse as he evangelized around Harrismith. And, lest this connection to his past be lost on anyone, Shembe named one of his gift horses "Free State."[85] This name stood out as one of many ways that Shembe regularly reminded people of his past. Not only did his history point to the miracle of all that had happened, but it also underscored what he had already given up by following God. As he explained in one sermon, "I left my home and my wives and my children and my life-stock [sic]; I left many things behind which I loved and were dear to my heart; I put them all down and went off to come to this Nazaretha faith."[86] Such stories raised the question: If he had given up so much in the past, why would he take from others in the present? Even a gift that marked Shembe as an elite could help him make this point if it gestured toward what had once been.

By the late 1920s, something else—already mentioned in the photograph of the foot washing ceremony—complemented the messages that Shembe sent through his modes of transportation: his clothes. Shembe did sometimes don the

FIGURE 9. Shembe on horseback in the early 1930s at Ekuphakameni. Shembe purportedly refused a car from his congregation but did accept a horse, named Free State, as a gift instead. The horse's name referred to Shembe's home region and his former success as a horseman.

PHOTOGRAPH INCLUDED WITH PERMISSION OF CAMPBELL COLLECTIONS, UKZN.

white gowns that everyone else wore for worship, but photographs from the era show that Shembe had an impressive wardrobe, with a variety of robes and church gowns that were, more often, different colors from the standard white. Indeed, the most elaborate had a top that looked like a cowboy-style fringe shirt—albeit with cattle tail fur instead of leather strips.[87] The similarity was likely a coincidence, but it might have offered evidence of the ways that fictionalized images of the US West were already percolating through South African popular culture—and how the people making Shembe's clothes were within the reach of these influences.[88] Shembe also frequently wore beaded bracelets and necklaces and often something on his head, whether a head wrap, a bowler hat, a pith helmet, or even a kufi. (The last option for headwear probably reflected items available to purchase from his

FIGURE 10. Shembe in the early 1930s in a robe and bowler hat. Shembe's clothing was often distinct from church members', church leaders' of other denominations, and other African elites'.

South Asian neighbors in Inanda.)[89] And, in most of the photographs of Shembe, as in the footwashing photograph, tailored, ironed pants and sharp-looking, shining shoes peeped out below the hem of his robes.[90]

Shembe's clothes were different from other African elites.' At a time when military garb was commonly worn by Inkosi Solomon at big events and many chiefs wore some combination of suits and skins, Shembe opted for none of these possibilities.[91] Nor did he opt for the standard three-piece suits of a John Dube or even the formal clerical garb of ordained African clergy.[92] Still, Shembe's clothes did often come closest to formal clerical garb, with robes and neckwear that looked like collars. Of course, in his last years, Shembe could have easily afforded the items that ordained African Christians wore. But, for Shembe, distinguishing himself from other African Christian leaders had taken additional meaning in the 1920s and 1930s, as more Africans became skeptical of church leaders who might go out and "put on a collar" to disguise themselves.[93] Shembe's clothes projected the idea that he did not need to pretend to be someone he was not. The absence of such pretending had, in fact, been central to his popularity since his first days in Ndwedwe.

Shembe's clothes made him singular within his community but also a product of it. The sheer variety of Shembe's clothes—and the number of items in his ensembles—set him apart from most South Africans. These clothes allowed him both to stand out in a crowd and to assert his importance. And yet, key elements of his clothing likely would have been made by churchwomen. Girls and women had been sewing at Ekuphakameni since the time of its founding; it was possible that some of the most talented seamstresses among them had made his robes. And if the Nazaretha women were not doing beadwork already, they would be very soon, linking them and their skills to the beads he wore too.[94] The material of the cattle-tail fringe was significant, as well, not only as furs and skins had become more acceptable in the church but also as a symbol of the Zulu royal family and Shembe's status, however fraught, as a father-in-law of the Zulu king.[95]

Shembe's ensemble that most resembled outfits worn by other members of the church sent messages about his consumption too. On days when church members danced, Shembe sometimes wore something like the clothing of the young, unmarried men. His clothes and the young men's included pith helmets, pleated skirts, and white shirts with high socks and shoes for dancing.[96] (These were some of the few photographs that showed many people in shoes—in part because young men would have needed shoes to go to work.) The similarities underscored how Shembe no longer considered himself to be a married man and was, in some ways, like the young, unmarried men of the church. Such similarity implied that Shembe, then, did not consume resources to support his wives and households. Perhaps such clothing suggested, too, that he owed his earnings to a higher power, much as he preached by then that sons should give their wages to their fathers.[97] But, if the Nazaretha did not see in his dancing uniform a message about how he refrained from consuming resources, he found other ways to make this point.

The Conduit

Shembe set himself apart in a region where other important men often displayed their authority through excess. Indeed, this excess might extend to the number of their wives and children, the amount of their cattle, or even the size of their bodies.[98] Such displays of excess had, ideally, been linked to rituals of redistribution. That is, the same chiefs and important men who acquired wives, cattle, food, and weight on their bodies also very publicly gave resources away.[99] As another way of emphasizing his sacrifice, Shembe very publicly recalibrated the ratio of consuming to giving. Indeed, this man who had spent so much time on the move framed himself as a conduit: someone who moved resources to others rather than using them himself.

People noticed, for example, that Shembe's body was "slender" and "agile," allowing him to walk quickly and dance in spritely ways.[100] For someone so often on the move, such a body shape was perhaps not a surprise. In fact, another reason why some chiefs could have large bodies reflected, again, the politics of movement—and how people moved to them. But on top of Shembe's frequent movement, he also engaged in a different kind of "politics of the belly" that helped explain his slender form.[101] He took food made for him by members of the church and gave it to other people. Even though he did not eat the food, moreover, the women who made it bragged saying still, "The Servant of God has eaten what I cooked!"[102] By redistributing it to others, then, he had "eaten" it.[103]

Shembe's role as a conduit casts his growing involvement in lobola loans in the 1920s and 1930s in a different light too. While, on one hand, Shembe had reasons to be uncomfortable as a church leader playing such a role in lobola exchanges, the influx of cattle from southern Zululand gave him another way to show how he moved resources.[104] Indeed, the importance of such displays for Shembe meant that he almost certainly did not stop them when the loans were discovered by a magistrate, who called Shembe "a danger to the peaceful government of the natives" as a result of his involvement in lobola.[105]

Rituals in the church surrounding money emphasized Shembe's role as a conduit too. People remembered that Shembe did not get a bank account until near the end of his life. They saw him, moreover, pay for large purchases with bags of "three-penny pieces."[106] On one hand, the size and number of the bags of money suggested his access to wealth. On the other hand, they also reflected the small offerings in coins of thousands of church members. Thus, the bags were so many and so large because Shembe had not touched the money before delivering it to its next source. Shembe's rituals of accountability surrounding money allowed him to show how he was different not only from other leaders, but also from other men in the Nazaretha Church who sometimes stole people's offerings.[107]

Where people could not see evidence of the movement of resources, problems emerged for Shembe. As the last chapter suggested, Shembe did not use all the land he acquired in the last years of his life. Some former members of the church sued him because of their questions about what was happening to the land they had helped buy.[108] In the absence of documentation or written evidence, they did not have much of a case and Shembe won.[109] Still, aware of the problem, Shembe might have begun prioritizing care for "needy people" and "needy widows" as one way to show where the money he collected was going instead.[110] This also fed back into the promise that Shembe made to care for any women abused by their husbands as he expanded polygyny in the church.

Shembe's promise to care for the vulnerable also helped explain one controversial target for his resource redistribution: his former wives and children. His account of leaving them and making them like widows and orphans allowed him to explain why they got some degree of special treatment. Much as he paid for his own sons to go to school, for example, he paid for some other orphaned boys to go to school too—if not all the way through finishing their bachelor's degrees.[111] And, much as he paid for other widowed and abandoned women to live at Ekuphakameni, he paid for his former wives to do the same.[112] As Shembe neared the end of his life, however, people began to ask pointed questions about the resources that his former wives and children would acquire after he died. As he explained before a government commission in 1931, he planned for most of his land to be left to his church: "I have given others more than I have given my children."[113] But while this was true of the total acreage, Shembe planned to give each of his surviving sons three hundred acres of land. As he said after a pointed line of questioning: "I have felt it my duty to make proper provision for the children which have been vouchsafed to me."[114] He added, a "father who has been given children, as in my case, who was at one time well off, should not leave his children poorly off and leave other people outside his family better off than his own children."[115] What this answer elided was just how much better off than other people his own children would be as a result of their inheritances.

By focusing on what he still owed his biological children, one sees yet another contradiction in Shembe's public image. This man, who had left his wives and children behind and no longer considered himself married, had become for many African women an exemplar of a husband and father: one who did not drink paychecks or pursue extra wives. One who took care of the otherwise marginal and abandoned even if they were sick and could not have children. One who would continue to suffer and sacrifice to try to find the people left behind, the majority of whom were still women and children in the 1930s. This interpretation of Shembe's public image helped explain the enduring appeal of the church to girls and women even as their roles in the Nazaretha community changed and, in some cases, as their authority diminished.[116] But, as with so many areas of his life, not everyone agreed that Shembe represented this ideal.

Truths and Consequences

Shembe also experienced troubles and suffering in ways that did not fit as neatly into narratives of sacrificing for God and his people—and that opened space for questions and criticism. The story of his daughter running off to marry the Zulu king offers an example of such trouble. On one hand, it could make Shembe seem relatable: even this powerful man had problems like other fathers who could not control their children either. On the other, if he could not control his own daughter, some might ask, what of other girls and young women who came to Ekuphakameni? More difficult experiences, too, opened space for varying interpretations. In the last years of his life, Shembe experienced the loss of another child—this time a grandson, named Benjamin.[117] Again, this showed how even Shembe experienced common forms of suffering that others faced, too. But the links between sin and illness upheld by people in his community meant that this death had the potential to raise questions about what was happening in his family as well. The foundational role of Shembe's life story for the Nazaretha and, with it, the loss of his own children made the potential questions more pointed.

There is little evidence to suggest whether or not the Nazaretha further pried open space to ask questions about Shembe's grandson's death or his daughter's marriage. One striking feature of Shembe's public image in the last decade of his life was how few minds it seemed to change. Everything mentioned above could simply be interpreted as adding more evidence to what one already thought. Shembe's most devoted followers could look to his sacrificing and his suffering to see a godly man and spiritual father, perhaps even wondering if he might be a Black Messiah or Christ. His detractors could look to the same examples and scoff at how Shembe was a pretender and cheat who thought he was God.

What all of these people could agree upon, however, was the main point that John Dube would make in the introduction to the book about Shembe published the year after Shembe's death: that whatever one thought about Shembe and what he had done, no one could deny that he was important.[118] The crowds, the cameras, the company Shembe kept, and the crafting of a complex public image all made this clear. Dube's own role in writing the introduction to the book affirmed Shembe's importance too. It represented yet another way that the celebrities of Natal and Zululand collided with and jostled against each other even, in this case, after one of them had died.

Conclusion

ISAIAH SHEMBE DIED ON MAY 2, 1935, ON A MISSION JOURNEY TO ZULULAND. IN THE 1930s, he had continued pressing north along the railway, nearing the Eswatini border in his travels. Shembe and his companions, a group of older men, were making their way back to Ekuphakameni but stopping at friendly homesteads and chiefdoms along the way. Shembe stopped last in the Mbonambi chiefdom in southern Zululand, one of the chiefdoms that had exploded with support for the Nazaretha in the 1920s.[1]

The Nazaretha remembered Shembe's final months as difficult ones. He had sometimes wandered off and been found by himself in strange places.[2] He had stopped walking as much on mission journeys and traveled, more often, by donkey. But what the Nazaretha remembered on this last stop was not any strange behavior, slowing down, or weakness. Instead, they remembered how Shembe kept going as long as he could. He presided over a marriage ceremony, he led dancing, and he baptized people.[3] He did this, moreover, after he started to feel unwell and when others with him were too sick to continue. Simon Mngoma, one of the older men traveling with Shembe on the last journey, remembered that he too had fallen ill. Mngoma had pain "in the head over the eyes" and "was unable to rise by [him] self." Shembe had carried on conducting services without Mngoma until Shembe himself collapsed.[4]

While Shembe could still speak, he found ways to preside despite his illness. He commanded the people around him to laugh and to show their joy despite the difficulty of the moment. When they struggled with this command, he told them to "laugh louder!"[5] He also admonished some of them who tried to proceed with worship without his permission. Someone remembered him saying, "You begin to do what you want to do already while I am still alive. What shall you do when I shall be no longer there?"[6] More than a joking prod, these words pointed to a concern that had grown in the last years of Shembe's life.[7]

Historians are poorly equipped to diagnose disease, whether in the past or in the present. Nevertheless, the descriptions of fever and headaches, Shembe's route through a region with endemic malaria, and the timing of his journey at the end of the rainy season make one wonder if he was sick from the effects of the common parasite in the region.[8] Whatever the specific cause of his death, the circumstances fit easily into narratives of his willingness to sacrifice. Shembe, the Nazaretha could say, had died for them. He was nearing his seventieth year.

South Africa in the Making

Born in the late 1860s to a people on the edge of disaster in a place on the edge of wrenching change, Shembe's life pierced through a set of astonishing transformations: diamonds and then gold, the conquest of the last independent African polities, the South African War, the unification of the South African state, the First World War, and the Great Depression. In Shembe's last years, the problem of white poverty, ideas coming out of Afrikaner seminaries, and anxieties about Africans' urbanization were already coalescing to widen the appeal of South Africa's brand of extreme white nationalism. South Africa's entry on the side of the allies in the Second World War would stoke it farther, ushering in apartheid in 1948.

Shembe had spent nearly seven decades on the move—first as part of a family and chiefdom struggling to stay together, then as an itinerant preacher and missionary, and finally as a church founder whose congregation sought his presence and nearness, asking him to come to them. Throughout this time, movement had been a solution to and a cause of his struggles. New places held the promise of more souls to save, ears that might listen, mouths that might testify, and hands that might give offerings. But new places also demanded that he adapt to fit in not just as someone passing through, but as someone who hoped to be welcomed back, as someone who depended upon others for access to land, and as someone who was often hiding from something. Shembe's movement had consequences for the church he founded too. The Nazaretha had become, by the time Shembe died, a congregation of movers, using their feet, the trains, and cars and buses to be near him and each other. The church was a movement in many senses of the word.

Shembe's life on the move illuminated the contours of a changing South Africa. To return to the questions posed in the introduction, one might start with what his life reveals about Christianity and its transformative effects on South African public life. An oft quoted statistic is that nearly 80 percent of all South Africans are now, at the beginning of the new millennium, Christians, with the highest rates of conversion occurring in the twentieth century.[9] The conventional explanation is still, as Adrian Hastings wrote many years ago, that this was "a [B]lack advance or it was nothing."[10] In other words, such sweeping religious change could not have been possible without Africans themselves interpreting and carrying the Gospel. Already, scholars have begun to show how this sweeping religious change affected more than the number of people attending church, too, whether through refashioning Africans' intimate lives, driving their political commitments, or propelling the redemptive project of post-apartheid nationalism.[11]

Shembe's circuitous path does not change Hastings's central conclusion, but it does add elements that help clarify how Christianity so profoundly shaped public life. Consider the many channels for the spread of the faith that Shembe's life exposes and, perhaps most of all, how those channels reached outside of formal missions and churches: He learned about God from watching his white landlord. He learned about divine healing—whether directly or indirectly—from people passing through on the roads of the Orange River Colony. He then went to cities and towns where the laws about clothes and days off from work could help people more easily make the jump from nonbeliever to convert—and where worship in homes and front yards fueled declarations of evangelical autonomy. In rural Natal, he found people who had already made such declarations, too, using their homesteads and common ground. And, as a church leader himself, Shembe sought ways to reach outsiders, whether by taking bad land, promising to cure infertility, or arranging marriages for runaway daughters. Such promises helped him make converts, true, but they also added to the number of people on the edges of the Nazaretha community—touched by, although not fully within, the church. His example shows how elements of Christianity spread among people who did not convert, as they adjusted to a world in which many other people did. His example shows, too, how the state inadvertently pushed Christianity into the capillaries of public life. Limits, surveillance, and threats encouraged Shembe to go new places and find ways to reach out to more people.

The Nazaretha became, as a result, one of many broad, unwieldy coalitions in the early twentieth century. True, their left-behind status opened common ground, but it had to be staked out and claimed across fractured spaces and people still divided by many categories of belonging. The resultant compromises and concessions changed the shape of the church. If the demographics of Nazaretha membership were distinctive, one nevertheless finds parallels with other churches that emerged in the 1910s as well as with the Industrial and Commercial Workers Union (ICU) in the 1920s, and then, by the 1950s, with political parties such as the African National Congress (ANC).[12] The restrictions of the state from above—as well as varied pressures from below—meant that these organizations, too, grew across complicated geographies and struggled to link scattered people together. These circumstances explain why the leaders of these organizations spent so much time in cars, moving toward their people too—if using a different mode of transportation than Shembe.[13] These circumstances also explain why banning and physically isolating leaders became a frequently used tactic of a government attempting to stop the movement of individuals who helped knit disparate groups of people together.[14] And, as when Ezra Mbonambi left the Nazaretha or when others would leave later, South Africa's many fractures made lobes within these broad coalitions that easily peeled away. When the Natal branch split from the larger ICU, its members were driven not just by the charisma of A. W. G. Champion, the ICU leader in Natal, but also by the different possibilities for Africans in a region where many people still lived in chiefdoms and where buying land was not yet off the table.[15] And, as with the Nazaretha and other African Christians, histories of difference *and* similarity contributed to the making of stark divides. When, in 1959, the Pan Africanist Congress (PAC) split from the ANC, a shared history of personnel and ideas between the organizations meant that the leaders of both groups found new ways to emphasize their differences. This polarization would follow the PAC and the ANC into exile and shape the emergence of the global anti-apartheid movement.[16]

How and why did Shembe become a savior at the helm of one of South Africa's many unwieldy coalitions? Foremost, he shepherded left-behind people in a time of trouble, going out to find them and then bringing them into a fold. He related to them with his personal stories of sadness and sacrifice. And he used other people like him to draw contrasts, whether healers who had eaten a lot of food in rural homesteads; people promising land who could not deliver it; or, later, the Zulu king with his cars, wives, and cigarettes. But he also became a savior because of a coalescence of resonances and influences. Long before he became a church founder, he had been the inheritor—the chosen one in his family—with privilege and responsibility. Biblical examples contributed too—first of wandering prophets who acted as God's messenger and then of Jesus, whose example prioritized one man above them all. There was the colonial logic of indirect rule—govern many through one—that the state attempted to employ with Shembe. There was also the power of a brand in an age of advertising, seen in the way that Nazaretha testimonies focused their stories on Shembe himself as their medicine, their healing. In the last years of Shembe's life, there was the power of celebrity, too, where cameras and crowds alike focused on him.

If South Africa's other twentieth-century saviors did not share Shembe's qualities, influences, and resonances equally, they nevertheless shared many of them. Consider how the apartheid government's vicious targeting of Steve Biko echoed the enduring logic of "many through one."[17] And consider how the story of Nelson Mandela's continued sacrifice—not just staying in prison so long but staying when he could have been free—allowed him to become another shepherd of a struggling people in a time of trouble. Although the social basis of each man's authority was different, the parallels between Shembe and Mandela are especially striking. Mandela, too, wore disguises and hid from the state, becoming known as the "Black Pimpernel" while he was on the run.[18] Mandela, too, left a family behind—expressing some of his strongest regrets about leaving his mother—as he became not only a father of a people but also a celebrity and a global icon.[19] And Mandela, with a body slimmed from deprivation and an exercise regime in prison, also promised a new redistribution of resources.[20] Such similarities point to the kaleidoscopic configurations of leadership and authority produced in twentieth-century South Africa, some pieces of which are still visible in the support for popular and populist leaders today.[21]

And, finally, what does Shembe's life tell us about why—speaking to the news in late 2022—a South African president might hide money in a couch? This question is not yet fully answerable with the information available and is unlikely to become so. But Shembe's life suggests two issues worth addressing. First, one might consider the links between evasion and patriarchy. Shembe turned most frequently to elder African men when he needed shelter from the state. At first, those elder men were less likely to be converts, be they chiefs and homestead heads who could offer land or the angry fathers whom Shembe tried to appease. By the 1920s, however, patriarchs in the church had more authority, including the elder men who went to the magistrate for Shembe and the chiefs from southern Zululand who gave Shembe another place to hide. Of course, patriarchy did not just come in response to, or through the mechanisms of, the state. People also bolstered and remade patriarchy from below. Recall how the young women who gathered around Shembe in the 1910s hoped he could provide them with land for something better. One might look as well at how married women in the church later venerated Shembe as a patriarch who cared and sacrificed for people like them. And yet, other patriarchs played such an important role in the Nazaretha community because of the authority granted to them by the settler government. That is, because homestead heads and chiefs had been allocated authority over space and people, they were especially useful partners for Shembe's efforts to avoid trouble with the state. The growth of the Nazaretha shows how evasion and patriarchy became intertwined.

There is a bigger point still to make about the productive role of evasion in South Africa's history. The many ways that Shembe evaded authority—through clothes, names, movement, and the company he kept—were all remarkably common. Indeed, almost every form of evasion that Shembe used was used by someone else, whether for similar reasons or different ones. For many new Christians, strategies of evasion could emerge from the act of defying one's parents to practice a new faith. But, away from home and family too, the sheer variety of laws that mismatched the reality of people's lives meant that evasion was often what it took to survive in an industrializing South Africa. It was a fact of life. But Christianity also allowed people to justify their evasion as moral and driven by a higher power. Someone's parents or state officials, in other words, might say "no," but God would surely say otherwise. In Shembe's lifetime, many South Africans learned about God while they experienced the advances of an often arbitrary and violent, but porous and uneven state. For people such as Shembe, the state's moral bankruptcy justified the evasion that its inadequacies facilitated.

The idea that certain forms of evasion were righteous has had a long life in South Africa. Most notably, historians have followed the ways that people took evasion and transformed it into open expressions of defiance. South Africa's role as a crucible for Mohandas Gandhi's notion of satyagraha, or "truth force," comes from a parallel process.[22] Satyagraha made private acts of evasion public and just, as its practitioners sought a morality outside of the state's. Work slowdowns kept hidden, for example, became strikes, and evasion of state tax laws became a public commitment to tax avoidance. Nor was it a coincidence that, as the ANC began experimenting with civil disobedience in the 1950s, its leaders launched the Defiance Campaign against Unjust Laws, which took experiences of evasion in daily life—whether relating to the intricacies of the pass laws or being in places where one was not supposed to go—and made them public too.[23] The idea of making South Africa "ungovernable" in the 1980s, as apartheid jolted toward its messy end, suggested something similar as well: redirect all of the ways that South Africans were already living outside of the state's many complicated, brutal, unjust laws and channel them into a movement to bring down a hateful regime.[24] And yet, if evasion turned into public defiance has understandably captivated our imaginations, evasion kept hidden has persisted. In some cases, the moral coatings of evasion have persisted, too, whether one thinks he or she or God still knows better. This makes South Africa's remarkable history of protest and its struggles with the rule of law difficult to disentangle.

The Burial Place

A car carried Shembe's body from southern Zululand back to Ekuphakameni. The form of transportation that Shembe had rejected for much of his life thus helped him make his final journey. Shembe's neighbor, John Dube, had made the arrangements. Dube also put notices about Shembe's death and upcoming funeral in his newspaper, *iLanga lase Natal*, but information traveled in many ways—by word of mouth, telegraph, and letter—as one more indication of Shembe's celebrity.[25]

The people who gathered at Shembe's funeral on May 5, 1935, exposed the sedimented layers of a life on the move. There were his surviving sons and daughters as well as some of their children, spouses, and other relatives. Linah Mntungwa, the "leader of the maidens" from Ndwedwe, was there as well as a "leader of the Indians." Nellie Wells attended; her husband, William, was one of the speakers. The lawyer D. G. Shepstone came, as did the chiefs and members of chiefly families who had provided Shembe with refuge in southern Zululand. The elder men who had grown close to Shembe in his last years presided over the service. Groups of people from along the north–south railway, divided in the crowd by gender and generation, race and place, made up the majority. As people had been doing for more than a decade, some outside of the church also came to Ekuphakameni just to see such a big event.[26]

It is easy to imagine some who were not there. Despite Shembe's efforts to reconcile with men such as Peter Mnqayi and Ezra Mbonambi, they probably were not in attendance.[27] The families who had been evicted for accepting vaccination and some of the girls who had been spat upon or removed were probably not there either. Nor were the members who had sued Shembe likely to attend his funeral. There were also enemies and outsiders whose numbers had grown since 1913 and who would not think to sanction Shembe's authority by going to the service. Even absences offered a testament, however, to Shembe's profound influence.

The funeral provided another moment to show unity toward the church founder in the face of possible conflict. People wore their church uniforms, sang, and danced in formation, as Shembe had requested they would.[28] They did so, however, as new troubles were afoot. A dispute erupted immediately after Shembe's death about where his body should be buried. The conflict broke open upon predictable fault lines: the people of Zululand claimed he should be buried there while the people of Natal demanded that he be buried at Ekuphakameni. At stake were not only questions of proximity to the dead church leader but also questions of which form of land—chiefly or private property—was most secure.[29] Members of the church credited John Dube with convincing enough of them that Ekuphakameni should be Shembe's final resting place. Over time, a kind of conceptual compromise emerged that evoked stories of another famous Christian traveler, David Livingstone: some Nazaretha began to say that Shembe had left his heart in Zululand even if his body went back to Natal.[30]

If the debate over burial seemed easy to resolve, it fed into others that proved more stubborn. People wondered if Shembe's Christ-like nature meant that he would be resurrected and, if so, how: physically or spiritually? Rumors circulated that members of Shembe's inner circle might have stolen money from him, and people speculated about what would happen to church land. Questions of succession swirled in this mix, too.[31]

Succession

In his lifetime, Shembe did not say much about who would succeed him or the role his sons might play. This was not likely a negative evaluation of his sons' characters or capacities but, instead, an indication of how he wanted something different for them—and how, because he could afford to offer them something different, they were not like him or most of his left-behind congregation. But in the weeks and months after his funeral, J. G. Shembe became a frontrunner for succession in part because of his role settling his father's estate.[32] The very elder men whose authority had been propped up by the state were, in turn, sidelined by another legal process—one that prioritized sons.

Other Inanda luminaries tried to convince J. G. Shembe about what his role should be.[33] Some thought that, if he did not take over, the church would dissolve—and that would be for the best. Others feared that the widows and orphans and other poor people living on church land would suffer if the community fell apart.[34]

J. G. Shembe decided to take over the church. When he did, he was both known and unknown to the congregation he was about to lead. Many knew something of him and his story because they knew his father's story. And yet, J. G. Shembe was a university graduate living in a square house with one kholwa wife.[35] His first challenge, like his father's had been, was to make himself less of a stranger.

J. G. Shembe used his father's story and clothes as well as ceremonies to capture his father's spirit to make himself better known to the church he inherited. Still, he met with limited success at first.[36] In 1939, a church event exploded in violence that pitted the elder men and their supporters against J. G. Shembe and church women—especially those from southern Zululand.[37] Government officials watched the events and saw them as a sign of the imminent unraveling of the church.[38] Once again, however, those officials underestimated the importance of the church girls and women, who kept the community together amid a tense situation for their embattled leader. Because of their support, some of the elder men who had been purged in the violence in 1939 pledged loyalty to J. G. Shembe and came back to the church too.[39]

Over the following decades, J. G. Shembe used a variety of approaches to help the Nazaretha adapt to a changing South Africa. J. G. Shembe asserted new authority over mobility, using church funds to buy buses and petrol stations to control (and facilitate) the movement of people to and from Ekuphakameni and Nazaretha satellite communities.[40] And, at a time when buying land became more difficult, he got a windfall: access to the kinds of gathering spaces that had been closed to his father ever since Isaiah Shembe left the Harrismith location. In the 1930s, just as Isaiah Shembe died, the first segregated townships sprung up in Natal. With townships came homes, yards, slips of public space, and a host of places where the Nazaretha might worship together—and where circles of white rocks began to appear as they did. What is more, some of those townships bordered on Inanda. Construction in KwaMashu began in the 1950s, bringing tens of thousands of people to the region.[41] Many of them were recently removed from rural homes and looking for authenticity and connection. Nazaretha membership skyrocketed as the church became a meeting place for the people of the region's townships and its rural chiefdoms.

Through the 1950s, J. G. sought government recognition, trying to assert that the Nazaretha deserved a spot among the likes of the African Methodist Episcopal Church and other "respectable" congregations. The government rejected his applications again and again for predictable reasons: the ministers "were not educated," the Nazaretha met in "shack areas," and "prominent members indulge in polygamy."[42]

Eventually, J. G. Shembe stopped trying to get government recognition even as he continued with his own projects of respectability. He encouraged formal education and became the source of accounts that Isaiah Shembe had, in fact, learned to read—not through a miracle or memorization as Isaiah Shembe himself had said—but through careful study.[43]

J. G. Shembe also often wore a lab coat—an update to his father's doctor's bag—and dispensed health advice about the need for sanitation and handwashing.[44] He became the person who conceded to vaccination—or, at least, did not reject it altogether, much as government officials had long hoped would happen with his father.[45] Perhaps, however, J. G. Shembe was also more of a pragmatist than white officials, realizing that his personal decision to accept vaccination (or simply to say he agreed to it) might not lead to the sweeping change officials had envisioned for all of the Nazaretha community. There would still be ways to evade the law.

In the 1960s, J. G. Shembe began to fashion himself more like a chief, with fancy material possessions on display and a growing number of wives.[46] J. G. Shembe had come of age at a time when the Christian African elite and middle class had more confidence asserting cultural difference than generations before them. This explained some of the shift.[47] But he, too, became a prophet of the people, acting as a mirror of the congregation and their times. While Isaiah Shembe had presided over a congregation of people left behind, J. G. Shembe presided over a congregation of people more often looking behind: to tradition, to ancestors, to a rural past.[48] For people living in the townships during the apartheid era, J. G. Shembe's chiefly persona spoke powerfully to them, although some among them might have remembered how different Isaiah Shembe's approach to marriage had been—and how accepting polygyny had once been framed as a grudging compromise.[49]

Of Schism and Solidarity

J. G. Shembe saw some significant departures from the church, but it was not until after his death, late in 1976, that the Nazaretha Church saw rival Shembes fighting each other.[50] This era of Shembe family rivalry extends into the present, with various descendants of Isaiah Shembe still claiming his prophetic mantle. The very tools that Isaiah Shembe and J. G. Shembe used to expand their community contribute to making these conflicts unresolvable—as do the many persistent fractures in South Africa today. Who, after all, has final authority? The Zulu king? The Constitutional Court of a democratic South Africa? The Nazaretha themselves? And what is the Nazaretha faith: one of many similar divine healing churches, a new religion developed in South Africa alone, or something in between? People in the church can find support for many answers to these questions in their history and put their weight behind different people as a result.

The ongoing leadership battles matter to average congregants. Again, in late 2022, members of one branch of the church showed this, with thousands of them gathering in the streets of downtown Durban to back their chosen successor.[51] And yet that gathering, to demonstrate support for one leader, underscored something else too: how the horizontal connections—the marriages, the economic ties, the fun, the dancing—matter at least as much. By focusing on the sacrifices, deeds, and miracles of one man, the Nazaretha became a people who persist through and with each other.

Notes

INTRODUCTION

1. This reconstruction of Shembe's first four decades comes from his retelling of his life, church members' retellings, and corroborating sources. It is a summary of events described in this book, and the following chapters provide more detail about the sources used to chart Shembe's life. For accounts of Shembe's early life, see Robert Papini, "Carl Faye's Transcript of Isaiah Shembe's Testimony of His Early Life and Calling," *Journal of Religion in Africa* 29, no. 3 (1999): 243–84; Petros M. Dhlomo, "1. The Tradition of the Beginner of the Way of the Nazaretha Movement, the Suffering Servant Isaiah Mdliwamafa Shembe," in *The Story of Isaiah Shembe, Vol. 1: History and Traditions Centered on Ekuphakameni and Mount Nhlangakazi*, ed. Irving Hexham and G. C. Oosthuizen, trans. Hans-Jürgen Becken (Lewiston, NY: Edwin Mellen, 1996), 1 (henceforth *SIS* 1); Petros Dhlomo and Khaya Ndelu, "Shembe's Farewell from His Family," in *SIS* 1, 26–28; Petros Dhlomo, Muntuwesizwe Buthelezi, and Linah Mntungwa, "21. Shembe's Early Ministry in the Durban Region," in *SIS* 1, 43–47.

2. The work of the Baptists with whom Shembe was affiliated was generally "self-supporting." See Kevin Roy, *No Turning Back: A History of Baptist Missionary Endeavor in Southern Africa from 1820–2000* (Pinelands, ZA: South African Baptist Historical Society, 2001), 13–15. The mission organization leaders, too, emphasized that they "rendered . . . what material help [they] could." Rev. John H. Frank to Sir Godfrey Lagden, 8 May

1906, 2643/09, 448, Papers of the Secretary of Native Affairs (henceforth SNA), National Archives Repository, Pretoria (henceforth SAB).

3. Bheki-Mkhize and Muntuwesizwe Buthelezi, "20. Shembe Comes to Natal," in *SIS* 1, 42–43.

4. This mid-1910s date is different from the date many others cite for the founding of the church. This date comes, however, from isiZulu-language newspapers that described Shembe as "formerly of the Baptist church" in 1913. Ezra Mbonambi, letter to the editor, *iLanga lase Natal*, February 28, 1913.

5. On the vow of the Nazarite, see Num. 6:1–21.

6. Estimates of church members ranged from 20,000 to 50,000. See, for example, Esther Roberts, "Shembe: The Man and His Works" (master's thesis, University of Natal, 1936), 19.

7. John Mabuyakhulu, "26. The Vaccination Controversy at Ekuphakameni," in *SIS* 1, 145–51.

8. John Langalibalele Dube, *UShembe* (Pietermaritzburg, ZA: Shuter and Shooter, 1936), 2. For more on this book, Joel Cabrita, "Patriot and Prophet: John Dube's 1936 Biography of the South African Churchman Isaiah Shembe," *Journal of Southern African Studies* 38, no. 3 (September 1, 2012): 433–50.

9. "Herd Boy Turns Healer: Remarkable Claims of Shembe, the Zulu," *The Friend*, July 27, 1927.

10. Adam Payne, "A Prophet among the Zulus," *Illustrated London News*, February 8, 1930.

11. Dube, *UShembe*, i. The terminology used to describe different groups of people in South Africa is contested and complicated. This source uses "Black" to refer to people often categorized as "Africans." In general, I use "Black," by contrast, in the Black Consciousness sense: to refer to groups including African, Indian, and/or so-called Coloured people.

12. Many media and scholarly sources suggest more than four million church members. See, for example, Simangaliso Kumalo and Martin Mujinga, "'Now We Know That the Enemy Is from within': Shembeites and the Struggle for Control of Isaiah Shembe's Legacy and the Church," *Journal for the Study of Religion* 30, no. 2 (2017): 122–53. The last census data is from 1996 and 2001. The 2001 census counted the church at just over 200,000 members, a decrease of more than 50 percent from 1996. (It is difficult to know how to account for this drop, and it may be an error.) Statistics South Africa, "Census 2001: 1996 and 2001 Compared" (Pretoria: Statistics South Africa, 2004), 25–27. I met church members from Eswatini, Zimbabwe, and Mozambique in visits from 2007 to 2016.

13. Magnus Echtler, "Shembe Is the Way: The Nazareth Baptist Church in the Religious Field and in Academic Discourse," in *Bourdieu in Africa: Exploring the Dyanmics of Religious Fields* (Leiden, NL: Brill, 2016), 236–66; Andile Sithole, "Faith-Based Series 'Umkhokha'

an Insult to Shembe Church, Say Members," *Witness* (blog), October 11, 2021.

14. Thami Magubane, "Ramaphosa Asks Shembe Church to Pray for ANC," May 2, 2017, https://www.iol.co.za/capetimes/news/ramaphosa-asks-shembe-church-to-pray-for-anc-8927650.

15. Roberts, "Shembe." She was part of a cohort of such women. See also Eileen Jensen Krige, *The Social System of the Zulus* (Pietermaritzburg, ZA: Shuter and Shooter, 1936); Monica Hunter, *Reaction to Conquest: Effects of Contact with Europeans on the Pondo of South Africa* (London: David Philip, 1979).

16. Absolom Mthethwa Vilakazi, Bongani Mthethwa, and Mthembeni Mpanza, *Shembe: The Revitalization of African Society* (Johannesburg: Skotaville, 1986), 30; Carol Ann Muller, *Rituals of Fertility and the Sacrifice of Desire: Nazarite Women's Performance in South Africa*, (University of Chicago Press, 1999), 19.

17. For monographs in this vein, see Elizabeth Gunner, *The Man of Heaven and the Beautiful Ones of God = Umuntu Wasezulwini Nabantu Abahle Bakankulunkulu: Writings from Ibandla LamaNazaretha, a South African Church* (Leiden, NL: Brill, 2002); Joel Cabrita, *Text and Authority in the South African Nazaretha Church* (New York: Cambridge University Press, 2014); Nkosinathi Sithole, *The Nazaretha Church in South Africa: Isaiah Shembe's Hymns and the Sacred Dance in IBandla LamaNazaretha* (Leiden, NL: Brill, 2016). For additional monographs important for the study of the Nazaretha, see also Bengt Sundkler, *Bantu Prophets in South Africa*, 2nd ed. (New York: Oxford University Press, 1961); Bengt Sundkler, *Zulu Zion and Some Swazi Zionists* (New York: Oxford University Press, 1976); Gerhardus C. Oosthuizen, *The Healer-Prophet in Afro-Christian Churches* (New York: Brill, 1992); Andreas Heuser, *Shembe, Gandhi, und die Soldaten Gottes: Wurzeln der Gewaltfreiheit in Südafrika* (New York: Waxmann, 2003); Joel E. Tishken, *Isaiah Shembe's Prophetic Uhlanga: The Worldview of the Nazareth Baptist Church in Colonial South Africa* (New York: Peter Lang, 2013).

18. David Chidester, *Religions of South Africa* (New York: Routledge, 1992); Norman Etherington, "Recent Trends in the Historiography of Christianity in Southern Africa," *Journal of Southern African Studies* 22, no. 2 (1996): 201–19; Daniel R. Magaziner, *The Law and the Prophets: Black Consciousness in South Africa, 1968–1977*, (Athens: Ohio University Press, 2010); Natasha Erlank, *Convening Black Intimacy: Christianity, Gender, and Tradition in Early Twentieth-Century South Africa* (Athens: Ohio University Press, 2022).

19. Helen Bradford, *A Taste of Freedom: The ICU in Rural South Africa, 1924–1930* (New Haven, CT: Yale University Press, 1987); Peter Limb, *The ANC's Early Years: Nation, Class and Place in South Africa before 1940* (Pretoria: Unisa Press, 2010); Robert Trent Vinson, *The*

Americans Are Coming!: Dreams of African American Liberation in Segregationist South Africa (Athens: Ohio University Press, 2012).

20. Robert R. Edgar and Luyanda kaMsumza, eds., *Freedom in Our Lifetime: The Collected Writings of Anton Muziwakhe Lembede* (Athens: Ohio University Press, 1996); Amanda Alexander and Andile Mngxitama, eds., *Biko Lives!: Contesting the Legacies of Steve Biko* (New York: Palgrave Macmillan, 2008); Robert Trent Vinson, *Albert Luthuli* (Athens: Ohio University Press, 2018); Henry Dee, "'I Am a Bad Native': Masculinity and Marriage in the Biographies of Clements Kadalie," *African Studies* 78, no. 2 (2019): 183–204; Tom Lodge, *Mandela: A Critical Life* (New York: Oxford University Press, 2007); Thami ka Plaatjie, *Sobukwe: The Making of a Pan Africanist Leader*, vol. 1 (Sandton, ZA: KMM Review, 2019).

21. Emsie Ferreira, "Public Protector Has Completed Ramaphosa's Phala Phala Inquiry," *Mail & Guardian*, January 24, 2023, https://mg.co.za/politics/2023-01-24-public-protector-has-completed-ramaphosas-phala-phala-inquiry/.

22. Jacob Dlamini, "Life Choices and South African Biography," *Kronos* 41, no. 1 (November 2015): 339–46; Lisa A. Lindsay, "Biography in African History," *History in Africa* 44, no. 1 (2017): 11–26; Heather Hughes, "African Biography and Historiography," in *Oxford Research Encyclopedia of African History*, ed. Thomas Spear (New York: Oxford University Press, 2018); Klaas van Walraven, ed., *The Individual in African History: The Importance of Biography in African Historical Studies* (Boston: Brill, 2020).

23. Jacob Dlamini, *Askari: A Story of Collaboration and Betrayal in the Anti-Apartheid Struggle* (Auckland Park, ZA: Jacana, 2014), 16.

24. This was perhaps especially true of the "life history" genre. See Belinda Bozzoli and Mmantho Nkotsoe, *Women of Phokeng: Consciousness, Life Strategy, and Migrancy in South Africa, 1900–1983* (Portsmouth, NH: Heinemann, 1991).

25. Charles van Onselen, *The Seed Is Mine: The Life of Kas Maine, a South African Sharecropper, 1894–1985* (New York: Hill and Wang, 1996); Dlamini, *Askari*; Richard L. Roberts, *Conflicts of Colonialism: The Rule of Law, French Soudan, and Faama Mademba Sèye* (Cambridge, UK: Cambridge University Press, 2022).

26. Colony of Natal, *Evidence Taken before the Natal Native Commission, 1881* (Pietermaritzburg, ZA, 1882), 138.

27. G. C. Oosthuizen, "Isaiah Shembe and the Zulu World View," *The Healer-Prophet in Afro-Christian Churches* (New York: Brill, 1992). Vilakazi also references unified Zulu and African identities. Vilakazi, *Shembe*, 1, 9.

28. Marshall D. Sahlins, "Poor Man, Rich Man, Big-Man, Chief: Political Types in Melanesia and Polynesia," *Comparative Studies in Society and History* 5, no. 3 (1963): 290.

29. Max Weber, *Economy and Society: A New Translation*, ed. and trans. Keith Tribe

(Cambridge, MA: Harvard University Press, 2019), 374.

30. Max Weber, *The Theory of Social and Economic Organization*, ed. Talcott Parsons, trans. A. M. Henderson (New York: Oxford University Press, 1947).

31. Sahlins, "Poor Man, Rich Man," 294.

32. See, for example, David A. Bell, *Men on Horseback: The Power of Charisma in the Age of Revolution* (New York: Farrar, Straus, and Giroux, 2020).

33. Igor Kopytoff and Suzanne Miers, "African 'Slavery' as an Institution of Marginality," in *Slavery in Africa: Historical and Anthropological Perspectives*, ed. Igor Kopytoff and Suzanne Miers (Madison: University of Wisconsin Press, 1977), 14–16.

34. As one example of this use, Mimmi Söderberg Kovacs and Jesper Bjarnesen, *Violence in African Elections: Between Democracy and Big Man Politics* (London: Bloomsbury Academic and Professional, 2018). For examples of how historians of Africa have used the term—albeit in different ways than Sahlins—see, Jan M. Vansina, *Paths in the Rainforests: Toward a History of Political Tradition in Equatorial Africa* (Madison: University of Wisconsin Press, 1990), 73–4; Felicitas Becker, "Traders, 'Big Men' and Prophets: Political Continuity and Crisis in the Maji Maji Rebellion in Southeastern Tanzania," *Journal of African History* 45, no. 1 (March 2004): 1–22.

35. Barry Driscoll, "Big Man or Boogey Man? The Concept of the Big Man in Political Science," *Journal of Modern African Studies* 58, no. 4 (December 2020): 521–50.

36. Kathryn M. De Luna, "Hunting Reputations: Talent, Individuals, and Community in Precolonial South Central Africa," *Journal of African History* 53, no. 3 (November 2012): 282.

37. Shembe was likely born in the late 1860s. Shembe noted that in 1873, he was three or four years old. Papini, "Carl Faye's Transcript," 261. On this transformation, see William Beinart, *The Political Economy of Pondoland, 1860–1930* (New York: Cambridge University Press, 1982); Peter Delius, *The Land Belongs to Us: The Pedi Polity, the Boers, and the British in the Nineteenth-Century Transvaal* (Berkeley: University of California Press, 1984); Richard Rathbone and Shula Marks, eds., *Industrialisation and Social Change in South Africa: African Class Formation, Culture, and Consciousness, 1870–1930* (New York: Longman, 1982).

38. Dan O'Meara, *Volkskapitalisme: Class, Capital, and Ideology in the Development of Afrikaner Nationalism, 1934–1948* (New York: Cambridge University Press, 1983); Charles Bloomberg, *Christian Nationalism and the Rise of the Afrikaner Broederbond in South Africa, 1918–48* (Bloomington: Indiana University Press, 1989); Patrick J. Furlong, *Between Crown and Swastika: The Impact of the Radical Right on the Afrikaner Nationalist Movement in the Fascist Era* (Middletown, CT: Wesleyan University Press, 1991).

39. William Beinart and Saul DuBow, *Segregation and Apartheid in Twentieth-Century South Africa* (New York: Routledge, 1995); Bill Freund, "South Africa: The Union Years, 1910–1948—Political and Economic Foundations," in *The Cambridge History of South Africa: Volume 2, 1885–1994*, ed. Robert Ross, Anne Kelk Mager, and Bill Nasson (New York: Cambridge University Press, 2011), 211–53.

40. See Marks and Rathbone, *Industrialisation and Social Change*; Beinart, *Political Economy*; William Beinart and Colin Bundy, eds., *Hidden Struggles in Rural South Africa: Politics and Popular Movements in the Transkei and Eastern Cape, 1890–1930* (Berkeley: University of California Press, 1987).

41. Shula Marks, "Class, Culture, and Consciousness in South Africa, 1880–1899," in *The Cambridge History of South Africa*, ed. Robert Ross, Anne Kelk Mager, and Bill Nasson (New York: Cambridge University Press, 2011), 130.

42. Marc Epprecht, *"This Matter of Women Is Getting Very Bad": Gender, Development, and Politics in Colonial Lesotho* (Pietermaritzburg, ZA: University of Natal Press, 2000).

43. Union of South Africa, *Census of the Union of South Africa* (Pretoria: Government Printing and Stationary Office, 1911), clxxxv; Anthony J. Christopher, "A South African Domesday Book: The First Union Census of 1911," *South African Geographical Journal* 92, no. 1 (June 1, 2010): 22–34.

44. Bozzoli and Nkotsoe, *Women of Phokeng: Consciousness, Life Strategy*; Cherryl Walker, "Gender and the Development of the Migrant Labour System, c. 1850–1930," in *Women and Gender in Southern Africa to 1945*, ed. Cherryl Walker (Cape Town: David Philip, 1990), 168–96.

45. Walker, "Gender and Development."

46. G. H. Pirie, "Slaughter by Steam: Railway Subjugation of Ox-Wagon Transport in the Eastern Cape and Transkei, 1886–1910," *International Journal of African Historical Studies* 26, no. 2 (1993): 319–43.

47. Charles H. Feinstein, *An Economic History of South Africa: Conquest, Discrimination, and Development* (Cambridge, UK: Cambridge University Press, 2005), 107–8.

48. Statistics and Census Bureau, *Union Statistics for Fifty Years* (Pretoria: Bureau of Census and Statistics, 1960), o17–8; South Africa and Office of Census and Statistics, *Sixth Census of the Population of the Union of South Africa, Enumerated 5th May, 1936* (Pretoria: Printed by the government printer, 1938).

49. Statistics and Census Bureau, *Union Statistics*, o18.

50. Freund, "South Africa"; Beinart and Dubow, *From Segregation to Apartheid*.

51. On some of them—and efforts to govern more effectively—see Keith Breckenridge, *Biometric State: The Global Politics of Identification and Surveillance in South Africa, 1850*

to the Present (New York: Cambridge University Press, 2014). See also, Martin Chanock, *The Making of South African Legal Culture, 1902–1936: Fear, Favour, and Prejudice* (New York: Cambridge University Press, 2001).

52. Papini, "Carl Faye's Transcript," 263.

53. Joseph Ngcobo, letter to the editor, *iLanga lase Natal*, February 12, 1915.

54. Sundkler, *Bantu Prophets*, 98–99.

55. We might compare this to scholarship on individuals in the Black Atlantic and the African Diaspora. This scholarship has traced mobile lives of reinvention. On this, see Lisa A. Lindsay, "Biography in African History," *History in Africa* 44, no. 1 (2017): 17.

56. Henry Callaway, *The Religious System of the Amazulu: With a Translation into English and Notes* (London, 1868), 288, 311.

57. For an early example in Natal, see Linah Mntungwa and Dainah Shembe, "28. Early Healings of Shembe," in *SIS* 1, 57–9.

58. On their history: A. Manson, "A People in Transition: The Hlubi in Natal 1848–1877," *Journal of Natal and Zulu History* 2, no. 1 (January 1979): 13–26; John Wright and Andrew Manson, *The Hlubi Chiefdom in Zululand-Natal History* (Ladysmith, BC: Ladysmith Historical Society, 1983).

59. For one example of how Shembe drew upon stories of wandering prophets, see Joseph Ngcobo, letter to the editor, *iLanga lase Natal*, February 12, 1915. And for the broader salience of journeys and spiritual progress, see Isabel Hofmeyr, *The Portable Bunyan: A Transnational History of* The Pilgrim's Progress (Princeton, NJ: Princeton University Press, 2018).

60. For his own telling of this story, see Papini, "Carl Faye's Transcript."

61. G. A. Park Ross to Secretary of Public Health, June 13, 1931, 41/214, 1431, Papers of the Native Affairs Department (henceforth NTS), SAB.

62. Jacques Kornberg, *Theodor Herzl: From Assimilation to Zionism* (Bloomington: Indiana University Press, 1993); Mark H. Gelber and Vivian Liska, eds., *Theodor Herzl: From Europe to Zion* (Tübingen: Max Niemeyer, 2007); Marilyn M. Thomas-Houston, *"Stony the Road" to Change: Black Mississippians and the Culture of Social Relations* (New York: Cambridge University Press, 2005); Marti Corn, *The Ground on Which I Stand: Tamina, a Freedmen's Town* (College Station: Texas A&M University Press, 2020).

63. The clearest evidence for this date comes from: Mbonambi, letter to the editor.

64. One way to track the decline for these young men was through the diminished significance of "exemption from Native Law." Shula Marks, *The Ambiguities of Dependence in South Africa: Class, Nationalism, and the State in Twentieth-Century Natal* (Baltimore: Johns Hopkins University Press, 1986), 49–51.

65. Jean Comaroff and John Comaroff, *Of Revelation and Revolution, Vol. 1* (Chicago: University of Chicago Press, 1991); Norman Etherington, "Outward and Visible Signs of Conversion in Nineteenth-Century Kwazulu-Natal," *Journal of Religion in Africa* 32, no. 4 (2002): 422–39; T. J. Tallie, "Sartorial Settlement: The Mission Field and Transformation in Colonial Natal, 1850–1897," *Journal of World History* 27, no. 3 (2016): 389–410. One way to chart these changes comes from the vocabulary surrounding Christianity. For example, isiZulu vocabulary blurred preachers and teachers and identified African Christians and non-Christians as "clothed" and "unclothed."

66. See also Muller, *Rituals of Fertility*; Nkosinathi Sithole, "The Sacrifice of Flesh and Blood: Male Circumcision in Ibandla LamaNazaretha as a Biblical and African Ritual," *Journal of the Study of Religion* 25, no. 1 (2012): 15–30.

67. One can see evidence of this in analyses of homestead dynamics. John Lambert, *Betrayed Trust: Africans and the State in Colonial Natal* (Scottsville, ZA: University of Natal, 1995); Benedict Carton, *Blood from Your Children: The Colonial Origins of Generational Conflict in South Africa* (Charlottesville: University Press of Virginia, 2000); Benedict Carton, "The Wages of Migrancy: Homestead Dynamics, Income Earning, and Colonial Law in Zululand, South Africa," *African Studies* 73, no. 3 (2014): 365–86.

68. Lambert, *Betrayal of Trust*.

69. See examples of imagery in Gunner, *Man of Heaven*.

70. For an early description, see Letter from Deputy Commissioner, Natal Police to Secretary of Native Affairs, 20 September 1921, 24/241, NTS 1431, vol. 1, SAB.

71. Heather D. Curtis, "Houses of Healing: Sacred Space, Spiritual Practice, and the Transformation of Female Suffering in the Faith Cure Movement, 1870–90," *Church History* 75, no. 3 (2006): 598–611. Many people who used these spaces compared them to hospitals—as did the public health officials who tried to shut them down. Joel Cabrita, *The People's Zion: Southern Africa, the United States, and a Transatlantic Faith-Healing Movement* (Cambridge, MA: Belknap Press of Harvard University Press, 2018), 79–80, 223.

72. For a description of someone's experience, see Statement of the Indian Female Mannikam, 10 August 1922, NTS 1431, vol. 1, SAB.

73. Roberts, "Shembe," 80. This statement offers a different perspective too on the debates about politics in communities such as the Nazaretha. Matthew Schoffeleers, "Ritual Healing and Political Acquiescence: The Case of the Zionist Churches in Southern Africa," *Africa* 61, no. 1 (1991): 1–25.

74. For examples of more confrontational responses, see Bradford, *A Taste of Freedom*; Vinson, *The Americans Are Coming!*.

75. Roberts, "Shembe," 55.

76. Roberts, "Shembe," 39.

77. Some examples: Solomon Mdluli, "5. The Story of Alson Mlaba and Gwili Mhlongo"; Hloniphilie Mdluli, "17. Shembe Helps a Woman of the Apostolic Church," in *SIS* 2, 4–5, 17–9; Bhengu, interview by author and Constance Mkhize Dlamini, Inanda, KwaZulu-Natal, July 4, 2016; Mthembu, interview by author and Constance Mkhize Dlamini, Inanda, KwaZulu-Natal, July 6, 2016; Mgomezulu, interview by author and Constance Mkhize Dlamini, Inanda, KwaZulu-Natal, July 5, 2016.

78. The largest of these projects is the already cited Hexham and Oosthuizen, *SIS* 1 and 2. See also Irving Hexham and G. C. Oosthuizen, eds., *The Story of Isaiah Shembe, Vol. 3: The Continuing Story of the Sun and the Moon,* trans. Hans-Jürgen Becken (Lewiston, NY: Edwin Mellen Press, 2001); Isaiah Shembe and J. G. Shembe, *Shembe Hymns,* ed. Carol Ann Muller and Bongani Mthethwa (Scottsville, ZA: University of KwaZulu-Natal Press, 2010).

79. I heard accounts of Isaiah Shembe's life story too in 2010 and 2016. Mhlongo, interview by author and Constance Mkhize Dlamini, KwaDabeka, KwaZulu-Natal, May 17, 2010; Mafuleka, interview by author and Constance Mkhize Dlamini, Inanda, KwaZulu-Natal, July 4, 2016.

80. Cheikh Anta Babou, *Fighting the Greater Jihad: Amadu Bamba and the Founding of the Muridiyya of Senegal, 1853–1913* (Athens: Ohio University Press, 2007), 19. More broadly, the scholarship on Muslim brotherhoods in West Africa provides useful comparative fodder—not only for the similar chronology but also for the challenge of using miracles as sources.

81. For other uses of advertisements in South African history, see Lynn M. Thomas, *Beneath the Surface: A Transnational History of Skin Lighteners* (Durham, NC: Duke University Press, 2020); Katie Carline, "Wise Mothers and Wise Buyers: Marketing Tea and Home Improvement in 1930s South Africa," *Journal of African History* 63, no. 3 (November 2022): 291–308.

82. Sundkler, *Zulu Zion,* 21–56; Cabrita, *The People's Zion,* 55–93.

83. Zam-buk, *iLanga lase Natal,* September 20, 1907, 4; Refuge, *iLanga lase Natal,* March 16, 1906, 4.

84. Dr. Williams' Pink Pills, *iLanga lase Natal,* April 1, 1904, 3.

85. Paul, La Hausse, *Restless Identities: Signatures of Nationalism, Zulu Ethnicity, and History in the Lives of Petros Lamula (c. 1881–1948) and Lymon Maling (1889-c. 1936)* (Pietermaritzburg, ZA: University of Natal Press, 2000), 50–51.

86. As quoted in Cabrita, *The People's Zion,* 109.

87. Gunner, *Man of Heaven*, 14.

88. Liz Gunner, "New Wine in Old Bottles," trans. and ed. Liz Gunner and Mafika Gwala, *Musho!: Zulu Popular Praises* (East Lansing: Michigan State University Press, 1991); Sara Berry, *No Condition Is Permanent: The Social Dynamics of Agrarian Change in Sub-Saharan Africa* (Madison: University of Wisconsin Press, 1993).

89. In the Bible, the last account of a miraculous birth was Jesus's own.

90. Linah Mntungwa, "26. The Purchase of Ekuphakameni," in *SIS* 1.

CHAPTER 1. AN INHERITOR IN THE FREE STATE

1. Shembe said that he was "three or four years old" in 1873. Robert Papini, "Carl Faye's Transcript of Isaiah Shembe's Testimony of His Early Life and Calling," *Journal of Religion in Africa* 29, no. 3 (1999): 261. This chapter draws from many accounts of Isaiah Shembe's early life, some with conflicting stories and emphases. This chapter sticks most closely to an account relayed by Shembe at a meeting with a government official in 1929.

2. On the complexity of succession, however, see: Peter Delius, "Chiefly Succession and Democracy in South Africa: Why History Matters," *Journal of Southern African Studies* 47, no. 2 (2021): 209–27.

3. On ancestors and the importance of surviving children, see: Henry Callaway, *The Religious System of the Amazulu: With a Translation into English and Notes* (London, 1868), 225.

4. Native Economic Commission, "Native Economic Commission, Sitting at Pietermaritzburg, Minutes of Evidence" (Pretoria: Union of South Africa, 1931), 6539–40.

5. Petros Dhlomo, Khaya Ndelu, and Jeslinah Mchunu, "14. Shembe Relates How He Separated His Wives," in *The Story of Isaiah Shembe, Vol. 1: History and Traditions Centered on Ekuphakameni and Mount Nhlangakazi*, ed. Irving Hexham and G. C. Oosthuizen, trans. Hans-Jürgen Becken (Lewiston, NY: Edwin Mellen, 1996), 26 (henceforth *SIS* 1).

6. Petros Dhlomo and Khaya Ndelu, "15. Shembe's Farewell from His Family," in *SIS* 1, 26–28.

7. Heather Hughes, *First President: A Life of John Dube, Founding President of the ANC* (Auckland Park, ZA: Jacana, 2011); Brian Willan, *Sol Plaatje: A Life of Solomon Tshekisho Plaatje, 1876–1932* (Auckland Park, ZA: Jacana, 2018). Even some Christians who did not denounce polygyny could still read: Hlonipha Mokoena, *Magema Fuze: The Making of a Kholwa Intellectual* (Scottsville, ZA: University of KwaZulu-Natal, 2011).

8. See: James Campbell, *Songs of Zion: The African Methodist Episcopal Church in the United States and South Africa* (Chapel Hill: University of North Carolina Press, 1998), 224–25.

9. On Hlubi history, see: Andrew Manson, "A People in Transition: The Hlubi in Natal

1848–1877," *Journal of Natal and Zulu History* 2, no. 1 (January 1979): 13–26; John Wright and Andrew Manson, *The Hlubi Chiefdom in Zululand-Natal History* (Ladysmith, BC: Ladysmith Historical Society, 1983); John William Colenso, *Langalibalele and the Amahlubi Tribe: Being Remarks upon the Official Record of the Trials of the Chief, His Son and Induna, and Other Members of the Amahlubi Tribe* (London, 1875).

10. The quotation is from James Stuart, "Mabonsa Ka Sidhlayi," in *The James Stuart Archive of Recorded Oral Evidence Relating to the History of the Zulu and Neighboring Peoples, Volume Two*, ed. Colin de B. Webb and John Wright (Durban: Killie Campbell Africana Library, 1979), 16. On the Mfecane, see: J. D. Omer-Cooper, "Has the Mfecane a Future? A Response to the Cobbing Critique," *Journal of Southern African Studies* 19, no. 2 (June 1, 1993): 273–94; Elizabeth A. Eldredge, "Sources of Conflict in Southern Africa, c. 1800–30: The 'Mfecane' Reconsidered," *Journal of African History* 33, no. 1 (1992): 1–35; Norman Etherington, "A Tempest in a Teapot? Nineteenth-Century Contests for Land in South Africa's Caledon Valley and the Invention of the Mfecane," *Journal of African History* 45, no. 2 (July 2004): 203–19; Morgan Ndlovu, "Manufacturing Black-on-Black Violence in Africa: A Decolonial Perspective on Mfecane and Afrophobia/Xenophobia in South Africa," *International Journal of African Renaissance Studies* 12, no. 2 (July 3, 2017): 97–109. And on uses of the Mfecane later, Carolyn Hamilton, ed., *The Mfecane Aftermath: Reconstructive Debates in Southern African History* (Johannesburg: Witwatersrand University Press, 1995).

11. This regathering never included all Hlubi people, however. Some became part of Mfengu communities and other groups. Poppy Fry, "Siyamfenguza: The Creation of Fingo-Ness in South Africa's Eastern Cape, 1800–1835," *Journal of Southern African Studies* 36, no. 1 (March 1, 2010): 25–40; Jochen S. Arndt, *Divided by the Word: Colonial Encounters and the Remaking of Zulu and Xhosa Identities* (Charlottesville: University of Virginia Press, 2022), 207–9.

12. Manson, "A People in Transition," 15–16; Wright and Manson, *The Hlubi Chiefdom*; Jeff Guy, *Theophilus Shepstone and the Forging of Natal* (Scottsville, ZA: University of KwaZulu-Natal Press, 2013), 449–58. Guy suggests that amaHlubi were less desperate than they made their circumstances seem—in part because they timed their movement into Natal with their crop cycle.

13. Papini, "Carl Faye's Transcript," 263.

14. Papini, "Carl Faye's Transcript," 263.

15. On Inkosi Langalibalele's regiments, see Colenso, *Langalibalele and the Amahlubi Tribe*, 6. On regiments more broadly, see Elizabeth H. Timbs, "The Regiments: Cultural Histories of Zulu Masculinities and Gender Formation in South Africa, 1816–2018" (Ph.D.

dissertation, Michigan State University, 2019), 39–92.

16. Papini, "Carl Faye's Transcript," 261.

17. Wright and Manson, *The Hlubi Chiefdom*; Guy, *Theophilus Shepstone*. Henry Callaway recorded an interview with a man who mentioned that Africans prayed for three things: "cattle, children, and corn." Callaway, *The Religious System of the Amazulu*. Clifton Crais's work alerts us, however, to corn as an indicator of poverty instead of prosperity. Clifton Crais, *Poverty, War, and Violence in South Africa* (Cambridge, UK: Cambridge University Press, 2011).

18. See Colenso, *Langalibalele and the Amahlubi Tribe*, 7.

19. Wright and Manson, *The Hlubi*, 16–25. For other communities turning to these strategies, see Peter Delius, *The Land Belongs to Us: The Pedi Polity, the Boers, and the British in the Nineteenth-Century Transvaal*, (Berkeley: University of California Press, 1984), 62–3.

20. Colenso, *Langalibalele and Amahlubi*, 7.

21. Leonard Thompson, *A History of South Africa* (New Haven, CT: Yale University Press, 2014), 115.

22. John M. Smalberger, "The Role of the Diamond-Mining Industry in the Development of the Pass-Law System in South Africa," *International Journal of African Historical Studies* 9, no. 3 (1976): 419–34; Rob Turrell, "The 1875 Black Flag Revolt on the Kimberley Diamond Fields," *Journal of Southern African Studies* 7, no. 2 (1981): 194–235; Anneke Higgs, "The Historical Development of Diamond Mining Legislation in Griqualand West during the Period 1871 to 1880," *Fundamina* 24, no. 1 (2018): 18–56.

23. Papini, "Carl Faye's Transcript," 261.

24. Norman Herd, *The Bent Pine: The Trial of Chief Langalibalele* (Johannesburg: Ravan, 1976); N. A. Etherington, "Why Langalibalele Ran Away," *Journal of Natal and Zulu History* 1, no. 1 (January 1, 1978): 1–24.

25. Norman Etherington, Patrick Harries, and Bernard Mbenga, "From Colonial Hegemonies to Imperial Conquest, 1840–1880," in *The Cambridge History of South Africa: Volume 1, From Early Times to 1885*, ed. Bernard K. Mbenga, Carolyn Hamilton, and Robert Ross (New York: Cambridge University Press, 2009), 378–79.

26. Wright and Manson, *The Hlubi Chiefdom*, 73–74.

27. Wright and Manson, *The Hlubi Chiefdom*, 73–74.

28. Papini, "Carl Faye's Transcript," 261.

29. Etherington, Harries, and Mbenga, "From Colonial Hegemonies to Imperial Conquest"; Leonard Thompson, *Survival in Two Worlds: Moshoeshoe of Lesotho, 1786–1870* (Oxford, UK: Clarendon Press, 1975); William Beinart, *The Political Economy of Pondoland, 1860–1930* (New York: Cambridge University Press, 1982); Peter Delius, *The Land Belongs*

to Us: The Pedi Polity, the Boers, and the British in the Nineteenth-Century Transvaal, (Berkeley: University of California Press, 1984).

30. Norman Etherington, *The Great Treks: The Transformation of Southern Africa, 1815–1854* (New York: Longman, 2001).

31. Timothy Keegan, "White Settlement and Black Subjugation on the South African Highveld: The Tlokoa Heartland in the North Eastern Orange Free State, ca. 1850–1914," in *Putting a Plough to the Ground: Accumulation and Dispossession in Rural South Africa, 1850–1930,* ed. William Beinart, Peter Delius, and Stanley Trapido (Johannesburg: Ravan Press, 1986), 219. This was also a place where some Hlubi families had been going already as they ran out of land in Natal. Manson, "A People in Transition," 16–17.

32. Keegan, "White Settlement," 233–34.

33. Keegan, "White Settlement," 233–34. Evidence of this regathering comes from Shembe's life, too. See discussion of Shembe's wives following in this chapter.

34. Eric Foner, *Reconstruction: America's Unfinished Revolution, 1863–1877* (New York: Harper and Row, 1988), 406.

35. Timothy J. Keegan, *Rural Transformations in Industrializing South Africa: The Southern Highveld to 1914* (London: Macmillan, 1987), 52–53; Keegan, "White Settlement," 238–39; Colin Bundy, *The Rise and Fall of the South African Peasantry* (Berkeley: University of California Press, 1979), 200–21.

36. Keegan, "White Settlement," 231.

37. South African Native Affairs Commission, *South African Native Affairs Commission, 1903–1905: Minutes of Evidence Taken in Rhodesia, Bechuanaland Protectorate, British Bechuanaland (Cape Colony), Orange River Colony, Basutoland, Transvaal Colony, and Again in the Cape Colony,* vol. 4 (Cape Town, 1904), 357.

38. As quoted in Keegan, "White Settlement," 233.

39. Keegan, "White Settlement," 233.

40. Keegan, *Rural Transformations,* 53.

41. Keegan, *Rural Transformations,* 75.

42. Papini, "Carl Faye's Transcript," 263.

43. Charles van Onselen, "The Social and Economic Underpinning of Paternalism and Violence on the Maize Farms of the South-Western Transvaal, 1900–1950," *Journal of Historical Sociology* 5, no. 2 (1992): 134.

44. On trouble spots, Richard Roberts, *Litigants and Households: African Disputes and Colonial Courts in the French Soudan, 1895–1912* (New York: Heinemann, 2005), 7.

45. P. L. Lefebvre and Bedver B. L. Jackson, *The Statute Law of the Orange River Colony* (Bloemfontein, ZA, 1907), 617, 715–17.

46. This interpretation of Free State rural life comes from Charles van Onselen, "Race and Class in the South African Countryside: Cultural Osmosis and Social Relations in the Sharecropping Economy of the South Western Transvaal, 1900–1950," *American Historical Review* 95, no. 1 (1990): 99–123; van Onselen, "Underpinnings of Paternalism and Violence": 127–60; Charles van Onselen, *The Seed Is Mine: The Life of Kas Maine, a South African Sharecropper, 1894–1985* (New York: Hill and Wang, 1996); Irving Hexham and Karla Poewe, "The Spread of Christianity among Whites and Blacks in Transorangia," in *Christianity in South Africa: A Political, Social, and Cultural History*, ed. Richard Elphick and Rodney Davenport (New York: Oxford University Press, 1997), 121–34; Sandra Swart, "'Bushveld Magic' and 'Miracle Doctors': An Exploration of Eugène Marais and C. Louis Leipoldt's Experiences in the Waterberg, South Africa, c. 1906–1917," *Journal of African History* 45, no. 2 (2004): 237–55.

47. Papini, "Carl Faye's Transcript," 265; Dhlomo, "8. Prayer Experiences of Young Shembe," in *SIS* 1, 10–13.

48. Papini, "Carl Faye's Transcript," 267. On sex education: Catherine Burns, "Sex Lessons from the Past?," *Agenda*, no. 29 (1996): 79–91.

49. Papini, "Carl Faye's Transcript," 269; Dhlomo, "8. Prayer Experiences of Young Shembe," in *SIS* 1, 12.

50. Stuart, "Mabonsa Ka Sidhlayi," 29–30; Oskar Eduard Prozesky, "The Life, Work, and Influence of Johannes Julius August Prozesky (1840–1915), Missionary of the Berlin Mission Society in South Africa" (Pietermaritzburg, ZA: University of Natal, 1995), 94–95.

51. On this history: Karel Schoeman, *The British Presence in the Transorange, 1845–1854* (Cape Town: Human & Rousseau, 1992); Karel Schoeman, *The Wesleyan Mission in the Orange Free State, 1833–1854: As Described in Cotemporary Sources* (Cape Town: Human & Rousseau, 1991); David Chidester, Judy Tobler, and Darrel Wratten, *Christianity in South Africa: An Annotated Bibliography* (Westport, CT: Greenwood Press, 1997); David B. Coplan, "Erasing History: The Destruction of the Beersheba and Platberg African Christian Communities in the Eastern Orange Free State, 1858–1983," *South African Historical Journal* 61, no. 3 (2009): 505–20.

52. Anthony Trollope, *South Africa*, vol. 2 (Leipzig, Ger., 1878), 267.

53. Trollope, *South Africa*, 267.

54. Andre Du Toit, "No Chosen People: The Myth of the Calvinist Origins of Afrikaner Nationalism and Racial Ideology," *American Historical Review* 88, no. 4 (October 1983): 924; Irving Hexham and Karla Poewe, "The Spread of Christianity among Whites and Blacks in Transorangia," in *Christianity in South Africa: A Political, Social, and Cultural History*, ed. Richard Elphick and Rodney Davenport (New York: Oxford University Press,

1997), 121–34; Charles van Onselen, "Race and Class in the South African Countryside: Cultural Osmosis and Social Relations in the Sharecropping Economy of the South Western Transvaal, 1900–1950," *American Historical Review* 95, no. 1 (1990): 99–123.

55.   John Mackenzie, *Ten Years North of the Orange River: A Story of Everyday Life and Work Among the South African Tribes* (Edinburgh, 1871), 16.

56.   Charles Alfred Payton, *The Diamond Diggings of South Africa: A Personal and Practical Account* (London, 1872), 108.

57.   Papini, "Carl Faye's Transcript," 265.

58.   Papini, "Carl Faye's Transcript," 263.

59.   Papini, "Carl Faye's Transcript," 263. There is also a curious resemblance to the story of Lazarus, but this may be a coincidence. Luke 16:21–23.

60.   On links between favoritism and access to whites' domestic space—albeit in the mission field—see David Maxwell, "The Missionary Home as a Site for Mission: Perspectives from Belgian Congo," *Studies in Church History* 50 (2014): 428–55.

61.   Papini, "Carl Faye's Transcript," 264.

62.   "Agriculture in the Orange Free State," *Farming in South Africa*, December 1927, https:// journals.co.za/doi/pdf/10.10520/AJA00148490_2961.

63.   Du Toit, "No Chosen People," 947.

64.   Adam Kuper, "The 'House' and Zulu Political Structure in the Nineteenth Century," *Journal of African History* 34, no. 3 (1993): 477.

65.   For more on Shembe seeing this Bible, see Joel Cabrita, "Texts, Authority, and Community in the South African 'Ibandla LamaNazaretha' (Church of the Nazaretha), 1910–1976," *Journal of Religion in Africa* 40, no. 1 (2010): 64–65; Joel Cabrita, *Text and Authority in the South African Nazaretha Church* (New York, NY: Cambridge University Press, 2014), 92.

66.   Dhlomo, "8. Prayer Experiences of Young Shembe," in *SIS* 1, 12.

67.   Dhlomo, "8. Prayer Experiences of Young Shembe," in *SIS* 1, 12; Papini, "Carl Faye's Transcript," 265.

68.   Stephen Kay, *Travels and Researches in Caffraria: Describing the Character, Customs, and Moral Condition of the Tribes Inhabiting That Portion of Southern Africa* (New York, 1834), 140. William H. Worger, "Parsing God: Conversations about the Meaning of Words and Metaphors in Nineteenth-Century Southern Africa," *Journal of African History* 42, no. 3 (December 2001): 417–47.

69.   Dhlomo, "8. Prayer Experiences," in *SIS* 1, 12. For a similar story, Callaway, *The Religious System of the Amazulu*, 246.

70.   Petros Dhlomo, "6. The Stolen Belt," in *SIS* 1, 8–9. For a different interpretation of this

story, see Paul Landau, *Popular Politics in the History of South Africa, 1400–1948* (New York: Cambridge University Press, 2010). For the story of the peaches, Papini, "Carl Faye's Transcript," 267.

71. Papini, "Carl Faye's Transcript," 267.

72. Scholars have pushed toward understanding Africans' spiritual autobiographies as literature and, as a result, often involving fabrication to fit genre. See, Derek Peterson, *Ethnic Patriotism and the East African Revival: A History of Dissent, c. 1935 to 1972* (New York: Cambridge University Press, 2012), 44, 212, 291. My approach to Shembe's spiritual autobiography involves, instead, attempting to distinguish between different layers of verifiable events, possible events, and likely additions or reinterpretations, among others.

73. For a comparable example as well as African Christians who thought it was fine to eat such meat, see Robert Houle, *Making African Christianity* (Bethlehem, PA: Lehigh University Press, 2011), 26, 105–6.

74. Papini, "Carl Faye's Transcript," 263.

75. Papini, "Carl Faye's Transcript," 263.

76. And some white landlords wanted to expose tenants to Christianity. See van Onselen, "Race and Class," 114.

77. Some tenants also tried to use church to get out of work. South African Native Affairs Commission, *South African Native Affairs Commission, 1903–1905*, vol. 4, 354.

78. One might compare Shembe to someone such as the Xhosa Prophet Nxele who also learned about Christianity on a Boer farm. J. B. Peires, "Nxele, Ntsikana and the Origins of the Xhosa Religious Reaction," *Journal of African History* 20, no. 1 (1979): 56.

79. James Campbell, *Songs of Zion: The African Methodist Episcopal Church in the United States and South Africa* (Chapel Hill: University of North Carolina Press, 1998), 162.

80. Papini, "Carl Faye's Transcript," 261. Shembe said he thought his father died before an important event in 1888, meaning that Shembe would have been less than twenty. Dhlomo, "9. The Youth of Shembe," in *SIS* 1, 14.

81. Dhlomo, "11. Shembe Gets Married," in *SIS* 1, 18–9; Papini, "Carl Faye's Transcript," 269.

82. Papini, "Carl Faye's Transcript," 261.

83. Families without a married male household head could seldom secure these arrangements, although there were exceptions. Solomon T. Plaatje, *Native Life in South Africa: Before and Since the European War and the Boer Rebellion*, ed. Alan Light (Project Gutenberg, 1998) https://www.gutenberg.org/ebooks/1452.

84. Papini, "Carl Faye's Transcript," 269; Petros Dhlomo, Khaya S. Ndelu, and Jeslinah Mchunu, "15. Shembe's Farewell from His Family," in *SIS* 1, 26–28.

85. Campbell, *Songs of Zion*, 166–68.

86. Peter Warwick, *Black People and the South African War, 1899–1902* (New York: Cambridge University Press, 1983), 145.

87. Warwick, *Black People and the South African War*, 158–59.

88. Tim Keegan, "The Restructuring of Agrarian Class Relations in a Colonial Economy: The Orange River Colony, 1902–1910," *Journal of Southern African Studies* 5, no. 2 (1979): 234–54.

89. Papini, "Carl Faye's Transcript," 275, 281–83; Dhlomo, "11. Shembe Gets Married," in *SIS* 1.

90. Union of South Africa, *Census of the Union of South Africa* (Pretoria: Government Printing and Stationary Office, 1911), 359.

91. Papini, "Carl Faye's Transcript."

92. Dhlomo, "11. Shembe Gets Married," in *SIS* 1, 17.

93. Manson and Wright, *The Hlubi Chiefdom*, 80–81.

94. Other chiefdoms had outposts across the border with the Free State as well. See Keegan, *Rural Transformations*, 52.

95. Papini, "Carl Faye's Transcript," 276, 279; Dhlomo, Ndelu, and Mchunu, "14. Shembe Relates," in *SIS* 1, 25.

96. Papini, "Carl Faye's Transcript," 261.

97. Dhlomo, "9. The Youth of Shembe," in *SIS* 1, 13.

98. Native Economic Commission, *Report of the Native Economic Commission* (Pretoria: Government Printer, 1932), 6542.

99. Keegan, *Rural Transformations*, 53.

100. Papini, "Carl Faye's Transcript," 281–83.

101. Papini, "Carl Faye's Transcript," 283.

102. M. Rodwan Abouharb and Anessa L. Kimball, "A New Dataset on Infant Mortality Rates, 1816–2002," *Journal of Peace Research* 44, no. 6 (2007): 743–54; Clifton Crais, *Poverty, War, and Violence in South Africa* (Cambridge, UK: Cambridge University Press, 2011), 94.

103. Vincent J. Cirillo, "'Winged Sponges': Houseflies as Carriers of Typhoid Fever in 19th- and Early 20th-Century Military Camps," *Perspectives in Biology and Medicine* 49, no. 1 (2006): 52–63; Aatekah Owais, Shazia Sultana, Umber Zaman, Arjumand Rizvi, and Anita K. M. Zaidi, "Incidence of Typhoid Bacteremia in Infants and Young Children in Southern Coastal Pakistan," *Pediatric Infectious Disease Journal* 29, no. 11 (November 2010): 1035–39.

104. Petros Dhlomo and Khaya Ndelu, "15. Shembe's Farewell from His Family," in *SIS* 1, 26–28.

105. For a detailed description: Callaway, *The Religious System of the Amazulu*, 348–57.

106. Dhlomo and Ndelu, "14. Shembe Relates," 23.

107. Papini, "Carl Faye Transcript," in *SIS* 1, 269.

108. Dhlomo, "11. Shembe Gets Married," in *SIS* 1, 16.

109. Papini, "Carl Faye's Transcript," 273; Dhlomo, "12. Shembe's Dream on the Mountain," in *SIS* 1, 16.

110. Petros Dhlomo, "13. Lighting Experiences," in *SIS* 1, 19–21.

111. Dhlomo and Ndelu, "14. Shembe Relates," in *SIS* 1, 24–25.

112. Cabrita makes this point, too, although in a different way and emphasizing the role of people affiliated with the Christian Catholic Apostolic Church in Zion. See Cabrita, *Text and Authority*, 99.

113. As quoted in James Robinson, *Divine Healing: The Holiness-Pentecostal Transition Years, 1890–1906—Theological Transposition in the Transatlantic World* (Eugene, OR: Pickwick, 2013), 2.

114. Andrew Murray, *Divine Healing: A Series of Addresses* (New York, 1900), 42.

115. Papini, "Carl Faye's Transcript," 281.

116. J. Du Plessis, *The Life of Andrew Murray of South Africa* (New York: Marshall, 1920).

117. Houle, *Making African Christianity*, 147–9.

118. Joel Cabrita, *The People's Zion: Southern Africa, the United States, and a Transatlantic Faith-Healing Movement* (Cambridge, MA: Belknap Press of Harvard University Press, 2018).

119. Elly Wynia, *The Church of God and Saints of Christ: The Rise of Black Jews* (New York: Garland, 1994).

120. William Burton, *When God Makes a Missionary: Being the Life Story of Edgar Mahon* (London: Victory Press, 1938).

121. As quoted in Andrew Porter, "Missions and Empire, c.1873–1914," in *The Oxford History of the British Empire: Vol. 5. Historiography* (Oxford, UK: Oxford University Press, 2011), 565.

122. As quoted in Roberts Liardon, *Maria Woodworth-Etter: A Complete Collection of Her Life and Teachings* (Albany, NY: Harrison House, 2000), 35.

123. Wayne Warner, *The Woman Evangelist: The Life and Times of Charismatic Evangelist Maria Woodworth-Etter* (Metuchen, NJ: Scarecrow Press, 1986).

124. Porter, "Missions and Empire."

125. This description of the Mahons' movements is from Burton, *When God Makes a Missionary*, 13–95; Cabrita, *The People's Zion*, 137, 149.

126. Burton, *When God Makes a Missionary*, 42–43. For a less enthusiastic description of these gatherings, see Elijah, "To the Editor: Mormon and Dowie," *Harrismith Chronicle*, May 21, 1904.

127. See also Cabrita on Zionists in Johannesburg: Cabrita, *The People's Zion*, 166.

128. Burton, *When God Makes a Missionary*, 34.

129. Emma Dempcy Bryant, "Interesting Article from Pen of Elder Emma Dempcy Bryant," *Leaves of Healing*, October 8, 1904.

130. Jonathan R. Baer, "Redeemed Bodies: The Functions of Divine Healing in Incipient Pentecostalism," *Church History* 70, no. 4 (2001): 740–1.

131. Baer, "Redeemed Bodies," 735–71.

132. Shembe would say that God had taken his children because they "had not yet sinned." Dhlomo and Ndelu, "14. Shembe Relates," in *SIS* 1, 26.

133. Baer, "Redeemed Bodies," 769. Dowie would try, however, to blame his daughter's sins.

134. Dhlomo and Ndelu, "14. Shembe Relates," in *SIS* 1, 25.

135. Dhlomo and Ndelu, "14. Shembe Relates," in *SIS* 1, 25.

136. The author and African nationalist, Sol Plaatje, would poignantly describe some of them who had been evicted from their homes a few years after Shembe had left the Free State: Plaatje, *Native Life in South Africa*; Lefebvre and Jackson, *The Statute Law of the Orange River Colony*.

137. Johannes Galilee Shembe was born in 1904; Amos Shembe, in 1907. Simangaliso Kumalo and Martin Mujinga, "'Now We Know That the Enemy Is from within': Shembeites and the Struggle for Control of Isaiah Shembe's Legacy and the Church," *Journal for the Study of Religion* 30, no. 2 (2017): 137. Other connections place him in Harrismith in 1908–1909. This includes his connection to William Leshega. See Gunner, *Man of Heaven*, 18–21. See also, Letter to Assistant Magistrate Ndwedwe from Sergt. Natal Police, May 12, 1921, 917/912, 77, Papers of the Chief Native Commissioner, Natal (CNC), Pietermaritzburg Archive Repository (NAB), Pietermaritzburg, South Africa. And in Natal by 1911: S. B. Khumalo, letter to the editor, *iLanga lase Natal*, December 12, 1911.

138. "Police Report: A Native John Shembe from Harrismith Is Preaching to the Natives on the Location," May 25, 1912, 2155/1912, 77, CNC, NAB, Pietermaritzburg, South Africa. This report included a description of Shembe's certificate as a Baptist evangelist from Harrismith and dated in 1908.

139. Dhlomo, "12 Shembe's Dream," 19.

CHAPTER 2. A BAPTIST IN TOWN

1. This photograph was not available for inclusion in this book but is in Elizabeth Gunner, *The Man of Heaven and the Beautiful Ones of God = Umuntu Wasezulwini Nabantu Abahle Bakankulunkulu: Writings from Ibandla LamaNazaretha, a South African Church* (Leiden, NL: Brill, 2002), plate 1. On uses of the doctor's bag, see Aran S. MacKinnon, "Of Oxford Bags and Twirling Canes: The State, Popular Responses, and Zulu Antimalaria Assistants

in the Early-Twentieth-Century Zululand Malaria Campaigns," *Radical History Review* 2001, no. 80 (May 1, 2001): 76–100. Traditional healers also carried bags: A. T. Bryant, *Zulu Medicine and Medicine-Men* (Cape Town: C. Struik, 1966), 4.

2. For photos to compare: Santu Mofokeng, *The Black Photo Album: Look at Me, 1890–1950* (New York: Walther Collection, 2013). See too: Lorena Rizzo, *Photography and History in Colonial Southern Africa: Shades of Empire* (London: Routledge, 2019).

3. Petros Dhlomo, "17. The Baptism of Shembe on 22 July 1906," in *The Story of Isaiah Shembe, Vol. 1: History and Traditions Centered on Ekuphakameni and Mount Nhlangakazi*, ed. Irving Hexham and G. C. Oosthuizen, trans. Hans-Jürgen Becken (Lewiston, NY: Edwin Mellen, 1996), 31 (henceforth *SIS* 1); Khaya Ndelu, "17. The Baptism of Shembe on 22 July 1906," in *SIS* 1, 31–33; Johannes Galilee Shembe, "17. The Baptism of Shembe on 22 July 1906," in *SIS* 1, 33–34; Petros Dhlomo and Khaya Ndelu, "18. The Commission of Shembe," in *SIS* 1, 34–35.

4. Orange River Colony (ORC), *Census Report of the Orange River Colony* (Bloemfontein, ZA, 1904), vi, viii, ix, 10. This percentage was higher than any other slice of South Africa—other than perhaps the mission stations. Even some mission stations had, however, begun to allow residents who were not Christians.

5. Muntuwesizwe Buthelezi, "20. Shembe Comes to Natal," in *SIS* 1, 42; Bheki-Mkhize, "20. Shembe comes to Natal, in *SIS* 1, 42–43.

6. ORC, *Census Report*, 16.

7. ORC, *Census Report*, 16.

8. Kevin Wall, "The Evolution of South African Wastewater Effluent Parameters and Their Regulation: A Brief History of the Drivers, Institutions, Needs, and Challenges," *Journal of Transdisciplinary Research in Southern Africa* 14, no. 1 (2005): 1–11. The "lessons learned" about sanitation in the concentration camps prompted some of these conversations as well. Elizabeth van Heyningen, "A Tool for Modernisation? The Boer Concentration Camps of the South African War, 1900–1902," *South African Journal of Science* 106, no. 5/6 (2010), 1–10.

9. Timothy Keegan, "White Settlement and Black Subjugation on the South African Highveld: The Tlokoa Heartland in the North Eastern Orange Free State, ca. 1850–1914," in *Putting a Plough to the Ground: Accumulation and Dispossession in Rural South Africa, 1850–1930*, ed. William Beinart, Peter Delius, and Stanley Trapido (Johannesburg: Ravan Press, 1986), 218–58; Timothy Keegan, *Rural Transformations in Industrializing South Africa: The Southern Highveld to 1914* (London: Macmillan, 1987), 10.

10. Eliza Hawkins, *The Story of Harrismith, 1849–1920* (Harrismith, ZA: Harrismith Rotary Club, 1982), 110.

11. Hawkins, *The Story of Harrismith*, 104–5.

12. "Public Health," *Harrismith Chronicle*, May 7, 1904. See also, "Sewage Disposal: The Septic Tank System," *Harrismith Chronicle*, May 21, 1904; "Health of the Town: Sewage Farm," *Harrismith Chronicle*, June 25, 1904; "Sanitation," *Harrismith Chronicle*, June 25, 1904.

13. Isidore Frack, *A South African Doctor Looks Backwards and Forward* (Cape Town: Central News Agency, 1943), 39, 46.

14. Petros Dhlomo and Khaya Ndelu, "15. Shembe's Farewell from His Family," in *SIS* 1, 28.

15. Frack, *A South African Doctor*, 46.

16. Enteric fever (or typhoid) was a particular concern. "To the Editor—Harrismith Chronicle—Enteric Germs," *Harrismith Chronicle*, June 18, 1904.

17. Nazaretha sources record his name as "George Curwen," but he was "George Cowan" in the Harrismith newspaper. Dhlomo and Ndelu, "15. Shembe's Farewell," in *SIS* 1, 28; "Health of the Town: Sewage Farm," *Harrismith Chronicle*, June 25, 1904. Frack noted the bad reputations of many night-soil cart drivers, writing that they were often intoxicated. Frack, *A South African Doctor*, 46.

18. The 1904 census counted only seventeen "night soil men and night cart drivers." ORC, *Census*, 171.

19. Wages for night-soil workers were reported in "Town Sanitation: Compulsory Slop Service," *Harrismith Chronicle*, September 10, 1904; "Sanitary Contract," *Harrismith Chronicle*, October 22, 1904.

20. South African Native Affairs Commission (SANAC), *South African Native Affairs Commission, 1903–1905: Minutes of Evidence Taken In Rhodesia, Bechuanaland Protectorate, British Bechuanaland (Cape Colony), Orange River Colony, Basutoland, Transvaal Colony, and Again in the Cape Colony*, vol. 4 (Cape Town, 1904), 322.

21. "Sanitary," *Harrismith Chronicle*, October 1, 1904.

22. Joel Cabrita, *The People's Zion: Southern Africa, the United States, and a Transatlantic Faith-Healing Movement* (Cambridge, MA: Belknap Press of Harvard University Press, 2018), 30.

23. Native Economic Commission, "Native Economic Commission, Sitting at Pietermaritzburg, Minutes of Evidence" (Pretoria: Union of South Africa, 1931), 6543.

24. J. W. Craddock to district commander, July 31, 1922, 24/214, 1431, vol. 1, Native Affairs Archive (NTS), National Archives Repository (SAB); Letter from H. C. Lugg to Park Ross, 26 April 1929, 24/214, 1431, vol. 1, NTS, SAB. See too: Maynard W. Swanson, "The Sanitation Syndrome: Bubonic Plague and Urban Native Policy in the Cape Colony, 1900–1909," *Journal of African History* 18, no. 3 (1977): 387–410. For comparison: Stephanie Newell, *Histories of Dirt in West Africa: Media and Urban Life in Colonial and*

Postcolonial Lagos (Durham, NC: Duke University Press, 2020), 16–31.

25. The history of destruction makes the Orange Free State an understudied mission field. See, however, David B. Coplan, "Erasing History: The Destruction of the Beersheba and Platberg African Christian Communities in the Eastern Orange Free State, 1858–1983," *South African Historical Journal* 61, no. 3 (2009): 505–20; David Chidester, Judy Tobler, and Darrel Wratten, *Christianity in South Africa: An Annotated Bibliography* (Westport, CT: Greenwood, 1997), 174–79; Karel Schoeman, *The Wesleyan Mission in the Orange Free State, 1833–1854: As Described in Contemporary Sources* (Cape Town: Human and Rousseau, 1991); Karel Schoeman, *The British Presence in the Transorange, 1845–1854* (Cape Town: Human and Rousseau, 1992).

26. A. J. Christopher, "Roots of Urban Segregation: South Africa at Union, 1910," *Journal of Historical Geography* 14, no. 2 (April 1, 1988): 151–69.

27. E. L. Nel, "Racial Segregation in East London, 1836–1948," *South African Geographical Journal* 73, no. 2 (1991): 60–68; Alan Lester, "The Margins of Order: Strategies of Segregation on the Eastern Cape Frontier, 1806–c. 1850," *Journal of Southern African Studies* 23, no. 4 (1997): 635–53; Marc Epprecht, "The Native Village Debate in Pietermaritzburg, 1848–1925: Revisiting the 'Sanitation Syndrome,'" *Journal of African History* 58, no. 2 (July 1, 2017): 259–83.

28. Christopher, "Roots of Urban Segregation," 157, 165.

29. For some these laws, see SANAC, *South African Native Affairs Commission, 1903–1905*, vol. 4, 321–22.

30. Hawkins, *The Story of Harrismith*, 53, 63, 79–80; ORC, *Census*, xxix.

31. J. Whiteside, *History of the Wesleyan Church in South Africa* (London, 1906), 344–55; Archdeacon Balfour, "Work in the Diocese of Bloemfontein," *The Mission Field*, August 1906.

32. Some denominations tried to break these laws and got in trouble. See "Apostolic Faith Mission, 1909," 1985/2, 607, Papers of the Colonial Office of the Orange River Colony (CO), Free State Archives Repository (VAB), Bloemfontein, South Africa.

33. SANAC, *South African Native Affairs Commission, 1903–1905*, vol. 4, 323; Elijah, "The Mormons and Dowie," *Harrismith Chronicle*, May 21, 1904; "Ethiopians," *Harrismith Chronicle*, July 30, 1904.

34. Elijah, "The Mormons and Dowie," *Harrismith Chronicle*, May 21, 1904; "Ethiopians," *Harrismith Chronicle*, July 30, 1904. Hawkins, *The Story of Harrismith*, 100–101; Cabrita, *The People's Zion*; James Campbell, *Songs of Zion: The African Methodist Episcopal Church in the United States and South Africa* (Chapel Hill: University of North Carolina Press, 1998), 160–64.

35. Irving Hexham and Karla Poewe, "The Spread of Christianity among Whites and Blacks in Transorangia," in *Christianity in South Africa: A Political, Social, and Cultural History*, ed. Richard Elphick and Rodney Davenport (New York: Oxford University Press, 1997), 132; Rodney Stark and William Sims Bainbridge, *A Theory of Religion* (New Brunswick, NJ: Rutgers University Press, 1996).

36. SANAC, *South African Native Affairs Commission, 1903–1905*, vol. 4, 320–26.

37. SANAC, *South African Native Affairs Commission, 1903–1905*, vol. 4, 320–26.

38. Peter Limb, *The ANC's Early Years: Nation, Class and Place in South Africa before 1940* (Pretoria: Unisa Press, 2010), 100–103, 117–22; Brian Willan, *Sol Plaatje: A Life of Solomon Tshekisho Plaatje, 1876–1932* (Auckland Park, ZA: Jacana, 2018). Kimberley's proximity to Bloemfontein put Plaatje in contact with many of the people there and made him an important observer of them.

39. ORC, *Census*, xxiii, 99, 101, 107.

40. For forms of employment, ORC, *Census*, 154, 171.

41. Balfour, "Work in the Diocese of Bloemfontein."

42. Limb, *The ANC's Early Years*, 115–43.

43. As quoted in South Africa Native Churches Commission, *Report of Native Churches Commission* (Cape Town: Cape Times, 1925), 25.

44. Cabrita, *The People's Zion*, 130. Cabrita describes many of these leaders as "a class of progressive and self-consciously modernizing African farmers." One exception was Daniel Nkonyane. Cabrita, *The People's Zion*, 141.

45. Dhlomo and Ndelu, "14. Shembe Relates," in *SIS* 1, 26.

46. Dhlomo and Ndelu, "14. Shembe Relates," in *SIS* 1, 27.

47. Dhlomo, "16. Shembe's Ministry before His Baptism," 31; Dhlomo and Ndelu, "18. The Commission of Shembe," 34.

48. Robert Papini, "Carl Faye's Transcript of Isaiah Shembe's Testimony of His Early Life and Calling," *Journal of Religion in Africa* 29, no. 3 (1999): 281.

49. Wesleyan Methodist Church of South Africa, *Minutes of the Twenty-Sixth Annual Conference* (Cape Town, 1908), 48.

50. See photograph of wedding and building: F. J. B. Lee and E. C. Moffett, *With the Eighth Division: A Souvenir of the South African Campaign* (London, 1903), 123. The photograph was taken between 1899–1902. See, too, Whiteside, *History of the Wesleyan Church*, 351; Natasha Erlank, "The White Wedding: Affect and Economy in South Africa in the Early Twentieth Century," *African Studies Review* 57, no. 2 (2014): 29–50.

51. Some of them were affiliated with the Driefontein syndicate. Whiteside, *History of the Wesleyan Church*, 371–72.

52. SANAC, *South African Native Affairs Commission, 1903–1905*, vol. 4, 279.

53. Petros Dhlomo, "10. Shembe in the Wesleyan Church," in *SIS* 1, 16.

54. T. J. Tallie, "Sartorial Settlement: The Mission Field and Transformation in Colonial Natal, 1850–1897," *Journal of World History* 27, no. 3 (2016): 389–410.

55. Dhlomo, "16. Shembe's Ministry before His Baptism," in *SIS* 1. This had parallels in the life of Joseph Smith. Richard Lyman Bushman, *Joseph Smith: Rough Stone Rolling* (New York: Vintage, 2007).

56. SANAC, *South African Native Affairs Commission, 1903–1905*, vol. 4, 378.

57. Dhlomo, "16. Shembe's Ministry before His Baptism," in *SIS* 1.

58. For an example, Native Affairs Commission Colony of Natal, *Evidence* (Pietermaritzburg, ZA, 1907), 706, 828; Henry Callaway, *The Religious System of the Amazulu: With a Translation into English and Notes* (London, 1868), 12–3.

59. Dhlomo, "16. Shembe's Ministry before His Baptism," in *SIS* 1. A bit later, "Police Report: A Native John Shembe from Harrismith Is Preaching to the Natives on the Location," May 25, 1912, 2155/1912, 77, Papers of the Chief Native Commissioner, Natal (CNC), Pietermaritzburg Archive Repository (NAB), Pietermaritzburg, South Africa.

60. Dhlomo, "16. Shembe's Ministry before His Baptism," in *SIS* 1, 29.

61. Dhlomo, "16. Shembe's Ministry before His Baptism," in *SIS* 1, 29.

62. Dhlomo, "16. Shembe's Ministry before his Baptism," in *SIS* 1, 28–31.

63. Papini, "Carl Faye's Transcript," 277.

64. As one revivalist noted, healing required "right conditions and right asking." "The Prayer of Faith," *Leaves of Healing*, January 9, 1909, 5; Andrew Murray, *Divine Healing: A Series of Addresses* (New York, 1900).

65. For his history in his words, letter from William Leshega to Godfrey Lagden, September 20, 1902, 2058/02, 58, Papers of the Secretary of Native Affairs—Transvaal (SNA), National Archives Repository, Records of the Former Transvaal Province (TAB), Pretoria, South Africa. See, too, Gunner, *The Man of Heaven*, 18–21; Andreas Heuser, *Shembe, Gandhi, und die Soldaten Gottes: Wurzeln der Gewaltfreiheit in Südafrika* (New York: Waxmann, 2003), 154–57. On Christianity among Pedi people: Peter Delius, *The Land Belongs to Us: The Pedi Polity, the Boers, and the British in the Nineteenth-Century Transvaal* (Berkeley: University of California Press, 1984); Peter Delius, "Witches and Missionaries in Nineteenth Century Transvaal," *Journal of Southern African Studies* 27, no. 3 (2001): 429–43.

66. A. H. Bleksley and Johannesburg Gezondheids Comite (Sanitary Department), *Census, 15 July 1896: Report of Director of Census* (Johannesburg, 1896), ii.

67. Michiel Hendrik De Kock, *Selected Subjects in the Economic History of South Africa* (Cape

Town: Juta, 1924), 243–63; Charles van Onselen, *Studies in the Social and Economic History of Witwatersrand, 1886–1914* (New York: Longman, 1982).

68. Tshidiso Maloka, "The Struggle for Sunday," in *Christianity in South Africa*, ed. Richard Elphick and T. R. H. Davenport (Berkleley: University of California Press, 1997), 242–44.

69. H. J. Batts, *The Story of 100 Years, 1820–1920: Being the History of the Baptist Church in South Africa* (Cape Town: T. Maskew Miller, 1922), 100.

70. Batts, *The Story of 100 Years, 1820–1920*, 100.

71. Curtis D. Johnson, "The Protracted Meeting Myth: Awakenings, Revivals, and New York State Baptists, 1789–1850," *Journal of the Early Republic* 34, no. 3 (2014): 357.

72. Johnson, "The Protracted Meeting Myth," 371–73.

73. Chidester, Tobler, and Wratten, *Christianity in South Africa*.

74. Kevin Roy, *No Turning Back: A History of Baptist Missionary Endeavor in Southern Africa from 1820–2000* (Pinelands: South African Baptist Historical Society, 2001).

75. Compare to the American Board. James Dexter Taylor, *The American Board Mission in South Africa: A Sketch of Seventy-Five Years* (Durban, ZA: J. Singleton, 1911), 19–31.

76. Roy, *No Turning Back*, 15. This approach would not last. As the missionary wing of Baptist efforts became more organized, Baptists took greater control over African clergy—and made more demands. Albeit in the Belgian Congo, Simon Kimbangu established his own church after being expelled from the Baptist Church.

77. Batts, *The Story of 100 Years, 1820–1920*.

78. Letter from Sub-Native Commissioner to Secretary of Native Affairs, November 19, 1909, 3463/09, 448, SNA, TAB.

79. On such rumors, Esther Roberts, "Shembe: The Man and His Works" (master's thesis, University of Natal, 1936), 41.

80. On this period of legal flux: P. L. Lefebvre and Bedver B. L. Jackson, *The Statute Law of the Orange River Colony* (Bloemfontein, ZA, 1907); SANAC, *South African Native Affairs Commission, 1903–1905*, vol. 4. And to see Africans testing out possibilities: William Leshega to Secretary of Native Affairs, November 5, 1909, NA3463/09, 448, SNA, TAB.

81. William Leshega to Secretary of Native Affairs, September 26, 1902, NA2058/02, 2058, SNA, TAB.

82. Eric Michael Washington, "Heralding South Africa's Redemption: Evangelicalism and Ethiopianism in the Missionary Philosophy of the National Baptist Convention, USA, Inc. 1880–1930" (PhD dissertation, Michigan State University, 2010), https://doi.org/doi:10.25335/M5X921J8R.

83. D. E. Murff to Native Affairs Department, November 23, 1909, 3463/09, 448, SNA, TAB.

84. D. E. Murff to Godgrey Lagden, May 8, 1906, 3463/09, 448, SNA, TAB.

85. National Baptist Convention, *Journal of the Thirty-First Annual Session of the National Baptist Convention* (Nashville: National Baptist Publishing Board, 1911), 210–11. Not too far below Leshega's name was the name of the African continent's most famous Baptist before 1920: the leader of the anti-settler resistance in Nyasaland, John Chilembwe. On Chilembwe: George Shepperson and Thomas Price, *Independent African: John Chilembwe and the Origins, Setting and Significance of the Nyasaland Native Rising of 1915* (Edinburgh, UK: University Press, 1987); John McCracken, ed., *Voices from the Chilembwe Rising: Witness Testimonies Made to the Nyasaland Rising Commission of Inquiry, 1915,* (Oxford, UK: Oxford University Press, 2015).

86. Bengt Sundkler, *Bantu Prophets in South Africa*, 2nd ed. (New York: Oxford University Press, 1961), 69; Campbell, *Songs of Zion*.

87. It was not until 1909 that someone did. See Secretary of Native Affairs to Director of Native Labour Bureau, December 9, 1909, 3463/09, 448, SNA, TAB.

88. On Leshega's acquisition of such a pass, see Commandant Griffiths to Under Colonial Secretary, December 18, 1909, 2324, 619, CO, TAB. See, too, Lefebvre and Jackson, *The Statute Law of the Orange River Colony*, 138, 1270.

89. On criticisms of "buying a collar," see Cabrita, *The People's Zion*.

90. Hawkins, *The Story of Harrismith*, 92; Gordon Pirie, "Railways and Labour Migration to the Rand Mines: Constraints and Significance," *Journal of Southern African Studies* 19, no. 4 (1993): 713–30.

91. SANAC, *South African Native Affairs Commission, 1903–1905*, vol. 4, 271, 290; Dhlomo, "16. Shembe's Ministry Before His Baptism," in *SIS* 1.

92. Dhlomo, "16. Shembe's Ministry before His Baptism," in *SIS* 1.

93. Dhlomo, "16. Shembe's Ministry before His Baptism," in *SIS* 1.

94. For these efforts in the Free State, Mat. I. Fourie to Colonial Secretary, May 28, 1904, 3923/04, 292, CO, TAB.

95. An officer in Natal who encountered Shembe in 1912 wrote down the contents of Shembe's certificate from the Baptist Church of Harrismith. Sergt. Natal Police to Asst. Magistrate Ndwedwe, May 12, 1921, 206/12, 917, CNC, NAB.

96. ORC, *Census*, xxxii; Wesleyan Methodist Church, *Minutes of the Twenty-Sixth Annual Conference*, 46, 48.

97. Leshega eventually joined the Apostolic Faith Mission. Curry R. Blake, *John G. Lake's Writings from Africa* (Maitland, FL: Xulon Press, 2005), 31. This edited collection has a letter referencing a "Brother Lesheka" "with 65 local preachers and 4000 people."

98. National Baptist Convention (NBC), *Journal of the Thirty-First Annual Session of the National Baptist Convention* (Nashville: National Baptist Convention, 1911), 210–11;

National Baptist Convention, *Annual Session of the Baptist Congress, 1905* (New York: Leopold Classic Library, 2016).

99. NBC, *Annual Session*, 34.

100. Norman Etherington, "When Settlers Went to War against Christianity," in *Between Indigenous and Settler Governance*, ed. L. Ford, T. Rowse, and A. Yeatman (New York: Routledge, 2012), 83–94; Peggy Brock, Norman Etherington, Gareth Griffiths, and Jacqueline Van Gent, *Indigenous Evangelists and Questions of Authority in the British Empire, 1750–1940* (Leiden, NL: Brill, 2015), 83–94.

101. isiNtu meant "the language of the people." See Papini, "Carl Faye's Transcript," 262.

102. Petros Dhlomo, "17. The Baptism of Shembe on 22 July 1906," in *SIS* 1, 31; Petros Dhlomo and Khaya Ndelu, "18. The Commission of Shembe," in *SIS* 1, 34–35. On Shembe's certificate from the Baptist Church, see "Police Report."

103. Batts, *The Story of 100 Years, 1820–1920*; Roy, *No Turning Back*.

104. Union of South Africa, *Report of the Inter-Departmental Committee of the Native Pass Laws* (Cape Town: Government Printers, 1922), 29–30.

105. Keith Breckenridge, *Biometric State: The Global Politics of Identification and Surveillance in South Africa, 1850 to the Present* (New York: Cambridge University Press, 2014), 90–114.

106. Papini, "Carl Faye's Transcript," 283.

107. He would refer to this as "the Baptism of John" for a time. See Timothy Khuzwayo, "115. Shembe Comes to Groutville in 1913," in *SIS* 2, 120–21.

108. Elias Khawula, "43. The Name Nhlanzini was Changed to Gospel," in *SIS* 2, 41–44.

109. Another theory is that "Shembe" was a play on *isithembu*, or polygyny. See Papini, "Carl Faye's Transcript," 284.

110. Dhlomo, "16. Shembe's Ministry before His Baptism," in *SIS* 1, 29.

CHAPTER 3. AN EVANGELIST IN DURBAN

1. Petros M. Dhlomo and Linah Mntungwa, "21. Shembe's Early Ministry in the Durban Region," in *The Story of Isaiah Shembe, Vol. 1: History and Traditions Centered on Ekuphakameni and Mount Nhlangakazi*, ed. Irving Hexham and G. C. Oosthuizen, trans. Hans-Jürgen Becken (Lewiston, NY: Edwin Mellen, 1996), 43–47 (henceforth *SIS* 1); Petros Dhlomo, "23. Shembe's Second Mission Journey in the Durban Region," in *SIS* 1, 48–51; Petros Dhlomo, Johannes Duma, and Daniel Dube, "38. Shembe's Call to Mount Nhlangakazi," in *SIS* 1, 76–77; Esther Roberts, "Shembe: The Man and His Works" (master's thesis, University of Natal, 1936), 29.

2. J. F. Gairns, "The Railways of Natal," *Cassier's Magazine*, December 1904, 93; Charles

William Francis Harrison and Joseph Forsyth Ingram, *Natal: An Illustrated Official Railway Guide and Handbook of General Information* (London, 1903), 160–61.

3. The edges of the Rand, in particular, offered space for creative community-building. Charles van Onselen, "'The Regiment of the Hills': South Africa's Lumpenproletarian Army, 1890–1920," *Past & Present*, no. 80 (1978): 91–121.

4. Norman Etherington, "When Settlers Went to War against Christianity," in *Between Indigenous and Settler Governance*, ed. L. Ford, T. Rowse, and A. Yeatman (New York: Routledge, 2012), 83–94.

5. Bengt Sundkler, *Bantu Prophets in South Africa*, 2nd ed. (New York: Oxford University Press, 1961), 69–70. The African Methodist Episcopal Church barely ventured into Natal. James Campbell, *Songs of Zion: The African Methodist Episcopal Church in the United States and South Africa* (Chapel Hill: University of North Carolina Press, 1998), 224.

6. Paul La Hausse, "The Struggle for the City: Alcohol, The Ematsheni, and Popular Culture in Durban, 1902–1936" (master's thesis, University of Cape Town, 1984), 27–28. This is based on 8000 arrests per year with a population of 20,000 African men. La Hausse suggests that this was "perhaps proportionately more than anywhere else in the world."

7. Vanessa Künnemann and Ruth Mayer, *Chinatowns in a Transnational World: Myths and Realities of an Urban Phenomenon* (New York: Routledge, 2011); Simone Cinotto, *Making Italian America: Consumer Culture and the Production of Ethnic Identities* (New York: Fordham University Press, 2014); Susan Hautaniemi Leonard, Christopher Robinson, and Douglas Anderton, "Immigration, Occupation, and Inequality in Emergent Nineteenth-Century New England Cities," *Social Science History* 41, no. 4 (2014): 645–71; Brian Purnell, Jeanne Theoharis, and Komozi Woodward, *The Strange Careers of the Jim Crow North: Segregation and Struggle Outside of the South* (New York: New York University Press, 2019). La Hausse, "Struggle for the City," 75; A. J. Christopher, "Roots of Urban Segregation: South Africa at Union, 1910," *Journal of Historical Geography* 14, no. 2 (April 1, 1988): 153, 155, 160–61; Marc Epprecht, "The Native Village Debate in Pietermaritzburg, 1848–1925: Revisiting the 'Sanitation Syndrome,'" *Journal of African History* 58, no. 2 (July 1, 2017): 273.

8. La Hausse, "Struggle for the City," 35–37; M. W. Swanson, "'The Durban System': Roots of Urban Apartheid in Colonial Natal," *African Studies* 35, no. 3–4 (1976): 159–76. On segregation, incrimination, and colonial cities, see, too, Susan Pedersen and Caroline Elkins, *Settler Colonialism in the Twentieth Century: Projects, Practices, Legacies* (New York : Routledge, 2005); Carl Nightingale, *Segregation: A Global History of Divided Cities* (University of Chicago Press, 2012); Robert Home, *Of Planting and Planning: The Making of British Colonial Cities* (New York: Routledge, 2013); Toyin Falola, *The African Metropolis:*

Struggles over Urban Space, Citizenship, and Rights to the City (London: Taylor and Francis, 2017); Anders Ese and Kristin Ese, *The City Makers of Nairobi: An African Urban History* (New York : Routledge, 2020).

9. On this return: Dhlomo and Mntungwa, "21. Shembe's Early Ministry," in *SIS* 1.

10. House of Commons Parliamentary Papers, *Natal: Correspondence Relative to the Establishment of the Settlement of Natal* (London, 1848), 139, https://parlipapers.proquest.com/parlipapers/docview/t70.d75.1847-025182?accountid=12598.

11. Jeff Guy, *Theophilus Shepstone and the Forging of Natal* (Scottsville, ZA: University of KwaZulu-Natal Press, 2013), 241.

12. Natal Native Commission, *Evidence Taken before the Natal Native Commission, 1881* (Pietermaritzburg, ZA, 1882), 49.

13. Norman Etherington, "African Economic Experiments in Colonial Natal, 1845–1880," *African Economic History* 5, no. 5 (1978): 4–5; Paul La Hausse, *Restless Identities: Signatures of Nationalism, Zulu Ethnicity, and History in the Lives of Petros Lamula (c. 1881–1948) and Lymon Maling (1889–c. 1936)* (Pietermaritzburg, ZA: University of Natal Press, 2000), 160–62; Marc Epprecht, *Welcome to Greater Edendale: Histories of Environment, Health, and Gender in an African City* (Montreal: McGill–Queen's University Press, 2016), 14.

14. Harvey Feinberg, *Our Land, Our Life, Our Future: Black South African Challenges to Territorial Segregation, 1913–1948* (Pretoria: Unisa Press, 2015), 21.

15. Etherington, "When Settlers Went to War against Christianity," 255; Robert Houle, *Making African Christianity* (Bethlehem, PA: Lehigh University Press, 2011), 121–24.

16. Norman Etherington, "The Shepstone System in the Colony of Natal and Beyond the Borders," in *Natal and Zululand from Earliest Times to 1910*, ed. Andrew Duminy and Bill Guest (Pietermaritzburg, ZA: University of Natal Press, 1989), 170–92; Jeremy Martens, "Decentering Shepstone: The Eastern Cape Frontier and the Establishment of Native Administration in Natal, 1842–1849," *South African Historical Journal* 67, no. 2 (2015): 180–201.

17. On Shepstone: Thomas McClendon, *White Chiefs, Black Lords: Shepstone and the Colonial State in Natal, 1845–1878* (Rochester, NY: University of Rochester Press, 2010); Guy, *Theophilus Shepstone*; Thomas McClendon, "The Man Who Would Be Inkosi: Civilising Missions in Shepstone's Early Career," *Journal of Southern African Studies* 30, no. 2 (2004): 339–58; Carolyn Hamilton, *Terrific Majesty: The Powers of Shaka Zulu and the Limits of Historical Invention* (Cambridge, MA: Harvard University Press, 1998), 72–129.

18. David Welsh, *The Roots of Segregation: Native Policy in Colonial Natal, 1845–1910* (New York: Oxford University Press, 1971); Mahmood Mamdani, *Citizen and Subject:*

Contemporary Africa and the Legacy of Late Colonialism (Princeton, NJ: Princeton University Press, 1996).

19. For this number, William Henry Beaumont and Natives Land Commission, *Report of the Natives Land Commission*, vol. 1 (Cape Town: Cape Times, 1916), 5. On the supposed merits of the Shepstone system: James Stuart, *A History of the Zulu Rebellion 1906: And of Dinuzulu's Arrest, Trial, and Expatriation* (New York: Negro Universities Press, 1969), 25, https://catalog.hathitrust.org/Record/001260061.

20. As quoted in Bengt Sundkler, *Bantu Prophets*, 70.

21. The African Methodist Episcopal Church, as a result, generally steered clear. Campbell, *Songs of Zion*, 224.

22. Robert Houle, *Making African Christianity* (Bethlehem, PA: Lehigh University Press, 2011), 121–22.

23. Etherington, "When Settlers Went to War against Christianity," 83–94; Peggy Brock, Norman Etherington, Gareth Griffiths, and Jacqueline Van Gent, *Indigenous Evangelists and Questions of Authority in the British Empire, 1750–1940* (Leiden, NL: Brill, 2015), 247–58.

24. H. J. Batts, *The Story of 100 Years, 1820–1920: Being the History of the Baptist Church in South Africa* (Cape Town: T. Maskew Miller, 1922), 62–76.

25. See, for example, National Baptist Convention, *Twenty-Fifth Annual Session of the National Baptist Convention* (Nashville, 1906), 39–40; Benjamin W. Arnett, *The Budget of 1904* (Philadelphia, 1903), 297.

26. This estimate is from the 1911 census. Union of South Africa, *Census of the Union of South Africa* (Pretoria: Government Printing and Stationary Office, 1911), 918. The 1904 census of Natal/Zululand did not collect data on Africans' religion.

27. Maynard W. Swanson, "Urban Origins of Separate Development," *Race* 10, no. 1 (1968): 31–40; Paul La Hausse, *Restless Identities: Signatures of Nationalism, Zulu Ethnicity, and History in the Lives of Petros Lamula (c. 1881–1948) and Lymon Maling (1889–c. 1936)* (Pietermaritzburg, ZA: University of Natal Press, 2000), 47.

28. Union of South Africa, *Report of the Inter-Departmental Committee of the Native Pass Laws* (Cape Town: Government Printers, 1922), 29–30.

29. South Africa Native Affairs Commission, "Appendix A," in *South African Native Affairs Commission, 1903–1905: Report of the Commission with Annexures of Evidence and Appendices* (Cape Town, 1905), A.11–41.

30. One official estimated that African men gave the wrong name in "two-thirds of the passes issued throughout the Colony." Natal Native Affairs Commission, *Evidence: Colony of Natal, Native Affairs Commission* (Pietermaritzburg, ZA, 1907), 250.

31. Union, *Report of the Inter-Departmental Committee*, 29.

32. Undersecretary for Native Affairs to Magistrate Durban, July 15 1902, 1616/1902, I/1/296, Papers of the Secretary of Native Affairs (SNA), Pietermaritzburg Archives Repository (NAB).

33. Secretary of Native Affairs to Criminal Investigation Office, June 13, 1903; Declaration of Mguquka, April 19, 1901, 1616/1902, I/1/296, SNA, NAB.

34. J. B. Mfazwe to Magistrate Harding, April 12, 1901, 1616/1902, I/1/296, SNA, NAB.

35. Colonial Secretary to M. Fourie, July 2, 1904, 3923/04, 292, Papers of the Colonial Office (CO), Free State Archives Repository (VAB).

36. Magistrate Harding to Secretary of Native Affairs, 1901, 737/1901, I/1/291, SNA, NAB.

37. Magistrate Harding to Secretary of Native Affairs, 1901, 737/1901, I/1/291, SNA, NAB.

38. Brock, Etherington, Griffiths, and Van Gent, *Indigenous Evangelists*, 248–52.

39. National Baptist Convention, *Journal of the Thirty-First Annual Session of the National Baptist Convention* (Nashville: National Baptist Publishing Board, 1911), 210.

40. J. B. Mfazwe to Secretary of Native Affairs, July 11, 1902, 1616/1902, I/1/296, SNA, NAB.

41. Brock, Etherington, Griffiths, and Van Gent, *Indigenous Evangelists*, 253.

42. Statement of Rosie Mfazwe, June 13, 1903, 1616/1902, I/1/296, SNA, NAB.

43. For a later exploration of this idea in popular culture, see Judith A. Sebesta and Daniel Larlham, review of *Sizwe Banzi Is Dead*, by Athol Fugard, John Kani, Winston Ntshona, and Aubrey Sekhabi, *Theatre Journal* 60, no. 4 (2008): 659–61.

44. Petros Dhlomo, "22. Shembe Visits the Grave of the Prophet Mfazwe," in *SIS* 1, 47–48. Still, this detail does confirm something suspicious since Shembe would not likely have gone to Maputaland/Mozambique to visit the grave. Perhaps Mfazwe died elsewhere.

45. Mfazwe's and Solani's examples offer a reminder that writing could be dangerous. Amid the (rightful) attention to Africans' writing in much recent scholarship, it is worth remembering that sometimes they would have had reasons not to write.

46. Hein Heydenrych, "Railway Development in Natal to 1895," in *Enterprise and Exploitation in a Victorian Colony*, ed. Bill Guest and John Sellers (Pietermaritzburg, ZA: University of Natal, 1985), 47–69.

47. Keletso E. Atkins, *The Moon Is Dead! Give Us Our Money!: The Cultural Origins of an African Work Ethic, Natal, South Africa, 1843–1900* (Portsmouth, NH: Heinemann, 1993); Ralph Callebert, *On Durban's Docks: Zulu Workers, Rural Households, and Global Labor* (Rochester, NY: University of Rochester Press, 2017); David Hemson, "Class Consciousness and Migrant Workers" (PhD dissertation, University of Warwick, 1979); Paul La Hausse, "The Struggle for the City: Alcohol, The Ematsheni, and Popular Culture in Durban, 1902–1936" (master's thesis, University of Cape Town, 1984).

48. La Hausse, "Struggle for the City," 23–24.

49. Maynard W. Swanson, "'The Asiatic Menace': Creating Segregation in Durban, 1870–1900," *The International Journal of African Historical Studies* 16, no. 3 (1983): 401; Goolam Vahed, "Control and Repression: The Plight of Indian Hawkers and Flower Sellers in Durban, 1910–1948," *International Journal of African Studies* 32, 1 (1999): 19–48.

50. Ralph Callebert, "Livelihood Strategies of Dock Workers in Durban, c. 1900–1959" (PhD dissertation, Queen's University, 2011), 31.

51. Union of South Africa, *Census* (1911), clxxxv.

52. Union of South Africa, *Census* (1911), clxxxv.

53. La Hausse, "Struggle for the City," 46.

54. La Hausse, "Struggle for the City," 24–25, 63. Dhlomo, Buthelezi, and Mntungwa, "21. Shembe's Early Ministry in the Durban Region," in *SIS* 1, 43–44; Christopher, "The Roots of Urban Segregation," 155

55. Gordon Pirie, "Railways and Labour Migration to the Rand Mines: Constraints and Significance," *Journal of Southern African Studies* 19, no. 4 (1993): 713–30.

56. Paul La Hausse, "'The Cows of Nongoloza': Youth, Crime, and Amalaita Gangs in Durban, 1900–1936," *Journal of Southern African Studies* 16, no. 1 (1990): 86. La Hausse emphasizes the importance of generation as well as "ethnic ties."

57. Dhlomo, "22. Shembe Visits the Grave," in *SIS* 1, 47.

58. Lewis Grout, *Zulu-Land: Or, Life among the Zulu-Kafirs of Natal and Zululand* (Philadelphia, 1864); Josiah Tyler, *Forty Years among the Zulus* (Boston, 1891).

59. Houle, *Making African Christianity*, 147–49; Robert J. Houle, "From Burnt Bricks to Sanctification: Rethinking 'Church' in Colonial Southern Africa," *South African Historical Journal* 70, no. 2 (2018): 348–69.

60. Houle, *Making African Christianity*, 190–91.

61. Dhlomo, Buthelezi, and Mntungwa, "21. Shembe's Early Ministry in the Durban Region," in *SIS* 1, 47.

62. Natal Native Commission, *Evidence* (Pietermaritzburg, ZA, 1907), 38–39; as quoted in Shula Marks, *Ambiguities of Dependence* (Baltimore: Johns Hopkins University Press, 1986), 103.

63. Callebert, *On Durban's Docks*, 20–45.

64. A. J. Christopher, "Roots of Urban Segregation: South Africa at Union, 1910," *Journal of Historical Geography* 14, no. 2 (1988): 1151–69.

65. As quoted in Saul Dubow, *Racial Segregation and the Origins of Apartheid in South Africa* (New York: Palgrave Macmillan, 1989), 27.

66. SANAC, *South African Native Affairs Commission, 1903–1905*, vol. 3, *Minutes of Evidence*

Taken in Colony of Natal (Cape Town, 1904), 641.

67. Marc Epprecht, "The Native Village Debate in Pietermaritzburg, 1848–1925: Revisiting the 'Sanitation Syndrome,'" *Journal of African History* 58, no. 2 (July 1, 2017): 262.

68. M. W. Swanson, "'The Durban System': Roots of Urban Apartheid in Colonial Natal," *African Studies* 35, no. 3–4 (1976): 159–76.

69. On earlier plans for model villages, see Atkins, *The Moon is Dead! Give Us Our Money!*, 117; Epprecht, "Sanitation Syndrome." Baumannville was one of the small "model villages" for families, and it had only sixty houses. La Hausse, "Struggle for the City," 79.

70. Lamontville was the first large urban location, followed by Umlazi. Louise Torr, "Lamontville—Durban's 'Model Village': The Realities of Township Life, 1934–1960," *Journal of Natal and Zulu History* 10, no. 1 (1987): 103–17.

71. Christopher, "Roots of Urban Segregation," 166; La Hausse, "The Struggle for the City," 43.

72. Atkins, *The Moon is Dead! Give Us Our Money!*, 120–21, 124.

73. W. P. M. Henderson, *Durban: Fifty Years' Municipal History* (Durban, ZA, 1904), 116; La Hausse, "Struggle for the City," 39.

74. La Hausse, "The Cows of Nongoloza." Many scholars refer to these groups of young men as "gangs," an apt term if only because of how the city made many of their activities illegal.

75. La Hausse, *Restless Identities*, 45–48. La Hausse also mentions Petros Lamula's efforts to secure worship space by renting a building, but that was after some of the laws in Natal had become more permissive. La Hausse, *Restless Identities*, 136.

76. La Hausse, "Struggle for the City," 59.

77. Buthelezi and Bheki-Mkhize, "20. Shembe Comes to Natal," in *SIS* 1, 42–43.

78. Declaration of Mguquka, April 19, 1901, 1616/1902, I/1/296, SNA, NAB.

79. Buthelezi and Bheki-Mkhize, "20. Shembe Comes to Natal," in *SIS* 1.

80. Harrison and Ingram, *Natal*, 160–61.

81. Harrison and Ingram, *Natal*, 160–61.

82. There were Wesleyan and American Board Mission communities nearby. On the early distribution of Natal's mission stations, see Norman Etherington, *Preachers, Peasants, and Politics in Southeast Africa, 1835–1880* (London: Royal Historical Society, 1978).

83. Natal Colony (South Africa), *Statutes of Natal* (Pietermaritzburg, ZA, 1901), 16.

84. Dhlomo and Mntungwa, "21. Shembe's Early Ministry," in *SIS* 1, 46; Esther Roberts, "Shembe: The Man and His Works" (master's thesis, University of Natal, 1936), 29.

85. William Burton, *When God Makes a Missionary: Being the Life Story of Edgar Mahon* (London: Victory Press, 1938), 44.

86. Dhlomo and Mntungwa, "21. Shembe's Early Ministry," in *SIS* 1, 44–45.

87. Dhlomo and Mntungwa, "21. Shembe's Early Ministry," in *SIS* 1, 44–45.

88. On Mnqayi's literacy, see P. J. D. Mnqayi, letter to the editor, *iLanga lase Natal*, February 9, 1917.

89. For these relationships more broadly, see Joel Cabrita, *Text and Authority in the South African Nazaretha Church* (New York: Cambridge University Press, 2014), 108–47.

90. Dhlomo, Buthelezi, Duma, and Dube, "38. Shembe's Call to Nhlangakazi," in *SIS* 1, 76–77.

91. Bengt Sundkler, *Bantu Prophets in South Africa* (New York: Oxford University Press, 1961), 70–72; South Africa Office of Census and Statistics, *Official Year Book of the Union* (Pretoria: Government Printers, 1918), 438.

92. Dhlomo and Mntungwa, "21. Shembe's Early Ministry," in *SIS* 1, 45.

CHAPTER 4. A GUEST IN THE RESERVES

1. For a description of the train journey, see A. Samler Brown and G. Gordon Brown, *The Guide to South Africa: For the Use of Tourists, Sportsmen, Invalids, and Settlers* (London, 1907), 423–24.

2. For histories of these people, see Magema Fuze, *The Black People and Whence They Came*, ed. A. T. Cope and H. C. Lugg (Pietermaritzburg, ZA: University of Natal, 1979), 12–21.

3. Charles William Francis Harrison and Joseph Forsyth Ingram, *Natal: An Illustrated Official Railway Guide and Handbook of General Information* (London, 1903), 159, 162.

4. William Henry Beaumont and Natives Land Commission, *Report of the Natives Land Commission*, vol. 1 (Cape Town: Cape Times, 1916), 436, 454.

5. Ex. 19–20.

6. Mbonambi, letter to the editor, *iLanga lase Natal*, February 28, 1913.

7. For interpretations of this pilgrimage now, see Sanelisiwe Peta, "Women, Religion and Landscape: Reimagining Traditional Religious Spaces of the Shembe Church from Afrocentric Notions of the Female Body" (master's thesis, University of Johannesburg, 2021).

8. Isaiah Shembe and J. G. Shembe, *Shembe Hymns*, ed. Carol Ann Muller and Bongani Mthethwa (Scottsville, ZA: University of KwaZulu-Natal Press, 2010), 51.

9. Petros Dhlomo, Muntuwesizwe Buthelezi, Johannes Duma, Daniel Dube, and Solomon Mdluli, "38. Shembe's Call to Mount Nhlangakazi," in *The Story of Isaiah Shembe, Vol. 1: History and Traditions Centered on Ekuphakameni and Mount Nhlangakazi*, ed. Irving Hexham and G. C. Oosthuizen, trans. Hans-Jürgen Becken (Lewiston, NY: Edwin Mellen, 1996), 75–84 (henceforth *SIS* 1).

10. Dhlomo et al., "38. Shembe's Call to Mount Nhlangakazi," in *SIS* 1, 74–85.

11. In Natal specifically, see John Lambert, *Betrayed Trust: Africans and the State in Colonial Natal* (Scottsville, ZA: University of Natal, 1995). In South Africa more broadly: William Beinart and Colin Bundy, *Hidden Struggles in Rural South Africa: Politics and Popular Movements in the Transkei and Eastern Cape, 1890–1930* (Berkeley: University of California Press, 1987); Clifton Crais, *Poverty, War, and Violence in South Africa* (New York: Cambridge University Press, 2011).

12. John Lambert, "The Rise of African Indebtedness in Natal during the Late Colonial Period," *Kleio* 24, no. 1 (January 1, 1992): 19–39; Lambert, *Betrayed Trust*, 171.

13. Union of South Africa, *Census of the Union of South Africa* (Pretoria: Government Printing and Stationary Office, 1911), 53.

14. On problems with census numbers, see Anthony J. Christopher, "A South African Domesday Book: The First Union Census of 1911," *South African Geographical Journal* 92, no. 1 (June 1, 2010): 22–34.

15. In Natal and Zululand, see Benedict Carton, *Blood from Your Children: The Colonial Origins of Generational Conflict in South Africa* (Charlottesville: University Press of Virginia, 2000); Thomas McClendon, *Genders and Generations Apart: Labor Tenants and Customary Law in Segregation-Era South Africa, 1920s–1940s* (Portsmouth, NH: Heinemann, 2002); Benedict Carton, "The Wages of Migrancy: Homestead Dynamics, Income Earning, and Colonial Law in Zululand, South Africa," *African Studies* 73, no. 3 (2014): 365–86. In southern Africa: William Beinart, *The Political Economy of Pondoland, 1860–1930* (New York: Cambridge University Press, 1982); Philip Bonner, *Kings, Commoners and Concessionaires: The Evolution and Dissolution of the Nineteenth-Century Swazi State* (New York: Cambridge University Press, 1983). Peter Delius, *The Land Belongs to Us: The Pedi Polity, the Boers, and the British in the Nineteenth-Century Transvaal* (Berkeley: University of California Press, 1984); Alan H. Jeeves, *Migrant Labour in South Africa's Mining Economy: The Struggle for the Gold Mines' Labour Supply, 1890–1920* (Kingston, ON: McGill–Queen's University Press, 1985); Patrick Harries, *Work, Culture, and Identity: Migrant Laborers in Mozambique and South Africa, c. 1860–1910* (Portsmouth, NH: Heinemann, 1994); Peter Delius, Laura Phillips, and Fiona Rankin-Smith, *A Long Way Home: Migrant Worker Worlds, 1800–2014* (Johannesburg: Wits University Press, 2014); Peter Delius, "The Making and Changing of Migrant Workers' Worlds (1800–2014)," *African Studies* 73, no. 3 (September 2, 2014): 313–22.

16. Carton, *Blood from Your Children*, 7.

17. Marc Epprecht, *"This Matter of Women Is Getting Very Bad": Gender, Development, and Politics in Colonial Lesotho* (Pietermaritzburg, ZA: University of Natal Press, 2000); Dorothy Hodgson and Sheryl McCurdy, eds., *"Wicked" Women and the Reconfiguration of*

Gender in Africa (Portsmouth, NH: Heinemann, 2001); Brett Shadle, *Girl Cases: Marriage and Colonialism in Gusiiland, Kenya, 1890–1970* (Westport, CT: Praeger, 2006).

18. Native Affairs Commission Colony of Natal, *Evidence* (Pietermaritzburg, ZA, 1907), 848.

19. Native Affairs Commission Colony of Natal, *Evidence*, 848.

20. Carton, "The Wages of Migrancy"; Aran MacKinnon, "The Persistence of the Cattle Economy in Zululand, South Africa, 1900–50," *Canadian Journal of African Studies* 33, no. 1 (1999): 107.

21. Jeremy Martens, "'Almost a Public Calamity': Prostitutes, 'Nurseboys,' and Attempts to Control Venereal Diseases in Colonial Natal, 1886–1890," *South African Historical Journal* 45, no. 1 (November 2001): 27–52. For fertility scares elsewhere, see Nancy Rose Hunt, *A Nervous State: Violence, Remedies, and Reverie in Colonial Congo* (Durham, NC: Duke University Press, 2016), 13–15. On sexually transmitted infections, see Shula Marks, "Patriotism, Patriarchy, and Purity: Natal and the Politics of Zulu Ethnic Consciousness," in *The Creation of Tribalism in Southern Africa*, ed. Leroy Vail (Berkeley: University of California Press, 1989), 215–34. Marks notes rates of syphilis. See, however, Vaughan on the possibility of misdiagnosis in much of colonial Africa. Megan Vaughan, "Syphilis in Colonial East and Central Africa: The Social Construction of an Epidemic," in *Epidemics and Ideas*, ed. Terence Ranger and Paul Slack (New York: Cambridge University Press, 1996), 269–303. And on malnutrition and infant mortality, see Diana Wylie, *Starving on a Full Stomach: Hunger and the Triumph of Cultural Racism in Modern South Africa*, (Charlottesville: University Press of Virginia, 2001), 173–75.

22. Native Economic Commission, "Native Economic Commission, Sitting at Pietermaritzburg, Minutes of Evidence" (Pretoria: Union of South Africa, 1931), 6244. On such anxieties in other colonial contexts, see: Hunt, *A Nervous State*, 12–15.

23. South Africa Department of Native Affairs, *Blue Book on Native Affairs* (Cape Town: Cape Times, 1911), 23.

24. Fuze, *The Black People*, 38.

25. Virginia van der Vliet, "Growing up in Traditional Society," in *The Bantu-Speaking Peoples of Southern Africa* (Boston: K. Paul, 1974), 212–13.

26. Not all African Christians disagreed with older ways of managing infertility because they saw examples in the Bible that resembled their methods. Norman Etherington, "Education and Medicine," in *Missions and Empire*, ed. Norman Etherington (New York: Oxford University Press, 2008), 267.

27. On chiefs in and near Ndwedwe: Native Affairs Commission, *Evidence*, 832, 849; Shula Marks, *Reluctant Rebellion: The 1906–8 Disturbances in Natal* (Oxford, UK: Clarendon, 1970), 198, 225–30, 325; Jeff Guy, *The Maphumulo Uprising: War, Law, and Ritual in the*

Zulu Rebellion (Scottsville, ZA: University of KwaZulu-Natal Press, 2005), 3.

28. On how these efforts played out near Ndwedwe, see Jill E. Kelly, *To Swim with Crocodiles: Land, Violence, and Belonging in South Africa, 1800–1996* (East Lansing: Michigan State University Press, 2018), 43–58, 63–74. See also, Norman Etherington, "When Settlers Went to War against Christianity," in *Between Indigenous and Settler Governance*, ed. L. Ford, T. Rowse, and A. Yeatman (New York: Routledge, 2012), 83–94; Robert J. Houle, "From Christian Brother to Native: Claiming and Rejecting Christianity, Commerce, and Civilization in Early Twentieth-Century Natal," *Journal of the Middle East and Africa* 8, no. 1 (January 2017): 41–56.

29. Native Affairs Commission, *Evidence*, 834.

30. It had not, however, left them behind evenly, as is suggested below.

31. On these stations: Lewis Grout, *Zulu-Land: Or, Life among the Zulu-Kafirs of Natal and Zululand* (Philadelphia, 1864); Josiah Tyler, *Forty Years among the Zulus* (Boston, 1891).

32. Robert Houle, *Making African Christianity* (Bethlehem, PA: Lehigh University Press, 2011), 106, 209.

33. Norman Etherington, "African Economic Experiments in Colonial Natal, 1845–1880," *African Economic History* 5, no. 5 (1978): 2, 4. Meghan Elisabeth Healy, "'To Control Their Destiny': The Politics of Schooling in Colonial Natal, 1885–1910," *Journal of Southern African Studies* 37, no. 2 (2011): 252–53; Meghan Healy-Clancy, *A World of Their Own: A History of South African Women's Education* (Charlottesville: University of Virginia, 2014).

34. American Board of Commissioners for Foreign Missions, *The Year at Home* (Boston, 1908), 40; James Dexter Taylor, *The American Board Mission in South Africa: A Sketch of Seventy-Five Years* (Durban, ZA: J. Singleton, 1911).

35. S. B. Kumalo, letter to the editor, *iLanga lase Natal*, December 15, 1911.

36. On the early schools, see Houle, *Making African Christianity*, 16–17. And on where girls from Ndwedwe began to go instead: Healy, "'To Control Their Destiny'"; Healy-Clancy, *A World of Their Own*.

37. Guy, *Maphumulo Uprising*, 133.

38. Shula Marks, *Reluctant Rebellion*, 239–40, 230, 325.

39. James Stuart, *A History of the Zulu Rebellion 1906: And of Dinuzulu's Arrest, Trial, and Expatriation* (New York: Negro Universities Press, 1969), 420, 521, https://catalog.hathitrust.org/Record/001260061.

40. Government of Great Britain, *Natal: Further Correspondence Relating to Native Disturbances in Natal* (London, 1906), 28–33, https://catalog.hathitrust.org/Record/100887758.

41. Guy, *Maphumulo Uprising*, 113.

42. Guy, *Maphumulo Uprising*, 165–217,

43. It is possible that Shembe's first hosts had been directly involved in the Bambatha Rebellion. Shembe worshipped at the home of July Mdletshe in Mona. A July from Mona, who often wore clerical garb, was arrested for involvement. Linah Mntungwa, "28. Early Healings of Shembe," in *SIS* 1, 59–60; Guy, *Maphumulo Uprising*, 169. On using homesteads for worship, see Houle, *Making African Christianity*, 115.

44. Mtnungwa, "28. Early Healings," in *SIS* 1; Linah Mntungwa, "29. More Healings," in *SIS* 1, 61–63.

45. Mtnungwa, "28. Early Healings," in *SIS* 1.

46. Mntungwa, "29. More Healings," in *SIS* 1.

47. We know that Shembe's life story was central to his early preaching because his detractors knew so much about him. See Kumalo, letter to the editor.

48. Dhlomo and Mntungwa, "21. Shembe Comes to Natal," in *SIS* 1.

49. Native Commissioner Ndwedwe to Chief Native Commissioner (CNC), November 15, 1933, NV 2/4/5, 3/3/2/1, Papers of the Magistrate of Ndwedwe (henceforth 1/NWE), Pietermaritzburg Archive Repository (NAB).

50. Mntungwa, "29. More Healings," in *SIS* 1.

51. Petros Mnqayi, letter to the editor, *iLanga lase Natal*, February 9, 1917.

52. Cherryl Walker, "Gender and the Development of the Migrant Labour System, c. 1850–1930," in *Women and Gender in Southern Africa to 1945*, ed. Cherryl Walker (Cape Town: David Philip, 1990), 173; Crais, *Poverty, War, and Violence in South Africa*.

53. Mntungwa, "28. Early Healings," in *SIS* 1.

54. Kumalo, letter to the editor.

55. Guy, *Maphumulo Uprising*, 169; Secretary of Native Affairs to Criminal Investigation Office, June 13, 1903, 1085/1901, I/1/291, Papers of the Secretary of Native Affairs (SNA), NAB.

56. This was in part due to the culture of healing in the region. See Karen Flint, *Healing Traditions: African Medicine, Cultural Exchange, and Competition in South Africa, 1820–1948* (Athens: Ohio University Press, 2008), 54.

57. Henry Callaway, *The Religious System of the Amazulu: With a Translation into English and Notes* (London, 1868), 326–27.

58. Mntungwa, "28. Early Healings," in *SIS*, 59.

59. Mntungwa, "28. Early Healings," in *SIS*, 59.

60. On his billycan: Dhlomo et al., "38. Shembe's Call," in *SIS* 1, 77.

61. Selina Nomahashi Mpanza, "24. The Conversion of Selina Nomahashi Mpanza," in *SIS* 2, 24–25.

62. Native Affairs Commission Colony of Natal, *Evidence* (Pietermaritzburg, ZA, 1907), 828.
63. Kumalo, letter to the editor.
64. E. Ntuli and Daniel Dube, "89. Chief Swayimane, the Son of Ziphuku, at Emqeku," in *SIS* 2, 83–86.
65. Mntungwa, "28. Early Healings," in *SIS* 1.
66. Police Report: A Native John Shembe from Harrismith Is Preaching to the Natives on the Location, May 25, 1912, 2155/1912, 77, Papers of the Chief Native Commissioner, Natal (CNC), Pietermaritzburg Archive Repository (NAB).
67. Callaway, *The Religious System*.
68. Flint, *Healing Traditions*, 136.
69. Dhlomo, Buthelezi, Duma, and Dube, "38. Shembe's Call to Nhlangakazi," in *SIS* 1.
70. Mbonambi, letter to the editor, *iLanga lase Natal*, February 28, 1913. Mbonambi was likely a descendant of one of the first Christian converts in Ndwedwe, but his family had joined many of the others who moved to a place where they could buy land. Tyler, *Forty Years*, 70, 125–27; Linah Mntungwa, "26. The Purchase of Ekuphakameni," in *SIS* 1, 54–57.
71. 2 Kings 4:8–37.
72. Joseph Ngcobo, letter to the editor, *iLanga lase Natal*, February 12, 1915.
73. John Mabuyakhulu and Hlanganisumuzi D. Mncwanga, "96. The Zulu King Comes to Ekuphakameni," in *SIS* 1, 155–57.
74. On chiefs (or traditional authorities) and Christians, Paul Stuart Landau, *The Realm of the Word: Language, Gender, and Christianity in a Southern African Kingdom* (Portsmouth, NH: Heinemann, 1995); James Campbell, *Songs of Zion: The African Methodist Episcopal Church in the United States and South Africa* (Chapel Hill: University of North Carolina Press, 1998), 181–83; David Maxwell, *Christians and Chiefs in Zimbabwe: A Social History of the Hwesa People* (Westport, CT: Praeger, 1999). And for a different take on Shembe and chiefs, see Joel Cabrita, *Text and Authority in the South African Nazaretha Church* (New York, NY: Cambridge University Press, 2014), 256–94.
75. Percy Ngonyama, "The Ward System: Redefining Chiefly Jurisdiction in the Lower Tugela Division (LTD) of Natal, 1906–1909" (paper, History and African Studies Seminar, University of KwaZulu-Natal, Durban, ZA, September 10, 2008), https://phambo.wiser.org.za/files/seminars/Ngonyama2008.pdf; Jill Kelly, *To Swim with Crocodiles* (East Lansing: Michigan State University Press, 2018), 71–72.
76. Natal Colony (South Africa), *Statutes of Natal* (Pietermaritzburg, ZA, 1901), 16.
77. Flint, *Healing Traditions*, 48.
78. For some examples of African Christians who approached the same chiefs as Shembe, James Stuart, *James Stuart Archive*, vol. 5, ed. Colin de B. Webb and John Wright

(Scottsville, ZA: University of KwaZulu-Natal, 2001), 120.

79. Dhlomo, Buthelezi, Duma, and Dube, "38. Shembe's Call to Nhlangakazi," in *SIS* 1, 76.

80. Dhlomo, Buthelezi, Duma, and Dube, "38. Shembe's Call to Nhlangakazi," in *SIS* 1, 75. Zeblon Khuzwayo, "91. Baptism and Healing at Emqeku," in *SIS* 2, 88–89.

81. H.-J. Becken, "On the Holy Mountain: A Visit to the New Year's Festival of the Nazaretha Church on Mount Nhlangakazi, 14 January, 1967," *Journal of Religion in Africa* 1, no. 2 (1968): 141.

82. Khuzwayo, "89. Chief Swayimane, the Son of Ziphuku, at Emqeku," in *SIS* 2, 84.

83. Khuzwayo, "89. Chief Swayimane, the Son of Ziphuku, at Emqeku," in *SIS* 2, 84.

84. Khuzwayo, "89. Chief Swayimane, the Son of Ziphuku, at Emqeku," in *SIS* 2, 84.

85. Khuzwayo, "89. Chief Swayimane, the Son of Ziphuku, at Emqeku," in *SIS* 2, 86.

86. Flint, *Healing Traditions*, 48.

87. Native Commission, *Evidence*, 833.

88. Native Commission, *Evidence*, 832. On this issue broadly: Sean Redding, "Deaths in the Family: Domestic Violence, Witchcraft Accusations and Political Militancy in Transkei, South Africa, 1904–1965," *Journal of Southern African Studies* 30, no. 3 (2004): 519–37; Adam Ashforth, *Witchcraft, Violence, and Democracy in South Africa* (University of Chicago Press, 2005); Timothy D. Stabell, "'The Modernity of Witchcraft' and the Gospel in Africa," *Missiology: An International Review* 38, no. 4 (2010): 460–74; Johanneke Kroesbergen-Kamps, "Witchcraft after Modernity: Old and New Directions in the Study of Witchcraft in Africa," *HAU* 10, no. 3 (December 2020): 860–73.

89. Ngcobo, letter to the editor.

90. This was Inkosi Mbango of the Hlophe. Magema Fuze labeled them "insignificant": Fuze, *The Black People*, 27. And albeit with numbers from a bit later, his chiefdom had only 160 people, while neighboring ones had between 1,500 to 2,000. N. J. van Warmelo, *A Preliminary Survey of the Bantu Tribes of South Africa* (Pretoria: Government Printer, 1935), 30.

91. This was Inkosi Swayimane Nyuswa. Guy, *Maphumulo Uprising*, 133–34.

92. Magwaza Gumede, Amos Qwabe, and Sheleni Nubane, "108. Shembe Visits Chief Meseni Qwabe at St. Helena," in *SIS* 2, 107–11.

93. This was the Qwabe family. Guy, *Maphumulo Uprising*, 251–53; Magwaza Gumede, Amos Qwabe, and Sheleni Nubane, "108. Shembe Visits Chief Meseni Qwabe at St. Helena," in *SIS* 2, 107–11.

94. Mntungwa, "28. Early Healings," in *SIS* 1. See also the description from Mbonambi, letter to the editor; Ngcobo, letter to the editor.

95. Guy, *Maphumulo Uprising*, 253.

96. See, for example, Bengt Sundkler, *Zulu Zion and Some Swazi Zionists* (New York: Oxford University Press, 1976), 167.
97. Mbonambi, letter to the editor.
98. Mbonambi, letter to the editor.
99. Ex. 19.
100. Ex. 34:29–35.
101. Mbonambi, letter to the editor.
102. Num. 6:1–21.
103. Judg. 6:16. Judg. 13:2–3; 1 Sam. 1:1–20; Luke 1:7–25.
104. Judg. 13:2–3; 1 Sam. 1:1–20; Luke 1:7–25.
105. The first references to him in Natal from other African Christians referred to him only as "Shembe." Kumalo, letter to the editor.
106. Isaiah 53:4.
107. Isaiah 35:5–8.
108. Isaiah 54:1.
109. Roberts, "Shembe," 79–81.
110. Carl Faye, memorandum, "UShembe," 1939, 24/214, 1431, Papers of the Native Affairs Department (NTS), National Archives Repository (SAB).
111. Carl Faye, memorandum, "UShembe."
112. Roberts, "Shembe."
113. For the earliest reference I found, A. B. Majola, letter to the editor, *iLanga lase Natal*, August 2, 1918.
114. Norman Etherington, "Outward and Visible Signs of Conversion in Nineteenth-Century Kwazulu-Natal," *Journal of Religion in Africa* 32, no. 4 (2002): 422–39; T. J. Tallie, "Sartorial Settlement: The Mission Field and Transformation in Colonial Natal, 1850–1897," *Journal of World History* 27, no. 3 (2016): 389–410.
115. Bengt Sundkler, *Bantu Prophets in South Africa* (New York: Oxford University Press, 1961), 55.
116. Ngcobo, letter to the editor; Report: John Shembe.
117. A magistrate finally figured out that Leshega was not ordained—but only after white missionaries aided the investigation. J. J. Ross to Under Colonial Secretary, December 22, 1909, 2324, 619, Papers of the Colonial Office (CO), Free State Archives Repository (VAB).
118. Sundkler, *Zulu Zion*, 45–56; Robert Edgar, *The Finger of God: Enoch Mgijima, the Israelites, and the Bulhoek Massacre in South Africa* (Charlottesville: University of Virginia, 2018), 61–62.
119. Colin Murray, "The Father, the Son and the Holy Spirit: Resistance and Abuse in the Life

of Solomon Lion (1908–1987)," *Journal of Religion in Africa* 29, no. 3 (1999): 348.

120. Edgar, *The Finger of God*, 78; William Beinart and Colin Bundy, *Hidden Struggles in Rural South Africa: Politics and Popular Movements in the Transkei and Eastern Cape, 1890–1930* (Berkeley: University of California Press, 1987), 1.

121. Joel Cabrita, *The People's Zion: Southern Africa, the United States, and a Transatlantic Faith-Healing Movement* (Cambridge, MA: Belknap Press of Harvard University Press, 2018).

122. Elizabeth Gunner, *The Man of Heaven and the Beautiful Ones of God = Umuntu Wasezulwini Nabantu Abahle Bakankulunkulu: Writings from Ibandla LamaNazaretha, a South African Church* (Leiden, NL: Brill, 2002), 11.

CHAPTER 5. A LANDOWNER IN INANDA

1. On Mntungwa's family, see Petros M. Dhlomo and Linah Mntungwa, "21. Shembe's Early Ministry in the Durban Region," in *The Story of Isaiah Shembe, Vol. 1: History and Traditions Centered on Ekuphakameni and Mount Nhlangakazi*, ed. Irving Hexham and G. C. Oosthuizen, trans. Hans-Jürgen Becken (Lewiston, NY: Edwin Mellen, 1996), 43–47 (henceforth *SIS* 1). Her age was estimated at forty in a record of people at Ekuphakameni in 1939. This record comes from Native Civil Court Cases, 1939, Papers of the Magistrate of Verulam (henceforth 1/VLM), Durban Archives Repository (henceforth TBD), Durban, ZA.

2. Dhlomo and Mntungwa, "21. Shembe's Early Ministry," in *SIS* 1, 45.

3. Because Linah Mntungwa was an early convert and still alive when foreign missionary scholars collected and translated Nazaretha histories and healing testimonies, she played a key role in describing Shembe's earliest day in Natal. Linah Mntungwa, "26. The Purchase of Ekuphakameni," in *SIS* 1, 54–57; Linah Mntungwa and Dainah Shembe, "28. Early Healings of Shembe," in *SIS* 1, 57–59; Linah Mntungwa and Esther Zungu, "29. More Healings," in *SIS* 1, 61–62. Still, other Nazaretha accounts mention her and attest to her importance. See, for example, Khesani Bhengu, "9. The Maidens Were Fighting for Shembe," in *The Story of Isaiah Shembe, Vol. 2: Early Regional Traditions of the Acts of the Nazarites*, ed. Irving Hexham and G. C. Oosthuizen, trans. Hans-Jurgen Becken (Lewiston, NY: Edwin Mellen, 1999), 9 (henceforth *SIS* 2); Hloniphile Mdluli, "15. The Marriage of Miss Agagi Shozi," in *SIS* 2, 13–15; Sophie Mtolo and Jestinah Mnyandu, "65. Shembe Comes to Thesalonika," in *SIS* 2, 68–70; and Emesiah Mthiya, "249. The Commission of Emesiah Mthiya to Swaziland," in *SIS* 2, 281–84.

4. This is surmisable from the first structures built at Ekuphakameni. Mntungwa, "26. The

Purchase of Ekuphakameni," in *SIS* 1.

5.   The son was Ezra Mbonambi. On the father's land holdings, Surveyor General Points out Balance of Survey Fees, SG1580A/1883, III/1/50, Papers of the Surveyor General's Office (henceforth SGO), Pietermaritzburg Archives Bureau (henceforth NAB), Pietermaritzburg, ZA; Native Land Act 1913: List of Native Land Owners, unnumbered folder, 3/3/2/1, 1/VLM, TBD.

6.   Mntungwa, "26. The Purchase of Ekuphakameni," in *SIS* 1.

7.   Mntungwa, "26. The Purchase of Ekuphakameni," in *SIS* 1.

8.   Mntungwa, "26. The Purchase of Ekuphakameni," in *SIS* 1.

9.   Esther Roberts, "Shembe: The Man and His Works" (master's thesis, University of Natal, 1936), 44–49; Bengt Sundkler, *Bantu Prophets in South Africa*, 2nd ed. (New York: Oxford University Press, 1961), 105–11; James W. Fernandez, "The Precincts of the Prophet: A Day with Johannes Galilee Shembe," *Journal of Religion in Africa* 5, no. 1 (1973): 32–53; H.-J. Becken, "Ekuphakameni Revisited: Recent Developments within the Nazaretha Church in South Africa," *Journal of Religion in Africa* 9, no. 3 (1978): 161–72.

10.   Luke 10:25–37.

11.   Paul La Hausse, *Restless Identities: Signatures of Nationalism, Zulu Ethnicity, and History in the Lives of Petros Lamula (c. 1881–1948) and Lymon Maling (1889–c. 1936)* (Pietermaritzburg, ZA: University of Natal Press, 2000), 17, 161, 200, 226.

12.   William Henry Beaumont and Natives Land Commission, *Report of the Natives Land Commission*, vol. 2 (Cape Town: Cape Times, 1916), 456. Such understandings might have also contributed to the ethnic nationalist turn of many politicians, including John Dube.

13.   Harvey Feinberg, *Our Land, Our Life, Our Future: Black South African Challenges to Territorial Segregation, 1913–1948* (Pretoria: Unisa Press, 2015).

14.   Cherryl Walker, "Critical Reflections on South Africa's 1913 Natives Land Act and Its Legacies: Introduction," *Journal of Southern African Studies* 40, no. 4 (July 4, 2014): 655–65.

15.   Walker, "Critical Reflections on South Africa's 1913 Natives Land Act," 35; Harvey M. Feinberg and André Horn, "South African Territorial Segregation: New Data on African Farm Purchases, 1913–1936," *Journal of African History* 50, no. 1 (2009): 41–60; William Beinart and Peter Delius, "The Historical Context and Legacy of the Natives Land Act of 1913," *Journal of Southern African Studies* 40, no. 4 (July 4, 2014): 667–88.

16.   Union of South Africa, *Minutes of Evidence of the Natal Natives Land Committee* (Cape Town: Cape Times, 1918), 149, https://catalog.hathitrust.org/api/volumes/oclc/12641608.html.

17.   Protocol No. 293/1935, Church of Nazareth Ecclesiastical Endowment Trust, 120/4/2537,

287, Papers of Director General Operations (henceforth DGO), NAB. This list includes more than forty properties all registered in Shembe's name, many with dates of purchase.

18. For example, assessing the Nazaretha for taxes was a problem. See J. W. Craddock to district commander, July 31, 1922, 24/214, 1431, vol. 1, Native Affairs Archive (henceforth NTS), National Archives Repository (henceforth SAB), Pretoria, ZA.

19. Roberts, "Shembe," 30; Absolom Mthethwa Vilakazi, *Shembe: The Revitalization of African Society* (Johannesburg: Skotaville, 1986); James W. Fernandez, "The Precincts of the Prophet: A Day with Johannes Galilee Shembe," *Journal of Religion in Africa* 5, no. 1 (1973): 35.

20. William Beinart and Peter Delius, "Introduction," in *Putting a Plough to the Ground: Accumulation and Dispossession in Rural South Africa, 1850–1930*, ed. William Beinart, Peter Delius, and Stanley Trapido (Johannesburg: Ravan Press, 1986), 38; Beinart and Delius, "The Historical Context and Legacy of the NLA," 668.

21. Roberts, "Shembe," 69, 72.

22. Karen Flint, *Healing Traditions: African Medicine, Cultural Exchange, and Competition in South Africa, 1820–1948* (Athens: Ohio University Press, 2008), 54.

23. La Hausse, *Restless Identities*; Helen Bradford, *A Taste of Freedom: The ICU in Rural South Africa, 1924–1930* (New Haven, CT: Yale University Press, 1987), 96.

24. William Burton, *When God Makes a Missionary: Being the Life Story of Edgar Mahon* (London: Victory Press, 1938), 51.

25. Sundkler, *Bantu Prophets in South Africa*, 90–91; Colin Murray, "The Father, the Son and the Holy Spirit: Resistance and Abuse in the Life of Solomon Lion (1908–1987)," *Journal of Religion in Africa* 29, no. 3 (1999): 348. For contrast: Robert Edgar, *The Finger of God: Enoch Mgijima, the Israelites, and the Bulhoek Massacre in South Africa* (Charlottesville: University of Virginia, 2018).

26. Lotha Zuma, "199. The Sermon of Shembe at Empuza in 1931," in *SIS* 2, 225–26.

27. The most famous example is Nongqawuse. J. B. Peires, *The Dead Will Arise: Nongqawuse and the Great Xhosa Cattle-Killing Movement of 1856–7* (Bloomington: Indiana University Press, 1989). See also, Julie Parle, "Witchcraft or Madness? The Amandiki of Zululand, 1894–1914," *Journal of Southern African Studies* 29, no. 1 (2003): 105–32.

28. Robert Houle, *Making African Christianity* (Bethlehem, PA: Lehigh University Press, 2011), 190–91.

29. Houle, *Making African Christianity*, 17.

30. Khesani Bhengu, "9. The Maidens Were Fighting for Shembe," in *SIS* 2, 9; Hloniphile Mdluli, "16. A Dispute with the Fathers of Marianhill," in *SIS* 2, 15–16.

31. Petros Dhlomo, "40. How the Congregation Was Allowed to Come to the Mountain," in

SIS 1, 84–85.

32. Helen Bradford, "Women, Gender and Colonialism: Rethinking the History of the British Cape Colony and Its Frontier Zones, c. 1806–70," *Journal of African History* 37, no. 3 (1996): 367; Karen Flint and Julie Parle, "Healing and Harming: Medicine, Madness, Witchcraft and Tradition," in *Zulu Identities: Being Zulu, Past and Present*, ed. Jabulani Sithole, Benedict Carton, and John Laband (London: C. Hurst, 2008), 312–21.

33. Dhlomo, "40. How the Congregation Was Allowed to Come to the Mountain," in *SIS* 1.

34. See, for example, Ula Yvette Taylor, *The Promise of Patriarchy: Women and the Nation of Islam* (Chapel Hill: University of North Carolina Press, 2017).

35. As quoted in Sean Redding, "Women as Diviners and as Christian Converts in Rural South Africa, c. 1880–1963," *Journal of African History* 57, no. 3 (November 1, 2016): 368. See also Robert Edgar and Hilary Sapire, *African Apocalypse: The Story of Nontetha Nkwenkwe, a Twentieth-Century South African Prophet* (Athens, OH: Ohio University Press, 2000).

36. Mntungwa, "26. The Purchase of Ekuphakameni," in *SIS* 1.

37. Mntungwa, "26. The Purchase of Ekuphakameni," in *SIS* 1.

38. Helen Bradford, *A Taste of Freedom: The ICU in Rural South Africa, 1924–1930* (New Haven, CT: Yale University Press, 1987), 247; Anne Kelk Mager, *Beer, Sociability, and Masculinity in South Africa* (New York: Cambridge University Press, 2010).

39. In 1912, the region had more than 20,000 acres of sugarcane and more than 2,000 African employees. (Because of where Inanda fit in Natal's districts, these numbers included statistics for Verulam.) Annual Report—Verulam–1912, VI 1/137/13—Annual Reports, 1/VLM 3/3/2/1, TBD; South African Native Affairs Commission (SANAC), *South African Native Affairs Commission, 1903–1905: Minutes of Evidence Taken In Rhodesia, Bechuanaland Protectorate, British Bechuanaland (Cape Colony), Orange River Colony, Basutoland, Transvaal Colony, and Again in the Cape Colony*, vol. 4 (Cape Town, 1904), 164.

40. Union of South Africa, *Third Census*, Vol. VIII, 143. Although from a later date, observers in the late 1920s and early 1930s, noted that many women and girls in the church worked as "cooks and nursemaids." Roberts, "Shembe," 59. The Phoenix settlement employed people too. Sita Gandhi, *In the Shadow of Mahatma: A Grand-daughter Remembers*, ed. Uma Dhupelia-Mesthrie (Calcutta: Sampark, 2005), 43.

41. Benedict Carton, *Blood from Your Children: The Colonial Origins of Generational Conflict in South Africa* (Charlottesville: University Press of Virginia, 2000), 3. The negative associations between girls and mobility might have limited the expectation that girls contribute to family survival strategies through cash.

42. SANAC, *South African Native Affairs Commission, 1903–1905*, vol. 4, 164, 744.

43. Jeremiah Gumede, "99. The Purchase of Ntanda," in *SIS* 2, 93–95.

44. Protocol No. 293/1935, Church of Nazareth Ecclesiastical Endowment Trust, 120/4/2537, DGO 287, SAB. This list includes more than forty properties all registered in Shembe's name.

45. For the criticism and Shembe's answer: Native Economic Commission, "Native Economic Commission, Sitting at Pietermaritzburg, Minutes of Evidence" (Pretoria: Union of South Africa, 1931), 6162, 6538–9. On women as "perpetual minors": Denys Shropshire, *The Bantu Woman under the Natal Code of Native Law: An Investigation* (Lovedale, ZA: Lovedale Press, 1941); "Natal Code of Native Law," *African Studies* 2, no. 1 (1943): 1–26.

46. Prabhudas Gandhi, *My Childhood with Gandhiji* (Ahmedabad, India: Navajivan, 1957), 37–38.

47. As quoted in Uma Dhupelia-Mesthrie, *Gandhi's Prisoner?: The Life of Gandhi's Son Manilal* (Cape Town: Kwela, 2004), 67.

48. Gandhi, *In the Shadow of Mahatma*, 34.

49. Mntungwa, "26. The Purchase of Ekuphakameni," in *SIS* 1. For confirmation, J. W. Craddock to district commandant, July 31, 1922.

50. Mntungwa, "26. The Purchase of Ekuphakameni," in SIS 1.

51. Hloniphile Mdluli, "15. The Marriage of Miss Agagi Shozi," in *SIS* 2, 13–15; Nozinkobe Samaria Jokini, "115. The Experience of the Indian Lady Nozinkobe," in *SIS* 1, 177–79; Elizabeth Gunner, *The Man of Heaven and the Beautiful Ones of God = Umuntu Wasezulwini Nabantu Abahle Bakankulunkulu: Writings from Ibandla LamaNazaretha, a South African Church* (Leiden, NL: Brill, 2002), 73.

52. Statement of the Indian Female Mannikam, August 10, 1922, 24/241, 1431, NTS, SAB; Roberts, "Shembe," 109.

53. Mdluli, "15. The Marriage of Miss Agagi Shozi," in *SIS* 2. Jokini, "115. The Experience of the Indian Lady Nozinkobe," in *SIS* 1.

54. Bertina Luthuli, "7. Intercession over a Deceased Baby," in *SIS* 2, 7–8.

55. Some people brought their own food and supplies, however. Statement of the Indian Female Mannikam.

56. H. C. Lugg to G. A. Park Ross, December 9, 1926, 24/241, 1431, NTS, SAB; Roberts, "Shembe," 59

57. Statement of Lloyd Mseleku, August 10, 1922, 24/241, 1431, NTS, SAB; Selina Mkhize, "148. On Snake Bite," in *SIS* 2; 163–64; Khaya Ndelu, Wellington Luthuli, and Elijah Shange,"74. No Nazaretha Will Be Killed by a Snake," in *SIS* 1, 120–25.

58. Irving Hexham and G. C. Oosthuizen, "34. Gospel," in *SIS* 2, 32; Gunner, *Man of Heaven*, 23–24.

59. Mdluli, "15. The Marriage of Miss Agagi Shozi," in *SIS* 2, 16–17.

60. Khesani Bhengu, "9. The Maidens Were Fighting for Shembe," in *SIS* 2, 9.

61. J. W. Carddock to district commandant.

62. American Board of Commissioners for Foreign Missions, *Annual Report of the American Board of Commissioners for Foreign Missions* (Boston: Board of Commissioners, 1917), 40; Meghan Healy-Clancy, *A World of Their Own: A History of South African Women's Education* (Charlottesville: University of Virginia, 2014); Meghan Elisabeth Healy, "'To Control Their Destiny': The Politics of Schooling in Colonial Natal, 1885–1910," *Journal of Southern African Studies* 37, no. 2 (2011): 247–64.

63. J. W. Craddock to district commandant.

64. Mntungwa, "26. The Purchase of Ekuphakameni," in *SIS* 1, 56.

65. Gumede, "99. The Purchase of Ntanda," in *SIS* 2, 95. He referenced Hlobane. Ron Lock, *Blood on the Painted Mountain: Zulu Victory and Defeat, Hlobane and Kambula, 1879* (London: Greenhill, 1995).

66. La Hausse, *Restless Identities*, 17–18.

67. On nursing, in particular, Shula Marks, *Divided Sisterhood: Race, Class and Gender in the South African Nursing Profession* (New York: St. Martin's Press, 1994); Catherine Burns, "'A Man Is a Clumsy Thing Who Does Not Know How to Handle a Sick Person': Aspects of the History of Masculinity and Race in the Shaping of Male Nursing in South Africa, 1900–1950," *Journal of Southern African Studies* 24, no. 4 (1998): 695–717; Leslie Anne Hadfield, *A Bold Profession: African Nurses in Rural Apartheid South Africa* (Madison, WI: University of Wisconsin Press, 2021).

68. Lynn M. Thomas, "The Modern Girl and Racial Respectability in 1930s South Africa," *Journal of African History* 47, no. 3 (November 2006): 461–90.

69. Jon Soske, *Internal Frontiers: African Nationalism and the Indian Diaspora in Twentieth-Century South Africa* (Athens: Ohio University Press, 2017), 138.

70. Andreas Heuser, *Shembe, Gandhi, und die Soldaten Gottes: Wurzeln der Gewaltfreiheit in Südafrika* (New York: Waxmann, 2003), 90; Andreas Heuser, "Recovered Narratives of an Inter-Cultural Exchange: Gandhi, Shembe, and the Legacy of Satyagraha," *Journal of the Study of Religion* 16, no. 1 (2003): 87–102. More broadly, see Heuser for a different treatment of relations between the Nazaretha and Indians.

71. Mntungwa, "26. The Purchase of Ekuphakameni," in *SIS* 1, 55–56.

72. Luke 10:25–37.

73. Muntuwesizwe Buthelezi, "76. The Well of Samaria at Ntanda," in *SIS* 2, 129–30.

74. For oral traditions relating to Indians in and around Ekuphakameni: Muntuwesizwe Buthelezi, "150. The Coming Lord," in *SIS* 2, 166; Elijah Shange, "74. No Nazaretha Will Be Killed by a Snake," in *SIS* 1; Mbuyisa, "59. Shembe Helps a Barren Woman," in *SIS* 1, 105.

75. John Mabuyakhulu, "91. The Vaccination Controversy at Ekuphakameni," in *SIS* 1, 145–51; Roberts, "Shembe," 43.

76. Jon Soske, *Internal Frontiers: African Nationalism and the Indian Diaspora in Twentieth-Century South Africa* (Athens: Ohio University Press, 2017), 64. See also Bill Freund, *Insiders and Outsiders: The Indian Working Class of Durban, 1910–1990* (Portsmouth, NH: Heinemann, 1995), 38. Another important body of scholarship emphasizes the many ways that the state and average people themselves manufactured difference: Nafisa Essop Sheik, "Customs in Common: Marriage, Law and the Making of Difference in Colonial Natal," *Gender and History* 29, no. 3 (2017): 589–604; T. J. Tallie, *Queering Colonial Natal: Indigeneity and the Violence of Belonging in Southern Africa* (Minneapolis: University of Minnesota Press, 2019).

77. Isabel Hofmeyr, *Gandhi's Printing Press: Experiments in Slow Reading* (Cambridge, MA: Harvard University Press, 2013), 8; Heather Hughes, "Violence in Inanda, August 1985," *Journal of Southern African Studies* 13, no. 3 (1987): 331–54.

78. Kalpana Hiralal, "'What Is the Meaning of the Word 'Wife?' The Impact of the Immigration Laws on the Wives of Resident Indians in South Africa 1897–1930," *Contemporary South Asia* 26, no. 2 (June 2018): 213–17; Sally Peberdy, "'A White Man's Land': Indian Immigration and the 1913 Immigrants Regulation Act," in *Selecting Immigrants: National Identity and South Africa's Immigration Policies, 1910–2005* (Johannesburg: Wits University Press, 2009), 31–56.

79. Michael Mahoney, *The Other Zulus: The Spread of Zulu Ethnicity in Colonial South Africa* (Durham, NC: Duke University Press, 2012), 123–25.

80. Gandhi, *In the Shadow of Mahatma*, 143.

81. Nongilishi Nokwanela Mdluli, "106. The Girl Who Took an Indian Lover," in *SIS* 2, 105–7; Gunner, *Man of Heaven*, 111.

82. Roberts, "Shembe," 43.

83. Daniel Dube, "80. Segregation Also in Heaven," in *SIS* 1, 132–34. He used this idea to try to recruit members of churches led by whites.

84. Jokini, "115. Experiences of the Indian Lady Nozinkobe," in *SIS* 1; Flint, *Healing Traditions*, 140. Healing practices in the region at once blurred and bolstered divisions of race. To address especially difficult problems, the sick and suffering might consult healers of other races. At the same time, healers of different races borrowed treatments and ingredients from each other but also used race (and other divisions) to market their claims. For example, some healers argued that certain kinds of medicine only worked for certain kinds of people: sometimes, for example, healers suggested that white doctors could heal white problems or Black doctors could heal Black ones.

85. Roberts, "Shembe," 76.

86. Mbongiseni Mdluli, "92. A White Manager Asks Shembe for a Child," in *SIS* 1, 151–52.

87. South Africa and Office of Census and Statistics, *Sixth Census of the Population of the Union of South Africa, Enumerated 5th May, 1936* (Pretoria: Printed by the government printer, 1938); Keith Buchanan and N. Hurwitz, "The Asiatic Immigrant Community in the Union of South Africa," *Geographical Review* 39, no. 3 (1949): 447; Hughes, "Violence in Inanda."

88. Flint, *Healing Traditions*, 156; Karen Flint, "Indian-African Encounters: Polyculturalism and African Therapeutics in Natal, South Africa, 1886–1950s," *Journal of Southern African Studies* 32, no. 2 (June 2006): 367–85.

89. Statement of the Indian Female Mannikam.

90. Freund, *Insiders and Outsiders*, 13; Bill Freund, "The Rise and Decline of an Indian Peasantry in Natal," *Journal of Peasant Studies* 18, no. 2 (1991): 263–87; Nile Green, "Islam for the Indentured Indian: A Muslim Missionary in Colonial South Africa," *Bulletin of SOAS* 71, no. 3 (2008): 529–53.

91. J. B. Brain and P. Brain, "Nostalgia and Alligator Bite: Morbidity and Mortality among Indian Migrants to Natal, 1884–1911," *South African Medical Journal* 65, no. 3 (1984): 98–102; J. B. Brain and P. Brain, "The Health of Indentured Indian Migrants to Natal, 1860–1911," *South African Medical Journal* 62, no. 20 (November 6, 1982): 739–42. On tuberculosis in South Africa broadly, Randall M. Packard, *White Plague, Black Labor: Tuberculosis and the Political Economy of Health and Disease in South Africa* (Berkeley: University of California, 1989).

92. Statement of the Indian Female Mannikam; Statement of Lloyd Mseleku.

93. Statement of the Indian Female Mannikam.

94. M. Martini, V. Gazzaniga, M. Behzadifar, N. L. Bragazzi, and I Barberis, "The History of Tuberculosis: The Social Role of Sanatoria for the Treatment of Tuberculosis in Italy between the End of the 19th Century and the Middle of the 20th," *Journal of Preventive Medicine and Hygiene* 59, no. 4 (December 15, 2018): E323–27.

95. Statement of the Indian Female Mannikam.

96. Barbara Bompani, "Religion and Development from Below: Independent Christianity in South Africa," *Journal of Religion in Africa* 40, no. 3 (2010): 307–30; Lindiwe Ngcobo and Joseph Chisasa, "The Nature and Benefits of Participating in Burial Society Stokvels in South Africa," *Acta Universitatis Danubius: Œconomica* 15, no. 2 (2019), 204–16.

97. Mabuyakhulu, "91. The Vaccination Controversy," in *SIS* 1, 148. On fanakalo: J. D. Bold, *Fanagalo: Phrase-Book Grammar Dictionary*, (Pretoria: J. L. van Schaik, 1990); Rajend Mesthrie, "Fanakalo as a Mining Language in South Africa: A New Overview,"

International Journal of the Sociology of Language 258 (August 2019): 13–33.

98. Jokini, "106. The Conversion of the Indian Lady."

99. Roberts, "Shembe," 49.

100. Brain and Brain, "Nostalgia for Alligator Bites," 102. This article makes derogatory references toward these Indian healers but notes the presence of a community of them in Verulam.

101. Nile, "Islam for the Indentured Indian"; Goolam Vahed, "Constructions of Community and Identity among Indians in Colonial Natal, 1860–1910: The Role of the Muharram Festival," *Journal of African History* 43, no. 1 (2002): 77–93; Preben Kaarsholm, "Zanzibaris or Amakhuwa? Sufi Networks in South Africa, Mozambique, and the Indian Ocean," *Journal of African History* 55, no. 2 (July 2014): 191–210.

102. Luke 10:25–37.

103. S. B. Kumalo, letter to the editor, *iLanga lase Natal*, December 15, 1911.

104. Norman Etherington, "African Economic Experiments in Colonial Natal, 1845–1880," *African Economic History* 5, no. 5 (1978): 1–15; Norman Etherington, *Preachers, Peasants, and Politics in Southeast Africa, 1835–1880* (London: Royal Historical Society, 1978); John Lambert, "The Attitude of the Kholwa Petty Bourgeois Elite to the Franchise and Authority in Late-Colonial Natal," *Kleio* 27, no. 1 (January 1, 1995): 70–96; Nicholas Cope, "The Zulu Petit Bourgeoisie and Zulu Nationalism in the 1920s: Origins of Inkatha," *Journal of Southern African Studies*, 1990; Hlonipha Mokoena, *Magema Fuze: The Making of a Kholwa Intellectual* (Scottsville, ZA: University of KwaZulu-Natal, 2011); Robert Houle, *Making African Christianity* (Bethlehem, PA: Lehigh University Press, 2011); Healy Clancy, *A World of Their Own*; Marc Epprecht, *Welcome to Greater Edendale: Histories of Environment, Health, and Gender in an African City* (Montreal: McGill–Queen's University Press, 2016). On clothes specifically: T. J. Tallie, "Sartorial Settlement: The Mission Field and Transformation in Colonial Natal, 1850–1897," *Journal of World History* 27, no. 3 (2016): 389–410. For other interpretations of Shembe's relationships with *kholwa*, see Joel Cabrita, "Isaiah Shembe's Theological Nationalism, 1920s–1935," *Journal of Southern African Studies* 35, no. 3 (2009): 609–25; Joel Cabrita, "Patriot and Prophet: John Dube's 1936 Biography of the South African Churchman Isaiah Shembe," *Journal of Southern African Studies* 38, no. 3 (September 1, 2012): 433–50; Joel Cabrita, *Text and Authority in the South African Nazaretha Church* (New York: Cambridge University Press, 2014).

105. Houle, *Making African Christianity*, 105–6.

106. Elias Khawula, "35. Shembe Comes to the Country of Mtwalume," in *SIS* 2, 33–34; Houle, *Making African Christianity*; Dean Jabulani Ndaba, "The Development of Umlazi Mission Station And Reserve, 1856–1948, With Special Reference To The Land Problem" (master's

thesis, University of Zululand KwaDlangezwa, 1993), 45–47; La Hausse, *Restless Identities*, 167. On assessments of the wealth of the land at Umvoti, see William Henry Beaumont and Natives Land Commission, *Report of the Natives Land Commission*, vol. 2 (Cape Town: Cape Times, 1916), 448.

107. Ndaba, "The Development of Umlazi."

108. La Hausse, *Restless Identities*, 167.

109. Heather Hughes, *First President: A Life of John Dube, Founding President of the ANC* (Auckland Park, ZA: Jacana, 2011); Heather Hughes, "Doubly Elite: Exploring the Life of John Langalibalele Dube," *Journal of Southern African Studies* 27, 3 (2001): 445–58; Shula Marks, "The Ambiguities of Dependence: John L. Dube of Natal," *Journal of Southern African Studies* 1, no. 2 (1975): 162–80; Shula Marks, *The Ambiguities of Dependence* (Johannesburg: Ravan, 1986). On Shembe and Dube, see Cabrita, "Patriot and Prophet."

110. Shula Marks, "Natal, the Zulu Royal Family and the Ideology of Segregation," *Journal of Southern African Studies* 4, no. 2 (April 1, 1978): 172–94; Cope, "The Zulu Petit Bourgeoisie."

111. Jacob Dlamini, *Safari Nation: A Social History of Kruger National Park* (Athens: Ohio University Press, 2020), 102–3.

112. La Hausse, "Death is Not the End," 261.

113. As quoted in testimony of Dhlamvuza Dhlamini, Native Constable, January 31, 1923, 24/241, 1431, NTS, SAB.

114. Timothy Khuzwayo, "115. Shembe Comes to Groutville," in *SIS* 2, 120–21; Khawula, "35. Shembe Comes to Umtwalume." See also Matsheni, "It's Easier Said Than Done," *iLanga lase Natal*, August 21, 1914.

115. Khuzwayo, "115. Shembe Comes to Groutville," in *SIS* 2. On McCord's, see Julie Parle and Vanessa Noble, *The People's Hospital: A History of McCords, Durban, 1890s–1970s* (Pietermaritzburg, ZA: Occasional Publications of the Natal Society Foundation, 2017).

116. On tensions with Martin Luthuli in Groutville, see La Hausse, *Restless Identities*, 167.

117. Khuzwayo, "115. Shembe Comes to Groutville," in *SIS* 2; Khawula, "35. Shembe Comes to Umtwalume"; Khuzwayo and Kunene, "116. In the Prison at Stanger," in *SIS* 2, 122. These areas were different because, unlike Inanda, they were spaces where communities of African Christians bought land together.

118. The magistrate allowed Shembe to keep evangelizing in Umtwalume where he was able to buy land—but not in Grouville, where he had converted more people. Elias Khawula, "38. A Colored Chief Accuses Shembe," in *SIS* 2, 36–7.

119. J. W. Craddock to district commandant.

120. Matsheni, "Easier Said Than Done."

121. Elder S. Mdaka, letter to the editor, *iLanga lase Natal*, April 5, 1917.

122. J. N. Mzimela, "A Church for Black People," *iLanga lase Natal*, March 29, 1915.

123. "Ay People!" *iLanga lase Natal*, August 10, 1917.

124. "Night Sentry," *iLanga lase Natal*, August, 21, 1914; Xaba, letter to the editor, *iLanga lase Natal*, May 9, 1914.

125. See also Andreas Heuser, "Staging African Prophets in South Africa: *iLanga lase Natal* as an Historical Archive of Early African Pentecostalism," in *Polycentric Structures in the History of World Christianity*, ed. Klaus Korschorke and Adrian Hermann (Wiesbaden, Ger.: Harrassowitz, 2014).

126. Khawula, "38. A Coloured Chief Accuses"; Muntuwesizwe Buthelezi, Edmond M. Dladla, and Chief Mfungelwa Mchunu, "93. The Child of Mafukuzela at Inanda," in *SIS* 1, 152–53.

127. Hughes, *First President*, 65.

128. Buthelezi, "93. The Child of Mafukuzela," in *SIS* 2.

129. Buthelezi, "93. The Child of Mafukuzela," in *SIS* 2.

130. In her work on Regina Twala, Joel Cabrita shows the consequences of this polarization for how later missionary scholars understood the Nazaretha—in large part because those later missionary scholars plagiarized from their "research assistants." Joel Cabrita, "Writing Apartheid: Ethnographic Collaborators and the Politics of Knowledge Production in Twentieth-Century South Africa," *American Historical Review* 125, no. 5 (December 29, 2020): 1668–97.

CHAPTER 6. A MATCHMAKER AT EKUPHAKAMENI

1. A. B. Majola, letter to the editor, *iLanga lase Natal*, August 2, 1918. The author might have been Albert Majola, a teacher at a mission school outside of Pietermaritzburg. See J. W. Howard, ed., *Twentieth Century Impressions of Natal: Its People, Commerce, Industries, and Resources* (Pietermaritzburg, ZA, 1906), 275, https://hdl.handle.net/2027/ien.35556012320313.

2. Philip Bonner, "South African Society and Culture, 1910–1948," in *The Cambridge History of South Africa*, ed. Robert Ross, Anne Kelk Mager, and Bill Nasson (New York: Cambridge University Press, 2011), 267–70.

3. Majola, letter to the editor.

4. For other discussions of young women's sexuality in the Nazaretha Church, see Carol Ann Muller, *Rituals of Fertility and the Sacrifice of Desire: Nazarite Women's Performance in South Africa* (Chicago: University of Chicago Press, 1999); Gerald O. West, "The Bible and the Female Body in Ibandla LamaNazaretha: Isaiah Shembe and Jephthah's

Daughter," *Old Testament Essays* 20, no. 2 (2007): 489–509; Nkosinathi Sithole, *The Nazaretha Church in South Africa: Isaiah Shembe's Hymns and the Sacred Dance in IBandla LamaNazaretha* (Leiden, NL: Brill, 2016).

5. Shula Marks, "Patriotism, Patriarchy, and Purity: Natal and the Politics of Zulu Ethnic Consciousness," in *The Creation of Tribalism in Southern Africa*, ed. Leroy Vail (Berkeley: University of California Press, 1989), 215–34; Gaitskell, "Devout Domesticity? A Century of African Women's Christianity in South Africa," in *Women and Gender in Southern Africa to 1945*, ed. Cherryl Walker (Cape Town: David Philip, 1990), 251–72. Jon Soske, *Internal Frontiers: African Nationalism and the Indian Diaspora in Twentieth-Century South Africa* (Athens: Ohio University Press, 2017), 137–44; Elizabeth Thornberry, *Colonizing Consent: Rape and Governance in South Africa's Eastern Cape* (New York: Cambridge University Press, 2018), 2–3. For examples of similar debates among white women, see S. E. Duff, "'Dear Mrs Brown': Social Purity, Sex Education and the Women's Christian Temperance Union in Early Twentieth-Century South Africa," *Social History* 45, no. 4 (October 1, 2020): 476–99. And elsewhere in colonial Africa: Dorothy Hodgson and Sheryl McCurdy, eds., *"Wicked" Women and the Reconfiguration of Gender in Africa* (Portsmouth, NH: Heinemann, 2001).

6. Marks, "Purity and Patriarchy," 231–33.

7. Majola, letter to the editor.

8. Robert Papini, "Carl Faye's Transcript of Isaiah Shembe's Testimony of His Early Life and Calling," *Journal of Religion in Africa* 29, no. 3 (1999): 243–84; Petros Dhlomo, Khaya Ndelu, and Jeslinah Mchunu, "14. Shembe Relates How He Separated His Wives," in *The Story of Isaiah Shembe, Vol. 1: History and Traditions Centered on Ekuphakameni and Mount Nhlangakazi*, ed. Irving Hexham and G. C. Oosthuizen, trans. Hans-Jürgen Becken (Lewiston, NY: Edwin Mellen, 1996), 22–26 (henceforth *SIS* 1).

9. On such accusations: J. W. Craddock to district commandant, July 31, 1922, 24/241, 1431, Papers of the Native Affairs Administration (henceforth NTS), National Archives Repository (henceforth SAB), Pretoria, ZA; Esther Roberts, "Shembe: The Man and His Works" (master's thesis, University of Natal, 1936), 41.

10. Ex. 19:15.

11. Statement of Testimony of Dhlamvuza Dhlamini, native constable, January 31, 1923, 24/241, 1431, NTS, SAB.

12. Petros Dhlomo and Linah Mntungwa, "21. Shembe's Early Ministry," in *SIS* 1, 45–46; Elizabeth Gunner, *The Man of Heaven and the Beautiful Ones of God = Umuntu Wasezulwini Nabantu Abahle Bakankulunkulu: Writings from Ibandla LamaNazaretha, a South African Church* (Leiden, NL: Brill, 2002), 75–77.

13. Many married just before departing. See Adrian Hastings, *The Church in Africa, 1450–1950* (New York: Oxford University Press, 1994), 260.

14. Nafisa Essop Sheik, "African Marriage Regulation and the Remaking of Gendered Authority in Colonial Natal, 1843–1875," *African Studies Review* 57, no. 2 (2014): 73–92; Nafisa Essop Sheik, "Customs in Common: Marriage, Law and the Making of Difference in Colonial Natal," *Gender and History* 29, no. 3 (2017): 589–604; Natasha Erlank, "The White Wedding: Affect and Economy in South Africa in the Early Twentieth Century," *African Studies Review* 57, no. 2 (2014): 29–50; Natasha Erlank, *Convening Black Intimacy: Christianity, Gender, and Tradition in Early Twentieth-Century South Africa* (Athens: Ohio University Press, 2022); Deborah Posel, "Marriage at the Drop of a Hat: Housing and Partnership in South Africa's Urban African Townships, 1920s–1960s," *History Workshop Journal* 61, no. 1 (2006): 57–76.

15. South Africa Office of Census and Statistics, *Official Yearbook of the Union* (Pretoria: Government Printers, 1921), 451.

16. Bengt Sundkler, *Bantu Prophets in South Africa*, 2nd ed. (New York: Oxford University Press, 1961), 69–70.

17. Petros Dhlomo and Johannes Duma, "37. Shembe Comes to the Home of Jan Dambuza," in *SIS* 1, 74–75.

18. Petros Dhlomo and Linah Mntungwa, "21. Shembe's Early Ministry," in *SIS* 1, 45.

19. Dhlomo and Mntungwa, "21. Shembe's Early Ministry," in *SIS* 1, 45.

20. Gertie Mbambo, "124. The Conversion of Gertie Mbambo," in *SIS* 2, 131; Testimony of Gertie Mbambo, 1967, 2B 25, Interviews with Healed MaNazaretha, H. J. Becken Papers (henceforth HJBP), Lutheran Theological Institute (henceforth LTI), Scottsville, South Africa.

21. Josiah Tyler, *Forty Years Among the Zulus* (Boston, 1891), 64.

22. Robert Houle, *Making African Christianity* (Bethlehem, PA: Lehigh University Press, 2011), 105–6.

23. Mbambo, "124. The Conversion of Gertie Mbambo," in *SIS* 2; Testimony of Gertie Mbambo.

24. Selina Nomahashi Mpanza, "24. The Conversion of Selina Nomahashi Mpanza," in *SIS* 2, 24–25.

25. Linah Mntungwa, "21. Shembe's Early Ministry in the Durban Region," in *SIS* 1, 45.

26. Khesani Bhengu, "9. The Maidens Were Fighting for Shembe," in *SIS* 2, 9; Timothy Khuzwayo, "114. Shembe Comes to Groutville," in *SIS* 2, 120–21; Hlanganisumuzi David Mncwanga and Nomabhece Zulu, "216. Shembe Builds the Temple of Linda," in *SIS* 2, 245.

27. Chief Native Commissioner to Secretary of Native Affairs, May 20, 1922, 24/241, 1431,

NTS, SAB; Craddock to district commandant. On similar complaints about missionaries, Amanda Porterfield, "The Impact of Early New England Missionaries on Women's Roles in Zulu Culture," *Church History* 66, no. 1 (1997): 73–77.

28. Interview with Isaiah Shembe, January 15, 1923, 24/241, 1431, NTS, SAB. For similar words from missionaries, Meghan Elisabeth Healy, "'To Control Their Destiny': The Politics of Schooling in Colonial Natal, 1885–1910," *Journal of Southern African Studies* 37, no. 2 (2011): 249.

29. Bhengu, "9. The Maidens Were Fighting for Shembe," in *SIS* 2; Khuzwayo, "115. Shembe Comes to Groutville in 1913," in *SIS* 2; Mabadimane Chiliza, "65. Shembe Comes to Thesalonika," in *SIS* 2, 68–70.

30. Khuzwayo, "115. Shembe Comes to Groutville in 1913," in *SIS* 2; Timothy Khuzwayo and Zachariah Kunene, "116. In the Prison at Stanger," in *SIS* 2, 123–4. Matsheni, "It's Easier Said Than Done," *iLanga lase Natal*, August 21, 1914.

31. Bhengu, "9. The Maidens Were Fighting for Shembe," in *SIS* 2.

32. Sheleni Ngubane, "114. The Headman Makhafula Ngubane Meets Shembe," in *SIS* 2, 117–20; Azariah Mthiyane, "202. An Attack on Shembe," in *SIS* 2, 229–30; Musawenkosi Mkhwanazi, "225. Shembe Comes to Chief Msibi," in *SIS* 2, 255–57; Musawenkosi Mkhwanazi, "226. Shembe Comes to Mtubatuba," in *SIS* 2, 257–60.

33. For a different interpretation of these relations, see Joel Cabrita, "Isaiah Shembe's Theological Nationalism, 1920s–1935," *Journal of Southern African Studies* 35, no. 3 (2009): 609–25. On Inkosi Solomon: Nicholas Cope, *To Bind the Nation: Solomon KaDinuzulu and Zulu Nationalism, 1913–1933* (Scottsville, ZA: University of Natal Press, 1993); Nicholas Cope, "The Zulu Petit Bourgeoisie and Zulu Nationalism in the 1920s: Origins of Inkatha," *Journal of Southern African Studies*, 1990; Shula Marks, *The Ambiguities of Dependence in South Africa: Class, Nationalism, and the State in Twentieth-Century Natal* (Baltimore: Johns Hopkins University Press, 1986).

34. Cope, *To Bind the Nation*, 24, 47.

35. Elijah Mdladlose seemed to have a closer relationship. Bengt Sundkler, *Zulu Zion and Some Swazi Zionists* (New York: Oxford University Press, 1976), 69–74.

36. Hlanganisumuzi David Mncwanga and Azariah Ndwandwe, "221. The Attempt to Burn the Village at Linda," in *SIS* 2, 251–52.

37. Hlanganisumuzi David Mncwanga and Bajabhisile Zulu, "217. Early Opposition at Linda," in *SIS* 2, 245–48; D. G. Shepstone to Chief Native Commissioner, October 27, 1931, 24/241, 1431, NTS, SAB.

38. Summary of decision: *Jeremiah Shandu v. Mtengeni Mhlonho*, December 17, 1925, 24/241, 1431, NTS, SAB.

39. Summary of decision: *Jeremiah Shandu v. Mtengeni Mhlonho*, December 17, 1925.

40. Cherryl Walker, "Gender and the Development of the Migrant Labor System, c. 1850–1930," in *Women and Gender in Southern Africa to 1945*, ed. Cherryl Walker (London: James Currey, 1990), 188–89.

41. Some parents had used Inanda Seminary similarly. Heather Hughes, "A Lighthouse for African Womanhood: Inanda Seminary, 1869–1945," in *Women and Gender in Southern Africa to 1945*, ed. Cherryl Walker (London: James Currey, 1990), 209.

42. Eileen Jensen Krige, *The Social System of the Zulus* (Pietermaritzburg, ZA: Shuter and Shooter, 1936), 142–43.

43. Elizabeth Thornberry, *Colonizing Consent: Rape and Governance in South Africa's Eastern Cape*, (New York: Cambridge University Press, 2018), 3.

44. Roberts, "Shembe," 92. In contrast, girls who had not reached adolescence wore no head coverings, and married women covered their heads with tied head wraps

45. Roberts, "Shembe," 54.

46. These words were *intombi* and *umakoti*. John William Colenso, *Zulu-English Dictionary* (London, 1861), 283, 353. Today *intombazana* is more commonly used to refer to unmarried girls and young women in the church. See also: Nongilishi Mdluli, "160. Shembe Cares for His Little Brides," in *SIS* 1, 237–39.

47. Krige, *Social System*, 155.

48. Krige, *Social System*, 104–6; Monica Hunter, *Reaction to Conquest: Effects of Contact with Europeans on the Pondo of South Africa*, (Cape Town: David Philip, 1979), 180–84. On age grades in African history: Corrie Decker, "A Feminist Methodology of Age-Grading and History in Africa," *American Historical Review* 125, no. 2 (2020): 418–26.

49. Magema Fuze, *The Black People and Whence They Came*, ed. A. T. Cope and H. C. Lugg (Pietermaritzburg, ZA: University of Natal, 1979), 29.

50. Nongilishi Nokwanela Mdluli, "106. The Girl Who Took an Indian Lover," in *SIS* 2, 105–7; Roberts, "Shembe," 80–88.

51. Chiliza, "65. Shembe Comes to Thesalonika," in *SIS* 2; Samariah Nozinkobe Jokini, "115. The Experiences of the Indian Lady Nozinkobe," in *SIS* 1, 177–78.

52. Timothy Khuzwayo, "159. Shembe Passes His Last Judgements," in *SIS* 1, 237. She was still at Ekuphakameni in in 1939. Native Civil Court Cases, 1939, Papers of the Magistrate of Verulam (henceforth 1/VLM), Durban Archives Repository (henceforth TBD), Durban, ZA.

53. Petros Dhlomo, "156. The Order of the Virgins in the Temples," in *SIS* 1, 232.

54. Fuze, *The Black People*, 29; Wilson, *Reaction to Conquest*, 183–4; Elizabeth Thornberry, "Virginity Testing, History, and the Nostalgia For Custom in Contemporary South Africa,"

African Studies Review 58, 3 (2015): 129–48.

55. Thornberry, "Virginity Testing," 137.

56. Dhlomo, "156. The Order of the Virgins."

57. Report: Examination of Native Girls as to Virginity, January 15, 1916, 57/1916, 227, Papers of the Chief Native Commissioner (CNC), Pietermaritzburg Archives Repository (NAB), Pietermaritzburg, ZA.

58. People used the words *ukuhlobonga, ukusoma,* and *ukuqoma.* Absolom Mthethwa
. Vilakazi, *Shembe: The Revitalization of African Society* (Johannesburg: Skotaville, 1986), 35.

59. Mdluli, "106. The Girl Who Had Chosen an Indian Lover."

60. Somali Mpahla, "31. The Burned Love Letters," in *SIS* 1, 65–6.

61. On love letters: Keith Breckenridge, "Love Letters and Amanuenses: Beginning the Cultural History of the Working Class Private Sphere in Southern Africa, 1900–1933," *Journal of Southern African Studies* 26 (June 1, 2000): 337–48; Erlank, *Convening Black Intimacy,* 77–81.

62. Catherine Burns, "Sex Lessons from the Past?," *Agenda: Empowering Women for Gender Equity,* no. 29 (1996): 79–91; Eileen Jensen Krige, "Girls' Puberty Songs and Their Relation to Fertility, Health, Morality and Religion among the Zulul," *Africa* 38, no. 2 (April 1968): 173–98; Wilson, *Reaction to Conquest,* 181.

63. Thandekile Shembe, "87. Shembe Gives Names to Girls," in *SIS* 2, 82; Esther Zungu, "44. The Trespass of the Girl at Mount Nhlangakazi," in *SIS* 1, 88–9.

64. Muntuwesizwe Buthelezi, "116. Nothing is Hidden from Shembe," in *SIS* 1, 179–80.

65. Roberts, "Shembe," 80.

66. Mdluli, "106. The Girl Who Chose."

67. Mdluli, "53. A Maiden Refuses the Invitation of Shembe," in *SIS* 1, 98–9.

68. Simon Mngoma, Khonzinkosi Mbuyazi, and Petros Dhlomo, "146. The Parable of the Bride Who Distributes Gifts," in *SIS* 1, 212–4.

69. Mbongiseni Mdluli, "144. The Parable of the Fine Girl who Played the Jew's Harp," in *SIS* 1, 211–12.

70. Johannes Duma, "135. The Parable of the Perilous Sweet," in *SIS* 1, 198–99.

71. Sita Gandhi, *In the Shadow of Mahatma: A Grand-Daughter Remembers*, ed. Uma Dhupelia-Mesthrie (Calcutta: Sampark, 2005), 43; Heather Hughes, "Violence in Inanda, August 1985," *Journal of Southern African Studies* 13, no. 3 (1987): 331–54.

72. Mdluli, "144. The Parable of the Girl Who Played the Jew's Harp," in *SIS* 1, 211–13.

73. Mngoma, Mbuyazi, and Dhlomo, "146. The Parable of the Bride"; Absolom Ndlovu, "137. The Parable of the Wife Who Had an Evil Heart," in *SIS* 1, 203–4; Khaya Ndelu, "31. The

Parable of the Young Man Who was Vaccinated," in *SIS* 2, 33–4.

74. Petros Dhlomo, Khaya Ndelu, and Jeslinah Mchunu, "14. Shembe Relates How He Separated His Wives," in *SIS* 1, 22–26.

75. For a photograph of Lutheran girls with similar head coverings in the 1910s, see Barry Morton, *Engenas Lekganyane and the Early ZCC: An Unauthorized History* (self-pub., BooksMango, 2018), 14.

76. Gaitskell, "Devout Domesticity? A Century of African Women's Christianity in South Africa," in *Women and Gender in Southern Africa to 1945* (Claremont: David Philip, 1990), 251–72.

77. Wilson, *Reaction to Conquest*, 183–4; Natasha Erlank, "The White Wedding: Affect and Economy in South Africa in the Early Twentieth Century," *African Studies Review* 57, no. 2 (2014): 29–50.

78. Bhengu, "9. The Maidens Were Fighting for Shembe," in *SIS* 2.

79. Jeremiah Gumede, "99. The Purchase of Ntanda," in *SIS* 2. On other invocations of Jephthah's daughter: Cornelis Houtman, "Rewriting a Dramatic Old Testament Story the Story of Jephthah and His Daughter in Some Examples of Christian Devotional Literature," *Biblical Interpretation* 13, no. 2 (April 2005): 167–90.

80. John Langalibalele Dube, *UShembe* (Pietermaritzburg, ZA: Shuter and Shooter, 1936).

81. Petros Dhlomo, Muntuwesizwe Buthelezi, and Khaya Ndelu, "4. Sitheya the Mother of Shembe," in *SIS* 1, 5–7.

82. Absolom Mthethwa Vilakazi, *Shembe: The Revitalization of African Society* (Johannesburg: Skotaville, 1986), 87; Robert Papini, "Dance Uniform History in the Church of Nazareth Baptists: The Move to Tradition," *African Arts* 37, no. 3 (2004): 48–64.

83. Fuze, *The Black People*, 29; Wilson, *Reaction to Conquest*, 181; Krige, *The Social System*, 144, 340.

84. Fuze, *The Black People*.

85. Majola, letter to the editor.

86. See also, Untitled, *iLanga lase Natal*, September 27, 1918; Mdluli, "15. The Marriage of Miss Agagi Shozi," in *SIS* 2.

87. By the 1910s, few kholwa were opposed to bridewealth. Erlank, *Convening Black Intimacy*, 21.

88. Majola, letter to the editor.

89. Veit Erlmann, "'Horses in the Race Course': The Domestication of Ingoma Dancing in South Africa, 1929–39," *Popular Music* 8, no. 3 (1989): 259–73; Veit Erlmann, "Migration and Performance: Zulu Migrant Workers' Isicathamiya Performance in South Africa, 1890–1950," *Ethnomusicology* 34, no. 2 (1990): 199–220; Veit Erlmann, "'The Past Is Far

and the Future Is Far': Power and Performance among Zulu Migrant Workers," *American Ethnologist* 19, no. 4 (1992): 688–709.

90. Majola, letter to the editor.

91. Testimony of Dhlamvuza Dhlamini.

92. Testimony of Dhlamvuza Dhlamini.

93. Bajabhisile Zulu, "217. Early Opposition at Linda," in *SIS* 2, 245–48.

94. Mdluli, "15. The Marriage of Miss Agagi Shozi," in *SIS* 2. Erlank, *Convening Black Intimacy*.

95. Mdluli, "15. The Marriage of Miss Agagi Shozi."

96. Untitled, *iLanga lase Natal*, September 27, 1918. For comparison, Erlank, "White Weddings," 31.

97. Untitled, *iLanga lase Natal*, September 27, 1918.

98. Untitled, *iLanga lase Natal*, September 27, 1918.

99. Vilakazi, *Shembe*, 68.

100. Sundkler also described how members of some denominations refused to use drums, for example, because they associated drums with churches like the Nazaretha. Sundkler, *Bantu Prophets*, 173.

101. Interview with Isaiah Shembe, January 23, 1923, 24/214, 1431, NTS, SAB.

102. Nellie Wells to Governor General, January 13, 1930, 50/1341, 1567, Papers of the Governor General (henceforth GG), NAB.

103. Vilakazi, *Shembe*, 28, 32, 78.

104. Craddock to district commandant.

105. Gaitskell, "Devout Domesticity," Porterfield, "The Impact of Early New England Missionaries on Women's Roles in Zulu Culture," 77; Terence Ranger, "'Taking on the Missionary's Task': African Spirituality and the Mission Churches of Manicaland in the 1930s," *Journal of Religion in Africa* 29, fascicle 2 (1999): 178.

106. Mdluli, "15. The Marriage of Miss Agagi Shozi," in *SIS* 2; Dorrit Posel and Stephanie Rudwick, "Marriage and Bridewealth (Ilobolo) in Contemporary Zulu Society," *African Studies Review* 57, no. 2 (2014): 51–72.

107. E. N. Braatvedt to Chief Native Commissioner, November 3, 1931, 24/214, 1431, NTS, SAB.

108. Wilson, *Reaction to Conquest*, 375; I. Schapera, *Married Life in an African Tribe* (London, Faber and Faber, 1966), 53.

109. As quoted in Marks, "Patriarchy and Purity," 28.

110. Jokini, "115. The Experience of the Indian Lady," in *SIS* 1.

111. Mdluli, "18. Agagi Shozi Leaves this Earth," in *SIS* 2, 17–8. Some of these women did play leadership roles in local branches of the church when they were older.

CHAPTER 7. A DISSIDENT IN SOUTHERN ZULULAND

1. Testimony of Masimini Zulu, February 13, 1922, 24/214, 1431, part 1, Papers of the Native Affairs Department (NTS), National Archives Repository (SAB), Pretoria, ZA.

2. Chief Native Commissioner to Magistrate Ndwedwe, December 15, 1922, 24/214, 1431, part 1, NTS, SAB.

3. Robert Edgar, *Because They Chose the Plan of God: The Story of the Bulhoek Massacre* (Johannesburg: Ravan Press, 1988); Robert Edgar, *The Finger of God: Enoch Mgijima, the Israelites, and the Bulhoek Massacre in South Africa* (Charlottesville: University of Virginia, 2018); Clifton Crais, *The Politics of Evil: Magic, State Power, and the Political Imagination in South Africa* (New York: Cambridge University Press, 2002), 117–21.

4. Edgar, *The Finger of God*, 77, 82.

5. Chief Native Commissioner to magistrate, Inanda Division, May 29, 1912, 917/12, 77, Papers of the Chief Native Commissioner (CNC), Pietermaritzburg Archives Repository (NAB), Pietermaritzburg, ZA.

6. Shula Marks, "War and Union, 1899–1910," in *The Cambridge History of South Africa*, vol. 2, ed. Robert Ross, Anne Kelk Mager, and Bill Nasson (New York: Cambridge University Press, 2011), 157–210; Bill Freund, "South Africa: The Union Years, 1910–1948," *Cambridge History of South Africa*, vol. 2 (Cambridge, UK: Cambridge University Press, 2011), 211–53.

7. G. A. Park Ross to Chief Native Commissioner, December 20, 1926, 24/214, 1431, part 1, NTS, SAB.

8. For some of the others, letter from M. Monger to district office police, November 13, 1922, 24/214, 1431, part 1, NTS, SAB; Charles Mckenzie to Chief Native Commissioner, 1922, NV2/26/22, 3/3/1/1, Papers of the Magistrate of Ndwedwe (1/NWE), NAB. See also South Africa Native Churches Commission, *Report of Native Churches Commission* (Cape Town: Cape Times,1925).

9. John Mabuyakhulu, "91. The Vaccination Controversy at Ekuphakameni in 1926," in *The Story of Isaiah Shembe, Vol. 1: History and Traditions Centered on Ekuphakameni and Mount Nhlangakazi*, ed. Irving Hexham and G. C. Oosthuizen, trans. Hans-Jürgen Becken (Lewiston, NY: Edwin Mellen, 1996), 145–51; G. A. Park Ross to Secretary for Public Health, December 9, 1926, 24/241, 1431, part 1, NTS, NAB.

10. Edwin G. Bain and Jan Venter, "Public Health Policy in a Time of Change and Disaster in South Africa: 1910–1920," *Jàmbá* 8, no. 1 (September 29, 2016): 1–8; James Duminy and Susan M. Parnell, "The Shifting Interface of Public Health and Urban Policy in South Africa," *Journal of Planning History* 21, no. 1 (February 1, 2022): 86–102.

11. M. Monger to District Officer, November 13, 1922, 24/241, 1431, part 1, NTS, SAB; Azariah Mthiyane and Gaslinah Cele, "201. Shembe Comes to the Country at Mbonambi," in *The*

Story of Isaiah Shembe, Vol. 2: Early Regional Traditions of the Acts of the Nazarites, ed. Irving Hexham and G. C. Oosthuizen, trans. Hans-Jurgen Becken (Lewiston, NY: Edwin Mellen, 1999), 227–29 (henceforth *SIS* 2); Mkhipheni Ndunakazi, "171. Shembe Comes to the Dube Tribal Area," in *SIS* 2, 185–92.

12. Freund, "South Africa"; Helen Bradford, *A Taste of Freedom: The ICU in Rural South Africa, 1924–1930* (New Haven, CT: Yale University Press, 1987); Jörn Leonhard, *Pandora's Box: A History of the First World War*, trans. Patrick Camiller (Cambridge, MA: Belknap Press of Harvard University Press, 2018); Ismee Tames and Maartje Abbenhuis, *Global War, Global Catastrophe: Neutrals, Belligerents and the Transformations of the First World War* (New York: Bloomsbury Academic, 2021); Barbara Foley, *Spectres of 1919: Class and Nation in the Making of the New Negro* (Urbana: University of Illinois Press, 2003).

13. Edgar, *Finger of God*, 2.

14. As quoted in Peder Anker, *Imperial Ecology: Environmental Order in the British Empire, 1895–1945* (Cambridge, MA: Harvard University Press, 2009), 51.

15. Jeremy Seekings, "'Not a Single White Person Should Be Allowed to Go Under': Swartgevaar and the Origins of South Africa's Welfare State, 1924–1929," *Journal of African History* 48, no. 3 (2007): 375–94; Jeremy Seekings, "The National Party and the Ideology of Welfare in South Africa under Apartheid," *Journal of Southern African Studies* 46, no. 6 (November 1, 2020): 1145–62.

16. This helps explain the "bewildering repetitiveness" of policy that Freund notes. Freund, "South Africa," 234.

17. South Africa Native Churches Commission, *Report of Native Churches Commission* (Cape Town: Cape Times, 1925).

18. C. W. H. Lansdown, H. A. Fagan, F. S. Tatham, H. Pring, V. Rosenstein, C. G. M. Place, and A. E. Speight, "South Africa," *Journal of Comparative Legislation and International Law* 12, no. 2 (1930): 143; "Union of South Africa: Medical Matters in Parliament," *British Medical Journal* 1, no. 3519 (1928): 1042–43. For earlier debates about the issue of conscientious objection in Britain, see Nadja Durbach, "Class, Gender, and the Conscientious Objectors to Vaccination, 1898–1907," *Journal of British Studies* 41, no. 1 (2002): 58–83.

19. Memorandum, "Vaccination: Shembe Sect," February 13, 1935, 24/241, 1431, part 1, NTS, SAB.

20. Lansdown et al., "South Africa."

21. Interview with Isaiah Shembe, January 15, 1923, 24/241, 1431, part 1, NTS, SAB.

22. Interview with Isaiah Shembe, January 15, 1923.

23. Magistrate Ndwedwe to Chief Native Commissioner, January 22, 1923, 24/241, 1431, part 1, NTS, SAB.

24. Interview with Isaiah Shembe, January 15, 1923.

25. Chief Native Commissioner to Secretary of Native Affairs, undated (but 1922), 124/307, 3192, NTS, SAB.

26. Chief Native Commissioner to Secretary of Native Affairs, undated (but 1922).

27. For comparison in colonial India: Paul D. Kenny, "The Origins of Patronage Politics: State Building, Centrifugalism, and Decolonization," *British Journal of Political Science* 45, no. 1 (January 2015): 141–71.

28. See, for example, Chief Native Commissioner to Secretary of Native Affairs, August 28, 1931, 24/241, 1431, Part I, NTS, SAB.

29. For Shembe's land purchases in this period, protocol no. 293/1935, Church of Nazareth Ecclesiastical Endowment Trust, 120/4/2537, 287, Papers of Director General Operations, SAB. Harvey M. Feinberg and André Horn, "South African Territorial Segregation: New Data on African Farm Purchases, 1913–1936," *Journal of African History* 50, no. 1 (2009): 48–49.

30. "Sale by and transfer from R. Monzali to Native I. Shembe and Passing of First Mortgage Bond," 1929, 2982, 1081, Papers of the Executive Council (URU), SAB. On the rarity of this, see Harvey Feinberg, *Our Land, Our Life, Our Future: Black South African Challenges to Territorial Segregation, 1913–1948* (Pretoria: Unisa Press, 2015), 107.

31. Chief Native Commissioner to Secretary of Native Affairs, February 1, 1930, 24/241, 1431, part 1, NTS, SAB.

32. Comparisons to the treatment of Sufi communities in West Africa are relevant. See David Robinson, *Paths of Accommodation: Muslim Societies and French Colonial Authorities in Senegal and Mauritania, 1880–1920* (Athens: Ohio University Press, 2000); Cheikh Anta Mbacke Babou, *Fighting the Greater Jihad: Amadu Bamba and the Founding of the Muridiyya of Senegal, 1853–1913* (Athens: Ohio University Press, 2007); Sean Hanretta, *Islam and Social Change in French West Africa: History of an Emancipatory Community* (Cambridge, UK: Cambridge University Press, 2009).

33. South Africa Police to District Officer, September 10, 1921, 24/241, 1431, part 1, NTS, SAB; G. A. Park Ross to Secretary for Public Health.

34. Magistrate of Inanda/Verulam to Chief Native Commissioner, April 24, 1922, 24/241, 1431, part 1, NTS, SAB; Commissioner of Police to Secretary of Native Affairs, June 12, 1922, 24/241, 1431, part 1, NTS, SAB.

35. G. A. Park Ross to Secretary for Public Health; Chief Native Commissioner to Secretary of Native Affairs, August 28, 1931, 24/241, 1431, part 1, NTS, SAB.

36. G. A. Park Ross to Chief Native Commissioner, December 20, 1926, 24/241, 1431, part 1, NTS, SAB.

37. Such relative assessments were a feature of many colonial governments and help explain why some of these governments confronted African-led religious movements and "therapeutic insurgencies," to borrow Nancy Rose Hunt's phrasing, with violence. See, George Shepperson and Thomas Price, *Independent African: John Chilembwe and the Origins, Setting and Significance of the Nyasaland Native Rising of 1915* (Edinburgh: University Press, 1987); Karen Fields, *Revival and Rebellion in Colonial Central Africa* (Portsmouth, NH: Heinemann, 1997); Nancy Rose Hunt, *A Nervous State: Violence, Remedies, and Reverie in Colonial Congo* (Durham, NC: Duke University Press, 2016).

38. Acting Chief Native Commissioner to Secretary of Native Affairs, January 7, 1935, 24/241, 1431, part 1, NTS, SAB.

39. H. C. Lugg, memorandum, "Vaccination—Shembe Sect," August 10, 1935, 24/241, 1431, part 1, NTS, SAB.

40. Acting Chief Native Commissioner to Secretary of Native Affairs, January 7, 1935.

41. Acting Chief Native Commissioner to Secretary of Native Affairs, January 7, 1935.

42. Acting Chief Native Commissioner to Secretary of Native Affairs, January 7, 1935.

43. In Natal, this stemmed in part from the myths surrounding the success of Theophilus Shepstone. Thomas McClendon, *White Chiefs, Black Lords: Shepstone and the Colonial State in Natal, South Africa, 1845–1878* (Rochester, NY: University of Rochester Press, 2010); Jeff Guy, *Theophilus Shepstone and the Forging of Natal* (Pietermaritzburg, ZA: University of KwaZulu-Natal Press, 2013).

44. Roberts, "Shembe," 76.

45. Chief Native Commissioner to Secretary of Native Affairs, May 26, 1939, 24/241, 1431, part 1, NTS, SAB.

46. Native Economic Commission, "Native Economic Commission, Sitting at Pietermaritzburg, Minutes of Evidence" (Pretoria: Union of South Africa, 1931), 6162.

47. Mabuyakhulu, "91. The Vaccination Controversy," in *SIS* 1.

48. H. C. Lugg to Assistant Health Officer, Durban, April 26, 1929, 24/241, 1431, part 1, NTS, SAB.

49. G. A. Park Ross to Secretary for Public Health.

50. Shula Marks, *The Ambiguities of Dependence in South Africa: Class, Nationalism, and the State in Twentieth-Century Natal* (Baltimore: Johns Hopkins University Press, 1986), 26.

51. The politics of the tightrope made state officials and Shembe unreliable narrators when it came to assessing how "political" the Nazaretha were. More broadly, Shembe's strategies for engaging with the state and evading its authority call for a reassessment of the politics of the Nazaretha and other divine healing churches.

52. Testimony of Masimini Zuzu, February 13, 1922, 24/214, 1431, NTS, SAB.

53. Mabuyakhulu, "91. The Vaccination Controversy," in *SIS* 1, 148.

54. Mabuyakhulu, "91. The Vaccination Controversy," in *SIS* 1, 148.

55. Roberts, "Shembe," 38.

56. H. C. Lugg to Assistant Chief Native Commissioner, October 1, 1929, 24/241, 1431, part 1, NTS, SAB.

57. For a biographical sketch, see Ruth Gordon, *Shepstone: The Role of the Family in the History of South Africa* (Johannesburg: A. A. Balkema, 1968), 384–91; E. J. Verwey, *New Dictionary of South African Biography* (London: Thorold's Africana Books, 1995), 565.

58. Jeff Guy, *Theophilus Shepstone and the Forging of Natal* (Pietermaritzburg, ZA: University of KwaZulu-Natal Press, 2013).

59. Native Economic Commission, "Native Economic Commission, Sitting at Pietermaritzburg, Minutes of Evidence" (Pretoria: Union of South Africa, 1931), 6366. Others recalled how Africans regularly lined up in his backyard in Pietermaritzburg to request favors and advice. Personal communication between the author and Jeff Guy, March 11, 2010.

60. Chief Native Commissioner to Secretary of Native Affairs, undated 1922, 24/241, 1431, part 1, NTS, SAB.

61. D. G. Shepstone to Chief Native Commissioner, October 27, 1931, 24/214, 1431, NTS, SAB.

62. William and Nellie Wells to J. B. M. Hertzog, September 8, 1925, 27/327, 7293, NTS, SAB; Joel Cabrita, "Texts, Authority, and Community in the South African 'Ibandla LamaNazaretha' (Church of the Nazaretha), 1910–1976," *Journal of Religion in Africa* 40, no. 1 (2010), 66.

63. For a brief description of some of her activities, see letter from H. C. Lugg to Chief Native Commissioner, February 7, 1930, 125/307, 3192, NTS, SAB.

64. For some of their names: Protocol no. 293/1935. On white women helping African men buy land, see Feinberg, *Our Land*, 3.

65. Nellie Wells to Governor General, January 13, 1930, 50/1341, 1567, Papers of the Governor General (GG), SAB.

66. Nellie Wells to Governor General.

67. Nellie Wells to Governor General. This logic did fit in many ways with how the segregation era government was articulating race relations. Papini, "Carl Faye's Transcript," 252.

68. For a later articulation of this idea, see Vilakazi, *Shembe*, 28–29.

69. G. A. Park Ross to Acting Secretary of Public Health.

70. Adam Payne, "A Prophet among the Zulus," *Illustrated London News*, February 8, 1930. (This was most likely Wells writing under a penname.)

71. Danie De Villiers, "'I See You': The Industrial and Commercial Workers Union of Africa, 1919–1930," *HIPSA* (blog); Helen Bradford, "Lynch Law and Labourers: The ICU in Umvoti, 1927–1928," *Journal of Southern African Studies* 11, no. 1 (October 1, 1984): 128–49; Helen Bradford, *A Taste of Freedom: The ICU in Rural South Africa, 1924–1930* (New Haven, CT: Yale University Press, 1987); Anusa Daimon, "'Ringleaders and Troublemakers': Malawian (Nyasa) Migrants and Transnational Labor Movements in Southern Africa, c. 1910–1960," *Labor History* 58, no. 5 (October 20, 2017): 656–75; Henry Dee, "'I Am a Bad Native': Masculinity and Marriage in the Biographies of Clements Kadalie," *African Studies* 78, no. 2 (2019): 183–204.

72. David Johnson, "Clements Kadalie, the ICU, and the Language of Freedom," *English in Africa* 42, no. 3 (2015): 44.

73. Bradford, *A Taste of Freedom*.

74. Bradford, *A Taste of Freedom*, 104.

75. Bradford, "Lynch Law and Labourers"; Bradford, *A Taste of Freedom*, 91. On the ICU and chiefs: Nicholas Cope, *To Bind the Nation: Solomon KaDinuzulu and Zulu Nationalism, 1913–1933* (Pietermaritzburg, ZA: University of Natal Press, 1993), 148.

76. On the ICU in Durban: Jonathan Hyslop, "The Politics of Disembarkation: Empire, Shipping and Labor in the Port of Durban, 1897–1947," *International Labor and Working Class History* 93 (Spring 2018): 188–89; Marks, *The Ambiguities of Dependence*, 76–108.

77. Gunner, *Man of Heaven*, 8.

78. Lotha Zuma, "199. Sermon of Shembe at Empuza in 1931," in *SIS* 2, 225.

79. G. A. Park Ross to Acting Secretary of Public Health.

80. Jock McCulloch, "Medicine, Politics and Disease on South Africa's Gold Mines," *Journal of Southern African Studies* 39, no. 3 (September 1, 2013): 543–56; Alan Cobley, "'Lacking in Respect for Whitemen': 'Tropical Africans' on the Witwatersrand Gold Mines, 1903–1904," *International Labor and Working-Class History* 86 (2014): 36–54; Randall M. Packard, *White Plague, Black Labor: Tuberculosis and the Political Economy of Health and Disease in South Africa* (Berkeley: University of California, 1989).

81. Mabuyakhulu, "91. Vaccination Controversy at Ekuphakameni in 1926," in *SIS* 1.

82. Mabuyakhulu, "91. Vaccination Controversy at Ekuphakameni in 1926," in *SIS* 1.

83. Compare Bhengu, "9. The Maidens Were Fighting," in *SIS* 2, to Simon Mngoma, "164. Shembe's Last Mission Journey to the North," in *SIS* 1, 242–7.

84. Secretary of Native Affairs to Commissioner of Police, Pretoria, June 12, 1922; Sub-inspector CI Dept. to Durban Deputy Commissioner, October 23, 1931, 24/214, 1431, NTS, SAB.

85. H. C. Lugg to Chief Native Commissioner, July 17, 1931; H. C. Lugg to G. A. Park Ross, April

26, 1929; C. L. Dube to senior Assistant Public Health Officer, September 10, 1935, 24/214, 1431, NTS, SAB.

86. On these allegations: Roberts, "Shembe," 79.

87. Mngoma, "165. Shembe's Last Days at Mikhaideni," in *SIS* 1.

88. Acting Chief Native Commissioner to Secretary of Native Affairs, January 7, 1935.

89. Notice the mismatch between the land in the trust document and Roberts description of church farms: protocol no. 293/1935, Church of Nazareth Ecclesiastical Endowment Trust, 120/4/2537, 287, Papers of Director General Operations, SAB; Roberts, "Shembe," 71–3.

90. On life at Gospel, Gunner, *Man of Heaven*, 153–57.

91. Consider, too, Shembe's description of fundraising for these purchases. These efforts involved fewer people: Native Economic Commission, "Sitting at Pietermaritzburg," 3538; Roberts, "Shembe," 71–2.

92. Chief Native Commissioner to Secretary of Native Affairs, September 28, 1930.

93. N. C. Mtunzini to Chief Native Commissioner, December 5, 1938; Chief Native Commissioner to Secretary of Native Affairs, January 25, 1940, 24/214, 1431, NTS, SAB.

94. Matthew A. Schnurr, "The Boom and Bust of Zululand Cotton, 1910–1933," *Journal of Southern African Studies* 37, no. 1 (2011): 119–34; David Lincoln, "Settlement and Servitude in Zululand, 1918–1948," *International Journal of African Historical Studies* 28, no. 1 (1995): 49–67; Aran S. MacKinnon, "The Persistence of the Cattle Economy in Zululand, South Africa, 1900–50," *Canadian Journal of African Studies* 33, no. 1 (1999): 98–135.

95. Marks, *Ambiguities of Independence*, 95.

96. MacKinnon, "Persistence of the Cattle Economy," 101.

97. MacKinnon, "Persistence of the Cattle Economy," 101.

98. "Annual Report of the Magistrate of Mtunzini," 1913, 1/26/13, 3/4/2/2, Papers of the Magistrate of Mtunzini (1/MTU), Durban Archives Repository (TBD), Durban, ZA.

99. Shula Marks, "Natal, the Zulu Royal Family and the Ideology of Segregation," *Journal of Southern African Studies* 4, no. 2 (April 1, 1978): 184; Aran S. MacKinnon, "Of Oxford Bags and Twirling Canes: The State, Popular Responses, and Zulu Antimalaria Assistants in the Early-Twentieth-Century Zululand Malaria Campaigns," *Radical History Review* 2001, no. 80 (May 1, 2001): 76–100. On yaws and syphilis: Katherine Paugh, "Yaws, Syphilis, Sexuality, and the Circulation of Medical Knowledge in the British Caribbean and the Atlantic World," *Bulletin of the History of Medicine* 88, no. 2 (2014): 225–52.

100. This was Inkosi Manqamu Mbonambi. For his history: "Report on Behavior of Mbonambi Regent," 1901, 299/1901, 3/2/6, Papers of the Magistrate of Empangeni (1/EPI), TBD.

101. Statement of Chief Manqamu, January 8, 1909, 53/1909, 3/2/13, 1/EPI, TBD; Julie Parle,

"'This Painful Subject': Racial Politics and Suicide in Colonial Natal and Zululand," in *Histories of Suicide: International Perspectives*, ed. John Weaver and David Wright (Toronto: University of Toronto Press, 2008), 170–71.

102. Joel Cabrita, "Isaiah Shembe's Theological Nationalism, 1920–1935," *Journal of Southern African Studies* 35, no. 3 (2009): 618.

103. E. N. Braatvedt to Chief Native Commissioner, November 3, 1931, 24/214, 1431, NTS, SAB.

104. E. N. Braatvedt to Chief Native Commissioner, November 3, 1931; Shepstone to Chief Native Commissioner, October 27, 1931; Mtunzini to Chief Native Commissioner, December 5, 1938.

105. Shepstone to Chief Native Commissioner, October 27, 1931.

106. Mtunzini to Chief Native Commissioner, December 5, 1938.

107. Paul La Hausse, *Restless Identities: Signatures of Nationalism, Zulu Ethnicity, and History in the Lives of Petros Lamula (c. 1881–1948) and Lymon Maling (1889–c. 1936)* (Pietermaritzburg, ZA: University of Natal Press, 2000), 131.

108. John L. Dube, memorandum, Cultivation of Sugar Cane in Reserve No. 8 (Chief Somshokwe), June 3, 1950, N2/8/3/2(2), 3/4/3/3, 1/MTU, TBD.

109. The phrase is a play on "away in the locations." William Beinart and Colin Bundy, *Hidden Struggles in Rural South Africa: Politics and Popular Movements in the Transkei and Eastern Cape, 1890–1930* (Berkeley: University of California Press, 1987).

110. On this history, Hlonipha Mokoena, *Magema Fuze: The Making of a Kholwa Intellectual* (Scottsville, ZA: University of KwaZulu-Natal, 2011), 217–21; Michael Mahoney, *The Other Zulus: The Spread of Zulu Ethnicity in Colonial South Africa* (Durham, NC: Duke University Press, 2012); Michael Mahoney, "Racial Formation and Ethnogenesis from Below: The Zulu Case, 1879–1906," *International Journal of African Historical Studies* 36, no. 3 (2003): 559–83.

111. Cope, *To Bind the Nation*, 151.

112. Cope, *To Bind the Nation*, 149; MacKinnon, "The Persistence of the Cattle Economy."

113. La Hausse, *Restless Identities*, 37; Norman Etherington, *Preachers, Peasants, and Politics in Southeast Africa, 1835–1880* (London: Royal Historical Society, 1978).

114. Ingie Hovland, *Mission Station Christianity: Norwegian Missionaries in Colonial Natal and Zululand, Southern Africa, 1850–1890* (Boston: Brill, 2013).

115. Cope, *To Bind the Nation*, 47, 122, 124. See too Max Gluckman, "Analysis of a Social Situation in Modern Zululand," *Bantu Studies* 14, no. 1 (January 1, 1940): 1–30.

116. Roberts, "Shembe," 89–112.

117. Testimony of Masimini Zuzu. Some branches of the church also had distinct traditions. Oosthuizen and Hexam, "64. Thesalonika," in *SIS* 2, 68.

118. Mkhipeni Ndunakazi, "171. Shembe Comes to the Dube Tribal Territory," in *SIS* 2, 190.

119. Ndunakazi, "171. Shembe Comes to the Dube Tribal Territory," in *SIS* 2, 191.

120. Statement of Mbanjwa Ngidi, undated [1931], 24/214, 1431, NTS, SAB.

121. H. C. Lugg to Chief Native Commissioner, September 18, 1931, 24/214, 1431, NTS, SAB.

122. Sophie Mtolo and Jestinah Mnyandu, "65. Shembe Comes to Thesalonika," in *SIS* 2, 68–69

123. Erlank, *Convening Black Intimacy*, 21.

124. Muntuwesizwe Buthelezi, "97. Shembe Gives His Daughter Zondi to Solomon," in *SIS* 1, 155–57; Cope, *To Bind the Nation*, 124; La Hausse, *Restless Identities*, 140.

125. Oliver Thabethe, "265. Bridewealth and Marriage Fees," in *SIS* 2, 307–9.

126. Philip Ngubane, Amoniah Nzimande, John Mabayakhulu, Solomon Mdluli, "60. The Angel of Mpondoland Calls Shembe South," in *SIS* 2, 56–57.

127. Thabethe, "265. Bridewealth and Marriage Fees," in *SIS* 2.

128. Thabethe, "265. Bridewealth and Marriage Fees," in *SIS* 2.

129. Gunner, *Man of Heaven*, 65, 73. This is a translation of the rules about marriage written down by a member of the church.

130. Gunner, *Man of Heaven*.

131. Gunner, *Man of Heaven*, 65.

132. Chief Native Commissioner to Acting Secretary of Native Affairs.

CHAPTER 8. A CELEBRITY IN SOUTH AFRICA

1. Adam Payne, "A Prophet among the Zulus," *Illustrated London News*, February 8, 1930, 203. "Adam Payne" was likely a pen name, and Nellie Wells was likely the author.

2. Reba N. Soffer, "Political Ideas and Audiences: The Case of Arthur Bryant and the Illustrated London News, 1936–1945," *Parliamentary History* 27, no. 1 (2008): 159.

3. On the long history of talent, fame, and reputation, see Jan M. Vansina, *Paths in the Rainforests: Toward a History of Political Tradition in Equatorial Africa* (Madison: University of Wisconsin Press, 1990), 274–75; Kathryn M. De Luna, "Hunting Reputations: Talent, Individuals, and Community in Precolonial South Central Africa," *Journal of African History* 53, no. 3 (November 2012): 279–99; Kathryn M. De Luna, "Affect and Society in Precolonial Africa," *International Journal of African Historical Studies* 46, no. 1 (2013): 123–50. Thanks in part to impressive work with word origins, some of the most influential studies about talent and fame draw upon examples in the precolonial period. For overlapping concepts, see, too, John Iliffe, *Honour in African History* (New York: Cambridge University Press, 2005).

4. Payne, "A Prophet among the Zulus."

5. For comparison, see South Africa Native Churches Commission, *Report of Native Churches Commission* (Cape Town: Cape Times, 1925).

6. Protocol no. 293/1935, Church of Nazareth Ecclesiastical Endowment Trust, 120/4/2537, 287, Papers of the Director General's Office, South African Archives Repository (henceforth SAB), Pretoria, South Africa. For comparison, see Harvey M. Feinberg and André Horn, "South African Territorial Segregation: New Data on African Farm Purchases, 1913–1936," *Journal of African History* 50, no. 1 (2009): 41–60; Harvey Feinberg, *Our Land, Our Life, Our Future: Black South African Challenges to Territorial Segregation, 1913–1948* (Pretoria: Unisa Press, 2015), 75.

7. On his daughter's marriage, see Muntuwesizwe Buthelezi, "97. Shembe Gives His Daughter Zondi to King Solomon," in *The Story of Isaiah Shembe, Vol. 2: Early Regional Traditions of the Acts of the Nazarites*, ed. Irving Hexham and G. C. Oosthuizen, trans. Hans-Jurgen Becken (Lewiston, NY: Edwin Mellen, 1999), 157–58 (henceforth *SIS* 2); Esther Roberts, "Shembe: The Man and His Works" (master's thesis, University of Natal, 1936), 38; John Langalibalele Dube, *UShembe* (Pietermaritzburg, ZA: Shuter and Shooter, 1936), 103–4; Joel Cabrita, "Isaiah Shembe's Theological Nationalism, 1920s–1935," *Journal of Southern African Studies* 35, no. 3 (2009): 614. And on his sons, see Roberts, "Shembe," 43; James W. Fernandez, "The Precincts of the Prophet: A Day with Johannes Galilee Shembe," *Journal of Religion in Africa* 5, no. 1 (1973): 32–51; G. C. Oosthuizen, "Succession Conflict within the Church of the Nazarites" (Institute for Social and Economic Research, University of Durban–Westville, 1981), 10–12; Joel Cabrita, *Text and Authority in the South African Nazaretha Church* (New York: Cambridge University Press, 2014), 295–335.

8. Simon Mngoma and Oliver Thabethe, "164. Shembe's Last Mission Journey to the North," in *SIS* 2, 242–47; J. G. Shembe and Muntuwesizwe Buthelezi, "165. Shembe's Last Days at Mikhaideni," in *SIS* 2, 247–49; Emesiah Mthiya, "249. The Commission of Emesiah Mthiya to Swaziland," in *SIS* 2, 281–84.

9. Joel Cabrita, "Texts, Authority, and Community in the South African 'Ibandla LamaNazaretha' (Church of the Nazaretha), 1910–1976," *Journal of Religion in Africa* 40, no. 1 (2010): 89.

10. Letter to Assistant Magistrate Ndwedwe from Sergt. Natal Police, May 12, 1921, 917/912, Papers of the Chief Native Commissioner, Natal (CNC) 77, Pietermaritzburg Archive Repository (NAB), Pietermaritzburg, ZA.

11. Dube, *UShembe*.

12. Papini and Gunner refer to Shembe as a "luminary" and a "celebrity" too. See Elizabeth Gunner, *The Man of Heaven and the Beautiful Ones of God = Umuntu Wasezulwini Nabantu Abahle Bakankulunkulu: Writings from Ibandla LamaNazaretha, a South African*

Church (Leiden, NL: Brill, 2002), 2; Robert Papini, "Carl Faye's Transcript of Isaiah Shembe's Testimony of His Early Life and Calling," *Journal of Religion in Africa* 29, no. 3 (1999): 254.

13. On the history of celebrity in the early twentieth century: Fred Inglis, *A Short History of Celebrity* (Princeton, NJ: Princeton University Press, 2010); Susan J. Douglas and Andrea McDonnell, *Celebrity: A History of Fame* (New York: New York University Press, 2019). And a particular apt contribution in post-apartheid South Africa: Fundiswa A. Kobo, "Spirituality Trapped in Androcentric Celebrity Cults in South Africa Post-1994," *HTS Theological Studies* 75, no. 3 (2019): 1–7.

14. On some of those chiefs and kings: Leonard Thompson, *Survival in Two Worlds: Moshoeshoe of Lesotho, 1786–1870* (Oxford, UK: Clarendon Press, 1975); Carolyn Hamilton, *Terrific Majesty: The Powers of Shaka Zulu and the Limits of Historical Invention* (Cambridge, MA: Harvard University Press, 1998). And on healers: Karen Flint, *Healing Traditions: African Medicine, Cultural Exchange, and Competition in South Africa, 1820–1948* (Athens: Ohio University Press, 2008), 48–54; Jeff Guy, *The Maphumulo Uprising: War, Law, and Ritual in the Zulu Rebellion* (Scottsville, ZA: University of KwaZulu-Natal Press, 2005), 4–7.

15. On King Shaka "testing" healers: Henry Callaway, *The Religious System of the Amazulu: With a Translation into English and Notes* (London, 1868), 390. In some cases, too, chiefs merged the roles of political leader and healer. John William Colenso, *Langalibalele and the Amahlubi Tribe: Being Remarks upon the Official Record of the Trials of the Chief, His Son and Induna, and Other Members of the Amahlubi Tribe* (London, 1875), 1; John Wright and Andrew Manson, *The Hlubi Chiefdom in Zululand-Natal History* (Ladysmith, ZA: Ladysmith Historical Society, 1983).

16. Within African communities, politicians, successful businesspeople, and journalists were often on the spectrum of celebrity too. Heather Hughes, *First President: A Life of John Dube, Founding President of the ANC* (Auckland Park, ZA: Jacana Media, 2011); Brian Willan, *Sol Plaatje: A Life of Solomon Tshekisho Plaatje, 1876–1932* (Auckland Park, ZA: Jacana, 2018). By the 1920s, labor leaders were as well: Henry Dee, "'I Am a Bad Native': Masculinity and Marriage in the Biographies of Clements Kadalie," *African Studies* 78, no. 2 (2019): 183–204; Shula Marks, *The Ambiguities of Dependence in South Africa: Class, Nationalism, and the State in Twentieth-Century Natal* (Baltimore: Johns Hopkins University Press, 1986).

17. Bajabhisile Zulu, "217. Early Opposition at Linda," in *SIS* 2, 245–48.

18. On Inkosi Solomon's marriages, see Nicholas Cope, *To Bind the Nation: Solomon KaDinuzulu and Zulu Nationalism, 1913–1933* (Pietermaritzburg, ZA: University of Natal

Press, 1993), 121–23. On his first wife: Rebecca Hourwich Reyher, *Zulu Woman: The Life Story of Christina Sibiya* (New York: Feminist Press at the City University of New York, 1999).

19. For these standards: Gunner, *The Man of Heaven*, 65–70.

20. Cope, *To Bind the Nation*.

21. I could not secure permission to use the image, but see Petros Lamula, *Uzulukamalandela: A Most Practical and Concise Compendium of African History* (Durban, ZA: Josiah Jones, 1931). Many thanks to Paul La Hausse for alerting me to this photograph. See also Paul La Hausse, *Restless Identities: Signatures of Nationalism, Zulu Ethnicity, and History in the Lives of Petros Lamula (c. 1881–1948) and Lymon Maling (1889–c. 1936)* (Pietermaritzburg, ZA: University of Natal Press, 2000), 140.

22. Lamula, *Uzulukamalandela*.

23. La Hausse, *Restless Identities*. Shembe had some of this memorabilia in his home at Ekuphakameni. Roberts, "Shembe," 55.

24. There were rumors that Zondi's "handmaid" produced an heir—but this raised questions too. See Carl Faye, memorandum, "UShembe," 1939, 24/214, 1431, Papers of the Native Affairs Department (NTS), SAB.

25. John Mabuyakhulu and Hlanganisumuzi David Mncwanga, "96. The Zulu King Solomon Comes to Ekuphakameni in 1930," in *SIS* 1, 155–57. John Mabuyakhulu, "98. The Cornerstone Ceremony at Ekuphakameni," in *SIS* 1, 158–59.

26. Cope suggests that 1928 was an important turning point. Cope, *To Bind the Nation*, 229. See also Marks, *Ambiguities of Dependence*, 36–37.

27. Muntuwesizwe Buthelezi, "97. Shembe Gives His Daughter to King Solomon," in *SIS* 1, 157–58.

28. Muntuwesizwe Buthelezi, "97. Shembe Gives His Daughter to King Solomon," in *SIS* 1.

29. Acting Chief Native Commissioner to Secretary of Native Affairs, January 7, 1935, 24/214, 1341, NTS, SAB.

30. Cope, *To Bind the Nation*, 137–39.

31. For good relations: Mkhipheni Ndunakazi, "171. Shembe Comes to the Dube Tribal Area," in *SIS* 2. Mkhipheni Ndunakazi, "172. Shembe Gets a Site for the Temple Gibizisila," in *SIS* 2; Mthiyane and Cele, "201. Shembe Comes to the Country of Mbonambi, " in *SIS* 2; Azariah Mthiyane, "203. Shembe Advises the Mbonambi Chief, " in *SIS* 2. Azariah Mthiyane, "204. Shembe Blesses the Mbonambi Chief," in *SIS* 2, 185–92, 192–93, 226–29, 230–31. For bad ones, Elias Khawula, "39. Shembe Restores the Chieftainship in the Luthuli Tribe," in *SIS* 2; Musawenkosi Mkhwanazi, "225. Shembe Comes to Chief Msibi," in *SIS* 2, 36–37, 254–57.

32. John Mabuyakhulu, "98. The Cornerstone Ceremony at Ekuphakameni," in *SIS* 1, 158–59.

33. Cope, *To Bind the Nation*, 231.

34. Marks, *The Ambiguities of Dependence*.

35. For a reconstruction of one of these crowds, see Hamilton, *Terrific Majesty*, 75–102.

36. Hamilton, *Terrific Majesty*. Adam Ashforth, *The Politics of Official Discourse in Twentieth-Century South Africa* (New York: Oxford University Press, 1990); Jeff Guy, *Theophilus Shepstone and the Forging of Natal* (Scottsville, ZA: University of KwaZulu-Natal Press, 2013).

37. Goolam Vahed, "'An Evil Thing': Gandhi and Indian Indentured Labour in South Arica, 1893–1914," *South Asia* 42, 4 (2019): 654–74; Jonathan Hyslop, "The Strange Death of Liberal England and the Strange Birth of Illiberal South Africa: British Trade Unionists, Indian Labourers and Afrikaner Rebels, 1910–1914," *Labour History Review* 79, no. 1 (April 2014): 97.

38. Helen Bradford, *A Taste of Freedom: The ICU in Rural South Africa, 1924–1930* (New Haven, CT: Yale University Press, 1987), 96; Veit Erlmann, "'Horses in the Race Course': The Domestication of Ingoma Dancing in South Africa, 1929–39," *Popular Music* 8, no. 3 (1989): 259–73.

39. Cope, *To Bind the Nation*, 115, 133.

40. Bhekinkonzo Zungu, "187. Healing a Vunizitha," in *SIS* 2, 211–12; Esau Madlopha, "189. Shembe comes to Zibindlela in 1927," in *SIS* 2, 213–14; Petros Dhlomo, "173. Shembe's Last Visit to Gibizisula in 1935," in *SIS* 2, 194–95.

41. For comparisons to downtown Durban: Paul La Hausse, "The Dispersal of the Regiments: Radical African Opposition in Durban, 1930," (paper presented at the African Studies Seminar, University of the Witwatersrand, Witwatersrand, ZA, March 1986), 1, https://core.ac.uk/download/pdf/39667913.pdf.

42. Jiniose Mzimela, "177. Shembe Comes to Emazimeleni" in *SIS* 2, 196–97.

43. Andy Rice, "Church and van Schalkwyk Settle Vuvuzela Battle with Minimum Fuss, Noise," Daily Maverick, June 23, 2010.

44. Cope, *To Bind the Nation*, 133–34.

45. La Hausse, "The Dispersal of the Regiments."

46. John Mabuyakhulu, "91. The Vaccination Controversy at Ekuphakameni," in *SIS* 1, 146–51.

47. Mabuyakhulu and Mncwanga "96. The Zulu King Solomon comes to Ekuphakameni in 1930," in *SIS* 1, 156.

48. Mabuyakhulu, "98. The Cornerstone Ceremony," in *SIS* 1.

49. Around the time of the ceremony, Shembe had been told to stop lobola loans and to tear down structures in Zululand. D. G. Shepstone to Chief Native Commissioner, October 27,

1931, 24/214, 1431, NTS, SAB.

50. As quoted in Papini, "Carl Faye's Transcript," 46.

51. Roberts, "Shembe," 80.

52. On first fruits: Eileen Jensen Krige, *The Social System of the Zulus* (Pietermaritzburg, ZA: Shuter and Shooter, 1936), 341; Jeremy C. Hollmann, "Allusions to Agriculturist Rituals in Hunter-Gatherer Rock Art? EMkhobeni Shelter, Northern UKhahlamba-Drakensberg, KwaZulu-Natal, South Africa," *African Archaeological Review* 32, no. 3 (September 1, 2015): 505–35.

53. Cope, *To Bind the Nation*, 126–29; Guillermo Giucci, Anne Mayagoitia, and Debra Nagao, *The Cultural Life of the Automobile: Roads to Modernity* (Austin: University of Texas Press, 2012), 66; Christine Jeske, "Are Cars the New Cows? Changing Wealth Goods and Moral Economies in South Africa," *American Anthropologist* 118, no. 3 (2016): 483–94.

54. They also traveled to government indabas, where the announcements began to recommend routes for travel "ngezimoto"—by cars. See Cope, *To Bind the Nation*, xiv.

55. Timothy Khuzwayo, "25. The Rules of Ekuphakameni," in *The Story of Isaiah Shembe, Vol. 3: The Continuing Story of the Sun and the Moon*, ed. Irving Hexham and G. C. Oosthuizen, trans. Hans-Jurgen Becken (Lewiston, NY: Edwin Mellen, 2001), 53–54.

56. Jacob Dlamini, *Safari Nation: A Social History of Kruger National Park* (Athens: Ohio University Press, 2020), 122.

57. This adds layers to Inanda's history as a tourist destination. Sabine Marschall, "An Inspiring Narrative with a Shadow: Tangible and Intangible Heritage at the Phoenix Settlement of Mahatma Gandhi," *Southern African Humanities* 20 (December 2008): 353–74; Sabine Marschall, "Sustainable Heritage Tourism: The Inanda Heritage Route and the 2010 FIFA World Cup," *Journal of Sustainable Tourism* 20, no. 5 (2012): 721–36; Sabine Marschall, "Woza ENanda: Perceptions of and Attitudes towards Heritage and Tourism in a South African Township," *Transformation* 83, no. 1 (2013): 32–55.

58. Nellie Wells, "A Sacred War Dance: New Zulu Prophet, Reform through Old Customs," *The Star*, July 15, 1924; Payne, "A Prophet among the Zulus."

59. Papini charts changes in church dance very helpfully: Robert Papini, "Dance Uniform History in the Church of Nazareth Baptists: The Move to Tradition," *African Arts* 37, no. 3 (2004): 48–64.

60. See, for example, Erlmann, "'Horses in the Race Course,'" 270. And for the longer history of looking traditional, see Jeff Guy, "A Paralysis of Perspective: Image and Text in the Creation of an African Chief," *South African Historical Journal* 47, no. 1 (2002): 51–74; Patricia Hayes, "Power, Secrecy, Proximity: A Short History of South African Photography," *Kronos*, no. 33 (2007): 139–62.

61. Mkhipeni Ndunakazi, "171. Shembe Comes to the Dube Tribal Territory," in *SIS* 2, 190.

62. A. B. Majola, letter to the editor, *iLanga lase Natal*, July 18, 1918.

63. Roberts, "Shembe," 92.

64. One expression of this re-discovery of tradition among African Christians was the Zulu Cultural Society. See Marks, "Patriotism, Patriarchy, and Purity," 216–21.

65. Erlmann, "'Horses in the Race Course,'" 267.

66. Erlmann, "'Horses in the Race Course'"; Bradford, *A Taste of Freedom*, 333.

67. The sacred meaning of dance was not diminished, however. See: Nkosinathi Sithole, *The Nazaretha Church in South Africa: Isaiah Shembe's Hymns and the Sacred Dance in IBandla LamaNazaretha* (Leiden: Brill, 2016).

68. This was conveyed to me when I tried to visit other church sites, including Ntanda in 2010.

69. "Depicts Isaiah Shembe Washing Male Followers' Feet," n.d., d09–016, Album D9/001–044 African Religion—Shembe, Killie Campbell Africana Collections (henceforth KCAC), University of KwaZulu-Natal, Durban, South Africa.

70. *Isicolo* is another word to describe this head-ring. For a discussion of them close to the time of the photo, see Magema Fuze, *The Black People and Whence They Came*, ed. A. T. Cope and H. C. Lugg (Pietermaritzburg, ZA: University of Natal, 1979), 27–29.

71. Cabrita also grapples with Shembe's imitation of Christ but to show his "religious innovation." Joel Cabrita, *Text and Authority in the South African Nazaretha Church* (New York, NY: Cambridge University Press, 2014), 148–84.

72. On this difference in the Nazaretha Church, Joel Cabrita, "Politics and Preaching: Chiefly Converts to the South African Nazaretha Church, Obedient Subjects, and Sermon Performance," *Journal of African History* 51, no. 1 (2010): 36.

73. "Depicts Isaiah Shembe washing male followers' feet."

74. For such complaints, Native Affairs Commission Colony of Natal, *Evidence* (Pietermaritzburg, ZA, 1907), 717, 826, 925, 947.

75. For one story, see Nelson Mandela, *Long Walk to Freedom* (New York: Back Bay Books, 1995), 124–26.

76. He reinforced this message in many ways too, whether by pursuing circumcision as an adult man to follow God's rules more perfectly or by highlighting examples of how his enemies still tried to persecute him. Roberts, "Shembe," 55.

77. On his circumcision: Roberts, "Shembe," 123. And on circumcision in the church now: Nkosinathi Sithole, "The Sacrifice of Flesh and Blood: Male Circumcision in Ibandla LamaNazaretha as a Biblical and African Ritual," *Journal of the Study of Religion* 25, no. 1 (2012): 15–30.

78. For more on people at these gatherings, see Shula Marks, "Natal, the Zulu Royal Family and the Ideology of Segregation," *Journal of Southern African Studies* 4, no. 2 (April 1, 1978): 172–94; Cope, *To Bind the Nation*; Cope, "The Zulu Petit Bourgeoisie."

79. Jill Kelly, *To Swim with Crocodiles* (East Lansing: Michigan State University Press, 2018).

80. Native Commissioner Ndwedwe to Chief Native Commissioner, November 15, 1933, N.V. 2/4/5, 3/3/2/1, Papers of the Magistrate of Ndwedwe (1/NWE), Pietermaritzburg Archive Repository (NAB), Pietermaritzburg, ZA.

81. Roberts, "Shembe," 55.

82. Joseph Kip Kosek, "Richard Gregg, Mohandas Gandhi, and the Strategy of Nonviolence," *Journal of American History* 91, no. 4 (2005): 1318–48. And for how Gandhi used technology differently, see Isabel Hofmeyr, *Gandhi's Printing Press: Experiments in Slow Reading* (Cambridge, MA: Harvard University Press, 2013).

83. Roberts, "Shembe," 63; Gunner, *Man of Heaven*, plates 2 and 7.

84. C. H. B. Marlow, "A Brief History of Equine Private Practice in South Africa," *Journal of the South African Veterinary Association* 81, no. 4 (December 2010): 190–200; Sandra Swart, "'High Horses': Horses, Class and Socio-Economic Change in South Africa," *Journal of Southern African Studies* 34, no. 1 (2008): 193–213.

85. Gunner, "Man of Heaven," plate 7.

86. Petros Dhlomo, Khaya Ndelu, and Jeslinah Mchunu, "14. Shembe Relates How He Separated from His Wives," in *SIS* 1, 22.

87. "Portrait of Isaiah Shembe," n.d., d10–164, Album D10/001–255 Zulu Customs, book 2, KCAC.

88. Chris Gibson, "How Clothing Design and Cultural Industries Refashioned Frontier Masculinities: A Historical Geography of Western Wear," *Gender, Place & Culture* 23, no. 5 (May 3, 2016): 733–52.

89. On the movement of shops into Inanda, Sita Gandhi, *In the Shadow of Mahatma: A Grand-Daughter Remembers*, ed. Uma Dhupelia-Mesthrie (Calcutta: Sampark, 2005), 43.

90. "Portrait of Isaiah Shembe," "Depicts Isaiah Shembe washing male followers' feet."

91. Cope, *To Bind the Nation*, 94, 134. On leaders and clothes in colonial Africa, see too Richard L. Roberts, *Conflicts of Colonialism: The Rule of Law, French Soudan, and Faama Mademba Sèye* (New York: Cambridge University Press, 2022), 15–16.

92. For images of Dube, see Hughes, *First President*; see also Peter Limb, *The ANC's Early Years: Nation, Class and Place in South Africa before 1940* (Pretoria: Unisa Press, 2010).

93. Joel Cabrita, *The People's Zion: Southern Africa, the United States, and a Transatlantic Faith-Healing Movement* (Cambridge, MA: Belknap Press of Harvard University Press, 2018).

94. Karen H. Brown, "White Robes for Worship: The Umnazaretha of the Nazareth Baptist Church in South Africa," *Textile Society of America Symposium Proceedings* (Lincoln, NE: Textile Society of America, 1996), 1–11, DigitalCommons@University of Nebraska–Lincoln 878, https://digitalcommons.unl.edu/tsaconf/878; Carol Boram-Hays, "Borders of Beads: Questions of Identity in the Beadwork of the Zulu-Speaking People," *African Arts* 38, no. 2 (June 22, 2005): 38–52.

95. Jeff Guy, *The View across the River: Harriette Colenso and the Zulu Struggle against Imperialism* (Charlottesville: University of Virginia Press, 2002), 317.

96. Payne, "A Prophet among the Zulus"; "Depicts group of men from the church of Nazarites. They are wearing white cassocks and carrying shields. Isaiah Shembe is on the right," n.d., d09–013, Album D9/001–044 African Religion—Shembe, KCAC.

97. Roberts, "Shembe," 69.

98. On accumulation: Sean Hanretta, "Women, Marginality and the Zulu State: Women's Institutions and Power in the Early Nineteenth Century," *Journal of African History* 39, no. 3 (1998): 389–415; Peter Delius and Stefan Schirmer, "Order, Openness, and Economic Change in Precolonial Southern Africa: A Perspective from the Bokoni Terraces," *Journal of African History* 55, no. 1 (March 2014): 37–54.

99. Delius and Schirmer, "Order, Openness, and Economic Change," 47–48.

100. Andreas Heuser, "'He Dances like Isaiah Shembe!' Ritual Aesthetics as a Marker of Church Difference," *Studies in World Christianity* 14, no. 1 (April 1, 2008): 35–54.

101. This is, of course, Bayart's phrase. See Jean-François Bayart, *The State in Africa: The Politics of the Belly* (New York: Longman, 1993).

102. Carl Faye, memorandum, "UShembe," 1939, 24/214, 1431, NTS, SAB.

103. This practice, although surely aimed to show Shembe's sacrifices, also perhaps suggested his concerns about poisoning.

104. Statement of Mbanjwa Ngidi, undated [1931], 24/214, 1431, NTS, SAB.

105. D. G. Shepstone to Chief Native Commissioner, October 27, 1931; E. N. Braatvedt to Chief Native Commissioner, November 3, 1931, 24/214, 1431, NTS, SAB. Instead, Shembe likely just stopped allowing people to write down the terms of these arrangements. The example of Hawukile and the written contract her father received contributed to the evidence against him.

106. Roberts, "Shembe," 77.

107. Roberts, "Shembe," 79.

108. Native Economic Commission (NEC), "Native Economic Commission, Sitting at Pietermaritzburg, Minutes of Evidence" (Pretoria: Union of South Africa, 1931), 6534, 6538; Roberts, "Shembe," 42.

109. Roberts, "Shembe," 42.

110. Roberts, "Shembe," 76. NEC, "Native Economic Commission, Sitting at Pietermaritzburg, Minutes of Evidence," 6534. This also relates back to Shembe's promise to support mistreated women, in polygynous marriages or otherwise.

111. Joseph Mthethwa, "143. Liberation by Education," in *SIS* 2, 157–58.

112. Dhlomo and Ndelu, "15. Shembe's Farewell from His Family," in *SIS* 1, 26–27.

113. NEC, "Native Economic Commission, Sitting at Pietermaritzburg, Minutes of Evidence," 6541.

114. NEC, "Native Economic Commission, Sitting at Pietermaritzburg, Minutes of Evidence," 6542.

115. NEC, "Native Economic Commission, Sitting at Pietermaritzburg, Minutes of Evidence," 6542.

116. This is a common pattern in patriarchal church communities. Jane Soothill, *Gender, Social Change and Spiritual Power: Charismatic Christianity in Ghana* (Boston: Brill, 2007).

117. Petros Dhlomo, "52. The Death of Benjamin Shembe," in *SIS* 1, 97–98.

118. Dube, *UShembe*, 2.

CONCLUSION

1. The Nazaretha preserved many oral traditions about Isaiah Shembe's death, in part because of its importance in their faith but also because of how the events of his death became a subject of dispute. Some of the oral traditions about his death provided ways of making claims about who should follow him as leader. J. G. Shembe, "161. J. G. Shembe's Last Visit with His Father"; Mdluli, "162. Shembe Announces His Death," Simon Mngoma and Oliver Thabethe, "164. Shembe's Last Mission Journey to the North," in *The Story of Isaiah Shembe, Vol. 2: Early Regional Traditions of the Acts of the Nazarites*, ed. Irving Hexham and G. C. Oosthuizen, trans. Hans-Jurgen Becken (Lewiston, NY: Edwin Mellen, 1999) (henceforth *SIS* 2); Oliver Thabethe, Simon Mngoma, Juliah Cele, Petros Dhlomo, J. G. Shembe, and Muntuwesizwe Buthelezi, "165. Shembe's Last Days at Mkhaideni"; Oliver Thabethe, J. G. Shembe, Dainah Shembe, Simon Mngoma, Elinah Gumede, France Ngongoma, Petros Dhlomo, and Muntuwesizwe Buthelezi, "166. The Death of the Prophet Shembe," in *The Story of Isaiah Shembe, Vol. 1: History and Traditions Centered on Ekuphakameni and Mount Nhlangakazi*, ed. Irving Hexham and G. C. Oosthuizen, trans. Hans-Jürgen Becken (Lewiston, NY: Edwin Mellen, 1996), 239–58 (henceforth *SIS* 1).

2. Shembe, "161. Shembe's Last Visit."

3. Mngoma, "164. Shembe's Last Missionary Journey," in *SIS* 2.

4.   Mngoma, "164. Shembe's Last Missionary Journey," in *SIS* 2.

5.   Shembe et al., "166. The Death of the Prophet Shembe," in *SIS* 1, 250.

6.   Shembe et al., "166. The Death of the Prophet Shembe," in *SIS* 1, 250.

7.   Roberts, "Shembe," 40–52.

8.   On the spread of malaria in the region, Paul La Hausse, *Restless Identities: Signatures of Nationalism, Zulu Ethnicity, and History in the Lives of Petros Lamula (c. 1881–1948) and Lymon Maling (1889–c. 1936)* (Pietermaritzburg, ZA: University of Natal Press, 2000), 249; Shula Marks, *The Ambiguities of Dependence in South Africa: Class, Nationalism, and the State in Twentieth-Century Natal* (Baltimore: Johns Hopkins University Press, 1986), 95.

9.   David Chidester, *Religions of South Africa* (New York: Routledge, 1992), xi; David Chidester, Judy Tobler, and Darrel Wratten, *Christianity in South Africa: An Annotated Bibliography* (Westport, CT: Greenwood, 1997); Richard Elphick and Rodney Davenport, eds., *Christianity in South Africa: A Political, Social, and Cultural History* (Berkeley: University of California Press, 1997).

10. Adrian Hastings, *The Church in Africa* (New York: Clarendon, 1996), 438.

11. Natasha Erlank, *Convening Black Intimacy: Christianity, Gender, and Tradition in Early Twentieth-Century South Africa* (Athens: Ohio University Press, 2022); Daniel R. Magaziner, *The Law and the Prophets: Black Consciousness in South Africa, 1968–1977* (Athens: Ohio University Press, 2010); Jaspal K. Singh and Rajendra Chetty, eds., *Trauma, Resistance, Reconstruction in Post-1994 South African Writing* (New York: Peter Lang, 2010).

12. Helen Bradford, *A Taste of Freedom: The ICU in Rural South Africa, 1924–1930* (New Haven, CT: Yale University Press, 1987); Peter Walshe, *The Rise of African Nationalism in South Africa: The African National Congress, 1912–1952* (Berkeley: University of California Press, 1971); Jon Soske, *Internal Frontiers: African Nationalism and the Indian Diaspora in Twentieth-Century South Africa* (Athens: Ohio University Press, 2017); Robert Trent Vinson, *Albert Luthuli*, Ohio Short Histories of Africa (Athens: Ohio University Press, 2018).

13. For example, Nelson Mandela, *Long Walk to Freedom* (New York: Back Bay Books, 1995), 124–26.

14. For this experience: Albert Luthuli, *Let My People Go* (New York: McGraw-Hill, 1962).

15. Bradford, *A Taste of Freedom*, 104–6.

16. Hugh Macmillan, *The Lusaka Years: The ANC in Exile in Zambia, 1963–1994* (Auckland Park, ZA: Jacana Media, 2013).

17. Xolela Mangcu, *Biko: A Life* (London: I. B. Tauris, 2014).

18. "'Black Pimpernel,'" *New York Times*, April 12, 1964.

19. Mandela, *Long Walk to Freedom*, 181.

20. Clive K. Corder, "The Reconstruction and Development Programme: Success or Failure?," *Social Indicators Research* 41, no. 1/3 (1997): 183–203; Colin Bundy, *Short-Changed?: South Africa since Apartheid* (Athens: Ohio University Press, 2015).

21. Tiffany Thames Copeland, *"We Are Not Scared to Die": Julius Malema and the New Movement for African Liberation* (New York: Peter Lang, 2021).

22. Kalpana Hiralal and E. S. Reddy, *Pioneers of Satyagraha: Indian South Africans Defy Racist Laws, 1907–1914*, 1st ed. (Ahmedabad, India: Navajivan, 2017); Andreas Heuser, "Recovered Narratives of an Inter-Cultural Exchange: Gandhi, Shembe, and the Legacy of Satyagraha," *Journal of the Study of Religion* 16, no. 1 (2003): 87–102. Heuser's role in seeing the connections between different forms of resistance is, I think, spot-on, but I see a different source of the connection.

23. Leo Kuper, *Passive Resistance in South Africa*. (New Haven, CT: Yale University Press, 1957), 21–22, 42–43; Mandela, *Long Walk to Freedom*, 128–39.

24. William Sales, "A Black Scholar Interview: Making South Africa Ungovernable," *Black Scholar* 15, no. 6 (1984): 2–14; Chitja Twala, "The Emergence of the Student and Youth Resistance Organizations in the Free State Townships during the 1980s: A Viable Attempt to Reorganize Protest Politics?" *Journal for Contemporary History/Joernaal Vir Eietydse Geskiedenis* 32, no. 2 (2007): 39–55; Thula Simpson, *History of South Africa* (New York: Oxford University Press, 2022), 267–78.

25. Roberts, "Shembe," 40–41. Misc. correspondence, May 1935, 27/3/35, 3/3/3/1, Papers of the Magistrate of Umzinto (1/UMZ), Durban Archives Repository (TBD).

26. Roberts, "Shembe," 44–52.

27. See, for example, Elizabeth Gunner, *The Man of Heaven and the Beautiful Ones of God = Umuntu Wasezulwini Nabantu Abahle Bakankulunkulu: Writings from Ibandla LamaNazaretha, a South African Church* (Leiden, NL: Brill, 2002), 77; Muntuwesizwe Buthelezi, "120. Ezra Mbonambi's Plan to Kill Shembe," in *SIS* 2, 185.

28. Roberts, "Shembe." Dhlomo, "167. The Burial of Isaiah Shembe," 256.

29. Dhlomo, "167. The Burial of Isaiah Shembe."

30. Dhlomo, "167. The Burial of Isaiah Shembe."

31. Dhlomo, "167. The Burial of Isaiah Shembe." Shembe, "161. J. G. Shembe's Last Visit with His Father"; Mdluli, "162. Shembe Announces His Death," Mngoma, "164. Shembe's Last Missionary Journey to the North," in *SIS* 2; Juliah Cele, "165. Shembe's Last Days at Mkhaideni."

32. Roberts, "Shembe," 51–52.

33. Fernandez, "Precincts of the Prophet," 34–35. In this context, Dube's publication of *UShembe* in 1936 might have been part of an effort to contribute to the church's dissolution. It mainly drew upon the stories that the Nazaretha already told about themselves, but also included some salacious rumors about Shembe. See also Joel Cabrita, "Patriot and Prophet: John Dube's 1936 Biography of the South African Churchman Isaiah Shembe," *Journal of Southern African Studies* 38, no. 3 (September 1, 2012): 433–50.

34. Fernandez, "Precincts of the Prophet."

35. Roberts, "Shembe," 40. J. G. Shembe married the daughter of Albert Ndlovu, who had been affiliated with the Tafamasi American Zulu Mission congregation.

36. Fernandez, "Precincts of the Prophet." See, too, how J. G. Shembe (or his supporters) inserted him into stories of his father's early struggles. Muntuwesizwe Buthelezi and Daniel Dube, "24. Shembe Acquires the Village of Ekuphakameni," in *SIS* 1, 51–53.

37. Statement of Peter Ngcobo, March 27, 1939, 24/241, 1431, Papers of the Native Affairs Department (NTS), National Archives Repository (SAB), Pretoria, ZA.

38. Inanda Magistrate to Chief Native Commissioner, April 29, 1939, 24/241, 1431, NTS, SAB.

39. Some of the men who had been removed from the church (according to Peter Ngcobo) were later listed as ministers in subsequent applications for recognition. See Application for Official Recognition, 1952, 24/241, 1431, NTS, SAB.

40. See, for example, Application for a Garage Site at Ingongweni, Ndwedwe, Johannes Galilee Shembe, 1947, 588/160, 1086, NTS, SAB.

41. Gavin Maasdoorp and A. S. B. Humphreys, *From Shantytown to Township: An Economic Study of African Poverty and Rehousing* (Cape Town: Juta, 1975); Jason Hickel, *Democracy as Death: The Moral Order of Anti-liberal Politics in South Africa* (Berkeley: University of California Press, 2015). In Hickel, see chapter 3.

42. Application for Government Recognition, 1952. On the politics of applying for official recognition, see Cabrita, *Text and Authority*, 295–335.

43. J. G. Shembe, "17. The Baptism of Shembe," in *SIS* 1, 34.

44. Fernandez, "Precincts of the Prophet."

45. Chief Native Commissioner to Secretary of Native Affairs, January 2, 1942, 24/241, 1431, NTS, SAB. The government forced the issue by refusing to grant a permit to allow the Nazaretha to go on pilgrimage.

46. Much as stories of Isaiah Shembe involved the train, donkeys, and horses, stories of J. G. Shembe involved his motor car. G. C. Oosthuizen, "Succession Conflict within the Church of the Nazarites" (Institute for Social and Economic Research, University of Durban–Westville, 1981), 20, 27.

47. Mandy Goedhals, "African Nationalism and Indigenous Christianity: A Study in the Life of James Calata," *Journal of Religion in Africa* 33, no. 1 (2003): 63–82.

48. On ancestors in the church today, see Edley J. Moodley, *Shembe, Ancestors, and Christ : A Christological Inquiry with Missiological Implications* (Eugene, OR: Pickwick, 2008).

49. Oliver Thabethe, "265. Bridewealth and Marriage Fees," in *SIS* 2; Gunner, *Man of Heaven*, 65–67.

50. Oosthuizen, "Succession Conflict."

51. Lethu Nxumalo, "Shembe Church Says It Will Not Be Dictated to by the Courts," IOL News, October 3. 2021, https://www.iol.co.za/sunday-tribune/news/shembe-church-says-it-will-not-be-dictated-to-by-the-courts-460c8d4a-bff6–4d3c-aae2-b16e6900512c.

Bibliography

ARCHIVAL SOURCES

Archives of the Republic of South Africa (Pretoria, South Africa) (SAB)
  Papers of the Decisions of the Executive Council (URU)
  Papers of the Department of Native Administration and Development (BAO)
  Papers of the Colonial Secretary (CS)
  Papers of the Governor General (GG)
  Papers of the Justice Department (JUS)
  Papers of the Secretary of Native Affairs (SNA)
Archives of the Province of KwaZulu-Natal (Pietermaritzburg, South Africa) (NAB)
  Papers of the American Board Mission (ABM)
  Papers of the Auditor General's Office (AG)
  Papers of Carl Faye
  Papers of the Chief Native Commissioner, Natal (CNC)
  Papers of the Department of Development Aid (DDA)
  Papers of Harry Lugg
  Papers of the Magistrate and Commissioner, Ixopo (1/IXO)
  Papers of the Magistrate and Commissioner, Ladysmith (1/LDS)
  Papers of the Magistrate and Commissioner, Ndwedwe
  Papers of the Magistrate and Commissioner, Umsinga (1/UMS)
  Papers of the Magistrate and Commissioner, Utrecht (1/UTR)
  Papers of the Master of the Supreme Court (MSC)
  Papers of the Master of the Supreme Court—Estates (MSCE)
  Papers of the Native High Court (NHC)
  Papers of the Natal Native Affairs Department (NSNA)
  Papers of the Office of the Attorney General (AGO)
  Papers of the Office of the Colonial Secretary (CSO)
  Papers of the Registrar, Supreme Court, Pietermaritzburg (RSC)
  Papers of the Surveyor General's Office (SGO)
  Papers of the Secretary of Native Affairs (SNA)
Archives of the Province of KwaZulu-Natal (Durban, South Africa) (TBD)

Papers of the Commissioner, Durban (2/DBN)

Papers of the Magistrate and Commissioner, Empangeni (1/EPI)

Papers of the Town Clerk, Empangeni (3/EPI)

Papers of the Magistrate and Commissioner, Eshowe (1/ESH)

Papers of the Magistrate and Commissioner, Mtunzini (1/MTU)

Papers of the Magistrate and Commissioner, Nongoma (1/NGA)

Papers of the Magistrate and Commissioner, Verulam (1/VLM)

Archives of the Province of the Orange Free State (Bloemfontein, South Africa) (BAR)

Papers of the Colonial Office (CO)

Papers of the Governor's Office (GO)

Durban Local History Museum (Durban, South Africa)

Photography Collections

Killie Campbell Africana Library (Durban, South Africa)

Photography Collections

Papers of John L. Dube

Papers of Esther Roberts

Papers of A. W. G. Champion

Papers of S. Bourquin

Lutheran Theological Institute (Scottsville, South Africa)

Papers of Hans-Jürgen Becken

University of Uppsala Special Collections (Uppsala, Sweden)

Papers of Bengt Sundkler

INTERVIEWS

Nazaretha history is complex and contested. I have included only first names or last names of interviewees as a result. When people shared the same last name, I included a number to indicate difference.

Anna, Bongi, Ma Dlamini, and Thobile. Interview by Constance Mkhize Dlamini and Lauren Jarvis. April 15, 2010 and May 15, 2010. Clermont. Written notes.

Bhengu. Interview by Constance Mkhize Dlamini and Lauren Jarvis. July, 4 2016. Inanda. Digital recording.

Gcibane. Interview by Constance Mkhize Dlamini and Lauren Jarvis. April 3, 2010. Inanda. Digital recording.

Gumede. Interview by Constance Mkhize Dlamini and Lauren Jarvis. July 13, 2016. Inanda.

Digital recording.

Hawukile. Interview by Constance Mkhize Dlamini and Lauren Jarvis. May 2010. Inanda. Digital recording.

Hlengwa. Interview by Constance Mkhize Dlamini and Lauren Jarvis. May 2, 2010. Esikawheni. Digital recording.

Khosa. Interview by Constance Mkhize Dlamini and Lauren Jarvis. July 13, 2016. Inanda. Digital recording.

Khumalo. Interview by Constance Mkhize Dlamini and Lauren Jarvis. July 29, 2016. Inanda. Digital recording.

Mafuleka. Interview by Constance Mkhize Dlamini and Lauren Jarvis. July 4, 2016. Inanda. Digital recording.

Magcaba, 1. Interview by Constance Mkhize Dlamini and Lauren Jarvis. May 15, 2010 and June 6, 2010. Inanda. Digital recording.

Magcaba, 2. Interview by Constance Mkhize Dlamini and Lauren Jarvis. July 9, 2010. Digital recording.

Majola. Interview by Constance Mkhize Dlamini and Lauren Jarvis. May 15, 2010 and June 9, 2010. Inanda. Digital recording.

Mbatha and Mbatha, 1. Interview by Constance Mkhize Dlamini and Lauren Jarvis. July 29, 2016. Inanda. Digital recording.

Mbatha, Mbatha, and Mbatha, 2. Interview by Constance Mkhize Dlamini and Lauren Jarvis. May 2, 2010. Esikhaweni. Digital Recording.

Mbatha, 3. Interview by Constance Mkhize Dlamini and Lauren Jarvis. July 4, 2016. Inanda. Digital recording.

Mchunu. Interview by Constance Mkhize Dlamini and Lauren Jarvis. July 6, 2016. Inanda. Digital recording.

Mdluli. Interview by Constance Mkhize Dlamini and Lauren Jarvis. July 4, 2016. Inanda. Digital recording.

Mgomezulu. Interview by Constance Mkhize Dlamini and Lauren Jarvis. July 5, 2016. Inanda. Digital recording.

Mhlongo, 1. Interview by Constance Mkhize Dlamini and Lauren Jarvis. May 17, 2010 and July 6, 2010. KwaDabeka. Digital recording.

Mhlongo, 2. Interview by Constance Mkhize Dlamini and Lauren Jarvis. July 8, 2016. Inanda. Digital recording.

Mkhize. Interview by Constance Mkhize Dlamini and Lauren Jarvis. July 29, 2016. Inanda. Digital recording.

Mpanza. Interview by Constance Mkhize Dlamini and Lauren Jarvis. July 29, 2016. Inanda.

Digital recording.

Mthembu, 1. Interview by Constance Mkhize Dlamini and Lauren Jarvis. July 6, 2016. Inanda. Digital recording.

Mthembu, 2. Interview by Constance Mkhize Dlamini and Lauren Jarvis. July 6, 2016. Inanda. Digital recording.

Mthembu, 3. Interview by Constance Mkhize Dlamini and Lauren Jarvis. July, 5, 2016. Inanda. Digital recording.

Msomi. Interview by Constance Mkhize Dlamini and Lauren Jarvis. July 6, 2016. Inanda. Digital recording.

Ndlovu. Interview by Constance Mkhize Dlamini and Lauren Jarvis. July 13, 2016. Inanda. Digital recording.

Nduma. Interview by Constance Mkhize Dhlamini and Lauren Jarvis. July 5, 2016. Inanda. Digital recording.

Ngcobo. Interview by Constance Mkhize Dlamini and Lauren Jarvis. July 13, 2016. Inanda. Digital recording.

Ngcongo. Interview by Constance Mkhize Dlamini and Lauren Jarvis. July 8, 2016. Inanda. Digital recording.

Ngobese. Interview by Constance Mkhize Dlamini and Lauren Jarvis. July 4, 2016. Inanda. Digital recording.

Ngubane. Interview by Constance Mkhize Dlamini and Lauren Jarvis. July 8, 2016. Inanda. Digital recording.

Ntuli, 1. Interview by Constance Mkhize Dlamini and Lauren Jarvis. July 8, 2010. Marianhill. Digital recording.

Ntuli, 2. Interview by Constance Mkhize Dlamini and Lauren Jarvis. July 8, 2016. Inanda. Digital recording.

Ntuli, 3. Interview by Constance Mkhize Dlamini and Lauren Jarvis. July 6, 2016. Inanda. Digital recording.

Ntuli, 4. Interview by Constance Mkhize Dlamini and Lauren Jarvis. May 5, 2010. Clermont. Digital recording.

Qwabe. Interview by Constance Mkhize Dlamini and Lauren Jarvis. April 3, 2010. Inanda. Digital recording.

Ratali. Interview by Constance Mkhize Dlamini and Lauren Jarvis. July, 29 2016. Inanda. Digital recording.

Shange, 1. Interview by Constance Mkhize Dlamini and Lauren Jarvis. July 6, 2016. Inanda. Digital recording.

Shange, 2. Interview by Constance Mkhize Dlamini and Lauren Jarvis. July 6, 2016. Inanda.

Digital recording.

Sibiya. Interview by Constance Mkhize Dlamini and Lauren Jarvis. May 16, 2010. Clermont. Digital recording.

Thokozile. Interview by Lauren Jarvis. June 12, 2010. Durban. Digital recording.

Vilakazi. Interview by Constance Mkhize Dlamini and Lauren Jarvis. July 6, 2016. Inanda. Digital recording.

Zulu, 1. Interview by Constance Mkhize Dlamini and Lauren Jarvis. July 5, 2016. Inanda. Digital Recording.

Zulu, 2. Interview by Constance Mkhize Dlamini and Lauren Jarvis. July 4 and 13, 2016. Inanda. Digital recording.

Zulu, 3. Interview by Constance Mkhize Dlamini and Lauren Jarvis. July 4, 2016. Inanda. Digital recording.

Zungu, 1. Interview by Constance Mkhize Dhlamini and Lauren Jarvis. July 13, 2016. Inanda. Digital recording.

Zungu, 2. Interview by Constance Mkhize Dhlamini and Lauren Jarvis. July 13, 2016. Inanda. Digital recording.

Zungu, 3. Interview by Constance Mkhize Dhlamini and Lauren Jarvis. July 4, 2016. Inanda. Digital recording.

PRINTED SOURCES

Abbenhuis, Maartje, and Ismee Tames. *Global War, Global Catastrophe: Neutrals, Belligerents and the Transformations of the First World War.* New York: Bloomsbury Academic, 2021.

Abouharb, M. Rodwan, and Anessa L. Kimball. "A New Dataset on Infant Mortality Rates, 1816–2002." *Journal of Peace Research* 44, no. 6 (2007): 743–54.

Adams, Kendall. "The Role of Izangoma in Bringing the Zulu Goddess Back to her People." *TDR* 43, no. 2 (1999): 94–117.

Adebanwi, Wale, and Rogers Orock. *Elites and the Politics of Accountability in Africa.* Ann Arbor: University of Michigan Press, 2021.

Adhikari, Mohamed. "Hope, Fear, Shame, Frustration: Continuity and Change in the Expression of Coloured Identity in White Supremacist South Africa, 1910–1994." *Journal of Southern African Studies* 32, no. 3 (2006): 467–87.

——. "'The Product of Civilization in Its Most Repellent Manifestation': Ambiguities in the Racial Perceptions of the APO (African Political Organization), 1909–23." *Journal of African History* 38, no. 2 (1997): 283–300.

Ajayi, J. F. Ade, *Christian Missions in Nigeria, 1841–1891: The Making of a New Elite.* London:

Longmans, 1965.

Alexander, Amanda, and Andile Mngxitama, eds. *Biko Lives!: Contesting the Legacies of Steve Biko*. New York: Palgrave Macmillan, 2008.

Allman, Jean, and John Parker. *Tongnaab: The History of a West African God*. Bloomington: Indiana University Press, 2005.

Anderson, Allan. "The Lekganyanes and Prophecy in the Zion Christian Church." *Journal of Religion in Africa* 29, no. 3 (1999): 285–312.

Anderson, David M. *Revealing Prophets: Prophecy in Eastern African History*. Athens: Ohio University Press, 1995.

Anker, Peder. *Imperial Ecology: Environmental Order in the British Empire, 1895–1945. Imperial Ecology*. Cambridge, MA: Harvard University Press, 2009.

Arndt, Jochen S. *Divided by the Word: Colonial Encounters and the Remaking of Zulu and Xhosa Identities*. Charlottesville: University of Virginia Press, 2022.

Arnett, Benjamin W. *The Budget of 1904*. Philadelphia, 1903. https://catalog.hathitrust.org/Record/008407188.

Asamoah-Gyadu, J. Kwabena. "Conversion, Converts, and National Identity." In *The Wiley Blackwell Companion to World Christianity*, edited by Lamin Sanneh and Michael McClymond, 176–89. New York: Wiley, 2016.

Ashforth, Adam. *The Politics of Official Discourse in Twentieth-Century South Africa*. Oxford, UK: Clarendon Press, 1990.

———. *Witchcraft, Violence, and Democracy in South Africa*. Chicago: University of Chicago Press, 2005.

Atkins, Keletso E. *The Moon is Dead! Give Us Our Money!: The Cultural Origins of an African Work Ethic, Natal, South Africa, 1843–1900*. Portsmouth, NH: Heinemann, 1993.

Austen, Ralph. "The Moral Economy of Witchcraft: An Essay in Comparative History." In *Modernity and Its Malcontents: Ritual and Power in Postcolonial Africa*, edited by Jean and John Comaroff. Chicago: University of Chicago Press, 1993.

Aylward, Alfred. *The Transvaal of To-Day: War, Witchcraft, Sport, and Spoils in South Africa*. Edinburgh, 1881.

Babou, Cheikh Anta. "Contesting Space, Shaping Places: Making Room for the Muridiyya in Colonial Senegal, 1912–45." *Journal of African History* 46, no. 3 (2005): 405–26.

———. *Fighting the Greater Jihad: Amadu Bamba and the Founding of the Muridiyya of Senegal, 1853–1913*. Athens: Ohio University Press, 2007.

Badassy, Prinisha. "'Is Lying a Coolie's Religion?' The Household Sammys and Marys of Colonial Natal, 1880–1920." *African Studies* 77, no. 4 (October 2, 2018): 481–503.

Baer, Jonathan R. "Redeemed Bodies: The Functions of Divine Healing in Incipient

Pentecostalism." *Church History* 70, no. 4 (2001): 735–71.

Ballard, Charles. "The Repercussions of Rinderpest: Cattle Plague and Peasant Decline in Colonial Natal." *International Journal of African Historical Studies* 19 (1986): 421–540.

Bank, Andrew. "The Politics of Mythology: The Genealogy of the Philip Myth." *Journal of Southern African Studies* 25, no. 3 (1999): 461–77.

Barnes, Teresa. "The History of South African Health Care." *Journal of African History* 50, no. 3 (2009): 449–51.

Barnett, Michael. *Empire of Humanity: A History of Humanitarianism*. Ithaca, NY: Cornell University Press, 2011.

Barrett, David B. "Two Hundred Independent Church Movements in East Africa." *Social Compass* 15, no. 2 (1968): 101–16.

Batts, H. J. *The Story of 100 Years, 1820–1920: Being the History of the Baptist Church in South Africa*. Cape Town: T. Maskew Miller, 1922. https://catalog.hathitrust.org/Record/007696518.

Bayart, Jean-François. *The State in Africa: The Politics of the Belly*. New York: Longman, 1993.

Becken, H. J. "Ekuphakameni Revisited: Recent Developments within the Nazaretha Church in South Africa." *Journal of Religion in Africa* 9, no. 3 (1978): 161–72.

———. "On the Holy Mountain: A Visit to the New Year's Festival of the Nazaretha Church on Mount Hlangakazi, 14 January 1967." *Journal of Religion in Africa* 1, no. 2 (1968): 138–49.

Becker, Felicitas. "Traders, 'Big Men,' and Prophets: Political Continuity and Crisis in the Maji Maji Rebellion in Southeast Tanzania." *Journal of African History* 45, no. 1 (March 2004): 1–22.

Beinart, William. "A Century of Migrancy from Mpondoland." *African Studies* 73, no. 3 (September 2, 2014): 387–409.

———. "Conflict in Qumbu: Rural Consciousness, Ethnicity and Violence in the Colonial Transkei, 1880–1913." *Journal of Southern African Studies* 8, no. 1 (1981): 94–122.

———. *The Political Economy of Pondoland 1860–1930*. Cambridge, UK: Cambridge University Press, 1982.

———. "Women in Rural Politics: Herschel District in the 1920s and 1930s." In *Class, Community, and Conflict: South African Perspectives*, edited by Belinda Bozzoli. Johannesburg: Ravan, 1987.

Beinart, William, and Colin Bundy. *Hidden Struggles in Rural South Africa: Politics & Popular Movements in the Transkei & Eastern Cape, 1890–1930*. London: J. Currey, 1987.

Beinart, William, and Peter Delius. "The Historical Context and Legacy of the Natives Land Act of 1913." *Journal of Southern African Studies* 40, no. 4 (July 4, 2014): 667–88.

Beinart, William, Peter Delius, and Stanley Trapido, eds. *Putting a Plough to the Ground:*

Accumulation and Dispossession in Rural South Africa, 1850–1930. Johannesburg: Ravan Press, 1986.

Beinart, William, and Saul Dubow. *Segregation and Apartheid in Twentieth-Century South Africa*. London: Routledge, 1995.

Bell, David A. *Men on Horseback: The Power of Charisma in the Age of Revolution*. New York: Farrar, Straus, and Giroux, 2020.

Bell, Morag. "The Pestilence That Walketh in Darkness: Imperial Health, Gender, and Images of South Africa c.1880–1910." *Transactions of the Institute of British Geographers* 18, no. 3 (1993): 327–41.

Bennett, T. W. *A Sourcebook for African Customary Law for Southern Africa*. Cape Town: Juta, 1991.

Benton, Lauren. *Law and Colonial Cultures: Legal Regimes in World History, 1400–1900*. New York: Cambridge University Press, 2001.

Berger, Iris. "Beasts of Burden Revisited: Interpretations of Women and Gender in Southern African Societies." In *Paths Toward the Past: African Historical Essays in Honor of Jan Vansina*, edited by Robert Harms. Atlanta: African Studies Association Press, 1994.

Berglund, Axel-Ivar. *Zulu Thought-Patterns and Symbolism*. Bloomington: Indiana University Press, 1989.

Berman, Bruce J. "Ethnicity, Patronage and the African State: The Politics of Uncivil Nationalism." *African Affairs* 97, no. 388 (1998): 305–41.

Berman, Bruce, and John Lonsdale. *Unhappy Valley: Conflict in Kenya and Africa*. Athens: Ohio University Press, 1992.

Berry, Sara. "Hegemony on a Shoestring: Indirect Rule and Access to Agricultural Land." *Africa* 62, no. 3 (1992): 327–55.

———. *No Condition Is Permanent: The Social Dynamics of Agrarian Change in Sub-Saharan Africa*. Madison: University of Wisconsin Press, 1993.

Berstein, Alison, and Jacklyn Cock. *Melting Pots & Rainbow Nations: Conversations about Difference in the United States and South Africa*. Urbana: University of Illinois Press, 2002.

Bickford-Smith, Vivian. "African Nationalist or British Loyalist? The Complicated Case of Tiyo Soga." *History Workshop Journal* 71, no. 1 (2011): 74–97.

———. "The Betrayal of Creole Elites, 1880–1920." In *Black Experience and the Empire*, edited by Philip D. Morgan and Sean Hawkins, 194–227. New York: Oxford University Press, 2006.

———. "South African Urban History, Racial Segregation and the Unique Case of Cape Town?" *Journal of Southern African Studies* 21, no. 1 (1995): 63–78.

Bloomberg, Charles. *Christian Nationalism and the Rise of the Afrikaner Broederbond in South Africa, 1918–48*. Bloomington: Indiana University Press, 1989.

Bonner, Philip. *Kings, Commoners and Concessionaires: The Evolution and Dissolution of the Nineteenth-Century Swazi State.* New York: Cambridge University Press, 1983.

Bonnin, Debby. "Claiming Spaces, Changing Places: Political Violence and Women's Protests in KwaZulu-Natal." *Journal of Southern African Studies* 26, no. 2 (2000): 301–16.

Booth, Alan. "European Courts Protect Women and Witches: Colonial Law Courts as Redistributors of Power in Swaziland, 1920–1950." *Journal of Southern African Studies* 18, no. 2 (1992): 253–75.

Bowler, Kate. *Blessed: A History of the American Prosperity Gospel.* New York: Oxford University Press, 2013.

Bozzoli, Belinda, and Mmantho Nkotsoe. *Women of Phokeng: Consciousness, Life Strategy, and Migrancy in South Africa, 1900–1983.* Portsmouth, NH: Heinemann, 1991.

Bradford, Helen. "Lynch Law and Labourers: The ICU in Umvoti, 1927–1928." *Journal of Southern African Studies* 11, no. 1 (October 1, 1984): 128–49.

———. "Mass Movements and the Petty Bourgeoisie: The Social Origins of ICU Leadership, 1924–1929." *Journal of African History* 25 (1984): 295–310.

———. A Taste of Freedom: The ICU in Rural South Africa, 1924–1930. New Haven: Yale University Press, 1987.

———. "Women, Gender and Colonialism: Rethinking the History of the British Cape Colony and its Frontier Zones, ca. 1806–70." *Journal of African History* 37 (1996): 351–70.

Breckenridge, Keith. *Biometric State: The Global Politics of Identification and Surveillance in South Africa, 1850 to the Present.* New York: Cambridge University Press, 2014.

———. "Love Letters and Amanuenses: Beginning the Cultural History of the Working Class Private Sphere in Southern Africa, 1900–1933." *Journal of Southern African Studies* 26 (June 1, 2000): 337–48.

Brenner, Louis. "Histories of Religion in Africa." *Journal of Religion in Africa* 30, no. 2 (2000): 143–67.

Brock, Peggy, Norman Etherington, Gareth Griffiths, and Jacqueline Van Gent. *Indigenous Evangelists and Questions of Authority in the British Empire, 1750–1940.* Leiden, NL: Brill, 2015.

Brookes, Edgar Harry. *A History of the University of Natal.* Pietermaritzburg, ZA: University of Natal Press, 1966.

Brookes, Edgar Harry, and Nathan Hurwitz. *The Native Reserves of Natal.* Cape Town: Oxford University Press, 1957.

Brookes, Edgar Harry, and Colin de B. Webb. *A History of Natal.* Pietermaritzburg, ZA: University of Natal Press, 1965.

Brookfield, H. C., and M. A. Tatham. "The Distribution of Racial Groups in Durban: The

Background of Apartheid in a South African City." *Geographical Review* 47, no. 1 (January 1957): 44.

Brown, A. Samler, and G. Gordon Brown. *The Guide to South Africa: For the Use of Tourists, Sportsmen, Invalids, and Settlers.* London, 1907.

Brown, Candy Gunther. "From Tent Meetings and Store-Front Healing Rooms to Walmarts and the Internet: Healing Spaces in the United States, the Americas, and the World, 1906–2006." *Church History* 75, no. 3 (2006): 631–47.

Brown, Karen H., "White Robes for Worship: The Umnazaretha of the Nazareth Baptist Church in South Africa." *Textile Society of America Symposium Proceedings*, 1–11. Lincoln, NE: Textile Society of America, 1996. DigitalCommons@University of Nebraska–Lincoln 878. https://digitalcommons.unl.edu/tsaconf/878.

Brown, Kenneth D. "An Unsettled Ministry? Some Aspects of Nineteenth-Century British Nonconformity." *American Society of Church History* 56, no. 2 (1987): 204–23.

Bryant, A. T. *A History of the Zulu and Neighbouring Tribes.* Cape Town: C. Struik, 1964.

———. *Olden Times in Zululand and Natal: Containing Earlier Political History of the Eastern-Nguni Clans.* Cape Town: C. Struik, 1965.

———. *A Zulu-English Dictionary.* Pinetown, ZA, 1905.

———. *Zulu Medicine and Medicine-Men.* Cape Town: C. Struik, 1966.

Buhlungu, Sakhela, and Malehoko Tshoaedi. *COSATU's Contested Legacy: South African Trade Unions in the Second Decade of Democracy.* Leiden, NL: Brill, 2013.

Bundy, Colin. "The Emergence and Decline of the South African Peasantry." *African Affairs* 71 (1972): 369–88.

———. *The Rise and Fall of the South African Peasantry.* Berkeley: University of California Press, 1979.

———. *Short-Changed? South Africa since Apartheid.* Athens: Ohio University Press, 2015.

Burns, Catherine. "'A Man Is a Clumsy Thing Who Does Not Know How to Handle a Sick Person': Aspects of the History of Masculinity and Race in the Shaping of Male Nursing in South Africa, 1900–1950." *Journal of Southern African Studies* 24, no. 4 (1998): 695–717.

———. "Sex Lessons from the Past?" *Agenda: Empowering Women for Gender Equity*, no. 29 (1996): 79–91.

Burridge, Kenelm. *Someone, No One: An Essay on Individuality.* Princeton, NJ: Princeton University Press, 2015.

Burton, William. *When God Makes a Missionary: Being the Life Story of Edgar Mahon.* London: Victory, 1938.

Bushman, Richard Lyman. *Joseph Smith: Rough Stone Rolling.* Reprint edition. New York: Vintage, 2007.

Cabrita, Joel. "Isaiah Shembe's Theological Nationalism, 1920–1935." *Journal of Southern African Studies* 35, no. 3 (2009): 609–25.

———. *The People's Zion: Southern Africa, the United States, and a Transatlantic Faith-Healing Movement.* Cambridge, MA: Belknap Press of Harvard University Press, 2018.

———. "Politics and Preaching: Chiefly Converts to the South African Nazaretha Church, Obedient Subjects, and Sermon Performance." *Journal of African History* 51, no. 1 (2010): 21–40.

———. *Text and Authority in the South African Nazaretha Church.* New York: Cambridge University Press, 2014.

———. "Texts, Authority, and Community in the South African Ibandla lamaNazaretha." *Journal of Religion in Africa* 40, no. 1 (2010): 60–95.

———. "Writing Apartheid: Ethnographic Collaborators and the Politics of Knowledge Production in Twentieth-Century South Africa." *American Historical Review* 125, no. 5 (December 29, 2020): 1668–97.

Callaway, Henry. *Nursery Tales, Traditions, and Histories of the Zulus, in Their Own Words, with a Translation into English, and Notes.* London, 1868.

———. *The Religious System of the Amazulu: With a Translation into English and Notes.* London, 1868.

Callebert, Ralph. *On Durban's Docks: Zulu Workers, Rural Households, and Global Labor.* Rochester, NY: University of Rochester Press, 2017.

Camiller, Jörn Leonhard. *Pandora's Box: A History of the First World War.* Translated by Patrick Camiller. Cambridge, MA: Belknap Press of Harvard University Press, 2018.

Campbell, James T. *Songs of Zion: The African Methodist Episcopal Church in the United States and South Africa.* New York: Oxford University Press, 1995.

Campbell, James, Matthew Pratt Guterl, and Robert G. Lee, eds. *Race, Nation, and Empire in American History.* Chapel Hill: University of North Carolina Press, 2007.

Carline, Katie. "Wise Mothers and Wise Buyers: Marketing Tea and Home Improvement in 1930s South Africa." *Journal of African History* 63, no. 3 (November 2022): 291–308.

Carton, Benedict. *Blood from Your Children: The Colonial Origins of Generational Conflict in South Africa.* Charlottesville: University Press of Virginia, 2000.

———. "'My Husband Is No Husband to Me': Divorce, Marriage, and Gender Struggles in African Communities of Colonial Natal, 1869–1910." *Journal of Southern African Studies* 46, no. 6 (October 22, 2020): 1111–25.

———. "The Wages of Migrancy: Homestead Dynamics, Income Earning, and Colonial Law in Zululand, South Africa." *African Studies* 73, no. 3 (2014): 365–86.

Carton, Benedict, John Laband, and Jabulani Sithole, eds. *Zulu Identities: Being Zulu, Past and*

Present. London: Hurst, 2009.

Cell, John. *The Highest Stages of White Supremacy: The Origins of Segregation in South Africa and the American South*. New York: Cambridge, 1982.

Chance, Kerry Ryan. "Sacrifice after Mandela: Liberalism and Liberation among South Africa's First Post-Apartheid Generation." *Anthropological Quarterly* 88, no. 4 (2015): 857–79.

Chanock, Martin. *Law, Custom, and Social Order: The Colonial Experience in Malawi and Zambia*. Cambridge, UK: Cambridge University Press, 1985.

———. *The Making of South African Legal Culture, 1902–1936*. New York: Cambridge University Press, 2001.

Chidester, David. *Religions of South Africa*. New York: Routledge, 1992.

Chidester, David, Judy Tobler, and Darrel Wratten. *Christianity in South Africa: An Annotated Bibliography*. Westport, CT: Greenwood, 1997.

Christopher, A. J. "Colonial Land Policy." *Annals of the American Geographers* 61, no. 3 (1971): 560–75.

———. "Port Elizabeth." In *Homes Apart: South Africa's Segregated Cities*, edited by Anthony Lemon, 43–57. Bloomington: Indiana University Press, 1991.

———. "Roots of Urban Segregation: South Africa at Union, 1910." *Journal of Historical Geography* 14, no. 2 (1988): 1151–69.

Cirillo, Vincent J. "'Winged Sponges': Houseflies as Carriers of Typhoid Fever in 19th- and Early 20th-Century Military Camps." *Perspectives in Biology and Medicine* 49, no. 1 (2006): 52–63.

Clark, Nancy. "The Limits of Industrialization under Apartheid." In *Apartheid's Genesis, 1935–1962*, edited by Philip Bonner, Peter Delius, and Deborah Posel. Johannesburg: Ravan, 1981.

———. "Society and Economy in South Africa through the Lens of the Beer Industry." *Journal of African History* 52, no. 2 (2011): 264–66.

Cohen, David William. "The Undefining of Oral Tradition." *Ethnohistory* 36, no. 1 (1989): 9–18.

Cohen, Thomas V. "The Macrohistory of Microhistory." *Journal of Medieval and Early Modern Studies* 47, no. 1 (2017): 53–73.

Colenso, John William. *Langalibalele and the Amahlubi Tribe: Being Remarks upon the Official Record of the Trials of the Chief, His Son and Induna, and Other Members of the Amahlubi Tribe*. London, 1875.

———. *Zulu-English Dictionary*. London, 1861.

Colony of Natal. *Evidence Taken before the Natal Native Commission, 1881*. Pietermaritzburg, ZA, 1882.

Comaroff, Jean. *Body of Power, Spirit of Resistance: The Culture and History of a South African*

People. Chicago: University of Chicago Press, 1985.

Comaroff, Jean, and John L Comaroff. *Of Revelation and Revolution, Volume 1: Christianity, Colonialism, and Consciousness in South Africa*. Chicago: University of Chicago Press, 1991.

———. *Of Revelation and Revolution, Volume 2: Christianity, Colonialism, and Consciousness in South Africa*. Chicago: University of Chicago Press, 1997.

Comaroff, John L. "Goodly Beasts, Beastly Goods: Cattle and Commodities in a South African Context." *American Ethnologist* 17, no. 2 (1990): 195–216.

Connolly, Jonathan. "Indentured Labour Migration and the Meaning of Emancipation: Free Trade, Race, and Labour in British Public Debate, 1838–1860." *Past and Present* 238, no. 1 (2018): 85–119.

Cooper, Barbara M. *Countless Blessings: A History of Childbirth and Reproduction in the Sahel*. Bloomington: Indiana University Press, 2019.

Cope, Nicholas. *To Bind the Nation: Solomon kaDinuzulu and Zulu Nationalism, 1913–1933*. Pietermaritzburg, ZA: University of Natal Press, 1993.

———. "The Zulu Petit Bourgeoisie and Zulu Nationalism in the 1920s: Origins of Inkatha." *Journal of Southern African Studies*. 16, no. 3 (1990): 431–51.

Copeland, Tiffany Thames. *"We Are Not Scared to Die": Julius Malema and the New Movement for African Liberation*. New York: Peter Lang, 2021.

Coplan, David B. "Erasing History: The Destruction of the Beersheba and Platberg African Christian Communities in the Eastern Orange Free State, 1858–1983." *South African Historical Journal* 61, no. 3 (2009): 505–20.

Corn, Marti. *The Ground on Which I Stand: Tamina, a Freedmen's Town*. College Station: Texas A&M University Press, 2020.

Couper, Scott. *Albert Luthuli: Bound by Faith*. Scottsville, ZA: University of KwaZulu-Natal Press, 2010.

Crafford, F. S. *Jan Smuts: A Biography*. London: Pickle Partners, 2017.

Crais, Clifton C. *The Culture of Power in Southern Africa: Essays on State Formation and the Political Imagination*. Portsmouth, NH: Heinemann, 2003.

———. *The Politics of Evil: Magic, State Power, and the Political Imagination in South Africa*. New York: Cambridge University Press, 2002.

———. *Poverty, War, and Violence in South Africa*. New York: Cambridge University Press, 2011.

Crais, Clifton C., and Shamil Jeppie. *Modernity's Magic: Paper, Bureaucracy, and the Culture of Resistance in Rural South Africa, 1900–1960*. Cape Town: Centre for African Studies, University of Cape Town, 1998.

Cunnigen, Donald, Rutledge Dennis, and Myrtle Glascoe, eds. *The Racial Politics of Booker T. Washington*. Boston: Elsevier, 2006.

Cunningham, Raymond. "From Holiness to Healing: The Faith Cure in America, 1872–1892." *Church History* 43, no. 4 (December 1974).

Curtis, Heather D. *Faith in the Great Physician: Suffering and Divine Healing in American Culture, 1860–1900.* Baltimore: Johns Hopkins University Press, 2007.

———. "The Global Character of Nineteenth-Century Divine Healing." In *Global Pentecostal and Charismatic Healing,* edited by Candy Gunther Brown, 29–46. New York: Oxford University Press, 2011.

———. *Holy Humanitarians: American Evangelicals and Global Aid.* Cambridge, MA: Harvard University Press, 2018.

———. "Houses of Healing: Sacred Space, Spiritual Practice, and the Transformation of Female Suffering in the Faith Cure Movement, 1870–90." *Church History* 75, no. 3 (2006): 598–611.

———. "Keeping the Faith, Discerning the Divine: Terms and Conditions in New Research on Christianity and Healing in North America." *Church History* 78, no. 3 (2009): 640–46.

De Luna, Kathryn M. "Hunting Reputations: Talent, Individuals, and Community in Precolonial South Central Africa." *Journal of African History* 53, no. 3 (November 2012): 279–99.

De Villiers, P. G. R. "Mysticism in a Melting Pot: Andrew Murray, a Mystic from Africa on the World Stage." *Spiritus* 16, no. 2A (2016): 94–111.

Decker, Corrie. "A Feminist Methodology of Age-Grading and History in Africa." *The American Historical Review* 125, no. 2 (April 1, 2020): 418–26.

Dee, Henry. "'I Am a Bad Native': Masculinity and Marriage in the Biographies of Clements Kadalie." *African Studies* 78, no. 2 (2019): 183–204.

Deflem, Mathieu. "Warfare, Political Leadership, and State Formation: The Case of the Zulu Kingdom, 1808–1879." *Ethnology* 38, no. 4 (1999): 371–91.

Delius, Peter. "Chiefly Succession and Democracy in South Africa: Why History Matters." *Journal of Southern African Studies* 47, no. 2 (March 4, 2021): 209–27.

———. *The Land Belongs to Us: The Pedi Polity, the Boers, and the British in the Nineteenth Century Transvaal.* Berkeley: University of California Press, 1983.

———. "The Making and Changing of Migrant Workers' Worlds (1800–2014)." *African Studies* 73, no. 3 (September 2, 2014): 313–22.

———. "Witches and Missionaries in Nineteenth Century Transvaal." *Journal of Southern African Studies* 27, no. 3 (2001): 429–43.

Delius, Peter, and Clive Glaser. "The Myths of Polygamy: A History of Extra-Marital and Multi-Partnership Sex in South Africa." *South African Historical Journal* 50, no. 1 (January 1, 2004): 84–114.

Delius, Peter, and Stefan Schirmer. "Order, Openness, and Economic Change in Precolonial Southern Africa: A Perspective from the Bokoni Terraces." *The Journal of African History* 55, no. 1 (March 2014): 37–54.

Denham, Bryan. "Magazine Journalism in the Golden Age of Muckraking: Patent-Medicine Exposures before and after the Pure Food and Drug Act of 1906." *Journalism & Communication Monographs* 22, no. 2 (June 1, 2020): 100–159.

Dhuphelia-Mesthrie, Uma. *Gandhi's Prisoner: The Life of Gandhi's Son Manilal.* Cape Town: Kwela, 2004.

Digby, Anne. *Diversity and Division in Medicine: Health Care from the 1800s.* Bern, CH: Peter Lang, 2006.

Dinnerstein, Myra. "The American Zulu Mission in the Nineteenth Century: Clash over Customs." *Church History* 45, no. 2 (1976): 235–46.

Dlamini, Jacob. *Askari: A Story of Collaboration and Betrayal in the Anti-Apartheid Struggle.* Auckland Park, ZA: Jacana, 2014.

———. "Life Choices and South African Biography." *Kronos* 41, no. 1 (November 2015): 339–46.

———. *Safari Nation: A Social History of Kruger National Park.* Athens: Ohio University Press, 2020.

Dooling, Wayne. "Poverty and Respectability in Early Twentieth-Century Cape Town." *Journal of African History* 59, no. 3 (November 2018): 411–35.

———. "Reconstructing the Household: The Northern Cape Colony before and after the South African War." *Journal of African History* 50, no. 3 (2009): 399–416.

Douglas, Susan J., and Andrea McDonnell. *Celebrity: A History of Fame.* New York: NYU Press, 2019.

Doyle, Shane. "The Child of Death: Personal Names and Parental Attitudes towards Mortality in Bunyoro, Western Uganda, 1900–2005." *Journal of African History* 49, no. 3 (2008): 361–82.

Draper, Jonathan. *Orality, Literacy, and Colonialism in Southern Africa.* Atlanta: Society of Biblical Literature, 2003.

Driscoll, Barry. "Big Man or Boogey Man? The Concept of the Big Man in Political Science." *Journal of Modern African Studies* 58, no. 4 (December 2020): 521–50.

Du Bruyn, D. and M. Oelofse. "'A Hygienic Native Township Shall Be Developed': The Founding and Development of Batho as Bloemfontein's 'Model Location' (c. 1918–1939)." *Historia* 64, no. 2 (2019): 47–81.

Du Plessis, J. *The Life of Andrew Murray of South Africa.* New York: Marshall, 1920.

Du Toit, Andre. "No Chosen People: The Myth of the Calvinist Origins of Afrikaner Nationalism and Racial Ideology." *American Historical Review* 88, no. 4 (October 1983):

920–52.

Du Toit, Brian M. "Missionaries, Anthropologists, and the Policies of the Dutch Reformed Church." *Journal of Modern African Studies* 22, no. 4 (1984): 617–32.

Dube, John. *UShembe*. Pietermaritzburg, ZA: Shuter and Shooter, 1936.

Dubow, Saul. "Holding 'a Just Balance between White and Black': The Native Affairs Department in South Africa c.1920–33." *Journal of Southern African Studies* 12, no. 2 (1986): 217–39.

———. *Racial Segregation and the Origins of Apartheid in South Africa, 1919–36*. New York: Palgrave Macmillan, 1989.

Duff, S. E. "'Dear Mrs Brown': Social Purity, Sex Education and the Women's Christian Temperance Union in Early Twentieth-Century South Africa." *Social History* 45, no. 4 (October 1, 2020): 476–99.

Duminy, Andrew, and Bill Guest, eds. *Natal and Zululand from Earliest Times to 1910: A New History*. Pietermaritzburg, ZA: University of Natal Press, 1989.

Durbach, Nadja. "Class, Gender, and the Conscientious Objector to Vaccination, 1898–1907." *Journal of British Studies* 41, no. 1 (January 2002): 58–83.

Echtler, Magnus. "Shembe in the Way: The Nazareth Baptist Church in the Religious Field and in Academic Discourse." In *Bourdieu in Africa: Exploring the Dyanmics of Religious Fields*, 236–66. Leiden, NL: Brill, 2016.

Edgar, Robert. *African Apocalypse: The Story of Nontetha Nkwenkwe, a Twentieth-Century South African Prophet*. Athens: Ohio University Press, 2000.

——— *Because They Chose the Plan of God: The Story of the Bulhoek Massacre*. Johannesburg: Ravan, 1988.

———. "The Fifth Seal: Enoch Mgijima, the Israelites, and the Bullhoek Massacre, 1921." PhD diss., University of California, Los Angeles, 1977.

———. *The Finger of God: Enoch Mgijima, the Israelites, and the Bulhoek Massacre in South Africa*. Charlottesville: University of Virginia, 2018.

———. "Garveyism in Africa: Dr. Wellington and the 'American' Movement in the Transkei." *Ufahamu* 4, no. 1 (1976): 31–57.

Edgar, Robert, and Luyanda kaMzumza, eds. *Freedom in Our Lifetime: The Collected Writings of Anton Muziwakhe Lembede*. Athens: Ohio University Press, 1996.

Elbourne, Elizabeth. *Blood Ground: Colonialism, Missions, and the Contest for Christianity in the Cape Colony and Britain, 1799–1853*. Montreal: McGill–Queen's University Press, 2008.

Erlank, Natasha. "Brought into Manhood': Christianity and Male Initiation in South Africa in the Early 20th Century." *Journal of Southern African Studies* 43, no. 2 (2017): 251–65.

———. *Convening Black Intimacy: Christianity, Gender, and Tradition in Early*

Twentieth-Century South Africa. Athens: Ohio University Press, 2022.

—. "The White Wedding: Affect and Economy in South Africa in the Early Twentieth Century." *African Studies Review* 57, no. 2 (September 2014): 29–50.

Erlmann, Veit. "'Horses in the Race Course': The Domestication of Ingoma Dancing in South Africa, 1929–39." *Popular Music* 8, no. 3 (1989): 259–73.

—. "Migration and Performance: Zulu Migrant Workers' Isicathamiya Performance in South Africa, 1890–1950." *Ethnomusicology* 34, no. 2 (1990): 199–220.

—. "'The Past Is Far and the Future Is Far': Power and Performance among Zulu Migrant Workers." *American Ethnologist* 19, no. 4 (1992): 688–709.

Essop Sheik, Nafisa. "African Marriage Regulation and the Remaking of Gendered Authority in Colonial Natal, 1843–1875." *African Studies Review* 57, no. 2 (2014): 73–92.

—. "Customs in Common: Marriage, Law and the Making of Difference in Colonial Natal." *Gender and History* 29, no. 3 (2017): 589–604.

Etherington, Norman. *The Great Treks: The Transformation of Southern Africa, 1815–1854.* New York: Longman, 2001.

—. "Missionary Doctors and African Healers in Mid-Victorian South Africa." *South African Historical Journal* 19, no. 1 (1987): 77–91.

—, ed. *Missions and Empire.* New York: Oxford University Press, 2005.

—. "Natal's Black Rape Scare of the 1870s." *Journal of Southern African Studies* 15, no. 1 (1988): 36–53.

—. "Outward and Visible Signs of Conversion in Nineteenth-Century Kwazulu-Natal." *Journal of Religion in Africa* 32, no. 4 (2002): 422–39.

—. *Preachers, Peasants, and Politics in Southeast Africa, 1835–1880: African Christian Communities in Natal, Pondoland, and Zululand.* London: Royal Historical Society, 1978.

—. "Recent Trends in the Historiography of Christianity in Southern Africa." *Journal of Southern African Studies* 22, no. 2 (1996): 201–19.

—. "A Tempest in a Teapot ? Nineteenth-Century Contests for Land in South Africa' s Caledon Valley and the Invention of the Mfecane." *Journal of African History* 45, no. 2 (2004): 203–19.

—. "When Settlers Went to War against Christianity." In *Between Indigenous and Settler Governance,* edited by Lisa Ford and Tom Rowse, 95–106. London: Routledge, 2012.

—. "Why Langalibalele Ran Away." *Journal of Natal and Zulu History* 1, no. 1 (January 1, 1978): 1–24.

Epprecht, Marc. *"This Matter of Women Is Getting Very Bad": Gender, Development, and Politics in Colonial Lesotho.* Pietermaritzburg, ZA: University of Natal Press, 2000.

—. "The Native Village Debate in Pietermaritzburg, 1848–1925: Revisiting the 'Sanitation

Syndrome.'" *Journal of African History* 58, no. 2 (July 1, 2017): 259–83.

———. *Welcome to Greater Edendale: Histories of Environment, Health, and Gender in an African City*. Montreal: McGill–Queen's University Press, 2016.

Faure, Veronique. "De la communauté des convertis amakholwa à la naissance de l'Inkatha (From the Converted Amakholwa Community to the Birth of the Inkatha)." In "La démocratie déclinée." Special issue, *Cahiers d'Etudes Africaines*, vol. 35, cahier 137, (1995): 133–61.

Feinberg, Harvey. *Our Land, Our Life, Our Future: Black South African Challenges to Territorial Segregation, 1913–1948*. Pretoria, ZA: UNISA Press, 2015.

Feinberg, Harvey M., and André Horn. "South African Territorial Segregation: New Data on African Farm Purchases, 1913–1936." *Journal of African History* 50, no. 1 (2009): 41–60.

Feinstein, Charles H. *An Economic History of South Africa: Conquest, Discrimination, and Development*. New York: Cambridge University Press, 2005.

Fernandez, James. "The Precincts of the Prophet: A Day with Johannes Galilee Shembe." *Journal of Religion in Africa* 5, no. 1 (1973): 32–53.

Fields, Karen E. *Revival and Rebellion in Colonial Central Africa*. Princeton, NJ: Princeton University Press, 1985.

Flint, Karen. *Healing Traditions: African Medicine, Cultural Exchange, and Competition in South Africa, 1820–1948*. Athens: Ohio University Press, 2008.

———. "Indian-African Encounters: Polyculturalism and African Therapeutics in Natal, South Africa, 1886–1950s." *Journal of Southern African Studies* 32, no. 2 (June 2006): 367–85.

Foley, Barbara. *Spectres of 1919: Class and Nation in the Making of the New Negro*. Urbana: University of Illinois Press, 2003.

Freeman, Edward. *The Epoch of the Negro Baptists and the Foreign Mission Board*. Kansas City, MO: Central Seminary Press, 1953.

Freund, Bill. "Inequality and the Causes of Poverty in South Africa." *Journal of African History* 50, no. 1 (2009): 129–32.

———. *Insiders and Outsiders: The Indian Working Class of Durban, 1910–1990*. Portsmouth, NH: Heinemann, 1995.

———. "The Rise and Decline of an Indian Peasantry in Natal." *Journal of Peasant Studies* 18, no. 2 (1991): 263–87.

Furlong, Patrick J. *Between Crown and Swastika: The Impact of the Radical Right on the Afrikaner Nationalist Movement in the Fascist Era*. Middletown, CT: Wesleyan University Press, 1991.

Fuze, Magema. *The Black People and Whence They Came*. Edited by A. T. Cope and H. C. Lugg. Pietermaritzburg, ZA: University of Natal, 1979.

Gaitskell, Deborah. "Christian Compounds for the Girls: Church Hostels for African Women in

Johannesburg, 1907–1970." *Journal of Southern African Studies* 6, no. 1 (1979): 44–69.

———. "Devout Domesticity? A Century of African Women's Christianity in South Africa." In *Women and Gender in Southern Africa to 1945*, edited by Cherryl Walker, 251–72. Claremont, CA: David Philip, 1990.

———. "'Wailing for Purity': Prayer Unions, African Mothers and Adolescent Daughters 1912–1940." In *Industrialisation and Social Change in South Africa; African Class Formation, Culture, and Consciousness, 1870–1930*, edited by Shula Marks and Richard Rathbone, 338–57. Johannesburg: Ravan Press, 1982.

Gandhi, Sita. *In the Shadow of Mahatma: A Grand-daughter Remembers*. Edited by Uma Dhupelia-Mesthrie. Calcutta: Sampark, 2005.

Gibson, Chris. "How Clothing Design and Cultural Industries Refashioned Frontier Masculinities: A Historical Geography of Western Wear." *Gender, Place & Culture* 23, no. 5 (May 3, 2016): 733–52.

Giucci, Guillermo, Anne Mayagoitia, and Debra Nagao. *The Cultural Life of the Automobile: Roads to Modernity*. Austin: University of Texas Press, 2012, 66.

Gluckman, Max. *Analysis of a Social Situation in Modern Zululand*. Manchester, UK: Manchester University Press, 1958.

———. *Rituals of Rebellion in South-East Africa*. Manchester, UK: Manchester University Press, 1954.

Goedhals, Mandy. "African Nationalism and Indigenous Christianity: A Study in the Life of James Calata." *Journal of Religion in Africa* 33, no. 1 (2003): 63–82.

Green, Nile. "Islam for the Indentured Indian: A Muslim Missionary in Colonial South Africa." *Bulletin of SOAS* 71, no. 3 (2008): 529–53.

Grout, Lewis. *Zulu-Land: Or, Life among the Zulu-Kafirs of Natal and Zululand*. Philadelphia, PA, 1864.

Gunner, Elizabeth. "Hidden Stories in the Light of the New Day: A Zulu Manuscript and Its Place in South African Writing." *Research in African Literatures* 31, no. 2 (2000): 1–16.

———. *The Man of Heaven and the Beautiful Ones of God: Umuntu Wasezulwini Nabantu Abahle Bakankulunkulu; Writings From Ibandla Lamanazaretha, a South African Church*. Leiden, NL: Brill, 2002.

———. "Power House, Prison House: An Oral Genre and Its Use in Isaiah Shembe's Nazareth Baptist Church." *Journal of Southern African Studies* 14, no. 2 (1988): 204–27.

Gunner, Elizabeth, and Mafika Pascal Gwala. *Musho!: Zulu Popular Praises*. East Lansing: Michigan State University Press, 1991.

Guy, Jeff. *The Destruction of the Zulu Kingdom: The Civil War in Zululand, 1879–1884*. London: Longman, 1979.

———. *The Maphumulo Uprising: War, Law, and Ritual in the Zulu Rebellion.* Scottsville, ZA: University of KwaZulu-Natal Press, 2005.

———. "A Paralysis of Perspective: Image and Text in the Creation of an African Chief," *South African Historical Journal* 47, no. 1 (2002): 51–74.

———. *Remembering the Rebellion: The Zulu Uprising of 1906.* Scottsville, ZA: University of KwaZulu-Natal Press, 2006.

———. *Theophilus Shepstone and the Forging of Natal.* Pietermaritzburg, ZA: University of KwaZulu-Natal Press, 2013.

———. *The View across the River: Harriette Colenso and the Zulu Struggle against Imperialism.* Charlottesville: University of Virginia Press, 2002.

Guyer, Jane I., and Samuel M. Eno Belinga. "Wealth in People as Wealth in Knowledge: Accumulation and Composition in Equatorial Africa." *Journal of African History* 36, no. 1 (1995): 91–120.

Hale, Frederick, ed. *Norwegian Missionaries in Natal and Zululand: Selected Correspondence.* Cape Town: Van Riebeeck Society, 1997.

Hall, Catherine. *Civilising Subjects: Metropole and Colony in the English Imagination 1830–1867.* University Of Chicago Press, 2002.

Hall, Martin. "The Myth of the Zulu Homestead: Archaeology and Ethnography." *Africa* 54, no. 1 (1984): 65–79.

Hamilton, Carolyn, ed. *The Mfecane Aftermath: Reconstructive Debates in Southern African History.* Johannesburg: Witwatersrand University Press, 1995.

———. *Terrific Majesty: The Powers of Shaka Zulu and the Limits of Historical Invention.* Cape Town: David Philip, 1998.

Hamilton, Carolyn, and John B. Wright. "The Making of the *AmaLala*: Ethnicity, Ideology, and Relations of Subordination in a Precolonial Context." *South African Historical Journal* 22, no. 1 (1990): 3–23.

Hanretta, Sean. *Islam and Social Change in French West Africa: History of an Emancipatory Community.* New York: Cambridge University Press, 2009.

———. "Women, Marginality, and the Zulu State: Women's Institutions and Power in the Early Nineteenth Century." *Journal of African History* 39, no. 3 (1998): 389–415.

Harries, Patrick. "Imagery, Symbolism, and Tradition in a South African Bantustan: Mangosuthu Buthelezi, Inkatha, and Zulu History." *History and Theory* 32, no. 4 (1993): 105–25.

———. *Work, Culture, and Identity: Migrant Laborers in Mozambique and South Africa, c.1860–1910.* Portsmouth, NH: Heinemann, 1994.

Harrison, Charles William Francis, and Joseph Forsyth Ingram. *Natal: An Illustrated Official*

Railway Guide and Handbook of General Information. London, 1903.

Hastings, Adrian. *The Church in Africa, 1450–1950*. New York: Oxford University Press, 1994.

Hay, Margaret Jean, and Marcia Wright, eds. *African Women and the Law: Historical Perspectives*. Boston: Boston University Papers on Africa, 1982.

Hayes, Patricia. "Power, Secrecy, Proximity: A Short History of South African Photography." *Kronos*, no. 33 (2007): 139–62.

Healy, Meghan. "'A World of Their Own': African Women's Schooling and the Politics of Social Reproduction in South Africa, 1869 to Recent Times." PhD diss., Harvard University, 2011.

———. "'To Control Their Destiny': The Politics of Home and the Feminisation of Schooling in Colonial Natal, 1885–1910." *Journal of Southern African Studies* 37, no. 2 (June 1, 2011): 247–64.

Healy-Clancy, Meghan. *A World of Their Own: A History of South African Women's Education*. Charlottesville: University of Virginia, 2014.

Henderson, WPM. *Durban: Fifty Years' Municipal History*. Durban, 1904.

Herd, Norman. *The Bent Pine: The Trial of Chief Langalibalele*. Johannesburg: Ravan, 1976.

———. *1922: The Revolt on the Rand*. Johannesburg: Blue Crane, 1966.

Heuser, Andreas. "'He Dances like Isaiah Shembe!' Ritual Aesthetics as a Marker of Church Difference." *Studies in World Christianity* 14, no. 1 (April 1, 2008): 35–54.

———. "Memory Tales: Representations of Shembe in the Cultural Discourse of African Renaissance." *Journal of Religion in Africa* 35, no. 3 (2005): 362–87.

———. "Recovered Narratives of an Inter-Cultural Exchange: Gandhi, Shembe, and the Legacy of Satyagraha." *Journal of the Study of Religion* 16, no. 1 (2003): 87–102.

———. *Shembe, Gandhi und Die Soldaten Gottes*. Berlin: Waxmann, 2002.

———. "Staging African Prophets in South Africa: *iLanga lase Natal* as an Historical Archive of Early African Pentecostalism." In *Polycentric Structures in the History of World Christianity*, edited by Klaus Korschorke and Adrian Hermann, 239–56. Wiesbaden, Ger.: Harrassowitz, 2014.

Hexham, Irving, and G. C. Oosthuizen, eds. *The Story of Isaiah Shembe*. Translated by Hans-Jürgen Becken. 5 vols. Lewiston, NY: Edwin Mellen Press, 1996–2002.

Hickel, Jason. *Democracy as Death: The Moral Order of Anti-liberal Politics in South Africa*. Berkeley: University of California Press, 2015.

Higgs, Anneke. "The Historical Development of Diamond Mining Legislation in Griqualand West during the Period 1871 to 1880." *Fundamina* 24, no. 1 (2018): 18–56.

Hiralal, Kalpana. "'What Is the Meaning of the Word "Wife?"' The Impact of the Immigration Laws on the Wives of Resident Indians in South Africa 1897–1930." *Contemporary South Asia* 26, no. 2 (June 2018): 206–20.

Hiralal, Kalpana, and E. S. Reddy. *Pioneers of Satyagraha: Indian South Africans Defy Racist Laws, 1907–1914*. Ahmedabad: Navajivan, 2017.

Hobsbawm, Eric. *Primitive Rebels: Studies in Archaic Forms of Social Movement in the Nineteenth and Twentieth Centuries*. New York: Norton, 1965.

Hodgson, Dorothy, and Sheryl McCurdy, eds. *"Wicked" Women and the Reconfiguration of Gender in Africa*. Portsmouth, NH: Heinemann, 2001.

Hoehler-Fatton, Cynthia Heyden. *Women of Fire and Spirit: History, Faith and Gender in Roho Religion in Nyanza*. New York: Oxford University Press, 1996.

Hofmeyr, Isabel. *Gandhi's Printing Press: Experiments in Slow Reading*. Cambridge, MA: Harvard University Press, 2013.

———. *The Portable Bunyan: A Transnational History of The Pilgrim's Progress*. Princeton, NJ: Princeton University Press, 2018.

Hollmann, Jeremy C. "Allusions to Agriculturist Rituals in Hunter-Gatherer Rock Art? EMkhobeni Shelter, Northern UKhahlamba-Drakensberg, KwaZulu-Natal, South Africa." *African Archaeological Review* 32, no. 3 (September 1, 2015): 505–35.

Houle, Robert J. "From Burnt Bricks to Sanctification: Rethinking 'Church' in Colonial Southern Africa." *South African Historical Journal* 70, no. 2 (2018): 348–69.

———. "From Christian Brother to Native: Claiming and Rejecting Christianity, Commerce, and Civilization in Early Twentieth-Century Natal." *Journal of the Middle East and Africa* 8, no. 1 (January 2017): 41–56.

———. *Making African Christianity: Africans Reimagining Their Faith in Colonial South Africa*. Bethlehem, PA: Lehigh University Press, 2011.

Houtman, Cornelis. "Rewriting a Dramatic Old Testament Story the Story of Jephthah and His Daughter in Some Examples of Christian Devotional Literature." *Biblical Interpretation* 13, no. 2 (April 2005): 167–90.

Hughes, Heather. "Doubly Elite: Exploring the Life of John Langalibalele Dube." *Journal of Southern African Studies* 27, no. 3 (2001): 445–58.

———. *The First President*. Johannesburg: Jacana, 2011.

———. "Violence in Inanda, August 1985." *Journal of Southern African Studies* 13, no. 3 (1987): 331–54.

———. "Mbiya Kuzwayo's Christianity: Revival, Reformation and the Surprising Viability of Mainline Churches in South Africa." *Journal of Religion in Africa* 38, no. 2 (2008): 141–70.

Hunt, Nancy Rose. *A Nervous State: Violence, Remedies, and Reverie in Colonial Congo*. Durham, NC: Duke University Press, 2016.

Hunter, Monica. *Reaction to Conquest: Effects of Contact with Europeans on the Pondo of South Africa*. London: David Philip, 1979.

Hyslop, Jonathan. "The Politics of Disembarkation: Empire, Shipping and Labor in the Port of Durban, 1897–1947." *International Labor and Working Class History* 93 (Spring 2018): 176–200.

———. "The Strange Death of Liberal England and the Strange Birth of Illiberal South Africa: British Trade Unionists, Indian Labourers and Afrikaner Rebels, 1910–1914." *Labour History Review* 79, no. 1 (April 2014): 97–120.

Iliffe, John. *Honour in African History*. New York: Cambridge University Press, 2005.

———. "The South African Economy, 1652–1997." *Economic History Review* 52, no. 1 (February 1, 1999): 87–103.

Inglis, Fred. *A Short History of Celebrity*. Princeton, NJ: Princeton University Press, 2010.

Janzen, John M, and William Arkinstall, eds. *The Quest for Therapy in Lower Zaire*. Berkeley: University of California Press, 1978.

Jeske, Christine. "Are Cars the New Cows? Changing Wealth Goods and Moral Economies in South Africa." *American Anthropologist* 118, no. 3 (2016): 483–94.

Johnson, Curtis D. "The Protracted Meeting Myth: Awakenings, Revivals, and New York State Baptists, 1789–1850." *Journal of the Early Republic* 34, no. 3 (2014): 349–83.

Jolles, Frank, and Stephen Jolles. "Zulu Ritual Immunisation in Perspective." *Africa* 70, no. 2 (2000): 229–48.

Jorgenson, Sarah Corinne. "The American Zulu Mission and the Limits of Reform: Natal, South Africa, 1835–1919." PhD diss., Princeton University, 2009.

Kaarsholm, Preben. "Zanzibaris or Amakhuwa? Sufi Networks in South Africa, Mozambique, and the Indian Ocean." *Journal of African History* 55, no. 2 (July 2014): 191–210.

Kay, Stephen. *Travels and Researches in Caffraria*. New York, 1834.

Keegan, Timothy J. *Rural Transformations in Industrializing South Africa: The Southern Highveld to 1914*. London: MacMillan, 1987.

Kelly, Jill E. *To Swim with Crocodiles: Land, Violence, and Belonging in South Africa, 1800–1996*. East Lansing: Michigan State University Press, 2018.

Khumalo, Vukile. "Ekukhanyeni Letter-Writers: A Historical Inquiry into Epistolary Network(s) and Political Imagination in Kwazulu-Natal, South Africa." In *Africa's Hidden Histories*, edited by Karin Barber, 113–26. Bloomington: Indiana University Press, 2006.

Kiernan, J. P. "The Other Side of the Coin: The Conversion of Money to Religious Purposes in Zulu Zionist Churches." *Man* 23, no. 3 (1988): 452–68.

———. "The 'Problem of Evil' in the Context of Ancestral Intervention in the Affairs of the Living in Africa." *Man* 17, no. 2 (1982): 287–301.

———. *The Production and Management of Therapeutic Power in Zionist Churches within the Zulu City*. Lewiston, NY: Edwin Mellon, 1996.

————. "Prophet and Preacher: An Essential Partnership in the Work of Zion." *Man* 11, no. 3 (1976): 356–66.

————. "Spouses and Partners: Marriage and Career Among Urban Zulu Zionists." *Urban Anthropology* 8, no. 1 (1979): 95–110.

————. "Themes and Trends in the Study of Black Religion in Southern Africa." *Journal of Religion in Africa* 12, no. 2 (1981): 136–47.

————. "The Weapons of Zion." *Journal of Religion in Africa* 10, no. 1 (1979): 13–21.

————. "The Work of Zion: An Analysis of an African Zionist Ritual." *Africa* 46, no. 4 (1976): 340–56.

Kobo, Fundiswa A. "Spirituality Trapped in Androcentric Celebrity Cults in South Africa Post-1994." *HTS Theological Studies* 75, no. 3 (2019).

Kohler, M. *Marriage Customs in Southern Natal.* Pretoria: Government Printer, 1933.

Kopytoff, Igor, and Suzanne Miers, eds. *Slavery in Africa: Historical and Anthropological Perspectives.* Madison: University of Wisconsin Press, 1977.

Kornberg, Jacques. *Theodor Herzl: From Assimilation to Zionism.* Bloomington: Indiana University Press, 1993.

Kresse, Kai. "Izibongo. The Political Art of Praising: Poetical Socio-Regulative Discourse in Zulu Society." *Journal of African Cultural Studies* 11, no. 2 (1998): 171–96.

Krige, Eileen. "Girls' Puberty Songs and Their Relation to Fertility, Health, Morality and Religion among the Zulu." *Africa* 38, no. 2 (April 1968): 173–98.

————. *The Social System of the Zulus.* Pietermaritzburg, ZA: Shuter and Shooter, 1936.

Kumalo, Simangaliso, and Martin Mujinga. "'Now We Know That the Enemy Is from Within': Shembeites and the Struggle for Control of Isaiah Shembe's Legacy and the Church." *Journal for the Study of Religion* 30, no. 2 (2017): 122–53.

Kuper, Adam. "The 'House' and Zulu Political Structure in the Nineteenth Century." *Journal of African History* 34, no. 3 (1993): 469–87.

————. "Zulu Kinship Terminology over a Century." *Journal of Anthropological Research* 35, no. 3 (1979): 373–83.

Kuper, Leo. *Passive Resistance in South Africa.* New Haven, Yale University Press, 1957.

La Hausse, Paul. *Brewers, Beerhalls, and Boycotts: A History of Liquor in South Africa.* Johannesburg: Ravan, 1988.

————. "'The Cows of Nongoloza': Youth, Crime and Amalaita Gangs in Durban, 1900–1936." *Journal of Southern African Studies* 16, no. 1 (1990): 79–111.

————. *Restless Identities: Signatures of Nationalism, Zulu Ethnicity and History in the Lives of Petros Lamula (c.1881–1948) and Lymon Maling (1889–c.1936).* Pietermaritzburg, ZA: University of Natal Press, 2000.

Lalu, Premesh. *The Deaths of Hintsa: Post-Apartheid South Africa and the Shape of Recurring Pasts*. Johannesburg: Human Sciences Research Council, 2009.

Lambert, John. *Betrayed Trust: Africans and the State in Colonial Natal*. Pietermaritzburg, ZA: University of Natal, 1995.

———. "The Rise of African Indebtedness in Natal during the Late Colonial Period." *Kleio* 24, no. 1 (January 1, 1992): 19–39.

———. "The Undermining of the Homestead Economy in Colonial Natal." *Southern African Historical Journal* 23 (1990): 54–73.

Lamula, Petros. *Uzulukamalandela. A Most Practical and Concise Compendium of African History, Etc.* Pietermaritzburg, ZA: Josiah Jones, 1931.

Landau, Paul. "Explaining Surgical Evangelism in Colonial Southern Africa: Teeth, Pain and Faith." *Journal of African History* 37, no. 2 (1996): 261–81.

———. *Popular Politics in the History of South Africa, 1400–1948*. Cambridge, UK: Cambridge University Press, 2010.

———. *The Realm of the Word: Language, Gender, and Christianity in a Southern African Kingdom*. Portsmouth, NH: Heinemann, 1995.

Larlham, Peter. "Festivals of the Nazareth Baptist Church." *Drama Review* 25, no. 4 (1981): 59–74.

Lefebvre, P. L., and Bedver B. L. Jackson. *The Statute Law of the Orange River Colony*. Bloemfontein, ZA, 1907.

Lelyveld, Joseph. *Great Soul: Mahatma Gandhi and His Struggle with India*. New York: Vintage, 2012.

Lester, Alan. "The Margins of Order: Strategies of Segregation on the Eastern Cape Frontier, 1806–c. 1850." *Journal of Southern African Studies* 23, no. 4 (1997): 635–53.

Liardon, Roberts. *Maria Woodworth-Etter: The Complete Collection of Her Life Teachings*. Shippensburg, PA: Harrison House, 2021.

Limb, Peter. *The ANC's Early Years: Nation, Class and Place in South Africa before 1940*. Pretoria: UNISA Press, 2010.

———. "The Empire Writes Back: African Challenges to the Brutish (South African) Empire in the Early 20th Century." *Journal of Southern African Studies* 41, no. 3 (2015): 599–616.

Lincoln, David. "Settlement and Servitude in Zululand, 1918–1948." *International Journal of African Historical Studies* 28, no. 1 (1995): 49–67.

Lindsay, Lisa A. "Biography in African History." *History in Africa* 44, no. 1 (2017): 11–26.

Livingston, Julie. *Debility and the Moral Imagination in Botswana*. Bloomington: Indiana University Press, 2005.

Lodge, Tom. *Mandela: A Critical Life*. New York: Oxford University Press, 2006.

Loram, C. T. *The Education of the South African Native.* London: Longmans, Green, 1917.

Lukhaimane, Elias. "The Zion Christian Church of Ignatius (Engenas) Lekganyane, 1924 to 1948: An African Experiment with Christianity." Master's thesis, University of the North, 1980.

Lwandle, P. S. "Concepts of Christ in Africa as Reflected in the Shembe Church." PhD diss., University of South Africa, 2009.

MacKinnon, Aran. "Chiefly Authority, Leapfrogging Headmen, and the Political Economy of Zululand, ca. 1930–1950." *Journal of Southern African Studies* 27, no. 3 (2001): 567–90.

———. "The Persistence of the Cattle Economy in Zululand, 1900–1950." *Canadian Journal of African Studies* 33, no. 1 (1999): 98–135.

———. "Of Oxford Bags and Twirling Canes: The State, Popular Responses, and Zulu Antimalaria Assistants in the Early-Twentieth-Century Zululand Malaria Campaigns." *Radical History Review* 2001, no. 80 (May 1, 2001): 76–100.

Magaziner, Daniel R. *The Law and the Prophets: Black Consciousness in South Africa, 1968–1977.* Athens: Ohio University Press, 2010.

Magwaza, Thenjiwe. "Conversations with Women of the Shembe Church: Self Perceptions and the Role of Zulu Culture in Formulating Their Status." *Agenda* 60 (2004): 136–54.

Mahoney, Michael. "The Millennium Comes to Maphumulo: Popular Christianity in Rural Natal, 1866–1906." *Journal of Southern African Studies* 25, no. 3 (1999): 375–91.

———. *The Other Zulus: The Spread of Zulu Ethnicity in Colonial South Africa.* Durham, NC: Duke University Press, 2012.

Makhulu, Anne-Maria. *Making Freedom: Apartheid, Squatter Politics, and the Struggle for Home.* Durham, NC: Duke University Press, 2015.

Maloka, Tshidiso. "The Struggle for Sunday." In *Christianity in South Africa,* edited by Richard Elphick and T. R. H. Davenport, 242–60. Berkeley: University of California Press, 1997.

Mandela, Nelson. *Long Walk to Freedom: The Autobiography.* New York: Little, 2013.

Mann, Kristin, and Richard Roberts, eds. *Law in Colonial Africa.* Portsmouth, NH: Heinemann, 1991.

Manson, Andrew. "A People in Transition: The Hlubi in Natal, 1848–1877." *Journal of Natal and Zulu History* 2, no. 1 (1979): 13–26.

Marks, Shula. "The Ambiguities of Dependence: John L. Dube of Natal." *Journal of Southern African Studies* 1, no. 2 (1975): 162–80.

———. *The Ambiguities of Dependence in South Africa: Class, Nationalism, and the State in Twentieth-century Natal.* Johannesburg: Ravan, 1986.

———. "Natal, the Zulu Royal Family and the Ideology of Segregation." *Journal of Southern African Studies* 4, no. 2 (April 1, 1978): 172–94.

———. "Patriotism, Patriarchy, and Purity: Natal and the Politics of Zulu Ethnic Consciousness." In *The Creation of Tribalism in Southern Africa*, edited by Leroy Vail, 215–34. Berkeley: University of California Press, 1989.

———. *Reluctant Rebellion: The 1906–8 Disturbances In Natal.* Oxford, UK: Clarendon, 1970.

Marks, Shula, and Richard Rathbone, eds. *Industrialisation and Social Change in South Africa: African Class Formation, Culture, and Consciousness, 1870–1930.* New York: Longman, 1982.

Marschall, Sabine. "An Inspiring Narrative with a Shadow: Tangible and Intangible Heritage at the Phoenix Settlement of Mahatma Gandhi." *Southern African Humanities* 20 (December 2008): 353–74.

———. "Sustainable Heritage Tourism: The Inanda Heritage Route and the 2010 FIFA World Cup." *Journal of Sustainable Tourism* 20, no. 5 (2012): 721–36.

———. "Woza ENanda: Perceptions of and Attitudes towards Heritage and Tourism in a South African Township." *Transformation* 83, no. 1 (2013): 32–55.

Maxwell, David. *African Gifts of the Spirit: Pentecostalism & the Rise of Zimbabwean Transnational Religious Movement.* Athens: Ohio University Press: 2007.

———. *Christians and Chiefs in Zimbabwe: A Social History of the Hwesa People c.1870s–1990s.* Edinburgh, UK: Edinburgh University Press, 1999.

———. "Delivered from the Spirit of Poverty? Pentecostalism, Prosperity, and Modernity in Zimbabwe." *Journal of Religion in Africa* 28, no. 3 (1998): 350–73.

———. "Historicizing Christian Independency: The Southern African Pentecostal Movement c. 1908–1960." *Journal of African History* 40, no. 2 (1999): 243–64.

———, "The Missionary Home as a Site for Mission: Perspectives from Belgian Congo." *Studies in Church History* 50 (2014): 428–55.

———. "New Perspectives on the History of African Christianity." *Journal of Southern African Studies* 23, no. 2 (1997): 283–300.

———. "The Spirit and Scapular: Pentecostal and Catholic Interactions in Northern Nyanga District, Zimbabwe in the 1950s and early 1960s." *Journal of Southern African Studies* 23, no. 2 (1997): 283–300.

———. "Witches, Prophets, and Avenging Spirits: The Second Christian Movement in North-East Zimbabwe." *Journal of Religion in Africa* 25, no. 3 (1995): 309–39.

Maxwell, David, and Ingrid Lawrie. *Christianity and the African Imagination: Essays in Honour of Adrian Hastings.* Leiden, NL: Brill, 2002.

McClendon, Thomas V. *Genders and Generations Apart: Labor Tenants and Customary Law in Segregation-Era South Africa, 1920s to 1940s.* Portsmouth, NH: Heinemann, 2002.

———. "Tradition and Domestic Struggle in the Courtroom: Customary Law and Control over Women in Segregation Era Natal." *International Journal of African Historical Studies* 28, no.

3 (1995): 527–61.

———. *White Chief, Black Lords: Shepstone and the Colonial State in Natal, South Africa, 1845–1878*. Rochester, NY: University of Rochester Press, 2010.

———. "You Are What You Eat Up: Deposing Chiefs in Early Colonial Natal, 1847–58." *Journal of African History* 47, no. 2 (2006): 259–79.

McKittrick, Meredith. *To Dwell Secure: Generation, Christianity, and Colonialism in Ovamboland*. Portsmouth, NH: Heinemann, 2002.

Meyer, Birgit. *Translating the Devil: Religion and Modernity among the Ewe in Ghana*. Edinburgh, UK: Edinburgh University Press for the International African Institute, 1999.

———. "Christianity in Africa: From African Independent to Pentecostal-Charismatic Churches." *Annual Review of Anthropology* 33 (2004): 447–74.

Minnaar, A. de V. *Empangeni: A Historical Review to 1983*. Pretoria: Human Sciences Research Council, 1984.

———. *Ushukela! A History of the Growth and Development of the Sugar Industry in Zululand: 1905 to the Present*. Pretoria: Human Sciences Research Council, 1992.

Moffett, F. C., and J. B. Lee. *With the Eighth Division: A Souvenir of the South African Campaign*. Westminster, UK, 1903.

Moguerane, Khumisho. "Black Landlords, Their Tenants, and the Natives Land Act of 1913." *Journal of Southern African Studies* 42, no. 2 (March 3, 2016): 243–66.

Mokoena, Hlonipha. *Magema Fuze: The Making of a* Kholwa *Intellectual*. Scottsville, ZA: University of KwaZulu-Natal Press, 2011.

———. "Zuluness on Trial: Re-reading John W. Colenso's 1874 *Langalibalele and the Amahlubi Tribe: Being Remarks Upon the Official Record*." *Journal of African History* 60, no. 1 (March 2019): 67–85.

Moodie, T. Dunbar. *Going for Gold: Men, Mines, and Migration*. Berkeley: University of California Press, 1994.

Moodley, E. J. "Shembe, Ancestors, or Christ? A Missiological Inquiry into the Status and Role of Jesus Christ in the AmaNazaretha Church, KwaZulu-Natal, South Africa." PhD diss., Asbury Theological Seminary, 2004.

Morton, Barry. *Engenas Lekganyane and the Early ZCC: An Unauthorized History*. Self-published, BooksMango, 2018.

Mukonyora, Isabel. *Wandering a Gendered Wilderness: Suffering & Healing in an African Initiated Church*. New York: P. Lang, 2007.

Muller, Carol Ann. "Archiving Africanness in Sacred Song." *Ethnomusicology* 46, no. 3 (2002): 409–31.

———. *Rituals of Fertility and the Sacrifice of Desire: Nazarite Women's Performance in South*

Africa. University of Chicago Press, 1999.

Müller, Retief. *African Pilgrimage*. London: Routledge, 2021.

———. "Constructing Separatism in South Africa's Racially Charged Religiosity: 20th Century Afrikaner Discourses on African Initiated Christianity." *Religion Compass* 11, nos. 1–2 (2017): e12231.

Murray, Andrew. *Divine Healing: A Series of Addresses*. New York, 1900.

Ndaba, Dean Jabulani. "The Development of Umlazi Mission Station And Reserve, 1856–1948, With Special Reference To The Land Problem." Master's thesis, University of Zululand KwaDlangezwa, 1993.

Ndlovu, Sifiso Mxolisi. "Women, Authority, and Power in Precolonial Southeast Africa." In *A Companion to African History*, 93–117. Hoboken, NJ: Wiley, 2018.

Ndlovu-Gatsheni, Sabelo, and Busani Ngcaweni, eds. *The Contested Idea of South Africa*. London: Routledge, 2022.

Newell, Stephanie. *Histories of Dirt in West Africa: Media and Urban Life in Colonial and Postcolonial Lagos*. Durham, NC: Duke University Press, 2020.

Ngonyama, Percy. "The Ward System: Redefining Chiefly Jurisdiction in the Lower Tugela Division (LTD) of Natal, 1906–1909." In *History and African Studies Seminar*. Durban, ZA: University of KwaZulu-Natal–Howard College, 2008.

Ngubane, Harriet. *Body and Mind in Zulu Medicine: An Ethnography of Health and Disease in Nyuswa-Zulu Thought and Practice*. London: Academic, 1977.

O'Meara, Dan. *Volkskapitalisme: Class, Capital, and Ideology in the Development of Afrikaner Nationalism, 1934–1948*. New York: Cambridge University Press, 1983.

Oosthuizen, G. C. *Baptism in the Context of the African Indigenous/Independent Churches (A.I.C.)*. KwaDlangezwa, ZA: University of Zululand, 1985.

———. *The Birth of Christian Zionism in South Africa*. KwaDlangezwa, ZA: University of Zululand, 1987.

———. *The Healer-Prophet in Afro-Christian Churches*. Leiden, NL: Brill, 1992.

———. *The Theology of a South African Messiah: An Analysis of the Hymnal of the Church of the Nazarites*. Leiden, NL: Brill, 1967.

Orange Free State. *Census Report of the Orange River Colony*. Bloemfontein, ZA, 1904.

Papini, Robert. "Carl Faye's Transcript of Isaiah Shembe's Testimony of His Early Life and Calling." *Journal of Religion in Africa* 29, no. 3 (1999): 243–84.

———. "Dance Uniform History in the Church of Nazareth Baptists: The Move to Tradition." *African Arts* 37, no. 3 (2004): 48–61, 90–92.

Parle, Julie. "This Painful Subject: Racial Politics and Suicide in Colonial Natal and Zululand." In *Histories of Suicide: International Perspectives on Destruction in the Modern World*, edited by John Weaver and David Wright, 156–77. University of Toronto Press, 2009.

———. "Witchcraft or Madness? The Amandiki of Zululand, 1894–1914." *Journal of Southern African Studies* 29, no. 1 (2003): 105–32.

Parle, Julie, and Vanessa Noble. *The People's Hospital: A History of McCords, Durban, 1890s–1970s.* Pietermaritzburg, ZA: Occasional Publications of the Natal Society Foundation, 2017.

Parpart, Jane, and Kathleen Staudt, eds. *Women and the State in Africa.* Boulder, CO: Lynne Reiner, 1989.

Paugh, Katherine. "Yaws, Syphilis, Sexuality, and the Circulation of Medical Knowledge in the British Caribbean and the Atlantic World." *Bulletin of the History of Medicine* 88, no. 2 (2014): 225–52.

p'Bitek, Okot. *African Religions in Western Scholarship.* Nairobi: East African Literature Bureau, 1970.

Peel, J. D. Y. *Aladura: A Religious Movement among the Yoruba.* London: International African Institute, 1968. Distributed by Oxford University Press.

———. *Religious Encounter and the Making of the Yoruba.* Bloomington: Indiana University Press, 2000.

Peires, Jeff. *The Dead Will Arise: Nongqawuse and the Great Xhosa Cattle-Killing Movement of 1856–7.* Bloomington: Indiana University Press, 1989.

———. *The House of Phalo: A History of the Xhosa People in the Days of Their Independence.* Cape Town: Jonathan Ball, 2003.

———. "Nxele, Ntsikana and the Origins of the Xhosa Religious Reaction." *Journal of African History* 20, no. 1 (1979): 51–61.

———. "'Soft' Believers and 'Hard' Unbelievers in the Xhosa Cattle-Killing." *Journal of African History* 27, no. 3 (1986): 443–61.

Perham, Margerie. *An African Apprenticeship: An Autobiographical Journey in Southern Africa, 1929.* London: Longman, 1974.

Peta, Sanelisiwe Buhlebemvelo Emily. "Women, Religion and Landscape: Reimagining Traditional Religious Spaces of the Shembe Church from Afrocentric Notions of the Female Body." Master's thesis, University of Johannesburg (South Africa), 2021.

Peterson, Derek. *Ethnic Patriotism and the East African Revival: A History of Dissent, c. 1935 to 1972.* New York: Cambridge University Press, 2012.

Pfeiffer, James. "African Independent Churches in Mozambique: Healing Afflictions of Inequality." *Medical Anthropology Quarterly* 16, no. 2 (2002): 176–99.

Phoofolo, Pule. "Epidemics and Revolutions: The Rinderpest Epidemic in Late Nineteenth–Century Southern Africa." *Past and Present* 138, no. 1 (1993): 112–43.

Pirie, Gordon. "Railways and Labour Migration to the Rand Mines: Constraints and Significance." *Journal of Southern African Studies* 19, no. 4 (1993): 713–30.

Plaatjie, Thami ka. *Sobukwe: The Making of a Pan Africanist Leader*. Sandton, ZA, KMM Review Publishing, 2019.

Pogrund, Benjamin. *Robert Sobukwe: How Can Man Die Better*. New York: Jonathan Ball Publishers, 2006.

Polak, Millie. *Mr. Gandhi: The Man*. London: Allen & Unwin, 1931.

Porter, Andrew. *Religion Versus Empire?: British Protestant Missionaries and Overseas Expansion, 1700–1914*. New York: Palgrave, 2004.

Posel, Deborah. "Marriage at the Drop of a Hat: Housing and Partnership in South Africa's Urban African Townships, 1920s–1960s." *History Workshop Journal* 61, no. 1 (2006): 57–76.

Ranger, Terence. "Connexions between 'Primary Resistance' Movements and Modern Mass Nationalism," parts 1–2. *Journal of African History* 9, nos. 3/4 (1968).

———. "The Invention of Tradition Revisited: The Case of Africa." In *Legitimacy and the State in Twentieth Century Africa*, edited by Olufemi Vaughn and Terence Ranger. London: MacMillan, 1993.

———. "Religious Movements and Politics in Sub-Saharan Africa." *African Studies Review* 29, no. 2 (1986): 1–68.

Ranger, Terence, and Isaria N. Kimambo. *The Historical Study of African Religion*. Berkeley: University of California Press, 1972.

Ranger, Terence, and John C. Weller. *Themes in the Christian History of Central Africa*. Berkeley: University of California Press, 1975.

Redding, Sean. "Deaths in the Family: Domestic Violence, Witchcraft Accusations and Political Militancy in Transkei, South Africa, 1904–1965." *Journal of Southern African Studies* 30, no. 3 (2004): 519–37.

———. *Sorcery and Sovereignty: Taxation, Power, and Rebellion in South Africa, 1880–1963*. Athens: Ohio University Press, 2006.

———. "Women as Diviners and as Christian Converts in Rural South Africa, c.1880–1963." *Journal of African History* 57, no. 3 (November 1, 2016): 367–89.

Reyher, Rebecca Hourwich. *Zulu Woman: The Life Story of Christina Sibiya*. New York: Feminist Press at the City University of New York, 1999.

Richardson, Peter. "The Natal Sugar Industry, 1849–1905." *Journal of African History* 23, no. 4 (1982): 515–27.

Roberts, Esther. "Shembe: The Man and His Work." Master's thesis, University of Natal, 1936.

Roberts, Richard. *Conflicts of Colonialism: The Rule of Law, French Soudan, and Faama Mademba Sèye*. Cambridge, UK: Cambridge University Press, 2022.

————. "Text and Testimony in the *Tribunal de Premiere Instance,* Dakar, During the Early Twentieth Century." *Journal of African History* 3 (1990): 447–63.

Robinson, David. *Paths of Accommodation: Muslim Societies and French Colonial Authorities in Senegal and Mauritania, 1880–1920.* Athens: Ohio University Press, 2000.

Robinson, James. *Divine Healing: The Holiness-Pentecostal Transition Years, 1890–1906: Theological Transpositions in the Transatlantic World.* Eugene, OR: Wipf and Stock, 2013.

Rotberg, Robert I. "Charisma, Leadership, and Historiography." Edited by Edward Berenson and Eva Giloi. *Journal of Interdisciplinary History* 42, no. 3 (2012): 419–28.

Roy, Kevin. *No Turning Back: A History of Baptist Missionary Endeavor in Southern Africa from 1820–2000.* Pinelands, ZA: South African Baptist Historical Society, 2001.

Schmidt, Elizabeth. *Peasants, Traders, and Wives: Shona Women in the History of Zimbabwe, 1870–1939.* Portsmouth, NH: Heinemann, 1992.

Sahlins, Marshall D. "Poor Man, Rich Man, Big-Man, Chief: Political Types in Melanesia and Polynesia." *Comparative Studies in Society and History* 5, no. 3 (1963): 285–303.

Schoeman, Karel. *The British Presence in the Transorange, 1845–1854.* Cape Town: Human & Rousseau, 1992.

————. *The Wesleyan Mission in the Orange Free State, 1833–1854, As Described in Cotemporary Sources.* Cape Town: Human & Rousseau, 1991.

Schoffeleers, Matthew. *Religion and the Dramatisation of Life: Spirit Beliefs and Rituals in Southern and Central Malawi.* Blantyre, ON: Claim, 2000.

————. "Ritual Healing and Political Acquiescence: The Case of the Zionist Churches in Southern Africa." *Africa* 61, no. 1 (1991): 1–25.

Scott, James. *Seeing Like a State: How Certain Schemes to Improve the Human Condition Have Failed.* New Haven, CT: Yale University Press, 1998.

————. *Weapons of the Weak: Everyday Forms of Peasant Protest.* New Haven, CT: Yale University Press, 1985.

Schnurr, Matthew A. "The Boom and Bust of Zululand Cotton, 1910–1933." *Journal of Southern African Studies* 37, no. 1 (2011): 119–34.

Scully, Pamela, and Clifton Crais. *Sara Baartman and the Hottentot Venus: A Ghost Story and a Biography.* Princeton, NJ: Princeton University Press, 2009.

Searing, James F. *"God Alone Is King": Islam and Emancipation in Senegal; The Wolof Kingdoms of Kajoor and Bawol, 1859–1914.* Portsmouth, NH: Heinemann, 2002.

Seekings, Jeremy. "'Not a Single White Person Should Be Allowed to Go under': Swartgevaar and the Origins of South Africa's Welfare State, 1924–1929." *Journal of African History* 48, no. 3 (2007): 375–94.

————. "The National Party and the Ideology of Welfare in South Africa under Apartheid."

Journal of Southern African Studies 46, no. 6 (November 1, 2020): 1145–62.

Shadle, Brett. "Bridewealth and Female Consent: Marriage Disputes in African Courts, Gusiiland, Kenya." *Journal of African History* 44, no. 2 (2003): 241–62.

————. *"Girl Cases": Marriage and Colonialism in Gusiiland, Kenya, 1890–1970.* Portsmouth, NH: Heinemann, 2006.

Shepperson, George, with Thomas Price. *Independent African: John Chilembwe and the Origins, Setting, and Significance of the Nyasaland Native Rising of 1915.* Edinburgh, UK: Edinburgh University Press, 1958.

Simons, H. J. *African Women: Their Legal Status in South Africa.* London: Hurst, 1968.

Simpson, Thula. *History of South Africa: From 1902 to the Present.* New York: Oxford University Press, 2022.

Sithole, Nkosinathi. *The Nazaretha Church in South Africa: Isaiah Shembe's Hymns and the Sacred Dance in Ibandla LamaNazaretha.* Leiden, NL: Brill, 2016.

————. "The Sacrifice of Flesh and Blood: Male Circumcision in Ibandla LamaNazaretha as a Biblical and African Ritual." *Journal of the Study of Religion* 25, no. 1 (2012): 15–30.

Slater, Henry. "Land, Labour, and Capital in Natal: The Natal Land Colonisation Company, 1860–1948." *Journal of African History* 16, no. 2 (1975): 257–83.

Smalberger, John M. "The Role of the Diamond-Mining Industry in the Development of the Pass-Law System in South Africa." *International Journal of African Historical Studies* 9, no. 3 (1976): 419–34.

Smith, R. H. "Native Farm Labour in Natal." *South African Journal of Economics* 9 (1941): 154–75.

Söderberg Kovacs, Mimmi. *Violence in African Elections: Between Democracy and Big Man Politics.* Chicago: Zed, 2018.

Soske, Jon. *Internal Frontiers: African Nationalism and the Indian Diaspora in Twentieth-Century South Africa.* Athens: Ohio University Press, 2017.

Spear, Thomas. "Neo-Traditionalism and the Limits of Invention in British Colonial Africa." *Journal of African History* 44, no. 1 (2003): 3–27.

Spear, Thomas T, and Isaria N. Kimambo. *East African Expressions of Christianity.* Oxford, UK: James Currey, 1999.

Stafford, W. G. *Native Law as Practiced in Natal.* Johannesburg: Witwatersrand University Press, 1935.

Stark, Rodney, and William Sims Bainbridge. *A Theory of Religion.* New Brunswick, NJ: Rutgers University Press, 1996.

Statistics and Census Bureau, *Union Statistics for Fifty Years.* Pretoria: Bureau of Census and Statistics, 1960.

Stephens, Rhiannon. *A History of African Motherhood: The Case of Uganda, 700–1900.* New

York: Cambridge University Press, 2013.

Swart, Sandra. "'Bushveld Magic' and 'Miracle Doctors': An Exploration of Eugène Marais and C. Louis Leipoldt's Experiences in the Waterberg, South Africa, c. 1906–1917." *Journal of African History* 45, no. 2 (2004): 237–55.

Swanson, Maynard. "'The Asiatic Menace': Creating Segregation in Durban, 1870–1900." *International Journal of African Historical Studies* 16, no. 3 (1983): 401.

———. "'The Durban System': Roots of Urban Apartheid in Colonial Natal." *African Studies* 35, no. 3–4 (1976): 159–76.

———. "The Sanitation Syndrome: Bubonic Plague and Urban Native Policy in the Cape Colony, 1900–1909." *Journal of African History* 18 (1977): 387–410.

———. "Urban Origins of Separate Development." *Race* 10, no. 1 (1968): 31–40.

Sweet, James H. *Domingos Álvares, African Healing, and the Intellectual History of the Atlantic World*. Chapel Hill: University of North Carolina Press, 2011.

Sundkler, Bengt. *Bantu Prophets in South Africa*. London: Lutterworth, 1948.

———. *Zulu Zion and Some Swazi Zionists*. London: Oxford University Press, 1976.

Tallie, T. J. "Sartorial Settlement: The Mission Field and Transformation in Colonial Natal, 1850–1897." *Journal of World History* 27, no. 3 (2016): 389–410.

———. *Queering Colonial Natal: Indigeneity and the Violence of Belonging in Southern Africa*. Minneapolis: University of Minnesota Press, 2019.

Thomas, Lynn. *Beneath the Surface: A Transnational History of Skin Lighteners*. Durham, NC: Duke University Press, 2020.

———. "The Modern Girl and Racial Respectability." *Journal of African History* 47 (2006): 461–90.

———. *Politics of the Womb: Women, Reproduction, and the State in Kenya*. Berkeley: University of California Press, 2003.

Thomas-Houston, Marilyn M. *"Stony the Road" to Change: Black Mississippians and the Culture of Social Relations*. New York: Cambridge University Press, 2005.

Thornberry, Elizabeth. *Colonizing Consent: Rape and Governance in South Africa's Eastern Cape*. New York: Cambridge University Press, 2018.

———. "Virginity Testing, History, and the Nostalgia for Custom in Contemporary South Africa." *African Studies Review* 58, no. 3 (2015): 129–48.

Timbs, Liz. "An In(Ter)Vention of Tradition: Medical Male Circumcision in KwaZulu-Natal, 2009–2016." *Journal of Natal and Zulu History* 32, no. 1 (2018): 1–23.

———. "The Regiments: Cultural Histories of Zulu Masculinities and Gender Formation in South Africa, 1816–2018." PhD diss., Michigan State University, 2019.

Tishken, Joel E. *Isaiah Shembe's Prophetic Uhlanga: The Worldview of the Nazareth Baptist*

Church in Colonial South Africa. New York: Peter Lang, 2013.

———. "The Nazareth Baptist Church as Subordinationist Christianity." *African Studies* 74, no. 3 (September 2, 2015): 449–69.

———. "Prophecy and Power in Afro-Christian Churches: A Comparative Analysis of the Nazareth Baptist Church and the Eglise Kimbanguiste." PhD diss., University of Texas at Austin, 2002.

———. "Whose Nazareth Baptist Church?: Prophecy, Power, and Schism in South Africa." *Nova Religio* 9, no. 4 (2006): 79–97.

Trollope, Anthony. *South Africa*, vol. 2. Leipzig, 1878.

Turner, Victor Witter. *The Drums of Affliction: A Study of Religious Processes among the Ndembu of Zambia.* Oxford, UK: Clarendon Press, 1968.

Tyler, Josiah. *Forty Years among the Zulus.* Boston, 1891.

Union of South Africa, *Census of the Union of South Africa.* Pretoria: Government Printing and Stationary Office, 1911.

Vahed, Goolam. "Constructions of Community and Identity among Indians in Colonial Natal, 1860–1910: The Role of the Muharram Festival." *Journal of African History* 43, no. 1 (2002): 77–93.

———. "'An Evil Thing': Gandhi and Indian Indentured Labour in South Africa, 1893–1914." *South Asia* 42, no. 4 (August 2019): 654–74.

———. "The Protector, Plantocracy, and Indentured Labour in Natal, 1860–1911." *Pacific Historical Review* 87, no. 1 (2018): 101–27.

Van Onselen, Charles. "Race and Class in the South African Countryside: Cultural Osmosis and Social Relations in the Sharecropping Economy of the South Western Transvaal, 1900–1950." *American Historical Review* 95, no. 1 (1990): 99–123.

———. "'The Regiment of the Hills': South Africa's Lumpenproletarian Army, 1890–1920." *Past & Present*, no. 80 (1978): 91–121.

———. "The Social and Economic Underpinning of Paternalism and Violence on the Maize Farms of the South-Western Transvaal, 1900–1950." *Journal of Historical Sociology* 5, no. 2 (1992): 127–60.

———. *The Seed Is Mine: The Life of Kas Maine, a South African Sharecropper, 1894–1985.* New York: Hill and Wang, 1996.

———. *Studies in the Social and Economic History of the Witwatersrand, 1886–1914.* New York: Longman, 1982.

Vansina, Jan M. *Paths in the Rainforests: Toward a History of Political Tradition in Equatorial Africa.* Madison: University of Wisconsin Press, 1990.

Van Walraven, Klaas, ed. *The Individual in African History: The Importance of Biography in*

African Historical Studies. Boston: Brill, 2020.

Van Warmelo, N. J. *Kinship Terminology of the South African Bantu*. Pretoria: Government Printer, 1931.

———. *A Preliminary Survey of the Bantu Tribes of South Africa*. Pretoria: Government Printer, 1935.

Vaughan, Megan. *Curing Their Ills: Colonial Power and African Illness*. Stanford, CA: Stanford University Press, 1991.

———. "Healing and Curing: Issues in the Social History and Anthropology of Medicine in Africa." *Social History of Medicine* 7, no. 2 (1994): 283–95.

Vilakazi, Absolom. *Zulu Transformations: A Study of the Dynamics of Social Change*. Pietermaritzburg, ZA: University of Natal Press, 1962.

Vilakazi, Absolom, Bongani Mthethwa, and Mthembeni Mpanza. *Shembe: The Revitalization of African Society*. Johannesburg: Skotaville, 1986.

Villalón, Leonardo Alfonso. *Islamic Society and State Power in Senegal: Disciples and Citizens in Fatick*. Cambridge, UK: Cambridge University Press, 1995.

Vinson, Robert Trent. *Albert Luthuli*. Athens: Ohio University Press, 2018.

———. *The Americans Are Coming!: Dreams of African American Liberation in Segregationist South Africa*. Athens: Ohio University Press, 2012.

Vinson, Robert Trent, and Robert Edgar. "Zulus Abroad: Cultural Representations and Educational Experiences of Zulus in America, 1880–1945." *Journal of Southern African Studies* 33, no. 1 (March 1, 2007): 43–62.

Walker, Cherryl. "Critical Reflections on South Africa's 1913 Natives Land Act and Its Legacies: Introduction." *Journal of Southern African Studies* 40, no. 4 (July 4, 2014): 655–65.

———, ed. *Women and Gender in South Africa to 1845*. Cape Town: David Phillips, 1990.

Warwick, Peter. *Black People and the South African War, 1899–1902*. New York: Cambridge University Press, 1983.

Washington, Eric Michael. "Heralding South Africa's Redemption: Evangelicalism and Ethiopianism in the Missionary Philosophy of the National Baptist Convention, USA, Inc. 1880–1930." PhD dissertation, Calvin College, 2010.

Webb, Colin de B., and J. B. Wright. eds. *The James Stuart Archive of Recorded Oral Evidence Relating to the History of the Zulu and Neighboring People*. 5 vols. Pietermaritzburg, ZA: University of Natal Press, 1976.

Weber, Max. *Economy and Society: A New Translation*. Edited and translated by Keith Tribe. Cambridge, MA: Harvard University Press, 2019.

———. *The Theory of Social and Economic Organization*. Edited by Talcott Parsons. Translated by A. M. Henderson. New York: Oxford University Press, 1947.

Welsh, David. *The Roots of Segregation: Native Policy in Colonial Natal, 1845–1910*. New York: Oxford University Press, 1971.

West, Gerald. "The Bible and the Female Body in Ibandla LamaNazaretha: Isaiah Shembe and Jephthah's Daughter." *Old Testament Essays* 20, no. 2 (January 2007): 489–509.

———. "Reading Shembe 'Re-Membering' the Bible: Isaiah Shembe's Instructions on Adultery." *Neotestamentica* 40, no. 1 (2006): 157–83.

White, Luise. *The Comforts of Home: Prostitution in Colonial Nairobi*. University Of Chicago Press, 1990.

———. *Speaking with Vampires: Rumor and History in Colonial Africa*. Berkeley: University of California Press, 2000.

White, Luise, Stefan Miescher, and David William Cohen, eds. *African Words, African Voices: Critical Practices in Oral History*. Bloomington: Indiana University Press, 2001.

Whiteside, J. *History of the Wesleyan Church in South Africa*. London, 1906.

Willan, Brian. *Sol Plaatje: A Life of Solomon Tshekisho Plaatje, 1876–1932*. Auckland Park, ZA: Jacana, 2018.

Wilson, Monica. *Reaction to Conquest: Effects of Contact with Europeans on the Pondo of South Africa*. London: Oxford University Press, 1936.

———. *Religion and the Transformation of Society: A Study in Social Change in Africa*. Cambridge, UK: Cambridge University Press, 1971.

———. "Xhosa Marriage in Historical Perspective." In *Essays on African Marriage in Southern Africa*, edited by Eileen Krige and John L. Comaroff. Cape Town: Juta, 1981.

Worger, William. "Parsing God: Conversations about the Meaning of Words and Metaphors in Nineteenth-Century Southern Africa." *Journal of African History* 42 (2001): 417–47.

———. *South Africa's City of Diamonds: Mine Workers and Monopoly Capitalism in Kimberley, 1867–1895*. New Haven, CT: Yale University Press, 1981.

Wright, John B. "Control of Women's Labour in the Zulu Kingdom." In *Before and After Shaka: Papers in Nguni History*, edited by J. B. Peires. Grahamstown, ZA: Institute of Social and Economic Research, 1981.

Wright, John B., and Andrew Manson. *The Hlubi Chiefdom in Zululand-Natal: A History*. Ladysmith, ZA: Ladysmith Historical Society, 1983.

Wylie, Diana. *Starving on a Full Stomach: Hunger and the Triumph of Cultural Racism in Modern South Africa*. Charlottesville: University Press of Virginia, 2001.

Zebrosko, Bob. *A Brief History of Pharmacy: Humanity's Search for Wellness*. London: Routledge, 2015.

Index

Italicized page numbers refer to figures.

A

accountability, 18, 74, 102–3, 129, 149

Act of Union, xix

African continent, xvii–xviii, 24, 55, 101, 190n85

African Diaspora, xxviii, 171n55

African history, xvi–xviii. *See also* South African history

African Methodist Episcopal Church, 26, 39–40, 162, 192n5, 194n21

African National Congress (ANC), xiv, 156, 158–59

African studies, xviii

Afrikaans language, 8, 25, 35

Afrikaner people, 154. *See also* Boer Republics

age-sets, 3, 8, 101–104

agriculture, 5–8, 28, 58–59, 124; crises, 22–23. *See also* farming

amaHlubi. *See* Hlubi people

American Board of Commissioners for Foreign Missions, 16, 39, 80, 197n82; American Zulu Mission, 56, 75, 87, 244n35

"Angel of Mpondoland," 128

"Angel of Zululand," 128–29

Anglican church, 25, 98, 107, 127

anthropology, xvi–xviii, 101, 108, 119

apartheid, xix, 25, 154–55, 157, 159, 162; anti-apartheid movement, 156

Apostolic Faith Mission, 69

archives, xxviii, xxx, 83

aristocracy, 126–27, 129

Ark of the Covenant, 68

Atkins, Keletso, 43, 47. *See also* "homeboy networks"

autobiography/life story (of Shembe), xxviii, 15–16, 59, 104, 144, 150–51, 173n79,

Salvation Army, 26, 137

Samaritans, 72, 82–86

sanitation, xiii–xiv, 14, 22–24, 162

Satyagraha, 159

Scotland, 9, 17

segregation, xiv, 3, 12, 38, 73, 83, 87, 100, 143,
    161; of the Free State, 30, 33; residential,
    25–27, 46–47. *See also* apartheid

serfdom, 5

sermons, xxviii, 9, 17, 88, 104, 128, 144

seTswana language, 2

settler colonialism, xxiv, 3–4, 7, 25, 38–40, 57,
    73, 88, 124, 158. *See also* Boer Republics;
    British Empire; British protectorates

sex, xxvi, 8, 56, 76, 83, 92–95; education,
    99–105; and morality, 61, 92–96, 106, 108;
    premarital, 101–2

sexual assault, 102–3

sexuality, xxv, 81–82

sexual purity, 92, 96, 104–5, 106, 108–9

Shakespeare, William, 2

shamans, xxvii

Shembe, J. G., 160–63

Shembe, Isaiah's children, 14–15, 23, 60,
    74, 104, 144, 149–150, 151, 159. *See also*
    Shembe, J. G.; Shembe, Zondi

Shembe, Isaiah's parents, 1–3, 12, 15, 19, 36,
    74, 105

Shembe, Isaiah's wives, 14–15, 74, 144, 149, 159

Shembe, Zondi, 133–34

Shepstone, Denis Gem, 118–19, 159

Shepstone, Theophilus, 39, 136

Shepstone system, 39–40

Simpson, A. B., 15

"skeleton man" story, 10–11

slavery, 5

smallpox, 112

Smith, Joseph, xvii

social history, xvii

sociology, xviii, 26

Solani, Funiselo, 40–43

South Africa, cities, protectorates,
    and provinces in: Cape Town, 40;
    Johannesburg, 30, 57, 119; Port Elizabeth,
    41, 113; Pretoria, 30; Transvaal, the, 21, 30,
    45, 69. *See also* Ndwedwe; Orange Free
    State, cities in

South African history, xix, xxi, 69, 75, 91, 124,
    158–59

South African War, 1, 12–13, 17, 31–34, 154

South Asian people, 45, 47, 85, 145, 147

"sponging" system, 47–48

succession, 160–63

sugar plantations, 77, 116, 124–26

Supreme Chief, 116

surveillance, xxiii, 48, 104–5, 112–13, 125, 156

syphilis, 125, 200n21

T

tenancy, xiii, xxiii, 1, 4–8, 11–12, 14–15, 17, 23,
    73–74, 180n77. *See also* farming

testimonies, xxviii–xxix, 17–18, 59–60, 126,
    157

theology, 11, 15–18, 26, 33–34, 50, 67, 70, 86,
    99, 112

Thornberry, Elizabeth, 99

Thukela River, 124–26, 129

togt jobs, 41

transportation, xx, xxvii–xviii, 23, 138, 144,
    156, 159. *See also* automobiles; horses;
    railway

"trousered Africans," stereotype, 38, 43, 119

Tshabalala (family name), 13

tuberculosis, 84–85

typhoid fever, 14

U

uniforms, *xxvi*–xxvii, 127, 148, 160

Union government, xx, 73, 94, 112. *See also* Act of Union

Union of South Africa, *xxi,* 13, 51, 69, 116, 125. *See also* Act of Union

United States of America, 5, 15–18, 32, 42, 87, 108; Western, 145

University of Natal, xvi, 118

urban space, xix–xx, 23–25, 38, 45–47, 49, 106, 122, 154

V

vaccinations, 112–15, 118, 136, 138, 160, 162; resistance to, 116–17, 120

Victorian era, xxv, 86–87, 99, 102–3, 131

vigilantism, xiii, xix, 4

violence, xxi, 57, 97, 99, 137, 141, 161; and Boers Republics, 7–8; and Mfecane, 2, 5, 19; state, 57, 111, 113, 158. *See also* sexual assault

virginity, 102–5

Virgin Mary, 100, 105, 107. *See also* mama kaJesu (Virgin Mary)

W

Weavers, George, 16

Weber, Max, xvii

Wells, Nellie, 119, 140, 159

Wesleyan Church, 25, 27–28, 33–34, 69, 95

widows, 129, 149, 161

witchcraft, 8, 64

Witwatersrand ridge, 23–24, 30–31, 34, 38, 40, 113, 192n3

Witzieshoek, 26, 28, 33

Woodworth-Etter, Maria, 17–18

World War I, 91, 94, 154

X

Xhosaland, 99, 180n78

Z

Zion Christian Church, 69

Zulu army, 81, 126

Zulu Kingdom, 2, 124, 126, 141